Two Dreams in One Bed

ASIA-PACIFIC:

CULTURE, POLITICS, AND SOCIETY

Editors: Rey Chow, H. D. Harootunian,

and Masao Miyoshi

Two Dreams in One Bed

EMPIRE, SOCIAL LIFE, AND THE ORIGINS

OF THE NORTH KOREAN REVOLUTION

IN MANCHURIA

HYUN OK PARK

DUKE UNIVERSITY PRESS

Durham and London

2005

© 2005 Duke University Press

All rights reserved

Printed in the United States of

America on acid-free paper ∞

Designed by Amy Ruth Buchanan

Typeset in Quadraat by Tseng

Information Systems, Inc.

Library of Congress Cataloging-in-

Publication Data appear on the last

printed page of this book.

✱

Duke University Press gratefully

acknowledges the support of the Korea

Foundation, which provided funds

toward the production

of this book.

In memory

of my mother,

KIM YANG RYE,

and for my father,

PARK RO TACK

CONTENTS

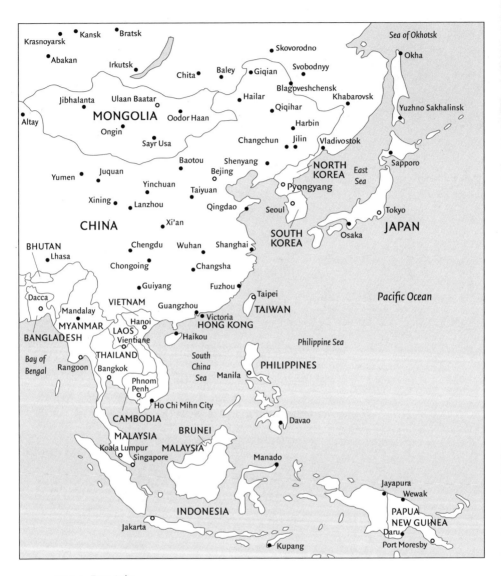

MAP 1. East Asia

MAP 2. Manchuria in the 1920s

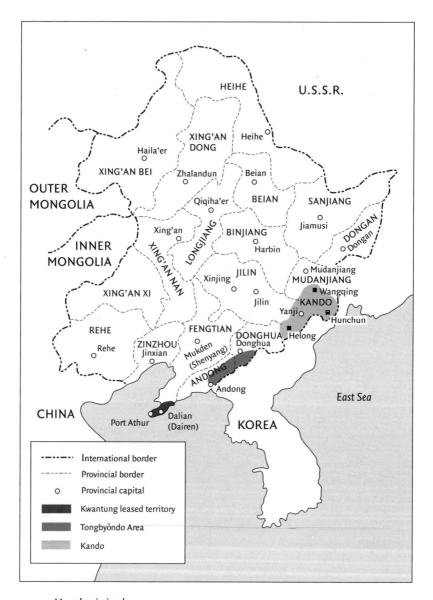

MAP 3. Manchuria in the 1930s

PREFACE

Manchuria has played a central role in the history and politics of East Asia in the twentieth century. This region is presently in the northeast portion of the People's Republic of China, an area of great importance for global politics and economy. In this century Manchuria has been home to Chinese, Koreans, and Japanese, whose collective histories as inhabitants are intertwined in complex relationships only partly described by nationalist and colonialist forces. Recent works have shed considerable light on the struggles of these national groups within Manchuria but as this book argues, an important dimension of their history has been neglected: global capitalism and their situation as actors within it.[1] Capitalism, this book shows, was the primary determinant of social relations in Manchuria. Grasping the nature of these relations is key to understanding the history of Manchuria from the late nineteenth century to the end of World War II. A new interpretation of social relations in Manchuria leads to a rethinking of the origins of the North Korean revolution and ultimately the origins of the current nationalism of the North Korean state. The revolution in North Korea that followed World War II saw itself as developing out of Korean resistance to Japan in Manchuria. Today, the North Korean state still represents its nationalism as based upon the Manchurian social experience.

This book considers the role of global capitalism in the processes of nation formation and colonization in two ways. Firstly, it involves a social approach to nationalism and colonialism, embedding them in the process of capitalist expansion, with a focus on the social sphere as the site of analysis. The clash between nationalist and colonialist forces over sovereignty took place not merely in the political arena of the struggle for independence but also in the social relations of commodity production and exchange. Recent cultural studies contribute to an understanding of nationalism and colonialism beyond their opposition and demonstrate their innate links, exposing the ways that new institutional learning under colonial rule framed the idea of the nation that the nationalists pursued.[2] In this book, I investigate the persistent gap between the political and cultural ideas of the nation and social practices. Organized simultaneously by nationalism and capitalism that both nationalists and colonizers pursued, social relations of production and exchange continued to deviate from state laws and policies that both Chinese and Japanese powers enacted to maintain national sovereignty. The rift between national ideas and social practices resulted from contradictory relations of nationalism and capitalism.[3]

Secondly, conceptualizing the social is imperative for my social approach to nationalism. Existing inquiries of nationalism and capitalism have mainly concerned the integrative effects that nationalism supplies for class politics of hegemony, e.g., inversion of class antagonism into universal identification with the national community. The social approach to nationalism ascribes nationalism not to the class politics of hegemony, but to the contradictory logic of capitalist expansion that simultaneously draws on and transcends national boundaries, a logic to which the Chinese states, Japanese colonizer, and Korean migrants adhered. Whereas an understanding of the ideological and political arenas of class politics is central to studies of class hegemony, the rethinking of the social is vital to the social approach. Because the contradictory logic of capital implies that the mediation of capitalist expansion by the nation is incomplete, social relations are not fixed by either national or capitalist forces but unstable. Instability of social relations, in turn, means the indeterminability of the nation whose imaginary ideas are actualized in the social process. In other words, inscribing the nation within the social process prescribes a different notion of spatio-temporality of the nation. If the notion of class hegemony hinges on the totalizing spatial effect of nationalism, imagining the nation as a stable whole, the social approach to nationalism exposes intrinsic indeterminability as a temporal marker of the nation.

Postulating the social and nation formation as a global problematic in this book exceeds the boundaries of existing studies of Manchuria. Available historical studies or historiographies of Manchuria are too nation-bound to offer insight on fleeting social relations in Manchuria. When situated in the nation formation of China, the study of Manchurian history concentrates on understanding the production of local discourses of the nation in Manchukuo and of Asian imaginaries in Asia within a global context. Since the global here refers to a system of nation-states, the relations of national discourses with global capitalism remain obscure. As for Japanese history, the study of Manchuria focuses on a range of complex domestic relations within Japan that constructed the social imaginary of Manchukuo as the jewel of the Japanese empire. Even when the contentious relationship between the Japanese state and capital is considered, the attention is exclusively on domestic politics in Japan. When concerned with Korea, Korean studies of Manchuria mainly regard the Manchurian experience as part of the national liberation struggle exploring it in terms of the genealogy of various organizations and their repertoires of anticolonial struggles. The social experiences of the masses are neglected in such studies as well as in new emergent postcolonial studies that uncover the vision of Korean modernity implicated in colonial knowledge.[4]

Instead this book draws on archival sources in Korea, China, and Japan to examine the triangular relationship of Koreans, Chinese, and Japanese whose social and national positions remained unstable. I specifically map out the social transformation of Manchuria in two regions at two historical moments: Kando (Jiandao in Chinese; currently the Yanbian Korean Autonomous Prefecture) and elsewhere before and after the Japanese occupation in 1931.[5] I trace the entwined formation of the private property system and national membership in Manchuria, and show how state policies of property and nationality deviated from actual laws, and in turn how social practices deviated from both the existing laws and the policies of the state. While both Koreans and Chinese tended to regard Manchuria as extensions of their home countries, the Japanese encouraged the immigration of Korean peasants into Manchuria (Japan ruled Korea at this time) as a way of fostering its own hegemony in the region. Showing how capitalism worked to determine social relations among Japanese, Korean, and Chinese peasant groups, this book demonstrates how these groups failed to transcend nationalistic perspectives and grasp their common interests. They were, in short, unable to create internal alliances. I argue that this tension between nationalism and internationalism prefigured the establishment of a North Korean state that would be much more historically nationalist than internationalist.

This book contributes to an understanding of Manchurian history, when historical memories of Manchuria have conveyed different meanings in different times to various national groups in East Asia: the origins of the revolution in North Korea; anti-imperialist and popular nationalism in South Korea; and the origins of Korean Chinese diaspora and the Asian community in neoliberal capitalism from the 1990s. The tenacity and various representations of Manchuria history bear testimony to the changing global forces that transformed Korean and Chinese politics and economies and their relations with the Manchurian experience. During the Cold War, the study of Manchurian history was both an academic and an activist inquiry in South Korea. North Korea's leadership has embraced the Korean communist struggle in Manchuria as the source of its revolution, elevating it as the crux of its official Juch'e (self-reliance) ideology. In contrast, the South Korean state has drawn on the non-communist exile movement in Shanghai as the foundation of its regime, banning any unauthorized studies of colonial Manchurian history. The American occupation from 1945 to 1948 and the establishment of the South Korean military state in 1961 not only maintained the Japanese colonial legacy—the colonial elites, bureaucratic and disciplinary institutions of the state, armies, police, and communist ideology—but also brought South Korean society under American hegemony. In such conditions, the symbolic elements of colonial Manchurian history that were idealized in North Korea and by South Korean radical groups encompassed anti-Japanese nationalism and mass politics. Such representation of Manchurian history had been integral to the democracy movement of the 1980s in South Korea, which aimed to decolonize society of both the Japanese colonial legacy and American domination and to establish a popular democracy. The study of Manchurian history among a radical group of South Korean historians served as much a critique of the South Korean regime as an endorsement of North Korea.[6]

Though developed as a critique of the official South Korean national history, the revisionist history project on Manchuria has succeeded another nationalist approach that has focused on the liberation movements. It has especially attended to the genealogy of exile communist organizations and activities, including the guerrilla struggles by Kim Il Sung, the former North Korean leader from 1948 until 1991, and by his comrades. Though seeking to contribute to the revisionist history project, this book reconsiders the meanings of anti-imperialist nationalism and mass politics, which were irreducible to the binary of colonialism and nationalism. Unlike the emblem of anti-imperialist nationalism, Korean politics in exile could not be reduced to the dichotomy of pro- and anti-Japanese stances, which equated anti-Japanese struggle in Manchuria with the struggle to liberate Korea from Japanese rule and create a new nation-state in Korea. Instead, exiled Koreans also persistently sought to improve the social conditions of Korean peasant migrants, who formed the majority of the population in Kando. Promoting the acquisition of Chinese nationality and stable landownership, they aimed at establishing self-rule within Manchuria. Furthermore, Korean peasants developed social as well as political networks with Japanese colonizers, as they relied on Japanese promises for low-interest loans, private ownership of land, and alternative modes of production and market exchange. While exiled communists were devoted to liberating Korea, social practices and identities of Korean peasants were not reducible to class or national interest but rather shaped by forms of everyday life that were embedded in the rapid commodification of Manchurian agriculture.

A wave of global and local changes since the mid-1990s has transformed the terrain of colonial Manchurian history within Korean national history. There has been a substantive shift in the relationship between the two Koreas from ideological war to economic cooperation. In tandem with the dissolution of the Soviet bloc and the declining appeal of socialism, economic crisis in North Korea has consolidated the legitimacy of the South Korean state now democratized since the late 1980s. The desire for continued economic development has also led South Koreans to seek further economic cooperation with North Korea rather than territorial integration. Interest in Manchurian communist history has dissipated. But these current changes have infused Manchurian history with the politics of both the Korean Chinese diaspora and the emergent Asian bloc. After the Cold War halted their repatriation to Korea, since the 1990s Korean Chinese have returned to South Korea as migrant laborers, comprising about 60 percent of the total 40 million foreign workers in South Korea. This reconnection of South Koreans and Korean Chinese results from the synergy of new South Korean global capitalism—especially transnational economic practices involving overseas production and the employment of an invited foreign guest workforce—and economic development in China.

Concurrent with this shift is the reconfiguration of the regional order in the post-Cold War, in which North and South Korea and China have joined Russia and Japan to envisage an Asian bloc as a counterweight to American hegemony. As East Asian countries and Russia aspire to create a regional bloc, they propose to establish a trans-Siberian freight route and sea tunnels across their countries, to create a single currency, and to develop the border region of Russia, China, and North Korea. Such interest in forming an economic bloc coincides with the proliferation of cultural Asian imaginaries in Japan, Taiwan, and Korea that invoke putative shared Asian customs. The current formation of an Asian community represses the memory of the first instance of the Asian community, which was the East Asia Co-Prosperity

Sphere (*Dai Tōa Kyōeiken*) put forward by the Japanese imperial power. Manchuria was at the heart of the first transnational imaginary of Asia as its new railways connecting Asia and Europe and burgeoning city life symbolized the form of modernity that Japan presented as an alternative to Western civilization. Together with the fear of imperial domination, the enchantment of a new future provided by the current form of global capitalism displaces the connection between these Asian imaginaries.

The comparability of the two Asian imaginaries—the East Asia Co-prosperity Sphere and the new one led by Russia and the present-day East Asian countries—in two historical moments lies in the fact that they are historical manifestations of a universal dynamic of capital expansion mediated by regionalism and nationalism. The regional imaginary is a trans-historical form that capital deploys to overcome its crises. Whether Japan or multilateral powers install the Asian network of the market, infrastructure, technology, and culture, the appeal to an Asian community signifies capitalist expansion in Asia. The nation-state system mediates capitalist regional expansion in both instances of Asian community formation. Although there are important differences in the two Asian imaginaries, such as the declining appeal to the nation, the exclusive focus on differences glosses over the underlying capitalist logic of its repetition. This book explicates the uncanny coalescence of global capitalism and nationalism that governs the formation of the Asian imaginary.

NOTE ON ROMANIZATION

Names and titles in Korean, Japanese, and Chinese are romanized in Korean, Japanese, and Chinese respectively. I follow the McCune-Reishauer system of romanization for Korean except for words or names that have their own specific conventions, for example, Kim Il Sung. I use the Hepburn system and Pinyin system for Japanese and Chinese respectively, except for names with other conventional usages such as the Kwantung Army.

ACKNOWLEDGMENTS

The work on this book took place in Berkeley and New York among a changing cohort of mentors, colleagues, and friends. The long and intermittent process of writing this book has delayed adequate expression of my gratitude toward them. Michael Burawoy, my dissertation advisor at Berkeley, taught me political economy through his immediate, meticulous critique of myriad drafts of chapters. His everyday devotion to students' projects and his public participation through teaching demonstrates an invaluable example of pedagogy for me. The members of Michael's 1991–1993 dissertation group—Bob Freeland, Mary Kelsey, Patrick Heller, Chris Rhomberg, Brian Rich, Suava Salameh, Anders Schuneiderman, Rob Wrenn, and Mona Yunis—helped me think Manchuria beyond the framework of area studies. I was also fortunate at Berkeley to receive warm hearted support from Arlie Hochschild, Tom Gold, Peter Evans, and Lowell Dittmer. I appreciate Troy Duster for his encouragement when I was writing my dissertation.

Since coming to New York University, I transformed part of my dissertation into this book. Harry Harootunian has rallied for the abundant institutional and intellectual support at NYU that was vital to completing new rounds of research in China and writing. My daily conversations with Harry and his enthusiastic reading of numerous drafts of all the chapters have made it possible for me to meld my learning of cultural studies with political economy. I appreciate Rebecca Karl for important and constructive suggestions on the entire final draft of the manuscript. Wolsan Liem offered an insightful reading of chapters. I thank colleagues and friends in the Departments of East Asian Studies and Sociology, especially Craig Calhoun, Doug Guthrie, Moss Roberts, Marilyn Young, Louise Young, Manu Goswami, Neil Brenner, Janet Poole, Yukiko Hanawa, and the late Dorothy Nelkin for their support. My special thanks also go to Osamu Nakano and Chia-jung Lin for their assistance in language.

This project would have been impossible to complete without the invaluable support from Korean Chinese scholars in Yanbian, China from 1998 to 2001. Professor Pak Changwuk has taught me the Korean history of Manchuria and made available precious archival sources, including those that he hand-copied many decades ago. His lifelong dedication to the writing and teaching of the Korean history of China has been an inspiration to me. I am grateful to Professor Chon Sinja who has always welcomed me to her home during my research trips, introduced me to many different groups of people, and supervised translations of archival sources. Her family and friends extended my understanding of Korean community beyond academic circles. I am also grateful to Professor Son Chunil who generously shared various archival documents with me. This book has benefited from new studies of Manchuria among Korean Chinese. Son Chunil's path-breaking study of landownership and Kim Songho's rigorous study of the Minsaengdan were essential to developing my own analysis. I thank Pang Hyang for her splendid assistance in my research in Shenyang. I also appreciate the various assistance and support from scholars at Yanbian University and its Institute of Ethnology.

Over the years I have presented some of the ideas in this book at workshops and conferences at the University of Toronto, Cornell University, Princeton University, and Harvard University, and Khabarovsk. I thank the organizers—Thomas Lahusen, Michael Shin, Charles Armstrong, and Dan Shao—and participants for their constructive feedback. I appreciate the encouragement from teachers and friends, including Hyunju Lee, Hagen Koo, Hong Yung Lee, Alvin So, Cho Uhn, Cho Haejoang, Cho Sunkyoung, Ching-Kwan Lee, Gwoshong Shieh, Michael Liu, Ronke Oyewumi, and Kim Eun Shil. Suava Salameh has been a source of strength from graduate school years to New York. I appreciate Elizabeth Cosslett for her timely and inspirational advice and support. Lim Kwangbin has kept me connected to the world with conversation and laughter during some of the most intense periods of writing.

During my post-doc years at the Department of Sociology and the International Institute at the University of Michigan, my exposure to interdisciplinary cultural studies laid the foundation for my later reworking of my dissertation into a book, although I was drawn into a different project at Ann Arbor. I wish to express gratitude to Gay Seidman, Michael Kennedy, Sonya Rose, Julia Adams, Howard Kimeldorf, Jeff Paige, Rick Lempert, Muge Gocek, Gretchen and David Cohen, whose hospitality made me feel so at home in a new town. I was blessed with the wonderful company of Gay and her family, Ben and Heinz, during dinners, weekends, and throughout my job interviews. I also would like to thank Arif Dirlik for his support during my stay at Ann Arbor.

Reynolds Smith, my editor at Duke University Press, has kept the faith in this book, giving me important suggestions along the way. His steadfast commitment to this book was indispensable to completing my revision. Four readers provided me with comments valuable to my revisions. Especially Stefan Tanaka's prudent readings and comments have expanded my thoughts on time, crises, and fascism. The writing of this book in its different stages has been improved by exceptional copyediting of Jim Shaefer and Lise McKean. Especially Lise not only made it possible for me to meet various writing deadlines on time but also turned a nerve-racking process into an exciting and gratifying one. In the end, of course I am responsible for any of the book's shortcomings or errors.

I am grateful to my family for their affection and trust over the years. Mija, Yoon Duckkeun, Hyunjoo, and Moon Seongho have enriched me with inspiration and unflagging support. Sookja, Namkyu, Kim Miheh, Hyun-Sook, and Stan Young have always provided me with a home away from home and ongoing encouragement. For their bountiful love and playfulness I thank my nieces and nephews, Jiyoun, Shin Wooseung, Eunjae, Hyewon, Kim Joosuk, Yonghoon, Justin, Minkyong, Amanda, Caroline, Seonghyun, and Jooyoung. Many thanks to Minje for his good company in New York. My parents have waited to see this book for a long time. With all my love and respect, I dedicate this book to my father, Park Ro Tack, whose everyday rhythms of work and life have been the foundation for my own, and to my mother, Kim Yang Rye, whose grace and passion for knowledge live with me.

INTRODUCTION

An old Asian saying, *tongsang imong*—bedfellows sleep in the same bed but have different dreams—provides a trope for this book's exploration of the ways in which colonialism and nationalism inhabit the same space yet envisage two different dream worlds. Postcolonial critics depict colonialism and nationalism as bedfellows, not enemies, with colonized elites embracing the Western modular form of the nation as the template for their own. The derivative idea of nation is seen to perpetuate the colonial condition in terms of their identities and cultures even after liberation from colonial rule. For postcolonial critics, the bed is the foundation of the modern nation, and the dreams of the bedfellows differ only to the extent that copies differ from the original.

In my study, the relationship between colonialism and nationalism involves more than their military and political opposition or the homology of original and copies. The shared bed has a temporal materiality that enables the bedfellows to sleep together but taints their dreams with the curse of making them unattainable. Capitalism is the bed. It draws together colonialists and their nationalist counterparts to work for a common goal—capitalist development of a given territory—but for different reasons. While colonialists desire a form of capitalist development that can benefit the entire empire, nationalists aspire to develop a national economy of their own. But their dreams are forever fleeting, and they become nightmares not just for the people whose surplus values are appropriated by those who represent them but also for the dreamers themselves. These bedfellows can neither control the speed of capitalist expansion nor fully resolve the social crises spawned by it. The trope of two dreams in one bed suggests that an analysis of colonial and national politics warrants the incorporation of global capitalism if we are to adequately account for their dyadic relationship.

NATIONAL AND COLONIAL DREAMS

Nationalism participates in the construction of colonial hegemony, especially in the ways in which colonial power, in cooperation and contention with nationalist power, embeds itself in social relations of work and exchange in everyday life. Frantz Fanon astutely observed the operation of colonial power in everyday life. He believed that social consciousness must accompany the national and anticolonial struggle if the colonized are to free themselves from forms of colonial rule that endure even after formal liberation. In his view, if nationalism does not accommodate viable social programs that address the true source of social inequality, it is nothing but an empty shell. If nationalism "is not enriched and deepened by a very rapid transformation into a consciousness of social and political needs, in other words into humanism, it leads up a blind alley. The bourgeois leaders of underdeveloped countries imprison national consciousness in sterile formalism. . . . The living expression of the nation is the moving consciousness of the whole of the people."[1] If social consciousness precedes this "authentic" nationalism, fierce demands for social justice turn into a festive tribalism that serves only national elites. Furthermore, an authentic national and social consciousness must rest on the critique of the uneven development of capitalism in which national and colonial bourgeoisies exploit peoples on the periphery.[2] This path to liberation remains a utopian humanist prescription.

In this study, I transpose the humanist prophecy for liberation into a problematic of colonial domination in everyday social life. If forms of national, social, and international consciousness are intrinsically bound together in Fanon's humanist prescription for liberation, they can also be understood as having an equally embedded relationship in the consolidation of colonial rule. Thus, my work elaborates the role played by nationalism in the colonial construction of social life. In his critique of nationalism as a tool of domination, Fanon distinguishes authentic from "narrow" forms. Narrow nationalism serves the national bourgeoisie, which acts as a middleman for the colonial bourgeoisie and claims to represent the universal rights of people only as a means of furthering its own interests. His work does not elaborate the specific ways in which nationalism affects everyday life, as everyday life on the periphery is so deeply enmeshed in colonial rule that only a radical rupture—violence—seems capable of triggering the development of an authentic national consciousness.

An inquiry into nationalism and everyday life demands clarification of the social. Despite its weight in Fanon's account of nationalism the social, as a concept, is largely undefined beyond the domain of class exploitation and antagonism. Social inequality is discussed most visibly in his analysis of the divide between rural and urban in *The Wretched of the Earth*. This divide refers to the division of colonized and colonizer. It also signifies socioeconomic relations that are construed as antagonistic and exploitative.[3] In Fanon's Manichaean analysis, colonialism intensifies the exploitation of labor power without introducing any means of modernization to develop technology, irrigation, and new crops and methods of production. For Fanon, this economic domination is maintained and reproduced by racial politics, which moves social antagonism into the political and ideological arena. The desire of people to overcome racism confounds their subjectivity and overshadows their social consciousness. But because he does not elaborate the ways in which national and racial politics constitute economic relations of exploitation, it is not clear in Fanon's work how the social differs from the economic and how cultural politics shapes the social experience of production and exchange. An understanding of everyday life under colonial rule compels us to ask how colonial rule is grounded not only in the racial inversion of social antagonism or the invocation of enlightenment but also in reforms in social relations that enable people to imagine new modes of agricultural production and consumption.

Numerous postcolonial studies distance their analyses of colonialism and nationalism from economic relations. A key concern is the dissemination of the idea of the nation from the "West to the Rest" through institutions such as traveling colonizers and the colonial state. A baseline for this orientation was provided by Benedict Anderson's conceptualization of nationalism as a popular consciousness circulating in public space without master agents. In his view, nationalism is not a product of a specific class or political mobilization but a cross-class identification that emerges through the simultaneous and repeated activities of reading print materials and seeing objects. It is through these activities that people come to imagine their connection with others living within a particular bounded territory and apprehend a world in which connections among events are not necessarily linked temporally or causally. Once it came to exist, this modular form of popular nationalism was imitated in colonized countries from Africa and Russia to Japan and Indonesia through many waves of colonization. As Machiavellian colonial states and creole elites consciously unified vernaculars, re-created their traditions and histories, and promoted modern education, the original popular and horizontal characteristic of modern nationalism became lost in the non-Western world.[4]

When accounts of colonial domination are reduced to the production of ideas of modernity, the analysis of nation and nationalism becomes dissociated from capitalist development. Anderson identifies print capitalism as the agent that creates a modular form of modernity. According to Harry Harootunian, this agency in Anderson's framework says "more about print than the political economy of capitalism, more about communicating commonalities than the destructive leveling of capitalist productive relations and forces."[5] Yet even this minimal sense of capitalism disappears in his analysis of derivative nationalisms in colonies, where nationalism has become the enlightenment project of modernization.

Subaltern studies shares a similar tendency to sideline capitalism. Partha Chatterjee seeks anticolonial nationalism in a spiritual domain untouched by colonial domination. Ranajit Guha examines how national elites appropriate the language and values of the metropole in their anticolonial movements, for example, Hindu rituals as a symbol of a new nation and the binary conception of civilized and uncivilized. The colonial discourse of enlightenment engenders a deep rift between national elites and laboring people. The opposition of unruly traditional behaviors and orderly modern ones is symptomatic of the distance between members of the elite and subalterns.[6] In such analyses, colonialism and anticolonial nationalism are removed conceptually and historically from their association with capitalism. Colonization integrates metropolitan society and its colonies while homogenizing the colonies and turning them into nations. But colonial integration also continues to maintain the differences between metropolitan and colonial societies, which are conditions for capitalist integration.

When capitalism is disregarded in studies of colonialism and nationalism, the people mainly refers to nationals whose subjectivities are detached from other elements of modern subjects: "free" labor, propertied people, and their relations. Although subaltern studies seeks to reinstate subaltern voices and experiences that were effaced from national historiographies, it recapitulates views on the subaltern conceived by national elites. Missing in these accounts is the process through which the representation of the subaltern by national elites shaped their social relationship in other domains of their everyday lives, where they were encountered as different socioeconomic groups. The enlightenment framework placed subject formation in a linear space, where the propertied, educated class is given precedence as the vanguard of colonized elites and laborers are relegated to the inferior position of latecomers. In this enlightenment framework, illiterate laborers pose a barrier to establishing a modern nation-state. They become objects of a national movement or colonial state project that seeks to instill in them new ethics and assign to them the new roles and status of modern subjects. This approach dispossesses laboring people of the means of conceiving their own subjectivity. When he charges Anderson with depriving the colonized of the means to imagine their own nation, Partha Chatterjee seems oblivious of his own tendency to divest laboring subalterns of the means to imagine their own sovereignty over their minds and bodies. The linear mapping of the modern subject conflates the relationship between colonizer and colonized with the familiar notion of the time lag of development, a notion that cannot account for uneven and mutually constitutive relations arising from the exchange of capital, labor, and other commodities.

When peoplehood is separated from the social relations of work and exchange, *the social* refers to the associations among "free" individuals that constitute civil society, which the colonized must learn from the colonizer in order to be modern. This problem of separating people from their material conditions arises from the practice of privileging written language over other modern experiences. For Henri Lefebvre, overemphasis on the written word and inattention to other social practices lead to the illusion of transparency, with its seeming fidelity between mental and social activities. Given the steps involved in channeling ideas into practices, there is no basis for assuming realization of the intended purposes of ideas. Nor is there any reason to assume that social experience can be equated with an enactment of consciousness.[7] The enlightenment approach to colonialism and nationalism also assumes such fidelity without examining how reading, imagination, and articulation of thoughts are constrained by social conditions and historical contingency. The cultural imaginary of the nation is given the status of a subject. The modern subject is seen to be formed mainly through the mental activities of reading and imagining and is removed from the social domain of work. This formulation of the subject erases the notion that colonialism is a form of political and economic domination that commodifies social relations.

Bringing capitalism into the analysis of nationalism enables us to place nationalism in the social domain. The relationship between capitalist modernity and nationalism is to be understood neither by the teleological intention of capital accumulation nor by the linear trajectory of enlightenment.

Rather, it is imperative to pursue both the representation of people by elites and the lived experience of those who use culture, history, and ideas to interpret the representation and transform their relations with others. The place of nationalism in the discussion of capitalism and the social is addressed in the next section.

THE CAPITALIST BED

Both nationalism and capitalism constitute the modern sovereignty of a people. Foremost among their functions and effects, they abstract social relations between people and between people and things. Taking people and land as examples, I explore commonalities and differences in the ways that nationalism and capitalism effect this abstraction. Both nationalism and capitalism standardize and homogenize social relations. Together nationalism and capitalism assign universality to people and land. To begin with, individuals are conceived to be members and producers whose relations with one another are standardized and homogenized. Nationalism designates individuals as members of a community whose identities are defined by universal rights and a homogeneous sense of belonging. Imagined attachments and notions of equality develop among nationals whose social relations may be separated by residence, particular traditions, and vernaculars but at the same time are interwoven through unequal transactions of things. Capitalism also integrates individuals of different locales into new organizations of production and circulation. New scales of production and systems of division of labor enforce new labor time and spatiality of work, without regard for the wide range of circumstances under which individual workers labor. The value of human labor is measured by its price in a market that deforms social relations into relations among things, relations that exist apart from and outside the producers.

Land also acquires the double abstraction of homogenization. Nationalism naturalizes land as territory, drawing a demarcation between the inside and the outside of a national community. The inside is regarded as a singular space, an entity determined by the inverse of its outside. This construction of territory as a national space is both an institutional and an imagined process, as national communication and transportation grids annihilate spatial distances and differences between individuals, binding the identities of individuals to territory. Severed from previous attachments to producers and histories, land also becomes commodified, entering the market in the same ways that people do. Protected by property law, the value of land is alienated from producers whose labor power, not the market, improves its productivity. As a commodity, land accrues its value through circulation, while its value is standardized through market exchange. Land is also monopolized as property owners exclude other potential users and producers.[8]

The social abstractions of nationalism and capitalism are driven by the opposite dynamics of spatio-temporality. The former fixes social relations as an absolute quality of an imagined entity, while the latter renders them ever changing and in constant circulation. Conceived as a system of closure, a national community is posited as a durable entity that binds its members with a solid structure of cultural idioms and unity.[9] Tradition, ethnic distinctions, and historical memory are presumed to endow a national community with symbolic qualities of spatial wholeness and temporal resilience. The spiritual metaphors of imagination and invocation represent this absolute spatial unity, which individuals and groups seem to be able to resurrect at any time. Nationalism is a thing that seems never to change, and more precisely it must not change if it is to maintain its existence. Without this constancy, the nation loses its value. People are invoked as timeless subjects, and their lives rooted in the land often provide the community with continuity over the generations. Land embodies the memory of people's experience: as subjective sentiments, repetitive work in farming, or the sovereignty of producers.[10] When the state constructs the boundary between nationals and nonnationals and removes foreigners from land, its legitimacy is grounded in part in its self-proclaimed right to represent the people and their historical memory.

Repetitive circulation marks the capitalist transformation of people and land. Separated from the means of production, individuals must continuously sell their labor, whose value is determined by its changing supply, the circulation of its products, and the reinvestment of profits into production. Capitalism transforms land from a mere source of wealth into a commodity. As a source of wealth, land is a means of production with which producers produce wealth and share it with landlords and the state. As a commodity, land becomes fictitious capital, altering its value through its endless exchange with money and other commodities. For instance, ground rent paid by renters to landowners is like interest on money spent to purchase land. Ground rent determines the necessary level of subsistence, rendering the surplus as profit. In contrast to feudal landlords, in the capitalist mode of production landlords are no different from investors in assets such as government bonds, stocks, and shares of enterprises. To the extent that land titles circulate in the market, land is also converted to money.[11] In an endless exchange of commodities and money, land becomes fictitious capital.

The overlapping abstractions of social relations made by nationalism and capitalism require an investigation of the specific historical configurations that emerge in their interactions. I elaborate this point as an alternative framework for understanding the relationship between nationalism and capitalism. But first, let me examine the existing scholarship on capitalism and nationalism, especially those concerned with class hegemony.[12] These received approaches draw on a spatial conception of the nation and a society-bound conception of the social, concepts that inhibit observation of the contradictions between capitalism and nationalism.

Scholarship on nationalism and capitalism primarily has been concerned with the effect of the nation on capitalism rather than their mutual constitution of social relations. A specific area of inquiry in the literature is the issue of how nationalism enables capitalism to create and reproduce its own conditions for production and circulation despite social inequality. While no inherent logic of capitalism is assumed in calling a nation or nation-state into existence, the political and ideological function of nationalism is portrayed as seamless to the degree that capitalism seems to depend on nationalism for its production and reproduction. Various studies of nationalism and capitalism still imply, though subtly, the ideological inversion of social relations from unequal and divided people to integrated and unified individuals. This tendency is particularly evident in the practice of locating the interaction of nationalism and capitalism in political and ideological terrains, as if social relations of production and circulation were governed only by the economic forces of capitalism.

The canonical notion of hegemony addresses the issue of how colonial and national power is embedded in social space. Classic discussions document the invention of hegemony as the historical metastasizing of a particular social consciousness. This specific social consciousness *inverts* class antagonism into a universal and horizontal membership in a national community, if not completely embodying a false recognition. In class politics, where a class cannot afford to attain dominance through coercion alone, nationalism enables the dominant class to represent its own interests as identical to the universal aims of community.[13] In this politics of hegemony, the invocation of national community neutralizes social antagonism. The dominant power bloc identifies itself not as a class but as the "other" of the opposed power, while presenting its class objective as the national-popular struggle against common enemies. The popular-democratic elements in hegemonic politics constitute subjects as "the people" rather than members of a class.[14] For instance, in the discourse of nazism, a German worker was construed as German and a worker in ways that separate these two identities; otherwise the fusion of the two identities would represent socialism as being in the historical interest of the German people.[15] In the domains of both the market and ideological politics, the discourse of nationalism performs in such a way as to secure the participation of the masses in a capitalist system.

The Achilles' heel in debates on hegemony is the issue of whether and how political and ideological leadership is grounded in material conditions. While various attempts have been made to clarify the issue, the linkage of the political and ideological with material conditions remains largely unexplored.[16] The inversion of class subjects into free individuals or the nation's people presumes a split of their identities, with each constituted separately as economic and political/ideological. The vexed question of inversion draws on the conceptualization of the social as a system of totality that consists of distinct economic, political, and ideological spheres. The conception of the political and ideological as semiautonomous domains — determined only in the last instance by material relations — justifies the analysis of the national-popular in the political and ideological domain only when their links to material relations of production are presumed. The analysis of the national-popular, for instance, tends to concentrate on the construction of people in political and ideological relations. More implicit than illustrated are linkages between hegemony and the concrete social programs that organize the system of private property and relations of production and circulation.[17]

An alternative conception of the social is provided by the notion of "articulation" or social formation, which helps us to understand nationalism as a force that constitutes the process of production. For Nicos Poulantzas, the Althusserian concept of the social as a structural totality of separate spheres risks representing economic relations as self-regulating and unchanging in different stages of capitalism. Poulantzas refutes the classic notion that, as ideals and representations, ideology mystifies, conceals, or inverts social relations, as if the economic were given. Instead he examines the ways in which the political and ideological intervene in the relations of production and the nation-state performs in the spatio-temporal matrix of the social division of labor. The Taylorist division of labor in the Fordist regime of production divides the production process into minute deskilled tasks performed by workers who are thus denied a vision of the whole. Social relations in this capitalist regime of production are fractured and parceled into cellular spaces and controlled by different kinds of time, including the operating schedules of machines, the stopwatches of foremen, and the turnover time of capital.

Serial and segmented space and time raise the problem of coordination and integration. It is assumed that the nation will take up this task. It is in the class struggle and state policy that the nation is articulated with relations of production. Conjured up by state apparatuses such as the military, schools, and prisons, the notion of national territory integrates individuals into the new space of a people-nation. Represented by the state, national history and tradition homogenize temporal sequences and provide a new frame of reference. According to Poulantzas, global capitalism depends on the nation to the degree that the transnational expansion of capital is a process of "inter-nationalization." Capital does not spread throughout the homogeneous space of the global but rather fills in the breaches between nations.[18] The state seeks to expand capital and territory by acquiring new frontiers. It encapsulates frontiers into national spaces, homogenizing, assimilating, and unifying the conditions of production and exchange.[19]

The theses of inversion and articulation are both derived from the notion of the spatio-temporality of the nation. The theses invariably consider the nation to be a fixed space. They reduce it to its function of homogenizing social difference and antagonism and assume this to be the ontological power of the nation. Conceived as a system of closure, the nation is seen to distill the inherent differences, oppositions, and antagonisms of capitalism into a unit called the national community. The presumed effect of unity or integration is to organize and maintain capitalist expansion. No type of institutional process or event is seen to transform the nation. In fact, instability and especially the transformability of the modern nation seem to be antithetical to the definition of the nation itself. The nation is thought to embody a distinct kind of populism, which, unlike the other popular discourses of democracy, liberty, and equality, is embedded in unique and irreducible historical experiences. It is therefore expected to provide an unusually stable frame of reference for historical discourse and the basis for a more "solid double structure of meanings than the social structure itself."[20] Furthermore, the nation's temporality of timelessness accentuates the image of spatial wholeness that transports the concrete present—where matters are often fragmented, contentious, and antagonistic—to a desired future. This notion depicts the nation as an empty, floating signifier whose contents are less relevant than the agents who articulate it. This is because it is not the content of the nation but class politics that determines the actual meaning of national discourses and political value. Depending on the nature of its class politics, the discourse of the nation could become a rhetorical abstraction for intellectuals or a basis for the formation of a national popular bloc.

This spatio-temporal conceptualization of the nation confounds spirituality with stability. As the nation must appear to remain stable in order to perform its unifying function, its ideological effect is confused with its stability. Neil Smith and Cindi Katz point out that space is "geometrically divisible into discrete bits," so the spatial conception of the nation renders the boundaries of inside and outside as if their categories are mutually exclusive rather than mutually constituted domains.[21] Similarly, the discussions of the nation and capitalism examined above presume that the national boundary between inside and outside is complete and uncontested. Spatial metaphors have become a primary means by which national experience is understood. For example, free laborers are "displaced" from the means and objects of production, while they are "reterritorialized" as free individuals in an internal market or as the sovereign people of a national community. Incorporation into national membership is assumed to be a one-time process. The divisions among those who are included are supposed to be erased. The conception of an absolute and singular space elides the fact that spatial practices in nation formation involve a complex politics in which the boundary between inside and outside continues to be contested by differences among insiders based on socioeconomic status, race, gender, and sexuality, as well as the differences between insiders and outsiders.[22]

The axiom of the stabilizing effect of the nation tends to equate the social with society. Capitalism is an inherently global process in which influxes of labor and capital transgress the territorial boundaries of national states while maintaining unevenness between places. Thus, the canonical function of the nation in integrating, inverting, and articulating capitalist processes is by no means absolute. The conception of a society as a self-contained entity is nothing but a desired effect of the nation in containing and stabilizing the dynamics of global capitalism. When the nation is imagined to maintain equilibrium and assimilate external forces in a given society, this effect is more about the requirements of capital than about actuality. When the instability of hegemonic leadership is recognized, it is often ascribed to interstate dynamics or intrasocietal politics. For Ernesto Laclau, class politics never completely determines the meaning of the nation. A certain openness in the ideological domain makes it impossible to settle the notion of a specific nation in hegemonic politics. Even when Poulantzas notes that global capitalism simultaneously requires and transcends the spatial restrictions imposed by national frontiers, his pathbreaking study does not address the implications of the contradictory dynamics of global capitalism for national-popular politics. We are left with unanswered questions. In what ways does nationalism fail to contain capitalist forces? What does the incomplete mediation of capitalism by nationalism mean for social relations? And what are its implications for the spatio-temporality of the nation?

In the next section, I elaborate on the mutual constitution or coeval articulation of global capitalism and nationalism in order to show their intrinsic tension, which is explicated in the terrain of the social. Although the origin and work of nationalism are irreducible to capitalist processes, my inquiry limits itself to the ways in which nation formation is pertinent to the dynamics of global capitalism.

TEMPORALITY OF THE NATION AND THE SOCIAL

The structural tension between nationalism and capitalism arises from contradictory dynamics of global capitalism that simultaneously homogenize and differentiate social relations of production and exchange. While capital must overcome barriers to its circulation, social barriers are a necessary condition for the mobility of capital, since social differences such as wages, labor and property laws, and infrastructure motivate capital to relocate production and market activities from one region to another.[23] Social differences between regions make it possible for people to move in search of economic opportunities. The nation creates social differences between places, turning a place into a nation and drawing firm boundaries between places. A nation-state creates infrastructure, communications networks, and laws that enable capital to be profitably invested within its boundaries. However, capital and labor also seek to relocate their economic activities abroad, threatening devaluation of investment in national infrastructures.

This structural tension has an effect on social relations. In the structural accounts, the nation is made consubstantial with the role of the state in creating a national market and infrastructure. Yet as a cultural and ideological force the nation abstracts social relations. When it is articulated with capitalism, the nation represents the capitalist relations among people and things. Nationalist discourses and politics may entail specific representations of capitalist relations. For instance, agrarian communitarianism, an archetypal nationalist discourse, critiques the private property system and market dynamics. It supplies an alternative way to redistribute surplus value, organizing a new division of labor and postulating small farmers as the backbone of a new national economy. It is through these conjunctural processes that we can examine specific forms of nationalist representation in order to imagine an alternative to capitalism. Because of the immanent effect of nationalism on the constitution of social experiences, the nation's articulation with capitalism cannot be reduced to a single function. Historical inflections of the coeval articulation of the nation and capitalism involve diverse cultural politics of representation through which capitalist relations are interpreted and modified in specific historical moments.

Whereas the relation between capitalism and nationalism has been explored mainly in terms of the effect of the latter on the former, it also involves the other side of the equation: the effects of contradictory capitalist forces on nation formation. The fact that the nation is inscribed in social space anchors nation formation in a historical and social process. I prefer to use the term *nation formation* rather than *nation*, since *formation* denotes a historical process that involves institutionalization and practices. What is troubling in discussions of the homogenizing effects of the nation or nationalism is that this presumed effect masks the absence of careful historical analysis. This enables the nation to be regarded as a floating signifier whose function is expected to bring about the intended effect. Once it is embodied in laws and policies, the institutionalization of national membership and other nationalist programs is supposed to more or less fulfill the projected function. However, the coeval articulation of capitalism and nationalism warrants attention to both the universal logic of capital and its historical articulation, mediated by specific nationalist discourses, mechanisms of power, and events. It also points to dynamic processes in which capitalism and nationalism develop their contentious roles in shaping social relations, even though nationalism projects an image of a completed process.

Nation formation also expresses its embeddedness in social practices that are simultaneously regulated by and subvert nationalist discourses and institutions. As the nation grounds itself in social relations, it is actualized as a set of concrete social practices in everyday life. The nation is a thing whose meaning is consigned and contested within a specific process of commodification of social relations. Although the nation is an imagined idea, it is institutionalized as laws and policies once it is invoked by social and state actors.

Analysis of social institutions is not sufficient, however. The institutionalization of national membership embodies the intentions of policymakers and
popular forces. Thus, nation formation also needs to be examined in the social space, where everyday activities develop responses to institutions and
struggle to modify them. Social practices in everyday life demonstrate the
historically specific ways in which people negotiate capitalist economic principles and national representations of capitalist dynamics.

The social is a global problematic. Ascribing the nation to the social process exposes its fleeting temporality. Economic principles of global capitalism and nationalist forces uncannily coexist in social life. Nationalist forces
shape practices but cannot assimilate capitalist dynamics completely, rendering forces that organize social relations contradictory. The social is therefore inherently unstable. The impossibility of determining the social is not
reducible to the multitude of cultural identities of people that, according
to the poststructuralist approach, arise from discursive struggles of groups
within a society.[24] The social is impossible also because individuals encounter
the contradiction of global capitalist and nationalist forces in their everyday
lives. It is in their social practices that we can follow the contentious process through which individuals subvert, modify, and assign meanings to laws
and social institutions. Social practices are marked with unfulfilled desires
of national and capitalist forces. The impossibility of the social implies that
nation formation is never complete. As the nation is inscribed in unsettled
social practices, capitalist forces within social institutions threaten the nation's actualization.

The intrinsic relationship between the nation and capitalism grounds
hegemony and subjectivity in a concretely historical and material form. The
nationalist construction of production and circulation confers hegemony
on capitalist relations by enabling individuals to imagine an alternative way
of attaining sovereignty over their own labor. The creation of individuals'
subjective will in realizing their sovereignty is one of the nation's historical
functions for capitalism. As an imagined popular consciousness or cultural
identity, the nation does not merely transpose unequal social relations onto
horizontal relations in a national community. Nor does it simply compensate or displace the absence of individuals' sovereignty over labor in capitalist relations. Rather, the nation enlists the consent of the people in the social
terrain. It provides individuals with a new vision and the will to create their
sovereignty in the workplace and the market. Agrarian communitarianism,
for instance, supplied new regimes of production and exchange and collec-

tive sovereignty as alternatives to capitalist relations in the Japanese empire of the early twentieth century, while its institutions paradoxically promoted a private property system. This means that national-popular hegemony is not separate from material foundations but rather involves an attempt to reinvent capitalist social relations.

Subjects are also constituted in specific historical conjunctures. In social space, an individual does not acquire a singular identity as either a class member or national subject, as if he or she were transposed from one spatial identity to the other. Rather, subjects are transformed simultaneously into economic and national subjects who submit to new rules of social relations, which are authorized by capitalist forces and their national representations. These subjectivities do not fit the ontological positions prescribed by economic and nationalist institutions. Subjects acquire a new social consciousness as they practice new nationalist prescriptions for material relations. They seek to establish sovereignty over their labor not just in political, cultural, and ideological spheres but also in their material relations.

My approach intersects with Michel Foucault's theory of power, especially the analysis of power in social space. Whether Foucault's theory is regarded as rectifying the notion of hegemony or as absconding from the problematic of ideology, his analysis of power is apt for my discussion here.[25] Following his insights, I inscribe power in a social space where individuals are disciplined rather than simply repressed. I explore, for instance, the ways in which various powers organized different nationalist regimes of production and circulation that appealed to the desires of migrant laborers, especially their quest for landownership. Instead of viewing nationalism as an ideological glue that binds people together, I specify techniques of power, such as communalism, the private property system, and the credit system, through which power concretely disciplines subjects.[26]

My analysis also differs from Foucault's in some respects. While Foucault believes that various power systems are "interwoven," "correlated," or "inseparable," I attempt to specify the relations of power, especially those involving nationalist and capitalist networks.[27] On one occasion, he states that power is so "consubstantial with the development of forces of production that it forms part of them" when the forces of production are meant to be capitalist material forces.[28] When Foucault suggests that there is mutual dependency among networks of power, this is primarily in reference to positive relations. He does not specify the caveats or tensions that might be present in the relations of networks of power. For example, when he states that the aim of the Panopticon is "to strengthen the social forces—to increase production, to develop the economy, spread education, raise the level of public morality; to increase and multiply," it is not clear under what conditions this objective is realized and whether it encounters power dynamics that inhibit it.[29] In this book, I consider the *disjuncture* of national governmentality and capitalist expansion, addressing the people *inside* the circuits of capitalist production and exchange. I investigate the subjectivity in social practices through which people respond to multiple forces of power that might not only propagate but also circumvent each other.

MANCHURIA

In light of the analytical framework presented so far, I now map out the social transformation of Manchuria at two historical moments: before and after the Japanese occupation of 1931. I present the formation of the private property system as a sublimation of the articulation of colonialism, nationalism, and capitalism. The private property system is the primary mechanism that separates people from the means of production, a process called primitive accumulation. Primitive accumulation is not a pure economic form; it depends on the existence of a nation-state to impose the private property system as law. The legalization of private property rights obscures the ideological and material process through which a property owner appropriates labor power deposited on land. As the right to appropriate surplus labor, the private property system is not restricted to the transaction of property assets but involves the regulation of wages and socially necessary times of labor. Karl Marx considers the importance of the role of the nation-state in a discussion that postulates the private property system as the ontological foundation of the nation-state: the state's existence came to rely on property laws to a greater extent than its power simply safeguards the law.[30] Karl Marx's account of primitive accumulation is more a genealogy of capitalism than an exposition of a historical process. According to many critics, primitive accumulation was not completed in the initial moment of capitalist development but continues in different forms, including the separation of people from both the material and nonmaterial means of production under imperial and postindustrial conditions.[31]

The Manchurian experience demonstrates historical processes of primitive accumulation in which nation formation played a key role. Marx's accounts of capital accumulation present the nation and the private property system as requirements of capital, yet the social practices of private property rights were never fixed in Manchuria. Although the nation made the property system seem natural, the private property system continued to be a main source of dispute among national elites, colonial power holders, and laborers. The formation of the private property system in Manchuria was marked by a series of *disjunctures* among law, policies, and social practices: state policies of the private property system deviated from the laws, and social practices deviated from laws and policies. The subsequent deviation signifies the tension between nation formation and global capitalism, which together constituted the social relations of production and exchange.

When the central Qing government of China legalized migration to Manchuria in 1884, a place previously preserved as the birthplace of the founder of the Qing, land gradually was privatized and sold to migrants from North China by local officials, who lacked government revenue and private income. Land became a commodity, whose sale and purchase were unrestricted, even though bribery of officials enabled purchasers to acquire larger parcels than could otherwise be obtained. Due to its lack of administrative power, the government did not fully establish legal protections for private property. Instead, property owners, especially large landlords, relied on private armies to protect their land. In addition, the shortage of labor to cultivate privately owned land as well as the availability of uncultivated land attracted peasant migrants from North China and Korea, who came to be the mainstay of agricultural production. In this initial stage of economic privatization, independent farmers tended to engage less in commercial than subsistence farming. The relationship between landlords and merchants in the commercialization of crops had not yet matured.

The gradual encroachment of Japanese colonial power and capital that began in the late nineteenth century had a paradoxical impact on social relations in Manchuria. It accelerated the incorporation of Manchuria into the global capitalist network, but it also provoked the intervention of the Chinese government (central and local) in relations of property and production. Through the interplay of the nationalization and privatization of land, commercial farming and the circulation of agricultural produce within and beyond Manchuria swiftly developed. By the early 1930s, Manchuria was producing almost half of all the soybeans traded in the world. The Chinese government intervened in social relations, representing itself as a national regime that could defend Manchuria and China proper from Japanese colonization.

This book investigates two moments in the incorporation of Manchuria into a global chain of production and market exchange: the period from the late nineteenth century to 1931; and the Manchukuo era, which lasted from 1932 to 1945. During the first period, Manchuria experienced a condensed form of accumulation in which primitive accumulation coexisted with export-oriented agricultural production. At the moment when wasteland was turned into arable land with market value, land became a primary form of capital in which landlords, merchants, the state, and Japanese business interests invested. Through the negotiation of various Chinese nationalist powers and Japanese capital, the relationship between land and labor in Manchuria was incorporated into the global market to such an extent that the worldwide depression, combined with the ongoing warfare of the warlord regime, precipitated a social crisis in the late 1920s. De facto colonization from 1932 marked a different moment, as it intensified the incorporation of Manchuria into a newly configured chain of global capital accumulation. Social relations based on the ground rent system were transformed into those based on the credit system, modifying the axis of social inequality.

In the following pages, I pursue the ways in which, during both moments of capital transformation in Manchuria, the double abstraction of the social gave birth to ethnic, national, regional, and temporal unevenness. In the representation of a would-be national state (whether it was a Chinese warlord regime, Manchukuo, or the new national state that the communists sought to create), land increasingly meant not just a resource for subsistence living or market exchange but the territory of the nation. Nationalization set an artificial price on land independent of the law of supply and demand: the nationalist government of China until 1931 set the terms of contracts, restricting the exchange of land to its nationals and imposing limits on the maximum number of years nonnationals (Koreans who had not been naturalized as Chinese nationals) could be employed and maximum wages they could be paid. The Manchukuo state, established in 1932, envisaged the establishment of small farmers, rather than merchants and rich farmers, as the bastion of the nation. This nationalization of social relations proceeded violently, as the government charged violators with treason and imprisoned them. The sovereignty of people over their bodies, labor, and products was appropriated by the state, which emerged with its alliance with merchants and landlords as a major agent of nationalism and capitalism.[32]

The national price set on land had contradictory effects on economic development. On the one hand, it was a barrier to capital accumulation since it inhibited the free circulation of the commodities of land and labor. On the other hand, it was a mechanism that created "free" labor separated from land and it increased rent. The national price killed the two birds of "anti-capitalist cancer"—a vast area of available land and a shortage of labor that Marx described in his analysis of the role of the colonial government in setting an artificial price on virgin soil.[33] By setting an exorbitant price, the nationalization of land compelled laborers to work for a long time despite the poor prospects of buying land of one's own. The artificial national price intervened in the process through which workers became landowners or landless free labor. Nation formation in Manchuria until 1931 enabled migrants from North China to become landowners while preventing their Korean counterparts from doing so. As Japan began to encroach on Manchuria, interventions such as funding Korean migrants and sending police and armies to protect them eliminated the customary rights to reside and own property in Manchuria that Koreans had previously possessed. Koreans' national membership and property rights came to occupy center stage in the negotiations between the Japanese colonial power and the Chinese nationalist government in Manchuria.

The ethnic/national axes of property relations were a historical form of the double abstraction of people, land, and their relations as the embodiment of the nation on the one hand and as a commodity on the other. The construction of national membership was inseparable from the value of one's labor power in agricultural production, which both the Japanese and Chinese powers tried to appropriate. For this reason, the construction of national membership was predicated on their relationship with nationals, who, as cultivators and wage laborers, had established relations with land. The production of people as labor was in turn predicated on their relationship with laborers, whose national identities circumscribed their chances for landownership and employment.

My discussion of the entwined abstraction of people, land, and their relations centers on two aspects: the ongoing construction of boundaries between national and nonnational members, which were inscribed in the relationship involving the exchange of land; and the forces that simultaneously shaped and destabilized national boundaries and social practices of production and exchange. The force that produced the entwined abstraction of people and land was the interplay of Japanese colonialism, Chinese nationalism, and capitalism. Neither the Japanese colonial power nor the Chinese nationalist power was a single, unified entity. Both were fraught with ten-

sions and conflicts within themselves. Although the Japanese empire portrayed itself as seamless, in fact it consisted of distinct administrative units
(e.g., Government General of Korea, the Manchukuo state, and the Kwantung Army) that represented different nationals and feuded with one another. The Chinese national power in Manchuria until 1931 was advanced by
the military government, civil bureaucrats, and merchants. The relationship
within and between the Japanese and Chinese powers determined the boundaries of the national and the nonnational, as well as their social relations.
Although the Japanese and Chinese powers competed for territorial sovereignty in Manchuria, they shared dreams of the capitalist development of
agriculture. It was within the entangled relationship between the Japanese
and Chinese powers that Koreans (and Chinese) found an interstitial space
where they sought to negotiate with both.

Chapter 1 presents Korean migration as a mechanism in the formation
of the Japanese empire and its capitalist expansion, which I term the territorial and capitalist politics of "osmosis." Setting the stage for this is my
reading of *Pukkando*, a representative novel in the South Korean nationalist
literature; the analysis foregrounds the politics of osmosis and the peasants'
sovereignty over their labor.

Chapters 2–5 examine the tensions between nation formation and capitalist expansion in the two phases of Japanese colonization of Manchuria—
territorial encroachment (1910s–1931) and de facto colonization (1932–45).
Nation formation in each period was marked by historically specific characteristics, for example, the distinctive triangular relationship among the Chinese national power, the Japanese colonial power, and Korean peasants, and
such cultural discourses of the nation as the nationalist representation of migrants and landed property until 1931 and agrarian communitarianism after
1931. The disparate nationalist politics and culture in the two periods drew
different distinctions between nationals and nonnationals and organized social relations of production and market exchange in various ways. While I de-
lineate the historical specificities of nation formation in each period, I also
focus on the perplexing relations of nation formation and capitalist expansion. The intrinsic tension between them finds its historical expression in
the persistent gulfs among the laws, policies, and social practices of national
membership and property rights. Although as a de facto colony Manchukuo
was thought of as bureaucratic, modern, and rational, the process of nation
formation was as incomplete as it had been under the preceding "warlord"
regime.

Chapters 2 and 3 compare regional variations in the national regime until 1931. Although they belonged to the same regional jurisdiction, headed by Zhang Zuolin, the Fengtian and Kando governments put the principle of national membership into practice through disparate policies and social practices. The principle of national membership considered private ownership of land to be the foremost right of nationals (*gongmin*). The right to elect political representatives was promised to nationals but never implemented. In the regions of South and East Manchuria, competition between the national and colonial powers for territorial sovereignty was translated into contestation over the rights of Koreans, whom both Japan and the Zhang government considered to be the vanguard of Japanese imperialism. The Fengtian government of South Manchuria adopted an exclusionary policy toward Koreans, prohibiting them from acquiring Chinese citizenship and owning land. In contrast, the Kando government in East Manchuria adopted an inclusive policy, encouraging Koreans to become naturalized as Chinese nationals. The disparate policies toward Koreans arose from the different relationships between the Zhang Zuolin government and Japan—a contending yet balanced one in South Manchuria and a competing one in the east.

The patterns of retreat from nationalist policies are also compared in chapters 2 and 3. Whether exclusionary or inclusive, the Korean population swelled in both regions, where most remained unnaturalized. Negotiations between the Zhang government and Koreans took many forms. The government improvised various measures requiring a few representatives of a Korean village or the heads of households to adopt Manchu customs. These cultural and communal national memberships were replaced over time with a legal and individually based form that required all male adults above the age of eighteen to apply for authorization at county offices. Koreans subverted such laws and policies by adopting aberrant forms of national membership and landownership: leasing land for long periods (*sangjogwŏn*) in South Manchuria and registering purchased land under the names of the few naturalized Koreans or Chinese (*Chŏnminje*) in Kando. Unnaturalized Koreans also survived by working as short-term tenants and low-wage laborers, frequently migrating to the periphery to evade the legal restrictions on settlement.

The fact that these seditious social practices were tolerated suggests that Koreans' bargaining power stemmed from their skill at rice farming, which both the Zhang government and Japan found valuable. The transformation of national membership from cultural and collective to legal and individual and the coexistence of legal and customary practices indicate the blurred distinction between nationals and nonnationals and, by extension, the incomplete formation of the (Chinese) nation in Manchuria. The transitory nature of its laws, policies, and social practices suggests a premodern, if not feudal, image of Manchuria. But I situate the fleeting instability and irregularity in the modern conundrum of nation formation and capitalist expansion.

Chapters 4 and 5 explore agrarian cooperatives as a new historical form of national membership entwined with landownership in which Koreans and Japanese were not only accepted as legal residents in Manchuria but also in principle elevated to small property owners. Dual nationality also characterized nation formation in the Manchukuo state. As the Japanese empire practiced division of labor among putative nation-states, the Government General of Korea and the Kwantung Army continued to represent, respectively, Koreans and Japanese in Manchuria who were also simultaneously governed by the Manchukuo state. Each administrative power built different agrarian cooperatives for Koreans, Japanese, or Chinese. Chapter 4 discusses the colonizer's territorial and capitalist desires, which prompted the various administrative powers to adopt agrarian communitarianism as a means of reinventing social relations and integrating Manchuria into the empire. Agrarian cooperatives fostered inequality in terms of the share of land and loans distributed to different nationals, which defied the pluralistic principle of national membership and universal private property rights. I attribute the hierarchical pattern to the unequal positions of different nationals in the Japanese empire and their dissimilar contributions to capitalist development in Manchuria and the empire as a whole.

Chapter 5 examines the formation of governmentality, which exposed a different layer of the schism between nation formation and capitalist expansion. The institution of agrarian cooperatives constituted a new governmentality. The cooperatives nationalized governance, while homogenizing a population divided by origin, socioeconomic status, and nationality, and created disciplinary techniques. But capitalist dynamics simultaneously thwarted the actualization of such nationalist institutions, engendering continuous differentiation and displacement of Korean and Chinese peasants from the land. Despite a plethora of adjustments, the administrative powers were incapable of standardizing the corporeal movement of Koreans. The practices of marking, coding, and registering Koreans had meager results, as they involved less than half the total number of Korean migrants.

The main body of this book provides a basis for establishing the link between Manchuria and Korean (and Chinese) communist politics in chapter 6.

Discussions of the origins of the North Korean revolution have always been preoccupied with the legendary anticolonial struggle in Manchuria led by the late Kim Il Sung and his comrades during the colonial period. Instead I explore the *social origins* of the Korean communist movement and the ways in which the nationalism espoused by the communists impeded their recognition of social relations in Manchuria and undermined their claims to internationalism. Colonial sovereignty was embedded in the creation of national subjects, whose labor power and property rights determined national membership. The viability of any communist critique depended on the elimination of social relations spawned by colonial capitalism. But both Korean and Chinese communists regarded Manchuria as an extension of their putative nation-states. Their inability to comprehend the commonalities and historical specificities of social relations in Korea, China proper, and Manchuria prevented them from creating international alliances across these places. The trauma of the purge of Koreans from the Chinese Communist Party exposed the tension between nationalism and internationalism. The communist struggle in Manchuria prefigured the establishment of the North Korean state that would be more nationalist than internationalist.[34]

The Politics of Osmosis:

Korean Migration

and the Japanese

Empire

Japan considered the occupation of Korea to be the first step in the colonization of Manchuria, China proper, India, and ultimately the rest of Asia.
In such a dream, the expansion of the Japanese empire hinged not on a dependent relationship between the metropole and each colony, with the latter
serving the former as a provider of resources or a market. Rather, the dream
rested on an intricate relationship between the colonizer and the colonized,
with the latter acting as a series of vessels that would allow Japan's sovereign
power to flow outward in succession, from one to the next, forming an extensive Asian community. I conceptualize this cascading strategy of empire
building as *the politics of osmosis*. In the osmotic process, the moving bodies
of Koreans, not immobile institutions or movable things per se, embodied
Japan's power in Manchuria like the cellular webs of a larger, expanding
body. This claim to power was mobilized as a strategy to displace Chinese
authority over Koreans and their lands and establish suzerainty over Manchuria. The politics of osmosis entailed the logic of territorial expansion and
the logic of capitalist expansion, for which a following reading of *Pukkando*,
a novel by An Sugil, works as an allegory. Issues pertinent to the reading of
the novel include the relationship between the Japanese power holders and
Korean peasants as bedfellows who both dream of obtaining land; the dual
position of Koreans as colonizers and colonized; and the social as a locus of

the triangular relations among Koreans, Chinese, and Japanese that is organized by nationalist and capitalist time.[1]

READING *PUKKANDO*

Manchuria occupied a new place in the Korean literary imaginary, since Korean writers settled in Kando (a district of Jilin Province in Manchuria and
currently the Korean Yanbian Autonomous Prefecture) during the colonial
period and wrote in Korean even after its use was banned in Korea. The lives
of the colonized on a new frontier galvanized the production of Manchurian
imaginaries. The plight of Koreans, their suffering at the hands of bandits
and Chinese landlords, and the allure of new, fertile land were familiar literary representations of Manchuria. As many of these writers went to live in
North Korea after liberation, their works were largely unavailable to South
Korean readers during the cold war.[2] One of the best-known writers who
moved to South Korea after liberation is An Sugil, who worked for *Mansŏn
Ilbo*, a Korean newspaper in Manchuria. Among An's key works, *Pukkando*
stands in opposition to *Pukhyangbo*, which is more controversial. Published
as a serialized novel from 1944 to 1945 in *Mansŏn Ilbo*, the latter portrays
Koreans as dedicated colonial subjects who embraced as their own Japan's
official project of creating new farms for relocated Korean peasants. While
Pukhyangbo branded the author as a collaborator, *Pukkando* can be counted
as a work of redemption. Written between 1959 and 1967 in South Korea,
Pukkando's two volumes narrate the epic of Korean migration to Manchuria
from the 1860s to 1945 and lives caught between Chinese nationalism and
Japanese imperialism. The second volume, which treats the period from the
early 1910s until 1945, is an orthodox nationalist narrative that depicts Koreans as victims of imperialism and heroes of anti-Japanese struggle. But the
first volume, the focus of my reading, offers a rare account of the preceding period, which has been largely overlooked in nationalist literature and
historical studies of Manchuria. More importantly, the representation of the
earlier period of Korean settlement offers essential insights into the dual
subjectivity of Koreans, who negotiated their lives as colonizers of Manchuria who were themselves colonized by Japan.

   Pukkando belongs to a nationalist literature that envisages peasants as the
subjects of a new history in which peasants not only secure their means of
living but also become enlightened constituents of a modern nation. In the

novel, the social life of peasants is dialectically opposed to that of modern citizens, as the inept government cannot protect impoverished peasants from natural calamities, forcing them to relocate on a new frontier. The generational unity of the family resolves this opposition, which leads to productive farming and a stronger nation. The genealogy of the protagonist family begins with its migration from southern Korea to a region bordering China. This migration is part of an official project of guarding Korean territory after the Choson state obtained the northern Tuman River region from China in 1432. The second uprooting of the family and its neighbors comes after four centuries of prosperity, when a persistent drought results in the family's financial devastation. This coincides with a new national crisis following the attacks by French, Russian, American, and Japanese warships. In the late nineteenth century, the family moves to (northern) Kando—Pukkando.

The migration to northern Kando represents the survival of the family and the nation. On the one hand, it is literally the final attempt at survival by the impecunious peasants. When migration is prohibited and violators are sentenced to death, the choice for the peasants is between dying of hunger and being executed by the state. On the other hand, the migration to Kando is figuratively the passage to a new Korean nation. Hanbok, a protagonist in Pukkando, was one of the few Koreans who risked his life to farm in Kando. As Kando is located just across the Tuman River from Hanbok's village in Korea, farming there requires crossing the river daily. He usually sets out for Kando in the dark and returns home before dawn, having farmed throughout the night. Hanbok's clandestine farming is inadvertently revealed by his son when the boy trades three potatoes for a friend's toy. When his exposure leads to an official investigation, Hanbok turns this misfortune into an opportunity to aver his belief that Kando is really Korean territory. In the end, he helps the Korean government to establish proof of its territorial right to Kando.

The reacquisition of this territory signifies a new period of nation building, as corrupted state officials have succumbed to the power of China and failed to refute the centuries-old claim of China to this land. Hanbok leads a wave of Korean migration that turns this frontier into yet another flourishing village. By obtaining land and operating schools for children, Hanbok resolves the conflict between farming and education that has spanned three generations and sown enmity between his grandfather and his father, as well as between his father and him. The Confucian principle considers the patrilineal family—especially the father-son lineage—to be the nucleus of the national community. According to Confucianism, rule of the whole world begins with command of one's own body and family and the ideal relationship between the state and its people must mirror the innate relationship between the patriarch and his family. Father-son conflict symbolizes the breakdown of the national community and subsequent threats to the survival of the patriline. The resolution of generational conflict in Hanbok's family in Kando connotes the resolution of this national crisis.

The following analysis of three episodes from the book offers three examples of bedfellow-type relationships that Koreans develop with the Chinese and Japanese. Although they take place in different historical contexts, these episodes are not necessarily a chronicle of fleeting triangular relationships. They can be considered synchronic metamorphoses in which national and capitalist time—though the latter is often suggestive—produce variant modes of the triangular relationship. All of the events within specific historical contexts inscribe Koreans to the a priori space of the Korean nation in different registers. Their national identity is brought into tension with their capitalist pursuits, including the maintenance of private property rights and the expansion of market activities. The first triangular relationship among Koreans, Chinese, and Japanese reinforces Korean nationalism, as it develops when China, fearing Japanese encroachment on Manchuria, stipulates naturalization of Koreans as Chinese nationals as a prerequisite for landownership. The compromise between Korean and Chinese nationalism yields aberrant forms of naturalization and landownership. The second triangular relationship involves the united front of Korean and Chinese nationalisms against the corrupt states of China and Korea. This new national and global consciousness is transformed into a popular politics coupled with material gain. The third relationship revolves around the pursuit by Chinese and Japanese policemen of a Korean felon in a city. The chase represents the increased exchange value of Koreans, their double oppression as a result of the territorial rivalry between China and Japan, and the advantages that Koreans carve out by turning these rivals against each other. These advantages can also be taken as a signifier of the commodification of Korean labor, which both the Chinese and Japanese powers sought to appropriate in order to develop Manchurian agriculture. In each relationship, international historical events coalesce with those of Koreans in Kando to dramatize emergent configurations of Korean subjectivity arising from their dual position as colonizer and colonized. Instead of standing apart from one another, the three episodes exhibit variant dimensions of the triangular relationship.

"Potato Tales": Social Life and the Nation

The episode of the potato incidents offers the first venue for the emergent opposition between Koreans and Chinese, which accelerates as Japanese imperialism advances. China had been defeated in the Sino-Japanese War (1894–95), which broke out when China and Japan sent troops to Korea allegedly to quell the Tonghak peasant rebellion. In the treaty signed at Shimonoseki in 1898, China conceded the full independence of Korea and transferred the Liaodong Peninsula of Manchuria and the island of Taiwan to Japan.[3] In 1870 and 1881, respectively, authorization of the migration of Korean and Chinese peasants by Korea and China had rekindled age-old territorial disputes. After its defeat in the war, China feared that Japan would intervene in these territorial disputes.[4] The Qing government therefore began to pressure the Koreans of Kando to become naturalized as Chinese citizens.

At that time, naturalization took the cultural form (*Hŭkpok pyŏnbal* or *Ch'ibal yŏkpok*) of enforcing Manchu clothing and hairstyles—black clothes with wide, long sleeves and hair shaved in front and worn in a long ponytail in back. This Manchu custom contrasts with the Korean practice of wearing white clothes and different hairstyles according to marital status—short hair in front and a long ponytail in back for unmarried men and hair tied and worn on top of the head for married men. In seeking a concession from the Koreans, the Qing authorities presented naturalization as a process as easy as cutting the front hair for unmarried men and untying hair for married men.[5] *Pukkando* relates that many Koreans felt that the soul of the nation "would not forgive such naturalization," since Confucian custom identifies one's hair as a bequest of the ancestors.[6]

The issue of naturalization, however, exceeded the matter of one's national identity. As the Qing government required it as a precondition for landownership, the matter of naturalization concerned the sovereignty of Koreans over their social lives. Being products of labor, potatoes in *Pukkando* symbolize the labor of producers, which increases the value of land. The property rights to one's land are equivalent to the sovereignty over one's social life since the value of land is inextricable from the labor one expends on it. The novel's potato incidents depict the tension between social life and national identity, which is posited as an opposition by the Chinese law that entwined nationality and landownership. In the novel, the issue of naturalization presents Koreans with the thorny dilemma of choosing between keeping their national identity and defending their rights to their lands. A deepening of this predicament, in tandem with mounting tensions between the Chinese and Koreans, sets the stage for a potato incident. During their play-time, Ch'angyun—Hanbok's grandson—and his friends steal potatoes from a farm owned by the village's richest Chinese landlord. Ch'angyun's action is triggered not just by hostility toward the landlord but also by disdain for his Korean neighbors, who increasingly seem to succumb to the landlord. The landlord's household members reprimand Ch'angyun by simulating his naturalization—changing his clothes and hair to the Manchu style.

Hanbok's death from the shock over this incident facilitates a compromise between social life and naturalization in his village. Before his death, the villagers had debated the contending positions on the best "method to love the village." In the first proposition, the one recommended by the Chinese government, a couple of their representatives would become naturalized and register under their names the land tilled by the unnaturalized village members. The opposition, led by Hanbok, not only reinvoked Kando as Korean territory but also affirmed Koreans' right to ownership of their land: "Regardless of whether the Korean government is too weak or corrupt to claim sovereignty over Kando, it is not feasible for us to give to China the land on which we poured our sweat and blood. Even though the naturalization of a couple of our representatives is a practical strategy to maintain our ownership, it would be grounds for the next generation to become slaves of the Chinese people."[7] Adopting this strategy after Hanbok's death, the Koreans elect their representatives and create their own land title—apart from the official title that the Chinese government had issued to nominal landowners—which will distinguish real and nominal landowners. The elected representatives at first help the Koreans in their negotiations with local Chinese officials over taxation and other legal matters. But, as Hanbok predicted, they increasingly exert power over the other Koreans.

Ch'angyun's potato incident brings his family back to the time of crisis in Korea by resuscitating the repressed memory of an earlier potato incident, one that involved his grandfather (Hanbok) and father (Changson) before their migration to Kando. In the repeated potato incidents, the crisis of the entwined national and social order is encoded on and resolved by the father-son relationship. As Hanbok once resolved the schism between his grandfather and father, Ch'angyun does the same for his grandfather and father. Ch'angyun's incident causes Hanbok to remember his own saga of illegal farming. Hanbok is overcome with pride, but it is mixed with apprehension over the conditions that are once again threatening the family's livelihood. Guilt over Hanbok's subsequent death induces Ch'angyun to fight with his best friend. They mock each other, calling each other "Chinese" (Ch'angyun once wore Manchu clothes and the father of his friend has adopted Chinese naturalization in his role as a village representative). Ch'angyun breaks his ankle after falling from a cliff and becomes ill. While Changson at first blames his son for his foolishness, Ch'angyun's remorse, even in delirium, leads Changson to a tearful reminiscence of an event that had been deeply suppressed for decades. Years ago, when Changson's trading of the potatoes for a toy led to the arrest of his father, the enraged Hanbok declared that he would "kill whoever reported my farming in Kando to the government, even my child." Changson now suspects that the lesson learned from this first potato incident must have nurtured the perseverance and determination necessary to survive in Kando. Ch'angyun's potato incident seems to bring closure to a generation-long tension in his family, as well as the conflict in the village over naturalization.

The repetition of potato episodes over three generations signifies the homogeneous and continuous time of the Korean nation, which is also marked by subtle ambiguity. National time binds the Koreans of Kando to the Korean nation. The potato incidents embody the persistent struggle of Korean migrants to maintain their social life within national time. In *Pukkando*, the repetition of the struggle is further accentuated by the fact that a childhood friend who tempted Ch'angyun's father with a toy is now a village representative who becomes naturalized, and that this friend's son is responsible for Ch'angyun's fall from the cliff. The dialectical resolution of the father-son conflict by the succeeding generation denotes the working of national time, which naturalizes the unity of peasants and the nation. When the villagers condemn the Korean state for failing even to protect their subjects' right to wear their own clothes, the resolution of the patrilineal friction implies that the author of *Pukkando* still preserves the agency of the nation itself in calling on the peasant migrants to reconcile their social life and national identity. Yet this work of the nation in the narratives of *Pukkando* remains incomplete. The pain inflicted on Korean bodies—Hanbok's death and Ch'angyun's broken ankle and illness—implies that the experience of the migrants cannot be contained by national time. The growing clash between the villagers and their naturalized representatives foretells a new crisis for the family, community, and nation. Hanbok's death intimates the end of the old national time and the inauguration of a new one.

"You and We Are the Same":
A Popular United Front of Koreans and Chinese

This episode depicts a new national time in Kando, Korea, and China, which is entwined with capitalist time. The issue of naturalization is reconfigured here into a popular politics, one in which Koreans' material concerns bind Korean with Chinese nationalism in everyday life. Events began to unfold when the Russo-Japanese Treaty of 1905 opened the door for Japan's advance on Manchuria and Korea. After the Sino-Japanese War, Russia launched military attacks on Manchuria and Korea. It acquired a number of rights from China and forced Japan to return the Liaodong Peninsula to China in 1895. Russia was permitted to build the eastern portion of the Trans-Siberian Railway through Manchuria, to lease Port Arthur and Dairen on the Liaodong Peninsula, to link these two major ports by rail, and to connect them both to the Trans-Siberian line. Exploiting the political crisis of the Boxer uprising in China in 1900, Russia dispatched its army to Manchuria to prepare for its occupation. Russia also threatened Korea, pressuring Japan to withdraw its forces and accept the proposition that Korea above the thirty-ninth parallel be designated as a neutral zone free from foreign powers. After allying itself with England and the United States to wage war against Russia in 1904, Japan signed the Portsmouth Treaty with Russia in 1905, under which it assumed all Russian rights and privileges in South Manchuria, including the lease of the Liaodong Peninsula. Designated the Kwantung Leased Territory, the peninsula became the base for Japanese penetration into Manchuria. The only concession offered by Japan was a compromise in which it agreed to retain control of only the southern half of the island of Sakhalin.[8]

In *Pukkando*, Koreans in Korea and Manchuria support Russia during the Russian invasion of Manchuria so as to defeat China and Japan. When Chinese officials and landlords in Kando flee Manchuria to escape Russian attacks, the Koreans are freed of the Chinese pressure to become naturalized. Again claiming Kando as its territory, the Korean government, closely allied with Russia, dispatches a commissioner to administer the Koreans. But Japan's victory in the Russo-Japanese War is followed by the return of Chinese officials and landlords and the resumption of the policy of naturalization in Kando. This change combines with other critical transformations in Korea and Japan. Japan forces Korea to sign the Protectorate Treaty in 1905, and Japan's encroachment drives the revolutionary movement in China.

The chapter "You and We Are the Same" (Tangsinnewa urinŭn katta) depicts the emergent politics of the united front forged between Koreans and Chinese against Japanese encroachment. The word *same* in the title represents the new global consciousness shared by Koreans and Chinese—the sharing of a common colonizer that encroaches on the territorial sovereignty of Korea and China. This global viewpoint is enabled by the new social consciousness of Koreans in Kando, which is portrayed through Ch'angyun's experiences. A trip to his grandfather's hometown in Korea provides Ch'angyun with the opportunity to distinguish Korea and the Koreans of Kando. When he steps onto the soil of Korea, Ch'angyun is overwhelmed by envy of people in Korea. In his initial impression, the land, people, and lifestyle in Korea are more authentic than in Kando. Whereas horror and menace by beasts and thieves define Kando's natural setting, "peace and comfort dwell in trees and forests" in Korea. "The air is tender and the sky is a more lucid blue in the [Korean] hometown."[9] The thinly layered clothing of the Koreans appears to Ch'angyun to be more stylish than his own heavily padded attire. However, this comparison is instantly reversed to favor Kando when Ch'angyun observes the despair and hardship suffered by his relatives. If he once denigrated his fellow villagers in Kando for their dark skin, the result of long hours toiling under the sun, Ch'angyun now appreciates their diligence and trust in one another. He mutters, "no matter what, ours [social life in Kando] is the best."[10] His bitter memories of hardship in Kando turn into a sense of achievement.

Recognizing "ours" foregrounds a new social consciousness among Koreans in Kando in recognition of the worth of their accumulated labor and their right to own the land that absorbs it. This social consciousness rests on differences between the Koreans of Kando and Korea that do not necessarily lead to contradiction and opposition. It means that the social experiences of the Koreans of Kando escape the homogenizing and territorializing parameters of the nation. It is from this position of difference that Ch'angyun mediates between the Koreans of Korea and the Chinese to forge a new national and global consciousness: "Koreans and Chinese are the same." It is also through didactic conversations with his former Korean teacher, Mr. Cho, and an imprisoned Chinese revolutionary, Mr. Wang, that Ch'angyun attempts to reconcile his social consciousness with the new Chinese and Korean nationalisms that entail global cooperation in the struggle against Japan. Mr. Cho is one of the vanishing breed of Confucian scholars who opposed the Protectorate Treaty between Korea and Japan. He advises Ch'angyun that the enemies of Koreans in Kando are no longer Chinese but Japanese and Russian and that

Koreans and Chinese must learn to cooperate. Despite its defeat by Japan, Russia shares with it the aspiration to colonize Korea and China. Whereas it is easy for Ch'angyun to understand that Koreans must prevent Japanese encroachment, he expresses misgivings about overcoming the animosity between the Koreans of Kando and the Chinese. When Mr. Cho is found dead the next morning, Ch'angyun "wants to believe" that his death was a suicide and that his appeal for the united front was his legacy to Ch'angyun. Determined to honor it, Ch'angyun tries to suppress his deep-seated hostility toward the Chinese.

Ch'angyun's doubts about an alliance with the Chinese are partially resolved by his encounter with a Chinese revolutionary, Mr. Wang. Returning to his village, Ch'angyun is arrested for an alleged link between a Korean self-defense group, which he organized during the Russian invasion of Manchuria, and Chinese revolutionary infiltrators. At this point, five or six years before the establishment of Republican China in 1911, Mr. Wang is a revolutionary from South China. Sharing the same prison cell, the two men intermittently converse during the night. Consoling Ch'angyun, who was tortured during his interrogation, Mr. Wang tells him that although the prison officials are thieves "all our Chinese people are not bad" and "there are more good people." Mr. Wang then repeats what Mr. Cho stated: "Chinese and Koreans are the same." In Ch'angyun's mind, Mr. Cho's thief is Japan and Mr. Wang's is the tyrannical Qing government.

Revolutionary Chinese nationalism overcomes the previous antagonism between Chinese and Koreans (of both Korea and Kando) by identifying Japan and the Qing government as their common enemies. Ch'angyun realizes that the Qing government is also the enemy of the Koreans of Kando. For Ch'angyun, the government deserves to be called a thief by Koreans, for it "asserts that others' [Koreans'] land is its own land. Asserting others' people as its own people, it also forced them to braid their hair and wear its own clothing styles. These crimes against Koreans are sufficient to make it a thief."[11] On their final night together, Mr. Wang observes that Japan is also a thief in the eyes of the Chinese people.[12] Ch'angyun and Mr. Wang tell each other that "Koreans and Chinese are the same." As Mr. Wang is finally about to expand on his thoughts, the conversation is interrupted by a prison guard, who calls Mr. Wang for his clandestine execution. Overwhelmed by empathy for this revolutionary, Ch'angyun repeats the phrase of Mr. Cho and Mr. Wang: "Koreans and Chinese are the same."

The embryonic social, national, and global consciousness of Koreans in

Kando appears to be analogous to the utopian and revolutionary formula necessary for genuine, simultaneous liberation from capitalist, national, and colonial oppression. Ch'angyun's social consciousness entails a new national and global consciousness about colonial power and the corrupt national governments of Korea and China. His social consciousness leads to a Korean national and global consciousness in which he identifies with the Koreans of Korea and the Chinese of Manchuria and China but nevertheless acknowledges the distinctive experiences of the Koreans of Kando. This distinction of Koreans in Kando exposes the impossibility of homogenizing them with either Korea or China. Earlier Korean and Chinese nationalisms subsumed the Koreans of Kando by regarding Kando as an extension of Korea (by refusing naturalization as Chinese nationals) and China (by forcing Koreans to become Chinese nationals). Ch'angyun's social consciousness is now capable of envisioning an alliance with the Koreans of Korea and the Chinese that will not require assimilation. If this social consciousness were to blossom, it could lead the Korean and Chinese "people" in a new national and global struggle. The new global alliance requires transcendence of national differences over territory, customs, and traditions. It must entail a simultaneous critique of colonialism, nationalism, and capitalism, whose complex interactions expel the laborers of Korea, Kando, and China from the land.

A viable global consciousness capable of liberating Koreans and Chinese from nationalist and colonial oppression must address not just commonalities among the colonized but also the differences and hierarchy within and between the oppressed and the oppressors. But homogenizing nationalism renders this possibility indefinite. Although Ch'angyun's recognition of the social distinction of Koreans of Kando lays the groundwork for a united front composed of Koreans and Chinese, Ch'angyun's social consciousness continues to be suppressed by his empathy for Mr. Cho and Mr. Wang. In the phrase, "you and we are the same," the categories "you" and "we" refer to national communities—Korea and China. Annexing Kando to Korea, the category "we" homogenizes the Koreans of both Korea and Kando as "Korean" (Han'gugin). The national consciousness of Mr. Cho and Mr. Wang remains bound to territorial and ethnic homogeneity. Although both recognize the distinctive value of Korean life in Kando, neither Mr. Cho nor Ch'angyun extends this egalitarian relationship to Korea and Kando. When Ch'angyun expresses his doubts about the united front, he quickly displaces them by embracing Mr. Cho's appeal as his legacy. This subdued doubt or hostility toward the Chinese symbolizes the incomplete nature of the new national and global consciousness. The interrupted conversation between Ch'angyun and the Chinese prisoner is also a metaphor for this insufficient consciousness. Though groundbreaking, Ch'angyun's insight into the distinction between Korea and Kando fails to problematize the singular category of "we" or "Han'gugin."

Capitalist time further unsettles the sensibility of the nascent social, national, and global consciousness. It operates during the metamorphosis of the united front into popular consciousness. In *Pukkando*, the unity of Koreans and Chinese is said to spread from mouth to mouth among Korean and Chinese peasants. Though petty conflicts between Koreans and Chinese often led to ruthless fights before, they now resolve them with laughter, saying, "you and I are the same." This popular sentiment is consolidated by an intriguing event involving a material and political compromise between Chinese and Koreans. Ch'angyun's villagers are cajoled into a general compact with the Chinese state and a landlord, coupling their popular consciousness with material gain. They are interested in bringing the local government office to their village. Unthinkable even a few years ago, this idea is fostered by their desire for economic development in their village, as the transformation of the village as an administrative center is expected to expand market activities. But when the largest Chinese landlord and the Korean representatives ask the villagers to submit a collective petition to the district government of Kando, they hesitate for fear of becoming subordinate to the Chinese government. In their minds, they ask, "How could we end the generations-long struggle with Chinese power in this manner?"[13] In the end, economic dynamics impel them to consent to the petition drive. When bandits steal most of the village's oxen—essential farming animals for Koreans—the Chinese landlord grants the villagers loans to purchase new ones. Even though the Chinese landlord charges a high rate of interest for the loans, the villagers find themselves obliged to support the efforts to bring the government office to their village. Festive moods prevail in the village for a while, though in a parallel development there are growing conflicts among the Koreans themselves.

The social and material concerns of the Korean peasants transpose a popular consciousness into a state of insensate assimilation by Chinese power. It turns out that after the Chinese local office is opened in Ch'angyun's village a naturalized Korean representative becomes its head. The office also shares the space with a Korean primary school. This transposition of a Korean national identity into a Chinese one in *Pukkando* powerfully exposes the power relations in the popular national and global consciousness of Koreans and Chinese against Japanese imperialism. The interplay of national and capitalist time implied here is further symbolized in the next episode.

"Our Value Must Have Increased":
The Exchange Value of Koreans

In this episode, the value of Koreans is determined by territorial and, it is suggested, capitalist competition between China and Japan. The historical context is the penetration of Kando by Japan around 1909. After dissolving the Korean armies in 1907, Japan had created a Korean police substation in Ryongjŏng, the largest city in Kando, ostensibly to protect the "lives and property of Koreans." Intended to settle the territorial disputes between China and Korea (now represented by Japan), the 1909 Kando treaty between China and Japan included three important clauses: Japan recognized Kando as part of China; China, in return, permitted Japan to establish consulates in four major cities in Kando; and China granted Koreans the right to reside and own property in Kando without becoming Chinese citizens. The Kando Treaty fell short of resolving the territorial disputes, let alone constraining Japanese colonization of the region. Japan continued to encroach on Chinese sovereignty, claiming that this was necessary to guard the lives and property of Koreans.

In *Pukkando*, the Kando Treaty consolidates the contradictory position of the Koreans that straddled Chinese and Korean (and Japanese) sovereignties. After Japan establishes its police substation in Ryongjong in the name of protecting Koreans, the Chinese begin to condemn Koreans as the forerunners of Japanese imperialism. Reiterating its sovereignty over Kando, China reimposes its naturalization policy and increases its military presence, although its forces are inferior to those of the Japanese. Some Koreans hold the Japanese police station accountable for growing Korean oppression by the Chinese, while others begin to think of Japan as their protector. After the station is opened, refugees from the Chinese oppression begin to migrate to the city. Even in Ch'angyun's village, Japan's help is discussed as an option when Chinese officials threaten Koreans in their search for the murderer of a Chinese man.

The episode, entitled "Our Value Must Have Increased" (Urido kapsi orŭn sem), takes place in Ryongjŏng in 1909. At this time, the city is the principal commercial center of Kando, as grain from nearby villages is gathered there and sold to merchants. Lined with stores, its streets and markets have become an emblem of commodification and urbanization in Kando. While visiting a friend, Ch'angyun witnesses a scene in which Japanese and Chinese policemen compete to arrest a Korean. A Japanese policeman is escorting a Korean felon, who, dressed in Chinese clothes (ch'ŏngbok), was involved in illegal gambling in the market. The Korean felon and Japanese policeman are chased by a group of Chinese policemen. Narrowing the chase, the Chinese policemen attempt to snatch the arrested Korean from the Japanese. One Chinese wrests away the rope that binds the hands and waist of the Korean gambler. Two others try to hold the criminal. To deter the Chinese from stealing the felon, a Japanese policeman fires gunshots in the air. In that moment, the Korean takes advantage of the chaos and escapes. Chinese and Japanese policemen are now running after the Korean. As Pukkando explains this event: "The Japanese policeman arrested the Korean since the latter was Korean despite his Chinese clothes, while Chinese policemen tried to steal him from the Japanese policeman because he violated Chinese law."[14]

The chase epitomizes the competition between Japan and China. It increased the exchange value of Koreans, as if they were commodities to be purchased by the highest bidder. Pukkando represents the exchange value of Koreans in terms of two contrary meanings that Ch'angyun and his friend, Hyŏndo, elaborate—the subjugation and advantages of Koreans. For Hyŏndo, the escape of the gambler is seen as advancing Koreans in the competition. In his words, "it is only the Korean who benefits from the fight between two groups of policemen,"[15] and the competition between Japan and China in courting Koreans "increases the worth of our people."[16] It turns out that the gambler initially took shelter with the Japanese policeman because the policeman was actually Korean. Hyŏndo is dismayed that a Korean defied the trust of another Korean. But he quickly hides his disappointment, saying that "these days, there are a lot of people who speak badly of Japanese consulates and they must have made up the story."[17] In contrast, for Ch'angyun the increased value of Koreans doubles their oppression, as the Korean gambler was betrayed by both the Korean-Japanese and Chinese powers. Thus, Koreans must endure being the victims of Japanese imperialism and Chinese domination. The price of oppression rises, as the competition between the two countries rapidly reduces the interstitial space where Koreans have been able to farm without adopting Chinese citizenship.

Along the lines of Ch'angyun's perspective, national time narrates the double position of Koreans in Pukkando. The familiar linear trope of nationalism dictates the depiction of the Korean experience in terms of oppression and resistance with the goal of liberating Korea. The story's narrative strategy juxtaposes the two conjoined paths taken by Ch'angyun and his son, Chŏngsu: Ch'angyun's continuous displacement and Chŏngsu's education and participation in the noncommunist resistance. When Koreans in Ch'angyun's village fail to identify the killer of the deceased Chinese man, Chinese officials levy fines on the whole village. Beleaguered by heightened tensions and penalties and motivated by rumors of a better life elsewhere, Koreans begin to migrate. Pukkando describes the migration in this way: "One family, two families, they abandon their Pibongch'on village without hesitation to leave for a place where they can live well. This is a kind of wind. It is a blustery wind. Driven by that wind, people in Pibongch'on, family by family, go forward with ragged hope." [18] Some leave for cities, new mining towns, or Russia. Others leave to farm in mountainous areas in northern Manchuria. During the relocations, Ch'angyun's family subsists by running a noodle shop in a city, making bricks, returning to farming, and then running a noodle shop again. The courageous resistance of Koreans is intertwined with this narrative of displacement. Uprooted from their land and family, Ch'angyun's brother even more than Ch'angyun vainly struggles to make a living in the city. He eventually joins the independence army to liberate Korea and finally dies in battle. Unlike Ch'angyun's brother, Ch'angyun's son obtains an education and earns a stable living as a teacher, but he also partakes in the anti-Japanese liberation movement.

National and Capitalist Time

In Pukkando, national time encapsulates the displacement of Koreans as a repetitive experience of a people without a nation. National time abstracts their experience into a single spatial consciousness for all Koreans, whether in Korea, Kando, or other parts of Manchuria. Except for the role of the Chinese government, Koreans' displacement within Manchuria is represented as indistinguishable from their prior displacement from Korea. Each moment of displacement is marked by a chain of events: Koreans are subject to extortion by landlords and officials, they accumulate debt, they lose their mortgaged land, and they flee to a new place. National time homogenizes the social experience of all displaced Koreans. The national representation of displacement dislodges both a local social consciousness of the rights to one's own labor and its products—the one that Ch'angyun and his neighbors had articulated earlier and a global consciousness about the united front with the Chinese people.

This narration of national time also presents the crisis of the nation, insinuating the departure of the Koreans of Kando from Korean nationalism. The narrative strategy of contrasting the passages of father and son — Ch'angyun as the devoted farmer and his son as a schoolteacher and activist — risks the separation of farming and enlightenment, which Ch'angyun's grandfather had unified. This unity worked as a symbol of a new Korean nationalism that was imagined to be realized in Kando, a new frontier for impoverished and uneducated peasants. The threat to the dialectical unity of social life and the Korean nation is further accentuated by the fact that Ch'angyun successfully persuades his son to defect to a Japanese consulate police station. This unfaithful act of Ch'angyun was forced by his anxiety that participation in the independence movement would jeopardize his son's education and future livelihood. Except for several months just before the liberation of Korea and Manchuria from Japan, during which time he would again be imprisoned for planning anti-Japanese activities, he stays away from politics despite the urging of his former comrades to join the guerrilla struggle. Ch'angyun's premature death is in part attributed to his guilt over influencing his son's decision to surrender to Japanese power. Ch'angyun's death is perhaps symptomatic of the dying Korean nation and withering nationalism of Koreans in Manchuria.

Transhistorical national time serves as a container for the diachronic time of capitalism. National time naturalizes the capitalist experiences of Koreans as a byproduct of national oppression. The displacement of Koreans in Ch'angyun's village is represented as the effect of mounting Chinese nationalism and Japanese imperialism. This makes the crucial relationship between national and capitalist time opaque. When Ch'angyun's family and former neighbors receive loans from a Japanese development company to purchase farmland, the narrative does not elaborate the implications for capitalist expansion of these economic ties between Koreans and Japanese. Other symptoms of commodification, such as wage and day labor and peddling in cities, are stated without exploring their capitalist significance. The absence of any reference to communist-led politics in Pukkando is perhaps another sign of a larger silence about capitalism in the linear nationalist narratives of the book.

The dual position of Koreans must be understood as a joint paradoxical effect of the commodification of land and labor, an effect to which all three parties — Koreans, Chinese nationalism, and Japanese imperialism — contributed. Korean migrants and Japanese power are bedfellows who share a capitalist dream. Japanese power has embedded in the dream of the colonized Koreans to secure social life and landownership. The exchange value of Koreans includes their perceived benefits in relation to Japanese power. Moreover, Chinese nationalism and Japanese colonialism are also bedfellows, sharing the dream of swiftly commercializing Manchuria. When the Chinese government banned unnaturalized Koreans from owning property and thus appropriated their land, Chinese nationalism was inseparable from capitalist expansion. In fact, the Chinese Northeast government invested heavily in land and agricultural commerce in Manchuria. Though repeatedly calling for the eviction of unnaturalized Koreans, it simultaneously retreated from this policy and even officially allowed Koreans to remain as agricultural laborers and short-term tenants. In tandem with Chinese oppression, the loans from the Japanese enabled Korean peasants to migrate from Kando to South and North Manchuria. Their transformation of wasteland into lucrative farmland hastened the pace of commodification. Displacement of Koreans from their land is the process whereby they lost control over their means of production. When they are forcibly removed from their land by Chinese oppression or the failure to repay the loans from Japanese organizations, they lost the products of the labor that they had applied to the land and infrastructure such as irrigation systems. The land taken away from Koreans or the high rents and land prices they had to pay in comparison with what their Chinese (and Japanese) counterparts paid are indicators of the exploitation that Koreans experienced in exchange relations at different times and places. An analysis of the dynamics of capital accumulation is necessary for a fuller understanding of the disputes between China and Japan over the citizenship and landownership of Koreans.

Displacement presents a different side of capitalist corporeality. Displacement is not nomadic movement per se but rather a form of movement that has definite forces and effects. National time naturalizes capitalist time, which then universalizes the social experience even as it concurrently distinguishes one moment of displacement from another. The corporeal movement of Koreans is a process of osmotic diffusion of commodification. It is a form of "social metabolism" that removes barriers to production and market exchange. Each migration journey is an instance in which the value of land and labor is created and appropriated. The repetition of displacement is an instance of capital accumulation in which land and labor are commodified along with their exchange value in the market. The exchange value of Koreans not only increased in response to the rivalry of the Japanese and Chinese powers per se. It was also determined by the unequal exchange of their labor power in the market.

Capitalist time authorized a new everyday politics for Koreans beyond their participation in the nationalist movement to liberate Korea. Their everyday politics is also to be assessed in their bargaining power as labor vis-à-vis landlords/capital and in their concrete relations of production and exchange. Even after Koreans migrated, they moved at least three or four times within Manchuria before they settled in one place. The multiple migrations of Koreans acquired a double meaning. The cycle of migration, cultivation, eviction, and remigration carried Japanese and Chinese power to peripheral areas in Manchuria, as the state powers chased after Koreans to claim sovereignty and ownership over the areas they had settled. It also embodied their subjectivities as displaced migrant laborers who desired to harmonize their Korean national identities (the evasion of both Japanese and Chinese pressure) and sovereignty over their labor (de facto ownership of the land to which they applied their labor). The multiple migrations of Koreans attest to their negotiating power with both the Japanese and Chinese, which was derived from the rice-farming skills of Koreans.

Koreans' social experience in Manchuria exceeded a prior spatial identification with their nation, as well as a linear temporality of displacement and nationalist politics. Their aberrant practices of nationality and landownership demonstrate the multiple places and temporalities of their subjectivities. Territorial rivalry between Japan and China (the Northeast Chinese government during the Qing and Republican periods) revolved around issues of the identities and institutional rights of Koreans. Neither Japan nor China, however, succeeded in controlling the direction of Korean migration, farming, and market exchanges, let alone totalizing their identities. Whether naturalized as Chinese nationals and whether before or during the Manchukuo period, Koreans continued to hold dual nationality. Even when they became naturalized as Chinese, their nationality took various cultural, legal, collective, and/or household-based forms. Moreover, naturalized Koreans continued to be identified as Koreans/Japanese. When the majority of Koreans remained unnaturalized, lacked secure rights to ownership of land, and were mobile, they were considered subjects of the Government General of Korea and the Japanese empire (including Manchukuo). Their landownership combined private ownership, long-term leasing, communal landownership, and various loans. The social formations of people as citizens and laborers are mutually constituted at different historical junctures.

National and capitalist times prescribe different kinds of global consciousness and actions. The former conceives globality as an amalgamation of different national communities bound to different territories and potently antagonistic in the case of border disputes. National time obliterates local experience. Capitalist time directs global consciousness by placing local experience in a global process. Because social relations are governed by capital dynamics, in principle and reality, social relations exceed national boundaries, making a global consciousness not just possible but necessary for the liberation of people in each locality. In the Japanese empire, peasants in Korea, Manchuria, Taiwan, and Japan were linked through their reliance on each other for production and reproduction. Agricultural production by each Korean peasant in Kando was regulated by the demand for crops in the world market, and reproduction increasingly depended on workers in Korea and Japan who produced the goods consumed by Koreans in Manchuria. The export of agricultural products produced by laborers in Manchuria transformed the relations of production and exchange in Korea and Japan.

While they bear a local distinction by virtue of their unique politics and culture, social relations in each locality are integrated with those of other localities through the chain of exchange. Global consciousness thus proceeds with the contradictory processes of local differentiations and global integration. A global movement capable of liberating people from capitalist oppression is not a single unified entity but a multiplicity of concrete struggles, each of which is embedded in the distinctive interconnections of local experience and the global context. The creation of this new community requires a dialectical resolution of the relationship between global and local consciousness, which territory-bound nationalism represents as the irreconcilable other. Local struggles in Manchuria must articulate the multiple temporalities of Koreans' experiences, as well as their relations with Chinese and Japanese.

The three episodes of *Pukkando* discussed here demonstrate that the spatial and temporal experiences of Koreans, arising from their double position as the colonized and the colonizer, demand careful analysis of the entangled national and capitalist dynamics. The next section conceptualizes the nation-state system (and nationalism) as the unit of territorial and capitalist expansion of the empire. It also elaborates the dialectical unity and tension between territorial and capitalist expansion. But let me first examine the proposition that Korean migration was a transnational mode of Japanese empire building.

THE POLITICS OF OSMOSIS

The osmotic expansion of the Japanese empire is demonstrated in the way Japan colonized Korea and then paired Korea and Manchuria for the next round of infiltration into China. Korean migrants to Manchuria, mainly peasants, served as "molecules" in the osmotic diffusion of Japan's power from Korea to Manchuria. Japan imagined Korean migrants as if they were fluid agents that could pass through the membrane of Korea's borders into Manchuria, where the solvent concentration (or resistance to Japan's intervention) was higher. In this way, Japan hoped that the migration and settlement of Koreans in Manchuria would neutralize Chinese resistance, making possible a gradual diffusion of Japan's power. The vast majority of the Korean migrants were landless peasants who wanted to escape poverty and debt. In one part of Manchuria, Kando, Koreans had comprised more than two-thirds of the total population since the 1900s. Japan's rule over Koreans in Kando was equated with colonization even before the establishment of Manchukuo in 1932.

The predicament for China was that it could neither evict Korean migrants nor ignore them, although they constituted at best less than 5 percent of the total population of Manchuria by 1931. As a temporary resolution of territorial disputes with Korea (Chosŏn) over Kando, the Qing government granted Koreans customary rights to farming and residence in Kando in the late nineteenth century. Before that time, Manchuria had been a sparsely populated hinterland preserved as the birthplace and hunting grounds of the Qing emperors. As the migration of Chinese to Manchuria was slow, the Qing government hoped that the Korean settlers would create a buffer from the threat of Russian imperialism. Even when the migration of peasants from North China rapidly expanded during the Republican period (1912–31), the Northeast Chinese government, led by Zhang Zuolin, vacillated between policies intended to prevent Korean migration and policies intended to utilize the migrants as rice growers. While vainly trying to evict Koreans from Manchuria, the government attempted to assert its sovereignty over them in order to thwart Japanese colonial ambitions. The confrontation between China and Japan became a competition over Koreans.

The main routes of Chinese and Korean migration in Manchuria were different. The development of ports and railways expedited migration from China proper. Chinese peasants in general moved from Northern China to southern Manchuria by ship or railway, especially via the railway line be-

TABLE 1. Estimates of the Population of Manchuria

Year	Korean population[a]	Total population[b]
1906		13,000,000
1910	202,070	
1916	328,288 (1.64%)	20,000,000 (100.00%)
1920	459,427	
1925	531,857	
1930	607,119 (1.96%)	31,000,000 (100.00%)
1935	826,570	
1942	1,500,570	

[a] Data are from Lee Hyŏngch'an, "1920–1930 nyŏndae Han'guginŭi manju imin yŏn'gu," 213.

[b] For detailed estimates, see Lee Chong Sik, *Revolutionary Struggle in Manchuria*, 22.

tween Beijing and Mukden (Shenyang, the capital of Fengtian Province in South Manchuria), which had been completed by the British in 1907. From South Manchuria, they spread east and north by taking the South Manchuria Railway or the Eastern Chinese Railway. In contrast, Korean migrants in Manchuria moved from the northeast to the southwest and north. From the late nineteenth century on, they initially concentrated in the Kando region in East Manchuria, not only because Kando was regarded as Korean territory but also because it was easy to cross the border at the Tuman River. Korean settlement in South Manchuria mainly began in the early twentieth century, as Koreans migrated from Kando or Korea, crossing the Apnok River, which ran between South Manchuria and Korea. Koreans moved from the mountainous border region of Fengtian Province, called Tongbyŏndo, to North and East Manchuria. Koreans in Kando also migrated to Jilin and Heilongjiang Provinces, fleeing from natural disasters and the Japanese suppression of exiled Korean independence movements.[19]

Korean migration is an important yet neglected theme in the study of Japanese imperialism.[20] The literature characterizes Japanese colonization in terms of formal and informal forms. Formal colonization refers to the annexation of a colony such as Korea or Taiwan by means of "blood and iron." Japan held exclusive sovereignty within the territory of each colony, requiring the colonized to obtain a Japanese passport or other identification, be

TABLE 2. Population in the Four Counties of Kando in 1926

Nationality	Yŏn'gil	Hwaryong	Wangch'ŏng	Hunch'un	Total	
Chinese	37,960	4,792	16,360	27,009	86,121	(19.37%)
Korean	169,427	111,605	31,580	43,598	356,210	(80.15%)
Japanese	1,418	61	103	379	1,961	(0.43%)
Others	70	20		38	128	(0.05%)
Total	208,875	116,478	48,043	71,024	444,420	(100.00%)

Source: Shim Yŏch'u, Yŏnbyŏn chosa sillok, 21.

liable for Japanese military conscription, provide donations and labor, and be subject to institutional assimilation and surveillance. Here Japan's sovereignty over its colonized peoples was territorial and institutional. Informal colonization denotes political and economic interventions brought about by unequal treaties. A paradigmatic case is the Japanese penetration into China proper from 1895 to 1937. Inaugurating Japanese dominance for the next half century, the Shimonoseki Treaty of 1895 provided Japan with the rights to access trading ports, build factories, engage in trade, and live and travel in the country. Japan's invasion of China in 1937 is considered to be the end of this informal rule.[21]

The binary mode of territorial and informal colonization obscures another form of extending rule—transnational territorial osmosis—in which Korean migrants constituted a transnational mechanism in the formation of the Japanese empire.[22] In the osmotic process, Japan's sovereignty did not reside in state institutions within a colony. Nor was it confined to the extra-territoriality of Japan's subjects and to protecting the circulation of capital, goods, and resources between metropole and Manchuria. The osmotic process reveals a transnational "body politics" through which Korean migrants carried Japan's power across the border from Korea to Manchuria. Another example of Japanese body politics is its assertion that sovereignty in Manchuria, Tibet, and Mongolia rested not with the Chinese state but with the princes of these regions. The prime minister of Japan stated in 1927 that "in the past although China speaks of the Republic of Five Races, yet Tibet, Sinkiang, Mongolia, and Manchuria have always remained special areas and the princes are permitted to discharge their customary functions. Therefore in reality the sovereign power over these resided with the princes. . . . So long as

TABLE 3. Places of Origin of Korean Migrants in 1932

	South Manchuria		
	Jiandao	South Manchuria	North Manchuria
From Northern Korea	396,745 (93.7%)	426,705 (90.8%)	12,023 (48.1%)
From Southern Korea	27,062 (6.3%)	43,280 (9.2%)	12,950 (51.9%)
Total	423,807 (100.0%)	469,985 (100.0%)	24,973 (100.0%)

Source: Lee Hyŏngch'an, "1920–1930 nyŏndae Han'guginui manju imin yŏn'gu," 214.
Note: When Manchuria was divided into southern and northern regions, Kando was often included in South Manchuria.

the princes there maintain their former administrations, the sovereign rights are clearly in their hands." In this stipulation, the bodies of princes, not state institutions, harbor sovereign power in these regions.[23] In this corporeal politics, Japan's exercise of power in Manchuria shows that sovereignty did not necessarily correspond to state power over the region.

Korean migration was not simply derivative of colonization; rather, it enabled Japan to strategize osmotic expansion. In this process, the annexation of Korea operated as a crucial step toward the colonization of Manchuria, which would form the basis for occupying China proper and eventually the whole of Asia. When complex political relations between Japan and the Western powers constrained the Japanese military from annexing Manchuria, Japan expanded its power there by pledging to protect Korean migrants. In the name of exercising its sovereignty over Koreans, Japan placed troops and consulates in Manchuria. As it had in Korea, Japan acquired farmland by making loans to Koreans and seizing mortgaged land when the debtors failed to repay them. Thus, Japan's osmotic domination of Manchuria was extended by establishing both administrative rule over Koreans and contractual relations with Koreans in an exchange of capital and labor.

In the politics of osmosis, Koreans were transformed not just into colonial agents but also into organic parts that constituted one Asian communal body. The notion of the politics of osmosis offers an additional insight into the Asian community. Interpreting the Japanese discourse of "the corporeal unity of the inner land and Korea" (in Japanese, *Naisen ittai*), Chungmoo Choi posits a discourse of assimilation in dyadic relations: Japan as a civilized inner land and Korea as an uncivilized hinterland.[24] For Choi, the unity of Korea and Japan entailed an undemocratic, dependent relationship in which Korea supplied human and natural resources to meet the capitalist needs of metropolitan Japan. But in my view the meaning of *Naisen ittai* needs to be understood in the context of building a larger imperial Asian community beyond Korea and Japan. In the 1930s, Japan placed *Naisen ittai* side by side with *Senman ittai* (the corporeal unity of Korea and Manchuria). The osmotic politics in the formation of an Asian community imparts a new interpretation of body politics. The relationship between Koreans and the Japanese empire cannot be reducible to the functions Koreans formerly served for metropolitan Japan. The bodily imaginaries of Asia, invoked by *Naisen ittai* and *Senman ittai*, construe all parts of the empire as one communal body. Under this putative organic unity, metropolitan Japan would be just another, albeit central, entity that relied on its colonies to function as an organism.

The formation of a transnational community distinguishes Japanese imperialism from its European counterparts. Japanese colonialism is often thought to mirror European colonialism in its drive to modernize itself and become like the West. Drawing on the trial and error of the European experience, Japan planned its colonial projects and tied them more closely to its metropolitan interests. Like its European counterparts, Japan used military force and violence to control its colonized subjects and then enshrouded these proceedings in terms of an enlightenment project for, and moral superiority over, the colonized.[25] This conventional view of Japanese colonialism elides the significance of its crucially distinct geographic and racial politics. European colonialism tended to colonize countries one by one and rule each as a separate entity. In Africa, the British integrated kingdoms, villages, languages, and tribes to redraw territorial boundaries and establish a state. They also established new institutions of governance, education, and communication, which engendered a sense of identification with the new territory and the modern state. In addition to this state-to-state relationship with each colony, Japan envisioned an organic unity, with the colonies forming an Asian community.

Japan represented the making of an Asian community as a reunion with Asian kin, however fictive that was. The colonial enactment of blood ties among Asians endowed this natural union with a consciousness of "we." The relationship between the Japanese colonizer and the colonized, therefore, escaped the simple binary opposition of self and other that was evoked

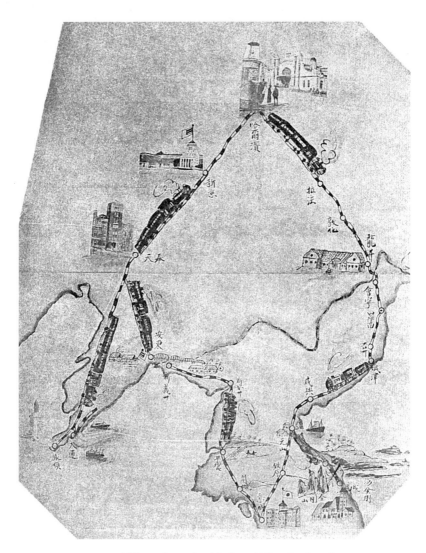

FIGURE 1. This 1938 travel guide for middle school students in Ryongjŏng illustrates the spatial integration of Korea and Manchuria. (From Ryu Eun Kyu, Ich'ojin hŭnjŏk, 277.)

in European empires. Instead of otherness, "sameness" was the idiom of rule in the Japanese empire. This imagined sameness was constructed through the evocation of racial and bodily unity between colonizer and colonized. The pious fiction of racial unity turned Japan and its colonies into an organic body called the Asian community. The elimination of differences within the community is not an effect but the main impetus in making this community. On the body politics in Japan, Harry Harootunian elucidates the logic of "immanentism" or "being in common," which imposed commonality on the Japanese communal body, leading the colonizer to the extreme of exterminating others in incidents such as the massacre in Nanjing.[26] The communal body, wrapped in the social fabric of folkism, rendered social relations as "natural," erasing all differences of class, gender, sex, and region. The portrayal of colonial expansion as an emotional reunion of folk with their kin invokes the naturalness of the osmotic formation of the Asian community.

The counterposing of Asia and the West reinforced the naturalized unity of colonizer and colonized. To create the spatial identity of the Asian community, since the nineteenth century Japan had supported ethnological projects, which pursued archaeological evidence for the shared origin of Japanese and Koreans. As Stefan Tanaka explores in detail, Japanese intellectuals have long debated whether Japanese and Koreans came from the Malay-Polynesian race or the early thalassocracy that comprised present-day Japan, Korea, and southeastern China.[27] For Japan, Asia was "the common ground and locus of comparison and contestation with regard to the West."[28] Although Japan's Orient embodied the moral and cultural superiority of the Japanese, it did not construe relations between Japan and its colonies, especially Koreans, in dichotomous terms in the way Europeans represented their colonial subjects as irreconcilably other. Fictive racial unity supplied Japan with a language of sameness that became the ideological basis of the territorial osmosis from Korea to Manchuria. Japan envisaged the Korean migrants of Manchuria as bearers of its colonial ambition to create a unified Asian community. The corporeal unity of Japanese and Koreans placed the formation of the Japanese imaginary of the communal body beyond its metropole. This early form of the Japanese imaginary of Asia prefigured the East Asia Co-Prosperity Sphere of the late 1930s.

Territorial Osmosis

The osmotic process evokes a natural progression. In this process, the Japanese imaginary of the Asian community was not complete; rather, it was always becoming actualized by the movement of people. The colonization of one region would disseminate Japanese power to another. In the discourse of the unity of the empire, the coordination of the parts was also seen to be simultaneous and natural. A threat to one part would be a threat to the others and the whole. This constitutive part was the nation-state. The logic of power in osmotic expansion tended to be fixed in the state's pursuit of national sovereignty within a specific territory. Each nation-state was like a nerve center regulating the circulation of power, capital, and people within its territory. Each one was expected not only to share the objective of expanding the empire but to synchronize its goals with those of the other members.

In fact, there were inherent constraints on the osmotic expansion of the Japanese empire. Specifically, the incoherence of territorial osmosis grew out of the nonhomologous relationships between the nation-state and the empire and between the nation and the state. Nation-states neither assumed an ideal form nor were equal to one another. Rivalry among nation-states developed as they pursued their interests in maintaining national sovereignty within their own territories. The state and the nation did not always correspond to each other, with apparatuses of the metropolitan state pursuing different national (and imperial) goals. These dynamics of the nation-state system accounted for the ineffective management of major critical elements of osmotic expansion—the nationality, landownership, and migration of Koreans. While the osmotic progression of the empire envisaged a synchronized singularity of the colonized and the colonizer, these disruptive dynamics destabilized the spatial and temporal experiences of Koreans.

The issue of Korean nationality demonstrated the disorderly nature of territorial osmosis. As a prelude to its osmotic strategy, Japan institutionalized an ethnic principle in defining Korean nationality. Two months prior to the annexation of Korea in 1910, the Cabinet in Tokyo defined Koreans as nationals of Korea, regardless of birthplace, residence, and acquisition of nationality in other countries. This resolution classified as Korean nationals all Koreans in Manchuria, regardless of whether they had been naturalized as Chinese nationals.[29] As exiled Koreans acquired national membership in their host countries (China, Russia, and America) to evade prosecution if they were arrested for their participation in the independence struggle after their return to Korea, Japan emphasized its recognition of the dual nationality of Koreans.[30] In 1922, Japan introduced a registration system, which stipulated that every Korean within and outside the country must register with the family registrar in their hometowns. The family registration system (hojŏk) became a new criterion for identifying Korean nationals in Manchuria during the Manchukuo period.

National membership of Koreans in Manchuria remained superfluous throughout the colonial period. Many Koreans held dual nationality in both Korea and China (meaning Northeast China prior to 1932 and Manchukuo afterward). The dual nationality of Koreans was an inherent product of the often conflict-ridden nation-state structure of the Japanese empire. While the Northeast Chinese government and Japan prior to 1932 ignored each other's stipulations on Korean nationality, the dual nationality of Koreans was not attributable entirely to the rivalry between the Japanese and Chinese powers. Nor was it merely the result of the ineffective administrative coordination of Japan. The tension between state apparatuses and nation-states rendered Korean nationality indeterminate. A double identification of Koreans with Korea and Manchuria destabilized their spatial and temporal experiences. Japanese state apparatuses stressed the viability of the naturalization of Koreans after Chinese laws established the naturalization of Koreans as Chinese nationals as a prerequisite for landownership. Administrators of the Japanese Cabinet, consuls, and the Government General of Korea before 1932 prioritized either the osmotic expansion or the maintenance of territorial sovereignty in an existing colony (see chapters 2 and 3). Beginning in 1932, Koreans were accepted as the members of the Manchukuo, but they were also required to enroll in the family registration system of Korea. The Government General of Korea continued to represent Koreans, coordinating and financing their migration, settlement, and agricultural production and exchange.

Korean migration was shaped by the dynamics of the nation-state system that constituted territorial osmosis. Colonial discourses construe the significance of the migration of people to Manchuria as benefiting their home states and the empire as a whole. Since the Russo-Japanese War in 1905, Japan had regarded the migration of Japanese to Manchuria as just as important to its colonization as the development of railways and mines. In his discussions with the Japanese foreign minister and the head of the South Manchuria Railway Company (SMRC), the commander of the Japanese army expressed the opinion that a "war can't be won every time" and "the permanent victory rests on the increase of the [Japanese] population in Manchuria."[31] The head of the SMRC, Goto Shinpei, supported this position, suggesting that immigration to Manchuria would consolidate Japan's position there.[32]

Three years later, in a Cabinet meeting in Tokyo, officials proposed the use of Korean migrants to further the osmotic expansion of Japanese power in Manchuria. It was decided that Japan must maintain its rights to protect Koreans at any cost. The report of the meeting stated: "A key in negotiating with China [over Kando] is not to insist on territorial rights but to secure our judicial rights over Koreans; this will enable us to protect Koreans."[33] In the same year, Japan declared that its police force would shelter the Koreans in Manchuria, who numbered about seventy thousand, while preventing them from rescinding their nationality.[34] A Japanese report in 1920 also states that "Koreans comprise the majority of the population in Kando and cultivate more than half of the arable land in Kando. If Koreans are assimilated into the Japanese, Kando will become another Korea. If Japan relocates Koreans to regions neighboring Kando and allows them to own land, those regions will become yet another Kando. This process would result in a concrete circle of Japanese power in Manchuria."[35] Moreover, migration to Manchuria was expected to alleviate agrarian conflicts at home and lessen the flow of landless peasants to cities with high unemployment. It was also expected to curb the migration of Koreans to Japan, where unskilled Japanese workers felt threatened by Korean migrants. The migration of people to a new frontier was adopted as a means of resolving the social crisis in the home country, thus defending the national sovereignty of the state.

The tendency of Korean migration to be in tension with Japanese migration reveals that the states in the Japanese empire developed conflicts over their national concerns. Although both the governor general of Korea and the commander of the Kwantung Army reported directly to the Japanese metropolitan army, they differed on the migration of Koreans. During the Manchukuo period, the Kwantung Army gave priority to the migration of Japanese over that of Koreans, despite the continued dissent of the Government General of Korea. It was only with the failure of the Japanese immigration project that the Kwantung Army condoned the systematic official sponsorship of Korean migration. The insistence on Japanese migration in spite of its lukewarm reception by the Japanese compromised the management of agricultural development in Manchuria. Furthermore, different powers—the Manchukuo state, the Government General of Korea, and the Kwantung Army, representing the metropolitan state—sponsored the establishment of agrarian cooperatives for their own subjects. The hierarchical positions of these administrative organizations produced inequalities among the cooperatives in terms of access to land and other agricultural essentials.

The territorial expansion of the empire involved sources of tension beyond the issues concerning Koreans. As is well known in the literature on Japanese imperialism, the Japanese policy toward Manchuria fluctuated during the 1920s. The Shidehara Cabinet (1924–27) is often compared to the Tanaka Cabinet (1927–29). The former tended to promote Japanese influence in Manchuria by diplomatic means, whereas the latter favored military measures to protect local Japanese interests and residents and attempted to prevent the Chinese revolution from spreading to Manchuria. Japan's policies during the 1930s were shaped by its autonomy from other imperialist powers, the breakdown of party rule, and the subsequent ascendancy of military power in both Japan and Manchuria.[36] Moreover, colonial institutions, including diverse Japanese state apparatuses and the military, developed complex relations of interdependency and competition in Manchuria. The dominance of the military in Japanese colonial affairs is ascribed to the absence of an effective centralized colonial administration under the civil government in Tokyo.[37] A team of Chinese scholars in 1934 compared the different hierarchical structures of colonial institutions over three periods during the first half of the twentieth century, which I summarize below not only because of their unfamiliarity in the literature but also because of their significance for the osmotic strategy of empire building.[38]

The first phase of Japanese penetration in Manchuria (1905–18) was marked by the dominance of the Kwantung Army, which consolidated power after its victory in the war against Russia. After obtaining all the rights that Russia had acquired from China, Japan established three major institutions in Manchuria: an administration (in Korean, Kwantong Todokpu), the SMRC, and consulates led by the consul general of Fengtian. The three institutions in principle engaged in a division of labor in which each undertook, respectively, the administration of the Liaodong Peninsula, the pursuit of economic interests, and the protection of Japanese residents and businesses. Although the armies were originally stationed to protect the South Manchuria Railway (SMR), they came to control all political, economic, and foreign affairs. The general served as the head of the administration and supervised the SMRC and the consulates.

During the period from 1918 to 1931, the power of the military in Manchuria was directed toward protecting the SMR. This period was characterized by the rule of four competing institutions: the Kwantung Administration, the Kwantung Army, the SMR, and the consulates. The party Cabinet in Japan divided the Kwandong Todokpu into the Kwandongch'ong (the Kwantung Administration) and the Kwantung Army in 1910. The Kwantung Administration was expected to manage all nonmilitary affairs in the Kwantung Leased Territory and to prevent the army from intervening in the affairs of the SMRC and the consulates.

Administrative disorder in Manchuria persisted during this period. The hierarchy of the Kwantung Administration, the SMRC, and the consulates was not clearly defined, even after the Ministry of Colonial Affairs (Takumusho) began to oversee both the Kwantung Administration and the SMRC. In order to rationalize the process of colonization in all parts of the empire, the metropolitan state in Tokyo created the Ministry of Colonial Affairs in 1929. The new ministry in theory presided over all aspects of territorial expansion of the empire. As just one of many ministries in Tokyo, however, its bureaucratic authority was too limited to accomplish comprehensive governance over the colonial expansion. The Ministry of Colonial Affairs remained largely a coordinating and reporting institution.[39] Although it administered both the Kwantung Administration and the SMRC, conflicts continued to develop. The Kwantung Administration was authorized to oversee the SMRC, but the company's president—served by former ministry-level bureaucrats—often disregarded the formal hierarchy and intervened in foreign affairs and the activities of the consulates. Furthermore, the Kwantung Administration did not have complete authority over the consulates, even when its regulation designated Japanese consulates as its secretaries—a regulation that enabled the Kwantung Administration to extend its authority to areas where the consulates had been established. This is because the consulates were under the jurisdiction of the Ministry of Foreign Affairs, whose position was parallel to that of the Ministry of Colonial Affairs.

After occupying Manchuria in 1931, the Kwantung Army regained its power over other Japanese state apparatuses. The army wanted to eliminate the three competing colonial institutions—the Kwantung Administration, the SMRC, and the consulates. It also attempted to install one governing body capable of overseeing all civil and military affairs, which would report directly to the Japanese emperor. Although opposed by the Ministries of Colonial Affairs and Foreign Affairs, the commander of the Kwantung Army at first occupied the top position in the Kwantung Administration rather than abolishing it. Yet after fierce debates within the Tokyo Cabinet in 1933 and 1934 the Kwantung Army broadened its jurisdiction. Adopted by the Tokyo Cabinet in which the prime minister also served as the minister of the Ministry of Colonial Affairs, the reform in 1934 extensively accommodated policy initiatives proposed by the military. The reform reduced the power of the Ministry of Colonial Affairs and its agent, the Kwantung Administration, replacing them with an office in the Cabinet and the local administration of the Kwantung Peninsula, respectively. Under the guidance of the ambassador and the prime minister of Japan, the local administration was expected to oversee administrative affairs only within the Kwantung Leased Territory.

The Kwantung Army also decreased the intervention of the Ministry of Foreign Affairs in the colonization of Manchuria in two ways: by creating the position of special ambassador and by abolishing the extraterritoriality of Japanese subjects in Manchuria. Even though the Kwantung Army failed to close down Japanese consulates, the commander restrained the consulates by serving as special ambassador. Ostensibly, the position of special ambassador was created to prepare for the formation of a new independent state in Manchuria. In 1934, the Kwantung Army also eliminated the extraterritoriality of Japanese subjects in Manchuria—a central task of the consulates—overriding the protests of Japanese merchants and officials in Manchuria, who joined the Kwantung Administration, the SMRC, and the Ministry of Foreign Affairs in opposition. Although the Ministry of Foreign Affairs retained the right to advise on foreign affairs, it lacked the authority to constrain the Kwantung Army, which reported to the prime minister.

The Kwantung Army's attempts at reform bore the most meager results on the issue of the SMRC. The Kwantung Army's original plan consisted of two measures: the creation of an office on the economy within the army and the transformation of the SMRC into a stock company. Under the direction of the office on the economy, the SMRC's various subsidiaries in coal, electricity, and transportation were prepared for independence. The SMRC would function as a financial institution providing loans to the newly created companies. This proposed reform was intended to prevent the investment of monopoly capital in the SMRC. Opposed by both the Ministry of Colonial Affairs and monopoly capital, the 1934 reform did not endorse the Kwantung Army's proposal. Ending their enmity during the 1920s, the Kwantung Army and monopoly capital collaborated on the development of Manchuria in the 1930s.

The innate disunity of the empire exposed the fictional reality of the whole. The empire sought to (re)create the nation-state in each colonized territory, which did not always serve the whole. Or, more precisely, there was no such a thing as the whole; the totality of the empire did not exist beyond the call for unity. The repeated invocation of unity—Korea and Manchuria as well as Korea and Japan—perhaps signifies the impossibility that such unity could be attained without causing unevenness within the empire. Until 1945, at different moments in Manchuria's colonization, the nation-state structure of the empire played havoc with the Japanese politics of osmosis.

Capitalist Osmosis

The osmotic expansion of the empire was a form of capital accumulation pursued by Japanese and Korean capital. Accordingly, Korean migration was more than a medium of territorial osmosis and a means of resolving the social crisis of the tenancy struggle and unemployment at home. It was geared primarily toward the production of surplus value for monopoly capital. The place of Korean migration in capitalist osmosis is best understood in the relationship between agricultural development and monopoly capital in the process of empire building. Together with Japanese industrial capital, finance capital from Japan and Korea was invested in development companies that acquired land and leased it to peasants, including Korean and Japanese migrants. The migration and settlement of Koreans bore contradictory results, as they were simultaneously the victims and agents of capital accumulation. On the one hand, they were evicted from the land in the process of primitive accumulation, as the capitalist integration of Korean and Japanese economies intensified the appropriation of surplus labor by colonial and comprador capital. Korean peasants served as the cheap supplier of rice to Japan and became the reserve armies of burgeoning urban industries. On the other hand, these Korean peasants were mobilized by Japanese and Korean capital to cultivate land and further capital accumulation in Manchuria.[40]

Development companies performed like financial institutions, whose purpose was to accumulate wealth and distribute profits to their stockholders. The companies generated profits from three sources: interest on loans, revenues from investments in other companies, and earnings from farming and logging.[41] To take an example, the Oriental Development Company (Tōyō takushoku kabushiki gaisha), which operated in Korea and the Kando region of Manchuria, invested in a total of fifty-two companies that were involved in electricity, transportation, mining, railways, chemicals, and wine making. As the primary stockholder of another major development company, the SMRC invested in similar industries in Manchuria. All the development companies collected rents from land leased to farmers. Perhaps the most important and controversial issue was the relation of loans to the accumulation of land, which was the main asset of the companies. Since land was the primary source of collateral for Koreans, the companies amassed land not so much by purchase as by confiscation. The companies preferred the seizure of mortgaged land to the collection of interest on loans. According to a director of the Ministry of Finance in the Government General of Korea, the Oriental Development Company was a unique financial institution. Unlike banks, it increased its wealth not through savings and loans but by hoarding mortgaged land, a practice that produced much resentment among Koreans.[42] It is said that the creditors adopted such ruses as manipulating their clocks to prevent debtors from repaying their loans on time.[43]

Capitalist social relations in Manchuria were constituted by the economic logic of accumulation and ideological and political forces such as colonialism, nationalism, and state politics. Japanese and Korean capital shared with the Chinese national power the dream of developing Manchurian agriculture. Land remained their primary means of capital accumulation even during the Manchukuo period, although the Manchukuo state stressed industrialization from the mid-1930s on. Japanese colonial development companies, the Northeast Chinese government of the Republican period, and the Manchukuo state invested their capital in land from 1932. They also endeavored to expand the labor force and organize the processes of production and market transactions. Chinese oppression combined with the Japanese promotion of Korean settlement to further capital expansion. When Chinese oppression prompted Koreans to leave their land and cultivate new wasteland, their migration inadvertently broke down such barriers to the market as the lack of transportation and communications facilities. The cycle of farming and displacement brought more land on the periphery into cultivation and expanded markets across Manchuria.

The complex interactions of colonial and national powers, which combined economic interests with territorial rivalry, produced a historically specific capitalist system. As a means of capital accumulation, the ground rent and credit systems coexisted in the early decades of the twentieth century, although the credit system became the primary mechanism of colonial governance in the Manchukuo period. The ground rent system involved two practices. One was fixing an absolute amount of each harvest as rent (chŏngjo). The other, more popular form (chipcho) set a percentage of the harvest as rent, with landlords (including Japanese development companies) and peasants sharing the risk of crop failure. Under the credit system, peasants received loans to purchase land from financial institutions, including colonial companies, and were expected to repay the loans on schedule. Both the ground rent and credit systems concealed the social content of commodified laborers—

the appropriation of their surplus value. Driven by the dynamics of capital accumulation, Korean and other migrants engaged in farming not merely to support themselves and their family members but also to pay rent and repay loans. Both systems determined the socially necessary time required to produce crops as commodities. The credit system was more rational and coercive in regulating labor time. Peasants were forced to adjust their production to meet detailed payment schedules.

The osmotic diffusion of colonial and national power through Korean multiple migrations engendered national and ethnic unevenness in the ground rent and credit systems. The land cultivated by Koreans before and after 1932 was often inferior compared to that occupied by Chinese and Japanese. Koreans prepared wasteland for farming and created irrigation systems to transform dry land into fields suitable for lucrative rice farming. When Koreans were forced to sign short-term tenancy contracts, when they were evicted, or when their contracts expired, landlords appropriated the labor they had invested in their land. When landlords hired new Chinese or Korean tenants, charging higher rent on land, the difference between the old and new rents denotes the level of exploitation. Furthermore, the peasants' relationship with the credit system was differentiated by nationality. Japanese migrants received more loans at lower interest rates than Korean migrants did; most Chinese residents did not qualify for any loans.

The nation-state system of the empire mediated the capitalist osmotic progression. In the overlapping division of labor, various colonial authorities administered and financed the development companies that operated in their jurisdictions. The complex relations of colonial authorities and the development companies are best illustrated by the organizational hierarchy of the companies. The participation of the nation-state powers and state apparatuses reflected the projected functions of the development companies, which required long-term planning and interstate coordination. The Government General of Korea exceeded other government agencies in its involvement with all of the development companies in employing and funding Korean migrants. Its extensive involvement derived from its goal of stabilizing social life in Korea and Manchuria so as to prevent Koreans from joining anti-Japanese movements. In 1908, the Japanese metropolitan state, in cooperation with the Government General of Korea, founded the Oriental Development Company with a total capital of 10 million won (two hundred thousand shares), which increased to 50 million won in 1919 (one million shares). The Government General of Korea initially acquired sixty thousand shares, and the Japanese and Korean monarchies also owned some shares.[44] The Government General of Korea had the authority, in principle, to license the main office and its branches. After the opening of its branch in Kando in 1917, its operations in Manchuria were confined to the Kando region.

In South Manchuria, the Asia Development Company (Tōa kangyō kabushiki gaisha) managed Korean settlement and farming. Created with a total capital of 20 million won in 1921, the company's primary stockholders included the Oriental Development Company and the SMRC. After the former transferred its stock to the latter in 1928, the SMRC owned 95 percent of the total shares. The administration of the Asia Development Company was divided among many Japanese authorities. Because the Kwantung Administration was the Japanese governing body in Manchuria during this period, it had authority over the Asia Development Company's revenues, loans, and financial relief programs for Koreans. It also approved the spending of the company's profits. The Government General of Korea not only had the official authority to supervise the company but it also provided the company with annual subsidies, which almost doubled those of the Kwantung Administration. To advise their businesses, the SMRC dispatched its agents to various companies owned and invested in by the Asia Development Company. The Ministries of Foreign Affairs and Colonial Affairs also provided supervision and assistance.[45]

In 1936, the Korea-Manchuria Development Company and its sister firm, the Manchuria-Korea Development Company, were established to expand and rationalize Korean migration. They replaced the Oriental Development Company and Asia Development Company. In 1932, the Government General of Korea proposed this reorganization to enact a long-term official program for large-scale Korean immigration. Its implementation was delayed for years because the Kwantung Army preferred Japanese immigration. The reshuffling of the companies involved the collaboration of the Ministry of Colonial Affairs in Tokyo, the armies in Japan, and the Kwantung Army. While the Government General of Korea nominated the president of the Korea-Manchuria Development Company, the Manchukuo state appointed three trustees. An army general served as the president of the Manchuria-Korea Development Company. The Government General of Korea supervised the business of the Korea-Manchuria Company, including the disbursement of profits, and the Ministry of Industry in Tokyo performed similar tasks for the Manchuria-Korea Development Company.[46]

The mediation of capitalist osmosis by the nation-state was not always

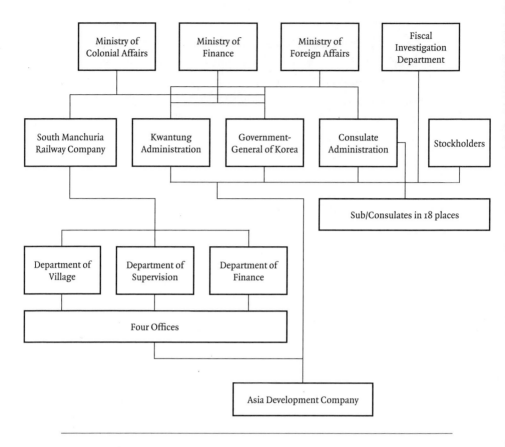

FIGURE 2. The Japanese administrative hierarchy and the Asia Development Company. (From *Tōa Kangyō Kabushiki Gaisha Jūnenshi*, 30.)

functional or complete. The participation of various administrative authorities led to confusion and conflict in coordinating agricultural development and immigration projects. Moreover, the incomplete mediation of capitalist osmosis resulted from the contradictory relationship between territorial and capitalist expansion. The nation-state system of empire both facilitated and constrained capitalist expansion. Some functional mediation included the following dynamics. By operating development companies, the colonial powers and their collaborators accumulated wealth through a series of interventions in production and market exchange. The companies introduced new farming methods and financed improvements in infrastructure. As mentioned earlier, the companies drew on the ground rent and credit systems to appropriate the surplus labor of cultivators who leased land or obtained loans from them. The practice of confiscating mortgaged land contributed to the displacement of cultivators from the land and their relocation to wasteland, transforming the displaced into productive laborers. In other words, the companies distributed laborers to the less-populated hinterland, expanding the amount of land under cultivation and involved in market transactions.

The mediation by the nation-state system also impeded capitalist expansion. As mentioned earlier, the Government General of Korea prioritized the preservation of national sovereignty in Korea over the osmotic expansion of territory and capital. Prior to 1931, the Government General of Korea's objection to the naturalization of Koreans as Chinese nationals reduced the number of Korean landowners, if not the number of Korean migrants, and the subsequent accumulation of land by the colonial development companies. During the 1930s, the conflict between the Government General of Korea and the Kwantung Army over the priority of Korean versus Japanese immigration also prevented them from effectively organizing Korean migration to strategic places in Manchuria. Furthermore, when each of the nation-state powers (the Government General of Korea, the Manchukuo state, and the Kwantung Army) organized agrarian cooperatives for its nationals (Koreans, Chinese, and Japanese, respectively) with the intention of settling displaced migrants, the hierarchy among them thwarted the intent of the policy. Land was expropriated from Koreans and Chinese and distributed to Japanese peasants, displacing the former once again.

Capitalist osmosis, in turn, intervened in the process of territorial osmosis. The organization of social life was a primary means through which the colonial powers—especially the Kwantung Army, the Government General of Korea, and the Manchukuo state—consolidated their national sovereignty over the territories of Korea and Manchuria. The reinvention of social relations of production was imbricated with the maintenance of national sovereignty over the territories of Korea and Manchuria. This was because the peasant economy was designed to deter the colonized from joining anticolonial resistance movements. National sovereignty did not, therefore, merely rely on the cultural and political assimilation of Koreans and Manchurian residents. More importantly, it was anchored in the social relations of production and market exchange. The colonial powers embedded their national sovereignties in the private property system, through which it was imagined that displaced peasants would become landowners.

Since capitalist forces organized social relations, they came to shape the national sovereignties of the colonial powers. The effect of capitalist forces on national sovereignties was paradoxical. Capitalist forces produced specific characteristics of colonial governance, but they also undermined it. For instance, agricultural cooperatives touted small landowners as the backbone of the new Manchuria. Separate agrarian cooperatives were established for different groups. This supported the ideology of the Manchukuo state, which encouraged the assimilation of five ethnic and national groups (Manchus, Han Chinese, Mongols, Koreans, and Japanese). The specific capitalist temporalities of the cooperatives—illicit landownership, a communal credit system, and collective market activities—enabled the Government General of Korea to rationalize its disciplinary techniques and penetrate the everyday lives of cultivators. At the same time, the capitalist system discouraged mixing among the various groups because capitalist expansion was predicated on maintaining differences among places (Korea, Japan, and Manchuria) and creating a social hierarchy. The hierarchy continued to displace Koreans and Chinese from land, even after the colonial powers pledged to territorialize them as productive laborers and landowners. The displacement turned on its head the promise to stabilize the social lives of peasants. It divested colonizers of the sovereign power embedded in their reinvention of social relations. With the contradictory territorial and capitalist osmosis and the incomplete mediation by the nation-state system, the formation of the Japanese empire encountered barriers within itself.

Given the contradictory relationship between the nation-state system and capitalism, understanding the process of capital accumulation requires an analysis capable of accounting for the complex processes negotiated by Japanese institutions, Chinese national power, and peasants. Through such an analysis, the anomalous social practices of Koreans—ambiguous citizenship, hybrid landownership, and displacement—can be explicated. The indeterminate social experiences of Koreans disclose a certain agency that empowered them. When Koreans were driven from their lands, their repetitive displacement set into motion the social metabolism of the osmotic expansion of the Japanese empire. This osmotic expansion progressed because Koreans envisioned a better life in a new place and invested their labor in wasteland to transform it into productive rice fields. The dreams of the Japanese and Chinese powers were embedded in the dreams of the Korean migrants themselves. Each instance of migration signifies a new relation with the spatio-temporality of colonialism, nationalism, and capitalism. The social practices of Korean migrants were therefore double edged: while Koreans pursued their dreams of landownership, their participation in the market was a process through which their surplus value was expropriated with each loan payment and every time they were displaced .

In this chapter, I have discussed Korean migration as a volatile engine of the osmotic expansion of the Japanese empire. While Koreans in Manchuria provided an important basis for exile movements to liberate Korea, they simultaneously became colonizers of Manchuria as Japan attempted to use them as the vanguard of its encroachment on Manchuria. The negotiation by Koreans of their paradoxical position complicates the prevailing binary view of them as victims of colonization and heroes of anti-Japanese struggle. Their repeated displacement served to territorialize Japanese power and capital, as each moment of displacement acquired a new value for the body and the land. This corporeal movement was governed not simply by the physical and mental endurance of migrant laborers and their ethnic or family allegiance—all qualities that diaspora studies explore as survival strategies of migrant laborers.[47] It was also dictated by national and capitalist time that determined the socially necessary time of production and the return time of capital investment. The distinction of Korean (Japanese) nationals and their "others" was never complete in Manchuria, although the diaspora literature portrays a binary distinction: nationals as localized, national, fixed, stable, and bounded by the national state; and nonnationals as global, cosmopolitan, floating, moving, hybrid, and deterritorialized. The indeterminable spatial and temporal experiences of the Korean diaspora in the early twentieth century arose not merely from their multiple national identities. They also resulted from the dual position of Koreans as both the colonized and the bedfellows of Japanese imperialism.

CHAPTER TWO

Between Nation and Market

In the midst of civil war and Japanese penetration during the first and second decades of the twentieth century, Manchuria was transformed from a sparsely populated hinterland into a highly commercialized region. Agricultural expansion was the backbone of its prosperous economy. The national and colonial powers had encouraged peasant migration from North China and Korea, respectively. When the Chinese and Korean migrants were displaced from their hometowns by crop failures and political crises, they were caught up in the political struggles between Japan and Chinese national powers. After Japan leased the Liaodong Peninsula and the South Manchuria Railway, its penetration into inner Manchuria relied on Korean migrants. To expand the Han Chinese population and bolster its sovereignty over the region, the Qing and subsequent Republican governments of China facilitated the migration of Han Chinese peasants to Manchuria.

Three shifts of emphasis characterized these national and colonial disputes: from political to social, from central to local, and from contention over Japanese penetration to contention over Korean migration. The Treaty on South Manchuria and East Inner Mongolia, which the Chinese and Japanese governments signed in 1915, delineated landownership and leasing rights by Japanese subjects as a primary site of contention between Japan and China. Although there was political opposition to the treaty, until 1931 the more persistent anticolonial politics concerned the social sphere and focused on land transactions. Contracts between Chinese and Japanese (Korean) subjects became the cornerstone of Chinese nation formation. This shift of national and colonial disputes from the political to the social arena reflected Japanese osmotic politics—a strategy of gradual expansion from the acquisition of land and expansion of police and military presence to the establishment of full sovereignty.

The social disputes moved from central China to the Manchurian region (China's three northeastern provinces). Building relative administrative autonomy, Zhang Zuolin, the chief Chinese administrator in the region, forced Japan to renegotiate the terms of the 1915 Treaty. In Manchuria, the governments of the three northeastern provinces (referred to as the Northeast government hereafter), Chinese merchants, and Japan negotiated and disputed with one another. Their triangular politics negated the simpler binary opposition of national and colonial politics. The balance of power revolved around both territorial and capitalist concerns. For instance, when Japan sought to expand its sovereign power over Manchuria, it assisted both the Northeast government and Chinese merchants, whose relations entailed both partnerships and conflicts. Despite their dissension, the three parties did share a desire for capitalist development of the region.

Triangular politics shaped national and colonial politics in two ways. First, territorial triangular politics translated national and colonial disagreements over the 1915 Treaty into a conflict over Koreans. Japanese osmotic politics supported Koreans and their occupation of the land, while the Chinese vowed to evict them. The exclusion of Koreans in the 1920s pledged to reverse a Chinese policy that had been in place since the mid–nineteenth century, one that encouraged Koreans to become naturalized as Chinese nationals. National politics in Manchuria in the 1920s pitted Chinese migrants against Koreans, the former as nationals and the latter as antinationals. The transformation of Chinese migrants as members of the Chinese nation represented by the Northeast government was predicated on regulating their land transactions with Koreans. The law that excluded Koreans from Manchuria differed from the law of Central Republican China, which permitted the naturalization of foreigners.

This triangular politics reconfigured the locus of the new Chinese nation formation in Manchuria. While the relationship between Manchus and Han Chinese was central under the Qing government, the relationship between Han Chinese and Koreans became prominent under the Northeast government during the Republican period.[1] The Manchu founders of the Qing regime maintained the Manchu identity of the government, directing Han Chinese residents in Manchuria to adopt Manchu customs. Under the Qing, the naturalization of Koreans as Chinese referred to their adoption of such customs, mainly Manchu clothing and hairstyles. During the Republican period, the government embraced a Han Chinese identity and assigned an inferior status to the Manchus. In Manchuria, the relationship between Chinese and Koreans emerged as the crucial principle defining the boundary of the Chinese nation.

Second, triangular politics constituted capitalist development while hindering Chinese nation formation in Manchuria. Its interest in Korean rice farming compelled the Northeast government to compromise its own nationality law. Although it continuously called for the eviction of Koreans, it concomitantly implemented policies that allowed Koreans to work as short-term tenants and agricultural laborers. This partial inclusion of Koreans had indelible effects on the development of capitalist relations and Chinese sovereignty. It produced national and ethnic unevenness in the social relations of landlords and tenants and laborers. The repeated retreat from the nationality law rendered Chinese sovereignty incomplete. This knotty compromise between capitalist and territorial interests was not attributable solely to the protests of Chinese landlords against the possible expulsion of Koreans. Instead, it was intrinsic to the character of Chinese national politics because the Northeast government was the primary investor in land, commerce, and financial institutions. In this sense, the common perception that Zhang Zuolin based his power on a feudalistic warlord clique obscures his Janus-faced interactions with Japan and Chinese merchants, through which he pursued his contradictory territorial and capitalist desires.

This chapter explores the national and colonial politics mediated by Koreans in the social sphere of Manchuria. It begins with an analysis of triangular politics, which entails a revision in the historiography of political and economic development and Chinese nation formation in Manchuria. After discussing the 1915 Treaty, I examine the struggle between the Japanese and Chinese powers over the social rights of Koreans. I also address the internal contradictions of Chinese nation formation.

THE BALANCE OF POWER

Zhang Zuolin secured power in Manchuria prior to 1920. In 1916, he assumed the military and civil governorships of Fengtian Province, a principal region of Manchuria. He also gained enough power to appoint his subordinates to the posts of governors, military chiefs of staff, leading secretaries, treasurers, and police chiefs in Jilin and Heilongjiang Provinces. The principal sources of revenue were companies, such as land and mining companies, and taxes on the sale of tobacco, wine, and salt. Under Zhang's rule, the three provinces illicitly kept a large proportion of their revenues for their own use; by the early 1920s, they had stopped remitting any revenue to the Beijing government. Zhang turned Manchuria into the military base for his power struggle with other militarists in China. His Fengtian clique, along with the Zhili and Anwei cliques, constituted the northern warlord group, whose leader was the president of the Republican government, Yuan Shikkai. After Yuan's death in 1916, the northern group became occupied with its own internal struggles. Zhang defeated his rivals to become the de facto ruler of the Beijing government in 1925.

A proper assessment of Zhang Zuolin's power and his relationship with Chinese merchants and Japan is important for understanding national and colonial politics in Manchuria. It is customary to contrast Zhang with his son and successor, Zhang Xueliang. The father is characterized as a gambler, bandit, opportunistic exploiter, and national traitor and the son as an educated modern patriot, peacemaker, and national hero who formed the anti-Japanese united front of the Kuomintang and Communist Parties.[2] Historiography also opposes Zhang Zuolin to the Chinese merchants, the former as a feudal militarist and Japanese collaborator and the latter as agents of Manchuria's economic development and anti-Japanese nationalists. However, Zhang Zuolin was no less national and modern than other militarists of his time. His triangular relationship with domestic foes and Japan was too complex to be simplified by a dichotomous notion of national and colonial politics. Zhang Zuolin, merchants, and Japan were bedfellows who simultaneously shared territorial and capitalist desires and competed to fulfill them.

Historiography

A principal analytical structure in the historiography of Manchuria is the opposition of warlords and the bourgeoisie, the former pursuing the territorial unification of China and the latter hoping to separate Manchuria from China in the interest of economic stability. Warfare is considered to have been a defining feature of Zhang Zuolin's Northeast government, which directed all its manpower and resources toward defeating its rivals in civil war. The term *warlord* presupposes that the Northeast government revolved around the personal allegiances and kinship ties of Zhang's Fengtian clique and its associates.[3] To finance wars, the Northeast government required merchants to make compulsory donations, and it frequently halted the trade of essential strategic goods in the interest of warfare. The Northeast government operated various provincial banks, issued its own currency, and manipulated the exchange rates of more than ten currencies in circulation. Incessant warfare debilitated the Manchurian economy, causing inflation, interrupting market activity, and diverting revenue from economic development.

The Northeast government acquired its economic and political independence from Japan in exchange for military aid. As a tactic meant to divide and weaken China, Japan supported Zhang Zuolin's military buildup, while also assisting his rivals in China proper so as to contain his power within Manchuria. In addition to financial assistance, Japan helped Zhang build arms factories. From 1913 to 1931, Japan also sent thirteen Japanese military advisers to the regimes of Zhang and his son. While helping Zhang Zuolin with his strategic plans, the military advisers gathered intelligence on his armies. For instance, one adviser, who assisted Zhang in his war with the Zhili faction in 1922, eventually became the commander in chief in the Kwantung Army and played a major role in the Manchurian Incident in 1931 and the subsequent Japanese occupation. Yet some dubious military advisers worked for Zhang as informants on Japanese politics or remained as his personal aides after completing their official terms as advisers.[4]

Chinese merchants survived by cooperating with Zhang Zuolin and his government. Chambers of commerce (*sanghoe* in Korean and *shanghui* in Chinese), associations of merchants and business owners, mediated relations between individual merchants and the warlord government. From 1904 to 1911, there were at least twenty chambers of commerce in Fengtian, seven in Jilin, and six in Heilongjiang Provinces. As noted, the chambers of commerce consisted of various types of business owners. For instance, in 1929 the chamber of commerce in Ch'ŏllyŏng county of Tongbyŏndo included 903 businesses, including bean curd shops, silk cloth stores, grain stores, moneylenders, pawnshops, coal shops, hairdressers, doctors, tobacconists, inns, and booksellers to name few.[5] The chambers of commerce promoted the interests of the business community, providing mutual assistance to its members and mediating disputes among them. Beyond these typical organizational functions, they carried out specific functions for the Northeast government. As Ronald Suleski writes, the chambers of commerce fixed the relative value of the several currencies in circulation. They regularly assessed market conditions, commodity prices, and trade practices and compiled reports for the Bureau of Industry. The chambers of commerce also negotiated with the government over tax rates and the amounts of special contributions for the military.[6]

Zhang Zuolin's northeastern armies were defeated by his military rivals in 1922. This tilted the balance of power toward the merchants. Allied with civil bureaucrats, they advocated nationalist economic reforms. They forced Zhang to declare the independence of Manchuria from China proper in 1922 and to sign a peace treaty with the Zhili faction in Beijing. A new civil governor of Fengtian Province successfully pressed Zhang to separate the civil and military governments there, which would in principle prevent the military from interfering in administrative and economic matters. Commanding other provincial governors, the civil governor of Fengtian played a leadership role in undertaking comprehensive reforms in administration, finance, agricultural development, and industrialization in Manchuria. The reforms gave unprecedented priority to the economic development of Manchuria, placing it ahead of warfare. Under new land registration and tax systems, the reserves of the Fengtian government doubled from 1923 to 1924.[7] To stabilize currencies, jurisdiction over official banks passed from the military to the Bureau of Finance. The development of the economy was another important area of reform. The Northeast government constructed more than half a dozen new railways that ran parallel to the South Manchuria Railway. To challenge the domination of Japanese cotton yarn, the government also built new textile mills and subsidized cotton industries and growers.[8] As will be elaborated later, peasant migrants were recruited from North China to expand the labor force.

The alliance of the military authority and economic reformers was brief. Breaking his promise, Zhang's armies resumed the war in 1924 with military budgets higher than before. Interfering again with civil affairs, he borrowed money from foreign banks in China proper, issued more currency, and added new taxes.[9] The fallout was worse than the previous economic crisis; by 1928, more than one-third of all businesses in Fengtian City, capital of the Fengtian provincial government, had to close. The literature on Manchuria describes the collaboration of the military and the merchant bourgeoisie as a tactic by Zhang to regain his strength. Because of the unusual level of cooperation by the warlord government, this reform is a central issue in the literature on Manchuria. Anti-Japanese protests led by merchants were seen to bolster the dichotomy between the warlords and the bourgeoisie. In 1915, the chambers of commerce in Manchuria organized widespread movements that called for a boycott of Japanese currency.[10] In 1924 and 1927,

these chambers also organized demonstrations to oppose Japan's establishment of consulates and to denounce the use of Japanese currency. One demonstration in front of the General Chamber of Commerce assembled about
twenty-five thousand people, including store clerks, officials, laborers, and
students.[11] In 1927, the General Chamber of Commerce in Fengtian ordered
all the other chambers to use the currencies issued by the Official Bank of
the Three Northeastern Provinces (Dongbeisansheng guanyinhao) and stop
using Dairen, the port monopolized by Japan.[12]

Historiography characterizes the Manchurian economy under warlord rule
and Japanese encroachment as semifeudal and semicolonial. According to a
recent major Chinese publication, *The Economic History of Northeast China* (*Dongbei jingjishi*), the despotic power of the warlords and colonial intervention
thwarted the initial role of the Chinese merchants in commencing the capitalist development of Manchuria in the Qing period.[13] The productivity of
agriculture increased not by improving methods of production but by feudalistic exploitation of cultivators. Herbert Bix defines the Manchurian economy in terms of the bifurcation of feudal agriculture and capitalist commerce
and industry under the control of domestic landlords and colonial capital.[14]
Owen Lattimore describes the Manchurian economy as anything but capitalist: nepotism prevailed rather than the dictated distribution of land; and
landlords who owned agricultural land but resided in cities lacked any entre-
preneurial spirit, considering land a source of wealth rather than a form of
capital.[15]

Triangular Politics

The dichotomy of the Zhang Zuolin government and the merchants, a
central construct of Manchurian historiography, elides the fact that both the
warlords and the merchant bourgeoisie pursued capitalist development. The
conflation of the Zhang Zuolin government with Japanese power obscures
their complex relationship with Chinese merchants. Addressing Zhang's simultaneous compromise with Japan and the merchants, Gavan McCormack
states that he was "more than a mere Japanese puppet but less than a nationalist."[16] This insightful observation can be deepened by paying attention to
the economic basis of the Northeast government. Although the term *warlord*
precludes acknowledging its capitalist character, Zhang, his family, and his
administration were major investors in all sectors of the economy, from agriculture and commerce to financial institutions. It is rare for historiography
to recognize the types of assets owned by warlords and their regimes. Even

when a warlord government's capital is noted, it is compared to private agricultural companies, which are considered capitalist.[17]

The material basis of the Northeast government reveals the structural framework of its alliance with the merchant bourgeoisie. The warlords and their families were the largest landlords, as they had amassed vast amounts of land. Zhang Zuolin exploited his power to grant land to his associates and their families. He also amassed land under the name of the Northeast Army.[18] Furthermore, the provincial governments invested in land, since agriculture was the basis of commerce and the emergent factories that processed agricultural products such as bean oil, flour, and silk and cotton yarn. A chief form of official investment was the operation of land companies. Established in the early 1900s, there were 137 official land companies in 1920 (71 in Fengtian, 51 in Jilin, and 15 in Heilongjiang). In addition to recruiting tenants and laborers, land companies pledged to increase agricultural output by conducting research on new crops and techniques of cultivation and teaching them to the peasants. Apart from their stated objectives, land companies were said to assist the warlord government in acquiring land and increasing rents.[19]

The provincial governments under Zhang Zuolin's leadership, often in partnership with the merchant bourgeoisie, established their own banks and other financial organizations throughout Manchuria. The Fengtian Official Bank (Fengtian guanyinhao), which opened in Shenyang in 1905 and was renamed the Official Bank of the Three Northeastern Provinces in 1924, had twenty-two branches and twelve subbranches in Manchuria. It invested in various sectors. Half of its total investment was in stores that traded soybeans, rice, and other grains, and one-seventh was in pawnshops, which, together with money-exchange stores, constituted the most rudimentary but widely used type of financial organization. Money-exchange stores run by the Official Bank earned profits by exchanging various currencies and selling bean oil and other merchandise.[20] The loans from official banks of provinces and the Official Bank enabled merchants who ran wholesale grain stores, called liangchan, to finance farmers who needed money during the agricultural season in return for a prearranged sale of their harvest. As bank loans were inaccessible to peasants who lacked sufficient collateral, they often put up their coming autumn harvest as security for their loans. When farmers defaulted on their loans, the lenders seized their harvests. With this practice, the banks and liangchan set the future price of crops when market prices for agricultural products were at their lowest point.[21]

Recognizing the material basis of warlord power and its partnership with the merchant bourgeoisie allows a new interpretation of the short-lived economic reform in effect from 1922 to 1925. It underscores the fact that the reform was a structural event. As the main investor in key sectors of the economy, the military had a vested interest in developing Manchuria's economy, including the promotion of national industries in competition with the Japanese. The tension between persistent warfare and economic development therefore signified an internal contradiction within the military, not just a conflict between the military and the merchants.

The ambiguous relationship between Japan and the merchant bourgeoisie completed the triangle of relationships. Joint ventures between Japan and the Chinese bourgeoisie in Fengtian Province predated the 1915 Treaty, although they expanded afterward.[22] Despite their differing goals and purposes, they shared the goal of separating Manchuria from China proper and halting Zhang's military buildup. The merchant bourgeoisie supported the movement opposed to Zhang Zuolin, which was far stronger in Jilin than in the two other provinces. Even though the merchant bourgeoisie originated in China proper, it supported the Jilin independence movement, rallying around its regional identity and calling for rule of the province by the people of the region.[23] When Zhang resumed the war in 1924, the merchant bourgeoisie found Japan making the same demand that Zhang withdraw his forces. Zhang deflected the threats from the merchant bourgeoisie and Japan by turning them against each other. Promising to suppress anti-Japanese demonstrations, he bargained with Japan for military aid. Simultaneously, he supported the Recovery Movement, which emerged in the late 1920s to nullify the 1915 Treaty. The fluctuating relations between Japan and Zhang Zuolin and the merchants continued until Zhang Xueliang formed an anti-Japanese front with the Kuomintang in 1929.

The surge of anti-Japanese sentiment after the 1920s provoked Japanese investors and residents of Manchuria to demand that the Japanese government intervene. Yet Japan's attempt to separate Manchuria from China proper surpassed its immediate goal of protecting its economic interests in Manchuria. From the 1910s to 1931, the independence of Manchuria remained the Kwantung Army's persistent strategy for the eventual occupation of all of China. Its first attempt took place in 1912, when the Republican government replaced the Qing. The Kwantung Army supported an abortive attempt by former imperial members and followers to establish a separate regime in Manchuria and Mongolia. When anti-Japanese protests increased in the aftermath of the 1915 Treaty, the Kwantung Administration and Kwantung

Army assisted in a similar futile initiative. At that time, Japanese factions were split between supporting the former imperial members and Zhang Zuolin. Following the recommendation of its consuls in Manchuria, the Tokyo Cabinet supported Zhang Zuolin. However, with support from the military and the imperial family in Tokyo, the Kwantung Army backed the followers of the former Qing government, who were soon pacified by Zhang. In 1931, the Japanese military finally succeeded in separating Manchuria when it occupied major cities there, allegedly to protect the South Manchuria Railway.[24]

The triangular relationship was more a dynamic balancing of power than a stalemate. In the pursuit of territorial and capitalist interests, the three parties entered into partnerships and disputes. This triangular shape of political relations gives rise to revisions of the analysis of national and colonial politics. First, the triangular politics anchored national and colonial politics in the social sphere. The balance of power translated incompatible territorial politics into the competing formations. Japan resorted to the osmotic strategy of gradual colonization by financing Korean migration and expanding its military forces in the name of protecting Koreans and their assets. To counter the Japanese strategy, the Northeast government tried not only to evict Koreans from Manchuria but also to consolidate its sovereignty over Chinese migrants and their property. An exclusive focus on military expansion and economic instability dissociates the formation of the Japanese empire or the Chinese nation from the construction of national subjects and their social experiences.

Second, the triangular politics demands attention to internal contradictions within national and colonial forces, as well as the complex relationships among them. The international contradiction rendered each force's sovereignty as only partial. Japanese osmotic politics was hampered by the inherent dilemma that arose when its administrative agents disputed their policies toward Koreans in the competition for power. Chinese nation formation also encountered hurdles, not just because of unstable relations between merchants and the Northeast government but also because of that government's contradictory territorial and capitalist aspirations. For instance, the Northeast government simultaneously enforced and retreated from the nationality law, as the eviction of Koreans would impede capitalist development of the region.

These revisions warrant a new perspective on the social experience of peasants. The conventional historiography of Manchuria represents the peasant experience in terms of the familiar cycle of exploitation, debt, poverty, and displacement. It identifies the polarization of society into landlords and peasants as a product of feudal and colonial exploitation. It employs a unitary category of peasants without differentiating their nationality as Chinese or Koreans, perhaps because Koreans comprised less than 5 percent of the total population. Yet even when historians focus on the specific experiences of Koreans of Manchuria their accounts resemble the more general descriptions of peasant impoverishment.[25] This existing approach obscures the fragmentation of the peasant social experience along ethnic and national lines, which in turn determined access to land and capital. The inequality of Chinese and Korean peasants emerged from the politics of the national and colonial forces, which competed for sovereignty over land and people. Contrary to the commonly assumed homogeneous experience, Chinese and Korean peasants were incorporated into different networks of capital—Chinese and Japanese. They also belonged to disparate social spaces. Korean peasants were restricted to being short-term tenants and cheap agricultural laborers, while Chinese peasants were transformed into landowners. The production of both Korean and Chinese peasants—as national subjects of Japan and China, respectively—took place within the parameters set by the 1915 Treaty.

PROPERTY RIGHTS AND EXTRATERRITORIALITY: THE 1915 TREATY

The Treaty on South Manchuria and East Inner Mongolia of 1915 set parameters for the disputes between Japan and the Northeast government of China until 1931. The treaty was the outcome of fierce negotiations over the so-called Twenty-one Demands that Japan presented to China. The negotiations involved twenty-five meetings and several revisions between January and May of 1915. Although historians have routinely focused on the disputes over the extension of the leasing of the Liaodong Peninsula and railways, other intensely disputed issues were the property rights and extraterritoriality of Japanese subjects.[26] Secret telegrams between Beijing and the Northeast provincial government during this period reveal the processes of intense negotiation over these issues.[27]

During negotiations over its Twenty-one Demands, Japan at first attempted to ensure land ownership of its subjects, then conceded the right to "purchase" land, and finally settled for the right to "lease" land. The Chinese central government objected to allowing Japanese subjects to purchase land. This was because the term *purchase* suggested the buyer's de facto ownership of the land. The settlement on the right to lease land (*sangjo* in Korean, *shangzu* in Chinese) was, however, anything but a clear resolution of the question of ownership. The unconditional renewal of a contract rendered leasing insufficiently distinguishable from ownership.

After signing the 1915 Treaty, the disputes over *sangjo* entailed three issues: its definition, the geographic area of its application, and the people subject to it.[28] Voicing its own definition of *sangjo*, each party relied on a different phrase in the attached explanation of Article 2 of the treaty: "The duration of the contract is limited to a maximum period of thirty years, while the renewal of the contract is permitted without conditions." To the Republican government, *sangjo* granted the right to use the leased land, which ruled out ownership by the lessee, and it referred to temporary leasing, which entitled the lessee to use someone else's property without the right to sublease the land. To Japan, *sangjo* meant permanent leasing with unconditional and continuous renewals of contract, and it would endow the lessee with the right to sell the leased land during the lease period.[29] Moreover, Japan insisted that *sangjo* be implemented in parts of South Manchuria and Inner Mongolia. In response, Zhang Zuolin issued a decree in 1923 that applied *sangjo* only to some parts of Fengtian Province.[30] The right of Koreans to lease land was another disputed issue, since China did not acknowledge Koreans as Japanese subjects.

A deeper concern in the disputes over leasing land was Japan's osmotic politics, which imagined the homology of landownership and territorial occupation. A Chinese intellectual in 1931 identified sangjo as a principal mechanism of Japan's territorial osmosis:

Sangjo is a classic strategy with which Japan can establish its sovereignty on a continent. This method will enable Japan to make territorial invasion a relatively peaceful and gradual process. Japan at first gradually acquires land. Then it attempts illegally to establish police stations in the areas where Japanese subjects reside, citing the judicial right of Japanese consulates to rule in court cases involving Japanese. Then Japan "Japanizes" the areas, turning them into Japanese territory. This process works the way a virus infiltrates a body, first penetrating the liver, then gradually taking over all parts of the body.[31]

Here the infection of the liver symbolizes Japanese acquisition of land, which laid the basis not just for profit making by landowners but also for the gradual colonization of Manchuria.

When the right of Japanese subjects to lease land was combined with their extraterritoriality, sangjo signified Japan's territorial sovereignty. Extraterritoriality of the lessee meant that Japanese consulates could hold sovereignty over both the lessee and the leased land itself unless the terms of the lease were clearly divorced from that of landownership. If the area of leased land were to increase, so would Japanese sovereignty. The 1915 Treaty left the door wide open to this possibility when it permitted extraterritoriality for Japanese subjects without a clear definition of *leasing*. Before signing the 1915 Treaty, Japan first demanded comprehensive extraterritoriality of Japanese subjects: its subjects would pay taxes to the Japanese government, its consuls would adjudicate all civil disputes involving Japanese defendants, and Japan and China would collectively rule on cases concerning land disputes between Chinese and Japanese landowners.

The Republican government proposed two alternatives: Japanese subjects would submit to Chinese laws and pay taxes to the Chinese government and Chinese courts would have sole authority over land disputes. In the words of the head of the Chinese Ministry of Foreign Affairs: "Japan seeks to infringe upon our sovereignty, demanding freedom in residence, trade, agriculture, and particularly landownership by Japanese subjects. . . . If it wishes its subjects to reside in Manchuria and own or lease our land, Japan must withdraw its demand that Japanese consuls decide the court cases involving Japanese." [32] In the end, each side compromised. The 1915 Treaty required Japanese subjects to observe Chinese laws and pay taxes to the Chinese government, while Japanese consuls would preside over all Japanese court cases except those involving land disputes, which were to be ruled on collectively by both Japan and China. When it lacked the sole authority to prosecute violators of the laws on land contracts, the Chinese government's loss of sovereignty over land and its occupants would be equal to its loss of territorial sovereignty.

After the treaty was signed, the continued disputes over landownership and extraterritoriality developed beyond the familiar spectacle of political protests against unequal treaties between China and foreign powers. In order to nullify the treaty, Beijing government officials appealed to the international community during international conferences in Paris in 1919 and New York in 1921. In fact, the Chinese Congress invalidated the treaty in 1923, though without any tangible effects. The issues of landownership and extraterritoriality did not incite the intense public outcry associated with anti-

Japanese protests against the leasing of railways and the Liaodong Peninsula. Instead the issues of leasing land and extraterritoriality were contested in the social space. Government regulation of the social practices of land transactions became the bedrock of Chinese nation formation. The Republican government, for instance, enacted the National Punishment Law (Kukchŏk chingbŏl chore), which sentenced to death those who traded land to foreigners on the grounds that such contracts would violate the territorial sovereignty of China.

The social regulation of land transactions mainly took place in Manchuria. Representing itself as the Chinese national government, the Northeast government under Zhang's rule transformed Chinese migrants into nationals as opposed to Japanese "others." Japan endeavored to convert Korean migrants into Japanese subjects. For both Japan and the Northeast government, the new relationship with the people not only involved political discipline such as the punishment of those who violated nationality laws and policies. It also constituted the national hegemony of the former over peasants by providing them with social programs. The social production of national subjects promised to mitigate political, economic, and cultural differences and inequality among migrants, whether Korean or Chinese.

PRACTICING OSMOTIC POLITICS

Japanese osmotic politics in the 1920s hinged on the operation of agricultural farms and consulates. Both measures were intended to make Korean cultivators into Japanese subjects while pacifying the exiled Korean movement. The expansion of farmland cultivated by Koreans was expected to bring more land under Japan's control; at the same time, consulates would augment Japanese military and police forces in the name of protecting Koreans. This osmotic politics faced both external and internal hurdles. Facing objections from the central and Northeast governments of China, Japan neither ensured the right of Japanese subjects to lease land, let alone own it, nor increased the number of consulates by as many as it had wished. Moreover, the dissension and ill-defined hierarchy among civilian Japanese administrators hampered their effective management of Korean settlement and the containment of Korean opposition. Since the Tokyo Cabinet was led by civil bureaucrats, who had pledged to forgo military intervention in Manchuria from 1918 until 1931, the Kwantung Army did not preside over the osmotic politics.

"Protecting" Koreans

Koreans in Manchuria numbered about one million in the mid-1920s. Dating back to an influx during the late nineteenth century, at least one-fourth of Manchuria's total Korean population resided in Fengtian Province, which was the base of the Northeast government and the main site of its contention with Japan. Japan regarded rice cultivation as the primary means of stabilizing the household economies of Korean migrants, who were held in thrall to debt and frequent migration.[33] According to Japanese reports, the majority of Koreans in southern Manchuria were too poor to buy even the seedlings for farming. They often used their share of the harvest as security to take out loans for almost every essential, including land, housing, grain, and farming tools. These Koreans usually traded the rice they harvested for millet and corn for their own consumption. Even in years with good harvests, they barely repaid their debts and had difficulty supporting their families. Bad harvests forced them to sell their possessions, including their clothing, before migrating to a new place.[34]

Japan represented its osmotic strategy as a way to turn Korean migrants into Japanese subjects. It separated good Koreans from undesirable ones, citing its obligation to protect trustworthy Koreans from oppression by Korean rebels and Chinese officials. The policy of protecting good Koreans and repressing rebellious ones (Pohoch'wich'e) denotes two constitutive elements of transforming Koreans into Japanese subjects. On the one hand, the protection of good Koreans corresponded to the first stage of the osmotic expansion of Japanese power because protection would require not merely their physical segregation from rebels and bandits but the improvement of their livelihood. Only stabilization of their household economies would discourage their support for the exiled Korean independence movement. Improvement of the Korean household economies necessitated the cultivation of fertile land. This task was coordinated by the colonial development companies, pro-Japanese Korean associations, and Korean credit unions, which purchased or leased land for Koreans and pledged to introduce new methods of agricultural production and meet basic needs for education and health. These economic and social measures were expected to bind Korean migrants to Japan. On the other hand, the pacification of recalcitrant Koreans would ensure another stage of osmotic expansion since it would bolster Japanese sovereignty over Koreans and enhance their military presence. In other words, the advancement of osmotic politics required that the two measures—the improvement of Korean social life and the suppression of Korean rebels—progress simultaneously. This was because the osmotic expansion of the Japanese empire required that Japanese sovereignty be wielded over all Koreans, their farmland, and the areas they inhabited.

The Northeast government's policies of naturalization introduced tension between the two measures. The government opposed the leasing of land by Japanese subjects and granted rights to ownership only to Chinese nationals. It also constrained Koreans from becoming naturalized as Chinese nationals. Without the naturalization of Koreans, the first act of territorial osmosis—the acquisition of land by Japanese subjects—would not be possible. Although naturalization would provide a necessary condition for the osmotic expansion of Japanese power, it would separate Koreans from Japan and thus obviate its claim to protect Koreans. Whether permitting or preventing Korean naturalization, the adoption of either approach alone would debilitate osmotic expansion. Japan's promise to protect good Koreans (through the provision of land) collided with its pursuit of sovereignty over them, jeopardizing the osmotic expansion of Japanese power.

This dilemma was never resolved, as Japanese powers debated throughout the 1920s the Japanese nationality of Koreans, or "imperial nationality" (cheguk kukchŏk). When the power of the Kwantung Army waned in the 1920s, the debates involved mainly the Government General of Korea and agents of the Japanese Ministry of Foreign Affairs. In November 1923, in Seoul, the Government General of Korea hosted the first comprehensive meeting on the issue of the Koreans of Manchuria, inviting the director of the East Asian Department of the Japanese Ministry of Foreign Affairs and ten Japanese consuls of Manchuria.[35] The consul general of Kando, where the exiled Korean resistance was concentrated, opposed the naturalization of Koreans as Chinese nationals on the grounds that it would divest Japan of the right to suppress the Korean independence movement. Their legal identity as Chinese nationals would shelter anti-Japanese Koreans from Japanese pacification. It would also turn Manchuria into a haven for defiant Koreans because the Chinese government would not cooperate with Japan to repress Korean resistance.

In contrast, the consul general of Fengtian—the head consul of Manchuria—proposed to permit Korean naturalization in South Manchuria. Although the consul general of Kando opposed naturalization primarily because of his concern over Korean politics there, the consul general of Fengtian considered South Manchuria and Mongolia to be the base of the Japanese empire's expansion. For the latter, situations in Kando and South Manchuria were different. In Kando, the naturalization of Koreans would not be nec-essary, since the Kando Treaty guaranteed landownership to nonnaturalized Koreans (see chapter 3). But in South Manchuria, even if Japan were to treat Koreans as its subjects, this would not substantively affect the Korean resis-tance movement unless the Chinese government—the sovereign power of Manchuria—agreed to accept Japan's sovereignty over Koreans. The consul general of Fengtian favored diplomatic negotiation with China in expanding Japanese influence in Manchuria.[36] In the end, the consul meeting of 1923 decided to oppose Korean naturalization. One year later the consul general of Fengtian reissued his proposal only to be rejected by the Government General of Korea. The government general was mainly preoccupied with consolidat-ing its sovereignty over the Korean nation and eliminating the threats from Korean rebels. In 1928, similar debates reaffirmed Japan's policy on Korean naturalization.

In principle, this Japanese policy would impede the acquisition of land by Koreans and thus the first stage of osmotic expansion. In reality, Japan at-tempted to invert this policy into an alternative strategy to guarantee both Korean landownership and Japanese sovereignty over Koreans. After the de-cision to reject Korean naturalization in 1923, Japan focused on invalidat-ing the Chinese nationality of naturalized Koreans rather than preventing Koreans from naturalizing. Simultaneously Japanese administrators envis-aged exploiting naturalized Koreans to purchase land. Japan's invalidation of Korean naturalization derived from the nationality law of the Chinese Re-publican government, which required foreigners to obtain the permission to become naturalized as Chinese nationals from their own governments.[37] This practice by Japan granted dual nationality to naturalized Koreans as Chi-nese nationals and Japanese subjects. Speaking about the dual nationality of Koreans as a tool used for the osmotic expansion of Japanese power, an offi-cial of the Government General of Korea stationed in the consulate of Harbin (in central Heilongjiang Province, which was referred to as North Manchu-ria) noted that "dual nationality of Koreans would benefit Japan for now, since it would contribute to consolidating both the economic and territorial interests of Japan. Japan can facilitate the migration of naturalized Koreans to North Manchuria and provide them with financial assistance to purchase land, and if the Chinese authorities protest this practice Japan can intervene militarily in the name of protecting Koreans."[38]

The disagreement over naturalization was not limited to Japanese admin-istrative agents in Manchuria but also involved their superiors in the Tokyo

Cabinet. For instance, when a new consensus over permission for Korean naturalization emerged in the Tokyo Cabinet in 1930, the Japanese Ministry of Colonial Affairs concurred. But the Japanese Ministry of Foreign Affairs opposed it on the grounds, among others, that it would intensify the oppression of Koreans by the Northeast government.[39] The dissension between these two ministries had been going on for several years. For instance, in 1918 they agreed to place the border region—Kando and Tongbyŏndo—under the jurisdiction of the Government General of Korea. But they competed in promoting the Kwantung Administration and consul general of Fengtian, respectively, as the foremost power in Manchuria except Kando.[40] Although the Japanese prime minister placed the Kwantung administration in charge of Manchurian affairs in 1919, this decision did not completely clarify the administrative hierarchy. According to the report of the police forces in Tongbyŏndo in 1922, they were required to report to both the Kwantung Administration and the consulates, which impeded effective control of the Korean resistance.[41] Moreover, although the ministries of the Japanese Cabinet tried to confine the authority of the Government General of Korea to the border region, the Government General of Korea continued to preside over Korean affairs in other parts of Manchuria.

As a result, osmotic expansion advanced without ensuring the Japanese nationality of Koreans or their rights to landownership. The Japanese attempt to use naturalized Koreans to purchase land prompted the Northeast government to restrain and even outlaw Korean naturalization, as will be discussed later. Japan never resolved the issue of Korean nationality during the 1920s.[42] Osmotic expansion in Manchuria (except in Kando) was directed by the Asia Development Company and Japanese consulates, which acquired land and developed sovereignty over Koreans and the region.

Attaining Sovereignty over Land

Land was the indispensable basis of Korean livelihood, as well as the principal vehicle of Japan's osmotic strategy of territorial expansion. Although Japanese individuals also acquired land and rented it to Koreans, it was mainly the Asia Development Company that interlaced Koreans with the Japanese osmotic strategy. As the Government General of Korea explained the purpose of the company: "Because of the importance of the expansion of rice farming, the protection of Korean agriculture and livelihood is central to the development of Manchuria and the Japanese policy to govern Koreans."[43] In 1921, the company was established by the Kwantung Administration, the

Ministry of Foreign Affairs, and the Oriental Development Company. In addition to the SMRC and the Oriental Development Company, the Government General of Korea and the Kwantung Administration were the primary financiers, although their annual contributions fell short of the pledged amount.

To evade the restriction on leasing land, the Asia Development Company adopted various methods. It leased land from Chinese landlords under the names of Chinese and naturalized Koreans. It also sought to establish joint ventures with Chinese individuals and the Northeast government. In addition, it hired Chinese as managers of its farms or Chinese peasants as tenants. Even after leasing land from landowners or in agreements with Chinese officials, the company was forced to renegotiate with the Northeast government to validate the contract and the use of the land.[44] In 1925, the company operated a total of nine farms (including one in Mongolia), though only six of them, four of which were run by Chinese managers or employed Chinese tenants, seemed to have achieved some stability.[45]

The company aspired to engage primarily in rice farming, although the proportion of paddy fields varied by farm due to the different conditions of land and facilities. Since paddy fields yield far more than dry fields and the price of rice was higher than other grains, the company preferred Koreans as tenants, as they were known for their expertise in irrigation and rice cultivation. The price of paddy fields was three times the price of dry fields and sixty times the price of untilled land. Hence Korean tenants added value to the land. By 1925, the company had hired 479 Korean households as tenants.[46] In the same year, the largest Fengtian farm hired about 450 Korean households to cultivate 1,339 chŏngbo of paddy fields.[47] The Asia Development Company transformed the relationship between Japan and Koreans into one between landlord and tenant. This transformation also affected the relationship between Koreans and Chinese, as irrigation facilities, for instance, became a source of conflict and led to the intervention of the Japanese authorities and the Northeast government.

The Asia Development Company became the major financial organization accessible to ordinary Koreans. Since they lacked assets to use as collateral for loans from Chinese banks, most Koreans had to borrow from Chinese landlords. The small Chinese creditors charged a monthly interest rate of 8 to 10 percent, although it was not rare for some landlords to charge an annual rate of 30 to 100 percent. The Asia Development Company offered Koreans an alternative. At an annual interest rate of 6 to 8 percent, the company loaned Koreans money to cover their expenses for cultivation and living. With an annual interest rate of about 1 percent, the company also funded credit associations run by Korean organizations. Furthermore, the Asia Development Company established eight Korean credit unions by 1932, which financed their members to transform untilled land and dry fields in paddy fields and collectively purchase necessities or sell harvested grain. The largest, Andong credit union, had 3,750 members, while others had a few hundred. In the words of the Government General of Korea, Koreans welcomed the credit unions as if they were the rain after a long drought.[48]

Osmotic expansion required administrative institutions that could translate the acquisition of land into Japan's sovereignty over the occupied land. Japanese consulates, which claimed judicial authority over Koreans, performed this task. They carried out diplomatic functions and mediated between the home government and its overseas residents, performing tasks such as issuing passports and protecting lives and property. Beyond these usual activities, the consulates also breached China's official sovereignty over the region. The 1915 Treaty permitted Japan to establish five consulates in South Manchuria. Japan's attempt to increase the number of consulates in the region in the 1920s renewed disputes over the treaty. The Chinese objection drew on a clause that required Japanese subjects to submit to Chinese laws. The Japanese demand for more consulates alluded to an auxiliary clause that provided for further negotiation between the two parties over this issue. Japan objected to the denial of its right to protect its own subjects.[49]

Over fierce opposition, Japan expanded its consulates. It asserted its right to station consular police as a corollary to the right of extraterritoriality on the grounds that police forces were necessary to perform the judicial functions of the consular courts. By 1931, Japanese consulates had been established at five locations in Manchuria, including Kando, and its subpolice stations numbered about six hundred, staffed with about thirty thousand policemen. The Chinese compiled a list of incidents of illegal expeditions by Japanese forces during the 1920s. For example, Japanese forces conducted military maneuvers across Manchuria, which destroyed farmland and injured Chinese civilians. They also assisted Mongol bandits who rebelled in South and Central Manchuria. In addition, they arrested Chinese civilians and launched attacks on Chinese forces.[50] Despite such encroachments on Chinese sovereignty, the capacity of the Japanese consulates hardly seems to have met the objective of administering the Korean population. For instance, even in the mountainous Tongbyŏndo area, which housed three of the four subconsulates in South Manchuria, in one county only one policeman was in charge of pacifying the Korean independence movement.[51] When Japan sought to create a consulate in Imgang County in Tongbyŏndo, the county magistrate evicted 110 households (560 people). This incident prompted other county magistrates to order their officials to expel Koreans and confiscate their lands.

To offset their low numbers, the Japanese consulates attempted to manage Korean organizations as subsidiaries. The relationship between Korean organizations and Japanese consulates is well illustrated by the history of the Association for the Protection of People (Pominhoe), which will be compared to the Korean Association in chapter 3.[52] The association was founded in 1921 on the initiatives of former members of Ilchinhoe of Korea—a pro-Japanese organization in Korea that promoted the annexation of Korea by Japan. Invoking Japan's general policy of protecting Koreans, the association aimed to help Koreans to improve their household economy and suppress various exile movements.[53] With financial support from the Government General of Korea and the Japanese Ministry of Foreign Affairs, the association established its headquarters in the consulate general in Fengtian, with more than one hundred branches in other parts of South Manchuria. The Government General of Korea not only supplied the association with weapons, but it also dispatched its policemen to the association's headquarters.

Japanese powers attempted to rationalize the administrative jurisdiction and unify Korean organizations. For sole control over the Association for the Protection of People by consulates, the Japanese Ministry of Foreign Affairs asked the Government General of Korea to withdraw weaponry given to the association and discontinue its financial assistance. Under the direction of the consul general of Fengtian, the association integrated other Korean organizations—the Korean Residents' Association (Chosŏnin kŏryumihoe) and the Farmers' Association (Nongmin chohap).[54] Yet these measures seem to have failed to ensure Japanese sovereignty over Koreans. The integration of Korean organizations was more nominal than actual. It was not rare for Korean organizations to retain their names while working for the Association for the Protection of People. The consul general of Fengtian failed to prevent illicit activities and corruption within the association. While condemning the exiled independence movement for collecting compulsory membership fees and extorting other donations, the association resorted to similar practices. Its leaders were also charged with infighting and appropriating official funds for private use. To prevent disorder and corruption, the consul general dismantled the association in 1923.

Japan collaborated with the Northeast government to suppress Korean independence movements, which led to the signing of a treaty in 1925 between the Government General of Korea and the Fengtian government. The 1925 treaty entailed two accords concerning the Tongbyŏndo region. The Fengtian government agreed to pacify rebellious Korean groups, while Japan promised not to cross the border to suppress them. In addition, the Fengtian government vowed to permit Koreans to reside and farm there if it were allowed to monitor the migration of Koreans. After the treaty, the Fengtian government proposed to organize Koreans into collective surveillance teams and issue residence permits with biennial inspections. If Koreans wished to move to other regions, they were required to obtain a migration permit. Despite its notoriety for the joint policing of Koreans by Chinese and Japanese, the 1925 treaty did not prevent Japan from sending its armies to suppress Korean resistance. It therefore did not assure the residency of Koreans, let alone their right to farm in the region.[55]

Osmotic politics straddled two strenuous efforts by Japanese administrative organizations to acquire land and expand the consulates. The significance of osmotic politics is that Koreans were bound to Japanese power not just through policing but also through social programs that supplied Koreans with land and loans. This means that extricating Koreans from Japanese power would require replacing the Japanese social program. Instead of embracing this option, the Northeast government aimed to make a distinction between Korean and Chinese migrants, eliminating the former and turning the latter into landowners.

PRODUCING THE CHINESE NATION

In the midst of Japan's osmotic advance, modern Chinese state sovereignty in Manchuria was expressed in terms of the triad of land, people, and territory. The increasing flow of Koreans to Manchuria fostered the fear of losing sovereignty over land and territory. In 1911, a report from Wangch'ŏng County, a border county between Manchuria and Korea, claimed that about one hundred Koreans were crossing the Tuman River and arriving in Kando every day.[56] According to the report, the initial attempt by Chinese policemen to slow Korean immigration had been futile, as the numbers were too large. In 1912, another report from the same county sardonically described the heavy flow of Koreans in terms of "reverse host-guest" relations between the Chinese and Koreans. It warned that the increase in Korean migration could inflame diplomatic disputes with Japan, which would use Koreans to infiltrate Kando.[57] In 1928, magistrates of the counties in Kando were still expressing alarm over swarming Korean emigrants.[58]

The territorial principle of national membership emerged as a unifier of land, people, and territory. The magistrate of Wangch'ŏng County in Kando, where the Japanese osmotic expansion advanced, summed it up in 1911:

> When Japan colonized Korea in 1910, Koreans lost their nation and thus Korean nationality. Japan is not entitled to force Koreans to become Japanese subjects. . . . While Japan might have the right to reprimand Koreans and the obligation to protect Koreans, it does not possess the prerogative to interfere with Koreans' own choice of nationality. . . . Contemporary intellectuals appraise the territorial principle [sokchi chuŭi in Korean, shudi zhuyi in Chinese] as a new idea of the present period of enlightenment as opposed to the obsolete ethnic principle [sogin chuŭi in Korean, shuren zhuyi in Chinese]. If Japan claims itself to be an enlightened country . . . it must accept the territorial principle. . . . When Japanese national membership has drawn on the territorial principle within Japan, why does Japan practice the ethnic principle in China [by claiming Koreans as its subjects]?[59]

The perceived threat of Koreans spread through Manchuria beyond Kando region. The territorial principle of national membership was enforced by Chinese national forces. Zhang Zuolin's Northeast government and the merchant community, despite their differences on the territorial boundaries and ethnic identity of the Chinese nation, collaborated to command the territorializing national membership in paradoxical territorial and capitalist politics. Whereas territorial politics diametrically opposed Chinese nationals and Korean migrants, capitalist politics brought both groups together in complex social relations of land exchange and labor that defied such a transparent dichotomy. While territorial politics fashioned the nationalist law that required Koreans to leave Manchuria, this law was limited by capitalist politics. Territorial and capitalist politics provided the Northeast government and merchant bourgeoisie with national hegemony over Chinese landowners and peasants.

National Hegemony over Landowners

Reforms dating from 1922 marked a key moment in the formation of the Chinese nation. In addition to the policies that promoted national industries, the Colonial and Development Plan expanded the Chinese workforce for the national development of Manchuria. Chinese peasants tended to be male adults from North China who stayed one season or a few years at most, though family migration was not absent. The Fengtian government motivated them, with some success, to settle in Manchuria for longer periods, if not permanently. As Ronald Suleski explains, the plan was intended to increase the number of Chinese migrants to 200,000 households, or at least 400,000 people annually, while lengthening the duration of their stay. To recruit migrants, government officials were sent to major ports and railway terminals in major cities, including Shenyang, Dairen, Changchun, and Harbin. The officials enlisted new recruits in government programs, providing them with special identification cards, reduced fares on Chinese-owned railways, and financial assistance for settlement. About half of the new migrants were sent to Jilin and Heilongjiang Provinces to reclaim wasteland and run ranches. The rest were directed to jobs in forestry, mining, and sugar refining. In addition, new migrants were offered tax exemptions for three to five years, as well as the opportunity to purchase land and dwellings at below-market prices after five years of residence. This migration policy enjoyed some success. The migration of Chinese peasants doubled from 1923 to 1930. By the late 1920s, about 40 percent of the entering migrants were staying for three years and 19 percent were staying for at least four years.[60]

Beyond its economic effects, the plan in my view created the hegemony of the Northeast government and merchant bourgeoisie over Chinese landowners and peasants. Just as Japan's sovereignty over Korean migrants rested on a social program that promised to help them become landowners, the Northeast government's sovereignty over the Chinese migrants hinged on a similar social program provided by the plan. The boundary between landowners and peasants was therefore fluid in Manchuria. In China proper, the powerful gentry class made up of large landlords inhibited capitalist development of agriculture. Its counterpart was absent in Manchuria. The domination of the Northeast government and bourgeoisie over landlords bore a distinctly capitalist character. As was explained earlier, the Northeast government was the primary financier for banks, grain stores, and food-processing factories. Landlords and producers depended on merchants or wholesale grain stores called liangchan, which controlled about 40 percent of the entire soybean trade in Manchuria, a primary cash crop.[61] Local merchants bought crops from the countryside and resold them to larger merchants of urban centers or near railway stations, who distributed them to stores, food processing factories, and exporters.[62]

The representation of land as "national territory" enabled the Northeast government and merchants to maintain control over landowners. The "nationalization" of property rights invoked a transparent distinction between citizens and national traitors. A statement by the Ministry of Foreign Affairs of the Republican government in 1925 captures the exigency of property law as the countermeasure to Japan's osmotic politics: "Japan has planned to purchase land and bring Koreans to live there so as to colonize the area forever. Ignorant Chinese have pursued only their greed by giving land to Koreans. As a result, our sovereignty is lost."[63] At least from 1924 until 1929, the Northeast government, in close communication with the central Republican government, repeatedly issued decrees on the social contract between Chinese landowners and foreigners, especially Koreans, over land and houses. Since unlimited renewals of leasing meant de facto ownership, renewal was forbidden.[64] The sale or lease of land and houses to foreigners required approval from county offices. The use of land as collateral for loans from Japanese financial organizations was also banned to preempt Japan's seizure of mortgaged land. Furthermore, the ban on the leasing of houses illustrates the determination to root out Koreans. Regulation of land transactions did not always come from the top but also was stipulated by civic associations. For instance, the Liaoning Association for Foreign Diplomacy in 1929 demanded that the Liaoning (previously Fengtian) provincial government issue laws to preserve the national territory and punish those who sold any of it to Koreans.[65] According to the association, the Japanese invasion not only used Koreans but also persuaded Chinese people to sell land.

This national construction of land and people continued during Zhang Xueliang's reign in Manchuria, with more emphasis on the responsibility of Chinese officials.[66] For example, ordered by the Kuomintang government, the Fengtian government decreed that "the South Manchuria Railway Company has amassed land along the Railway . . . which exemplifies its invasion of our land. If we do not stop the company from purchasing land now, we will face major difficulties in retrieving the South Manchuria Railway from Japan after expiration of the lease. Local officials will also be penalized for sales of land to foreigners."[67] In another decree, issued six months later, the Fengtian government reinforced this policy, announcing the death penalty for those who sold land, mountains, mines, buildings, or properties, as well as reductions in pay and dismissal for officials who failed to prevent such occurrences.[68]

Territorial Exclusion of Koreans

The hallmark of nation formation in the 1920s was the clear distinction between nationals and nonnationals. It consisted of shifts from customary and cultural to legal and social national membership, and from the inclusion to the exclusion of Koreans. From the late nineteenth century on, the adoption of Manchu customs signified naturalization as Chinese nationals. Some Koreans listed an unmarried son as head of the household and secured their landownership because unmarried Korean males adhered to the custom of wearing long hair, which resembled the Manchu hairstyle.[69] While adoption of Manchu customs was continuously imposed as a marker of naturalization, it became a supplementary measure in the 1920s. Instead, the distinction between Chinese nationals and nonnationals came to be legislated in the social domain, as the terms of transactions of land and labor defined the legal obligations of nationals. While Koreans had been ordered to become naturalized as Chinese nationals, various prerequisites for naturalization now constrained their Chinese national membership. Nonnaturalized Koreans were barred from owning and leasing land. Their customary rights to reside and work were also threatened.[70]

The Northeast government restricted the naturalization of Koreans. It scrutinized Korean applicants suspected of buying land for Japanese. It also reversed its previous promotion of naturalization for exiled Korean rebels. While it had once encouraged rebels to settle in Manchuria, in the 1920s the Northeast government feared that Japan would send military forces to suppress the anti-Japanese Korean movements. In 1925, the Fengtian government ordered county magistrates to prevent both pro-Japanese and anti-Japanese Koreans from becoming naturalized. A year later it raised the bar for Korean naturalization by requiring that each applicant receive approval from the provincial government instead of the county magistrate.[71] Moreover, the requirement that Koreans submit proof that they had "renounced registration as Japanese subjects" (ch'ulchŏk) added another barrier to their naturalization.[72] This was because Japan did not permit the naturalization of Koreans in Manchuria, let alone releasing proof that they were no longer Japanese subjects.

In the Tongbyŏndo region, where Japan strove to increase the number of its consulates as a means of containing the Korean resistance movements, the Northeast government intensified the exclusion of Koreans. Nonnaturalized Koreans were deprived of the right to association and landownership and faced eviction, while naturalized Koreans were limited in the amount of land they were permitted to own. Naturalized Koreans were permitted to own a maximum of 5.26 chŏngbo of land per household.[73] In Andong County, naturalized Koreans were permitted to own a maximum of 5.44 chŏngbo.[74] In some areas, associations of nonnaturalized Koreans were banned. For instance, Chinese officials shut down a Korean farmers' union in Hunggyŏng that had received loans for rice farming from the Asia Development Company and the Japanese consulate. This was the only credit union run by Koreans. The order was based on the charge that the union threatened public order. In addition, Chinese officials pressured Chinese homeowners to repossess houses rented to Korean associations.[75] In Imgang County from March to May in 1927, various groups of Chinese, including the county magistrate, police, students, and the chamber of commerce, participated in the eviction of Koreans. Even those who passed meticulous background checks and became naturalized were differentiated from native Chinese nationals. They were required to report their leases of land or houses to the Chinese police.

The defining of the Chinese people in terms of their difference from Koreans presumed the natural unity of Japanese and Koreans. It obscured the fact that the relationship between Japanese and Koreans was not only social but also unstable—a relationship that could be severed by an alternative social program. In fact, Korean representatives, in vain, urged the Fengtian and Jilin provincial governments to provide Koreans with social programs such as the distribution of land and low-interest loans. For these representatives, only assistance comparable to the financial support of Japan would discourage a close relationship between Japanese and Koreans. Underscoring the Koreans' contribution to Manchuria, they also called for the promotion of Korean naturalization by canceling the application fee for naturalization and establishing a special office to expedite it. A petition proclaimed their entitlement to social programs and naturalization: "Whether or not they are naturalized as Chinese nationals, most Koreans . . . have observed Chinese laws and fulfilled their duties. They have paid all taxes, such as the land tax, household tax, donation to the military, local security fee, and education fee. In addition, Koreans have paid extra fees such as those for the relocation, the residential permit, use of roads, and postal service. . . . Koreans have also cultivated an enormous amount of wasteland."[76]

The issuance of similar decrees on national membership throughout the 1920s suggests that there were persistent but unsuccessful attempts by the Northeast government to regulate land transactions between Chinese and

Koreans. It attests to the difficulty of fixing social relations according to national politics. This difficulty was affirmed by another trend, in which the government often issued decrees to override its own regulations of rights relating to Chinese landowners and Korean migrants. The ineffective enforcement of the rules of national membership might indicate the administrative incompetence of the Chinese government. More importantly, the simultaneous enforcement of and retreat from the rules reveal the predicament of the Northeast government, which was caught between its territorial and capitalist desires.

Capitalist Inclusion of Koreans

The territorial politics of the Northeast government embedded the production of people as nationals in the realm of social relations of production and exchange. Its significance lies in the ways in which Japan and the Northeast government embedded their sovereignty in the social lives of landowners and peasants. As territorial politics shaped social relations of production and exchange, it generated an unexpected effect on capitalist politics. In turn, the territorial politics of distinguishing nationals and non-nationals was regulated by capitalist imperatives that governed social relations of production. National and territorial politics did not necessarily facilitate capital accumulation, and vice versa. For instance, when the Chinese nationalized property ownership for Chinese landowners but not Koreans, in principle it posed a barrier to the capitalist development of agriculture. This barrier was especially significant because the Manchurian economy was built on agricultural production. The exclusion of Koreans meant less labor power available for reclamation and rice cultivation.

The discourse on rice farming by Koreans illustrates the recognition of their labor power by Japan and the Northeast government. Despite the nationality law that banned the sale and leasing of land to nonnaturalized Koreans, Chinese landlords invited Koreans, even migrants from Korea, to cultivate rice. A 1926 decree of the Fengtian government illustrates how Korean expertise in rice farming posed a dilemma to the Chinese: "Koreans have been pioneers in rice farming. During the early period of reclamation, we the Chinese government levied only a small amount of tax on them. . . . We decided to mobilize our Chinese people to repossess rice fields from Koreans. . . . But our people's rice farming is still so crude that they have to learn from Koreans. The immediate eviction of Koreans would halt the expansion of rice farming."[77] Japan also regarded rice farming as innate to Korean culture. *Contemporary Manchuria*, a Japanese magazine, characterized the paddy rice cultivation of Koreans as a "unique" way of life, while the Chinese were noted for their aversion to soaking their feet in wet paddy fields. With their natural gift, Koreans were seen to create irrigation facilities with perfect skill. They quickly discovered how to draw water from nearby rivers to their fields and never missed even the smallest stream. Once they found the water, they immediately proceeded to grow rice. Koreans cultivated about 85 percent of the paddy fields in Manchuria.[78]

Depictions of Korean rice farming as a natural talent obscure the commodification of Korean labor power and the land they cultivated. They fail to acknowledge the backbreaking labor and sacrifices Koreans made to convert wasteland into productive paddy fields. Reclaiming land was a gamble that required investing everything with no guarantee of return. Many Koreans were new to rice farming, having migrated from northern Korea, where dry field farming was predominant. Rice cultivation in Manchuria required a period of experimentation that involved building an adequate infrastructure and adjusting to local conditions such as its short but scorching summer. The unpopularity of rice farming among Chinese peasants does not signify any intrinsic lack of talent but more favorable material conditions, which relieved them of such a risky business. The losses incurred by Koreans from rice cultivation involved inputs of labor that were never compensated as use or exchange value. In South Manchuria, paddy fields comprised only 34 percent of the land that Koreans cultivated, which suggests the extent to which reclamation was unsuccessful. The situation was compounded by Koreans' unstable institutional status. which threatened their farming.[79]

Rice farming produced a specific mode of inclusion of Koreans in the Chinese national economy: the demotion of Koreans from independent farmers to tenants and agricultural laborers. This pattern of partial inclusion resulted from the Northeast government's attempt to resolve the tension between its national and capitalist desires. However, it is not clear how systematically it was applied across Manchuria. Although the Northeast government was determined to eradicate Korean landownership and residence, it still permitted the employment of nonnaturalized Koreans as tenants with restrictions on length of tenancy and the numbers of tenant households per landlord. According to a 1925 decree, a tenancy contract could not exceed one year, with seven to eight years as the maximum period of renewal. In a 1928 decree, the tenancy contract was reduced to five years for reclamation of wasteland or three years for rice farming. The maximum number of Korean tenant households per Chinese household was limited to ten. Landlords were obliged to evict at least three tenant households every year if they had hired more than the maximum number of tenants permitted by law. In addition, the rights of Korean tenants were circumvented from time to time, as they were required to pay higher rents in 1924, an additional fee for a long-term lease of land in 1925, and new taxes in 1927. To prevent Koreans from overstaying or paying rent late, in 1928 they were required to register at local offices their conditions of employment with the date of hire and the amount of land under their care.[80]

In Tongbyŏndo, where the eviction of Koreans resulted from the acute tension between Japan and the Northeast government, Koreans were restricted to rice farming at fixed wages.[81] Opposing the order of eviction, landlords in Imgang County proposed a variety of alternative measures that would sever the relationship between Japan and Koreans, such as the restriction of residence to one year, a biennial household survey, and a collective surveillance system that would group ten households together for mutual supervision.[82] Although the Northeast government rejected such proposals, it withdrew from its initial position of restricting the employment of Koreans to rice farming at fixed wages. In 1925, the Fengtian provincial government specified that hired Koreans were barred from doing anything other than rice farming.[83] In May 1926, the Fengtian provincial government ordered the county magistrate of Ryuha to replace "contracts for tenancy" between Chinese landlords and Koreans with "contracts for laborers," with a special condition that the annual wage for a hired laborer would be eighty yuan for a male and twenty yuan for a female.[84] This partial inclusion discloses compromise of national and capitalist interests by the Northeast government.

Between the nationality law and partial inclusion in markets, the number of Korean migrants swelled several times, even though the swarming throngs of Koreans continued to fuel apprehension among Chinese government officials. About 38 percent of the total of one million Koreans remained in South and North Manchuria (excluding Kando) by the end of the 1920s. Chinese nation formation was actualized in the domain of the social relations of agricultural production and market exchange. It obscured the unequal relationship between (Chinese) landlords and (Korean) tenants and agricultural laborers.

CONCLUSION

Japan, the Northeast government, and the Chinese merchants were bedfellows whose shared capitalist dream constrained their contentious national
politics. Capital accumulation set limits on territorial and national politics,
which were embedded in the social process of the exchange of land and labor.
Japan's sovereignty over Koreans therefore depended on the viability of the
social relations of production. Japan supplied capital to Korean peasants to
purchase land while attempting to increase its administrative presence. In
response, the Northeast government endeavored to regulate transactions of
land between Chinese landowners and Korean migrants and create a legal
distinction between the former as citizens and the latter as colonial subjects
of Japan. The implementation of nationalist law was constrained by the capitalist desires of the Chinese national forces.

What Manchuria witnessed was not a simple binary antagonism between
Japan and the putative Chinese national power, between Japan and Koreans,
or between Chinese and Koreans. The triangular politics of Japan, the Chinese bourgeoisie, and the Northeast government fragmented the social life of
Korean and Chinese migrants: Koreans as tenants and agricultural laborers
and Chinese as property owners. The opportunity to become landowners was
greater for Chinese migrants than for their Korean counterparts. Despite the
preference of Chinese landlords for rice farming by Koreans, Koreans were
distinguished from Chinese tenants, as they were restricted to short-term
tenancy and low-wage work.

The fragmented social spaces of Koreans and Chinese offer a new perspective on the Manbosan Incident, which is perhaps the best-known clash between Chinese and Korean peasants. In Manbosan, near Changchun City of
Jilin Province, Japan leased land from Chinese landowners through a Chinese
broker and subleased it to Koreans without formal approval from the Chinese
officials. To prepare for irrigation, Korean tenants began to dig a canal that
cut across unleased land between the nearest river and the leased land and to
build a dam across the river. Chinese landowners and farmers opposed the
irrigation project on the grounds that the dam would flood their land. The
conflict between the Koreans and Chinese resulted in the intervention of the
Japanese police and Northeast government officials. The Chinese authorities arrested several Koreans and filled in the canal. Chinese farmers armed
themselves with farming tools and pipes to evict Koreans. In response, the
Japanese consular police used force to prevent the Chinese from destroying

FIGURE 3. An irrigation channel at Manbosan dug by Korean farmers in preparation for rice farming. (From Ryu Eun Kyu, *Ich'ojin hŭnjŏk*, 73.)

the irrigation works. An exaggeration of Korean casualties in the incident mobilized Koreans in Korea to call on Japan to protect the migrants. What might have been a trivial dispute developed into a national dispute between China and Japan, with each dispatching separate police forces and spreading rumors about Korean and Chinese peasants massacring each other. The Manbosan Incident reflected an imagined antagonism between the Koreans and Chinese that originated in conflicts between Japan and China. Fixation on the conflict obscures the fragmentation of social life that resulted from the compromise by the Northeast government of its paradoxical desires for territorial sovereignty and capitalist development.[85]

CHAPTER THREE

Agency of Japanese Imperialism

Now known as the Yanbian Korean Autonomous Prefecture, with four counties of Jilin Province adjacent to northern Korea, Kando was the archetype of Japan's osmotic expansion. Extensive penetration by Japan marked Kando as perhaps the most contentious site of colonial and national politics in Manchuria in the first half of the twentieth century. As in other parts of Manchuria, the formation of modern subjects and national sovereignty was intertwined with the development of private property ownership. This resulted in disputes between Japan and Chinese national forces in Kando. Yet distinctive patterns of national and colonial politics drew on historical contingencies in Kando, such as the legacy of territorial disputes between Korea and China and Koreans as its majority population. Here the key political players included Japan, the Chinese administration in Kando (hereafter the Kando Administration), and Korean political groups that developed confrontational relationships through the medium of Korean nationality and landownership.

Japan's osmotic expansion in Kando accelerated with the selective adoption of the Kando and 1915 Treaties. The former ensured Koreans the rights of residence and landownership, and the latter ensured their extraterritoriality. The two treaties produced a paradoxical relationship between Kando and Koreans. On the one hand, Japanese consulates and the Oriental Development Company, the primary colonial development company in Kando, capitalized on Koreans' rights so as to consolidate economic bonds between Koreans and Japan by means of loans. On the other hand, the rights of Koreans laid the foundation for their militant anti-Japanese movements. Anti-Japanese activities signified osmotic "leakage" or the interruption of osmotic transfusion. But Japan turned this moment of breakdown into an opportunity for increasing osmotic expansion. In the name of pacifying Korean resistance, Japanese consulates and the Government General of Korea expanded their security forces and wielded sovereignty over Koreans. When the Korean population swelled in the mid-1920s to about 300,000, or two-thirds of Kando's population, Japan's claims on Koreans conjured its sovereignty over Kando.

Driven by territorial and capitalist quests, Chinese countercolonial politics in Kando progressed with a two-tiered policy of assimilation: the facilitation of naturalization of Koreans and the validation of nonnaturalized Koreans for farming wasteland and rice fields. The principal incentives for Korean naturalization in Kando were social programs available elsewhere only to Chinese migrants, such as exemption from the land tax and cultivation of wasteland free of charge. The assimilation policies in Kando included abolition of Korean schools and obligatory adoption of the Chinese language and customs. However, the nationality policy had limited results. The 10 to 15 percent rate of naturalization among Koreans in Kando was almost equal to the rate under exclusionary national policies elsewhere. When the Kando Administration regulated landownership by nonnaturalized Koreans, they purchased land under the names of naturalized Koreans. Despite the continual failures of its nationality policies, the Kando Administration did not seal its border with Korea but instead directed nonnaturalized Koreans to farm wasteland and rice fields.

Korean politics was not dictated completely by their national identification with Japan and China but also encroached on capitalist politics. Although Kando became a center of the exiled Korean independence movement, the Korean Association (a primary pro-Japanese organization) and various self-rule organizations continued to address concerns about social conditions in Manchuria. Japanese consulates exercised closer supervision of the Korean Association in Kando than in other parts of Manchuria. The Korean Association in Kando tended to encompass small landowners and destitute peasants, who relied on loans for acquiring land, farm equipment, or subsistence. In contrast, various Korean self-rule organizations, which supported the Chinese authorities and their policy of promoting Korean naturalization, were led by landowning elites. Participation of disparate social groups accentuated the polarization of Korean politics. However, the divided politics encompassed capitalist politics, as the desire for private property ownership foregrounded any competing partnership with Japan or China.

In this chapter, I first discuss the Kando Treaty and the 1915 Treaty, which supplied Japan with two instruments of osmotic expansion—Korean landownership and extraterritoriality. I then explore the confrontational triangular politics of Japan, China, and Koreans in Kando, which laid the political and economic foundations for Japan's osmotic expansion. I also examine the specific formation of the Chinese nation and the Korean self-rule movement through which Chinese and Koreans envisaged regaining territorial and capitalist sovereignty from Japan.

THE KANDO TREATY (1909 TREATY) AND THE 1915 TREATY

The Kando Treaty shaped distinctive national and colonial politics in Kando. After signing the Protectorate Treaty with Korea in 1905, Japan reopened age-old territorial disputes between China and Korea over Kando. Japan attempted to modify a resolution reached by China and Korea one year earlier, which allowed Koreans to reside in Kando, own land there, and pay taxes to the Kando Administration. This resolution neither stated the sovereign rights of Korea or China nor clarified the nationality of Koreans. Instead the resolution named the region Kando (literally the "middle land between China and Korea"), implying that it would not be claimed by either party.[1] After years of disagreement, in 1909 Japan signed the Tuman River China-Korean Boundary Treaty, also known as the Kando Treaty, which recognized Kando as Chinese territory. In return, China permitted the creation of Japanese consulates and the involvement of Japanese subjects in business.

A significant change for Koreans brought about by the Kando Treaty was the strengthening of Chinese sovereignty over them. As before, Koreans continued to reside and own land there without becoming naturalized as Chinese nationals. Article 3 of the treaty permitted "the residence of Koreans on agricultural lands lying north of the Tuman River." Yet, in accordance with China's territorial rights over Kando, Koreans were under Chinese administrative and judicial authority. Extraterritoriality for Koreans was thereby ruled out. In particular, Article 4 stated that "Koreans residing on agricultural lands in the mixed region [chapkŏ chiyŏk in Korean, zayu diyu in Chinese —the areas where Korean reclamation was allowed prior to 1880] shall submit to Chinese laws, pay taxes, and be adjudicated by Chinese authorities." Article 5 held Chinese officials responsible for protecting land and houses owned by Koreans.[2]

Although the Kando Treaty proclaimed Kando to be Chinese territory, this was anything but a resolution of the problem of territorial sovereignty.

The statement about Chinese administrative and judicial authority over Koreans was too weak to guarantee China's sovereignty. Although Japan had asserted that Koreans were its subjects one year earlier, the treaty did not specify their nationality. In the aftermath of the treaty, Japan's osmotic politics galvanized the dispute on sovereignty over Koreans into a dispute on sovereignty over the area. As Koreans constituted the majority of the population in Kando, Japan's osmotic politics posed a greater threat to Chinese sovereignty in Kando than elsewhere.

Despite this ambiguity, China was forced to defend the Kando Treaty by default in order to prevent Japan from asserting the extraterritoriality of Japanese subjects. Although the 1915 Treaty concerned South Manchuria and Mongolia, Japan insisted on extending it to Kando, which was often referred to as East Manchuria. Thus, the 1915 Treaty would grant Koreans extraterritoriality, which had been precluded by the Kando Treaty. In disputes over the applicability of the 1915 Treaty to Koreans, a key contention concerned whether Koreans were Japanese subjects and whether Kando was part of South Manchuria.[3] The Government General of Korea elaborated on the Japanese standpoint on Koreans. In an appeal to the Japanese Ministry of Foreign Affairs from June to August of 1915, the Government General of Korea reasoned that Japan's annexation of Korea converted Koreans into Japanese subjects and that asymmetrical Japanese administrative authority over Koreans in Kando and South Manchuria would thwart the effective suppression of the anti-Japanese activities of Koreans in Manchuria. It projected that the absence of Japan's judicial authority over Koreans in Kando would provide a sanctuary for the exiled Korean independence movement.

With the support of the consul general in Kando, the Government General of Korea asked that the Japanese Ministry of Foreign Affairs substitute the 1915 accord on extraterritoriality of Japanese subjects for Articles 3, 4, and 5 of the Kando treaty, which proclaimed Chinese administrative and judicial authority over Koreans in Kando. This appeal cited Article 8 of the 1915 Treaty, which annulled all preceding treaties. The Japanese Ministry of Foreign Affairs initially opposed the Government General of Korea's proposal so as to initiate conciliatory relations with China. Its objection drew on the distinction of Koreans and Japanese subjects, the former subject to the Kando Treaty and the latter to the 1915 Treaty. However, in August 1915 the Japanese Cabinet, in which the prime minister also served as the head of the Japanese Ministry of Foreign Affairs, endorsed the Government General of Korea's proposal and pressed the Beijing government to consent to it. The Chinese Republican government issued a challenge, stating that the 1915 Treaty concerned South Manchuria and Japanese subjects, not Koreans in Kando.

The Kando and 1915 Treaties both guaranteed the disparate prerequisites of Japan's osmotic politics—landownership and the extraterritoriality of Koreans. The specious adoption of both treaties equipped Japan with the tools of osmotic politics. Japan displayed its defiance of Chinese objections by using imprecise and evasive geographical references. In the 1915 Treaty, Japan introduced regional categories for Manchuria, such as South, North, and occasionally East Manchuria, instead of using China's administrative categories of Fengtian, Heilongjiang, and Jilin Provinces. Insisting that Kando was part of South Manchuria, Japan revoked three disputed provisions of the Kando Treaty while retaining landownership for Koreans prescribed by the Kando Treaty. It ordered its consulates in Manchuria to apply their juridical rights over Koreans. The move to assert the extraterritoriality of Koreans in Kando in 1915 affirmed the strategy of protecting Koreans, which Japan had identified earlier as an alternative to territorial rights over Kando. Prior to 1931, the renegotiation between China and Japan over territorial sovereignty was imbricated with capitalist development and took place within a new political context shaped by the Kando Treaty.

CONFRONTATIONAL TRIANGULAR POLITICS

National and colonial politics in Kando veered toward confrontational relations among Japan, the Kando Administration, and Koreans. The political and economic landscape in Kando was marked by the absence of the powerful Chinese merchants who had played a key role in national politics in Fengtian Province. Instead, Japanese capital subordinated Chinese and Korean merchants in Kando, making them mediators between peasant producers and Japanese buyers and traders. Since the Kando Treaty granted Japan the rights to trade and invest in four major cities in Kando, Japanese capital quickly flooded in and came to monopolize trade, exports, and the financial sector. Japan's economic domination in Kando has been depicted not just as an intervention but also, more aptly, as a sponge soaking up the wealth of Kando.[4] Japanese trading companies hired Chinese and Korean merchants to buy crops from farmers in the countryside, transport them to urban areas, and sell them to Japanese trading companies. The companies not only distributed these crops to grain stores and food-processing factories (bean oil and bean cake processors, flour mills, and so forth) but also exported them via the South Manchuria Railway to Korea, Japan, and Europe.[5]

Japanese merchants and financial institutions dominated the financial sector. Organizations such as the Choson Bank, a branch of the Oriental Development Company (known as the Kando Relief Association, Kando ku-jehoe), and the Hungnong Joint Company operated as giant pawnbrokers. Lending money to individual merchants and peasants, these organizations assigned asset values to houses and other properties for mortgages. In fact, Japanese financial organizations offered low-interest loans and became a major source of loans available to Korean and Chinese merchants and peasants. These organizations eventually absorbed the credit organizations run by Koreans. Furthermore, Japanese currency circulated freely and was favored over Chinese currency, whose value fluctuated widely.[6] Chinese financial organizations, such as a branch of the Official Bank of the Three Northeastern Provinces and a branch of Jilin Yonghung Official Bank, mainly engaged in exchanging the currencies their banks issued and transporting money between places. These institutions rarely loaned money to individual peasants.

Anti-Japanese politics in Kando unfolded within a confrontational framework. With a weak Chinese bourgeoisie, the key political player on the Chinese side was the Kando Administration. Because of territorial disputes with Japan over Kando, the Kando Administration was in direct communication not just with the Jilin provincial government, its immediate superior, but also with the Chinese Ministry of Foreign Affairs in Beijing, even in the 1920s, when Zhang Zuolin gained control over Jilin and other parts of Manchuria. The Kando Administration enacted policies to integrate Koreans into the Chinese community, coaxing them to become naturalized and adopt Manchu and Chinese customs.

Koreans emerged as pivotal political players. As Japan and local governments competed for control over them, Koreans were not merely objects of mobilization but also formed a political force in Kando. This development was in contrast to the ambiguous politics of Koreans in South Manchuria, where they neither protested Japanese claims on them (except in the border area of Fengtian Province called Tongbyŏndo) nor demanded that Chinese authorities ease the oppression of Koreans (except for a few petitions submitted by the representatives of naturalized Koreans of three northeast provinces). On the contrary, Koreans in Kando developed the region as a site of the Korean independence movement. Noncommunist nationalist groups dominated politics in the 1910s, advocating education for Koreans and operating guerrilla armies.[7] The massacre in Hunch'un County in the autumn of 1920, where Japan retaliated against exiled Korean resistance with a mass execution of more than 6,000 Korean civilians, marked a turning point in the Korean independence movement within and beyond Kando. After the massacre, Korean nationalists fled to North Manchuria and the Tongbyŏndo area, and communist activities in Kando increased during the 1920s. Japanese police forces and armies continued to disregard Chinese sovereignty in their suppression of Korean resistance.

The Kando Administration and Japanese consulates continued to negotiate their collective pacification of the Korean independence movement. The Kando Administration intended to root out those Korean resistance activities that led to Japanese police and military exercises. The head of the Kando Administration recruited new police and even asked Japan to arm them.[8] However, their joint operation was less forceful in Kando than in South Manchuria, especially the Tongbyŏndo region. More importantly, Chinese officials attempted to integrate Koreans into its national community. This Chinese national politics was accompanied by the favorable attitude of Koreans of Kando toward China. The rivalry between Japan and China divided Koreans' national politics along these two lines.

DE FACTO COLONIZATION

Social Sovereignty

Confrontational politics prepared Japan to make audacious encroachments in Kando. Administrative and financial subsidiaries enabled Japanese consulates to establish de facto sovereign power over Koreans and over Kando itself. Japan's sovereign power was anchored in social relations. The Oriental Development Company contributed to osmotic expansion by developing social ties with Koreans. Establishing its headquarters in Tokyo in 1908, the Oriental Development Company opened its branch in 1918 in Kando, absorbing the Kando Relief Association that the Government General of Korea created in 1911 ostensibly to assist fire victims in Ryongjŏng city. While the company invested in industries such as electrical power and mining, it became an indispensable provider of financial services to Koreans. In 1928, its Kando branch expended about half of its total 2.3 million won of investment on loans. The annual interest rate of loans made by the company differed by the type of security, with 8.2 percent for loans guaranteed by land and 10.2 percent by movable assets such as a house or future harvest. These annual interest rates were lower than the 17 to 30 percent rates charged by other financial organizations and 40 to 70 percent rates of usurers.[9]

As the Asia Development Company had done in South Manchuria, the Oriental Development Company accumulated land by confiscating mortgaged land in cases of default. The amount of land owned by the company in Kando was 58,170 mu, about four-fifths of which was rice fields. The practices of the Oriental Development Company differed according to the borrower's nationality, reflecting the resistance of the Chinese government to the company's acquisition of land. When Chinese borrowers failed to repay loans, the company was required to transfer the guaranteed land to the Chinese government, which then collected a portion of the harvest from the debtor or the tenants to repay the loans. When Korean landowners used land as collateral, the company usually kept the title or the leasing contract. When Korean debtors failed to repay their loans, the company seized the land and hired tenants to cultivate it.[10]

Supervised by consular police departments, the Korean Association enabled Japanese consulates to cultivate social ties with Koreans and penetrate the everyday lives of Koreans. The Korean Association fostered closer social relationships with the Japanese consulates in Kando than in other parts of Manchuria. In 1917, the consulates began to restructure the subsidiary Korean organizations in Kando. As the Korean Association and the Korean Residents' Association (Chosŏnin kŏryuminhoe) suffered from low membership, the restructuring attempted to coordinate the organizations and expand their social bases.[11] The thrust of the restructuring was to develop the Korean Association as a public organization capable of forcing the compulsory participation of Koreans. In May 1917, the consul general in Kando spoke of the anticipated benefits of this restructuring:

> As China and Japan contended over the issue of whether the 1915 Treaty overrides some provisions of the Kando Treaty, Chinese authorities began to integrate Koreans into Chinese society. If we neglect this situation, it could gradually detach Koreans from Japanese imperial officials. . . . Koreans in Kando are divided into pro-Japanese and pro-Chinese groups. . . . The public status of the envisaged Korean organizations would not only make membership obligatory but also would offer practical excuses for joining the organizations to Koreans who are fearful of Chinese retaliation. Furthermore, the public status of Korean organizations would authorize the collection of membership fees.[12]

From 1916 to 1920, a total of eighteen branches of the Korean Association were established in Kando. Some were dismantled during anti-Japanese protests on March 13, 1919, but were later resurrected.[13] The Korean Association integrated other organizations. Although a few branches of the association existed in other parts of Manchuria, their operations lagged far behind those of their counterparts in Kando. It was not until 1935 that the new Federation of the Korean Association (Chonsŏnin minhoe yŏnhaphoe) integrated the Korean Association in other parts of Manchuria.

Since the Korean Association was the auxiliary organization of the consulates, the Japanese Ministry of Foreign Affairs was responsible in principle for subsidizing their major activities. When the Government General of Korea offered subsidies to the Korean Association, they were intended to pay for other activities for Koreans such as public education and hygiene.[14] As for its primary work on behalf of the Japanese consulates, the Korean Association enforced orders and conducted surveys of Koreans on family origins, property ownership, amounts of land under cultivation, and economic conditions.[15] It carried out daily surveillance of Koreans so as to curtail the influence of the exiled independence movements and to prevent them from spreading to Korea. The Korean Association checked the identities of relatives and others visiting Korean households and scrutinized the meetings and activities of Koreans. It issued permits to residents for travel to Korea in order to prevent contacts among the partisans and nationalists in Kando and Korea. The Korean Association enabled the police of the Japanese consulates to monitor anti-Japanese activities among Koreans without leaving their offices. Shim Yŏch'u in the late 1920s testified about the overarching activities of the association: "Koreans who do not join the Korean Association are suspected of defying Japan. While anti-Chinese attitudes do not matter much in daily life, being implicated as anti-Japanese makes even one day unbearable. The mere expression of an anti-Japanese attitude can lead to immediate arrest by Japanese police."[16] This expansive authority over Koreans prompted Chinese officials to denounce the Korean Association for interfering with Chinese administrative sovereignty.[17]

The ubiquitous presence of the association in the everyday lives of Koreans continues to generate interest among historians. The activities of the Korean Association belied simple qualification of pro-Japanese.[18] Lim Yŏngsŏ, a South Korean historian, describes the Korean Association as an auxiliary unit serving Japanese consulates and a group promoting self-rule for Koreans. Lim's suggestion that the association was a self-rule organization draws

on the contrast between the leadership and activities of the Korean Association and those of other prominent pro-Japanese organizations, especially the
Association for the Protection of Koreans (Pominhoe) on the border of Fengtian Province and Korea. The leadership of the Korean Association was made
up of many schoolteachers who did not have obvious backgrounds working for Japan. However, the leadership of the Association for the Protection
of Koreans mainly included former members of the infamous pro-Japanese
organization Ilchinhoe, which advocated the annexation of Korea by Japan.
This leadership background makes it difficult to determine whether the Korean Association was entirely pro-Japanese. The fact that the major leaders
of the Korean Association migrated to Manchuria before the annexation of
Korea by Japan seemed to lead them to prioritize their concern for the Korean community over the liberation of Korea. Moreover, the Korean Association was geared toward eliminating the Chinese oppression that jeopardized
residence and farming for Koreans, while the Association for the Protection
of Koreans aimed to eradicate the exiled Korean movements. In Lim's analysis, this community character of the Korean Association is affirmed by their
participation in the self-rule movement in 1923.[19]

Although Lim's analysis is a significant attempt to explore the intricate
nature of the Korean Association, it remains incomplete. Improving the social life of Koreans was a motto not just for the Korean Association but also
for the Association for the Protection of Koreans. However, the crucial issue
for understanding Korean organizations is not whether they sought to enhance Korean social life. Instead, it is the fact that the call for improving
social life was the crux of Japan's osmotic expansion in the name of "protecting" Koreans. Distributing land to Koreans was the most basic element
of osmotic expansion, as a founder of the Association for the Protection
of Koreans clearly articulated in 1923: "Japan cannot establish sovereignty
over Koreans, unless it attends to the livelihood of Koreans depending on
farming. . . . The distribution of land to poor Koreans by Japan would not
only help stabilize Koreans' livelihood but also enrich Japan. Manchuria will
then belong to not just Koreans but also Japan."[20] He reiterated in 1924 that
Japan could win the support of Asians not merely by military means but also
through its investment in land reclamation.[21]

The community orientation shared by Korean organizations signified Japan's osmotic strategy. The promise to improve the lives of peasants enabled
Japan to embed its power in the social life of Koreans. Together with the Oriental Development Company, the credit unions of the Korean Association

carried out the policy of protecting Koreans. In 1920, it opened five credit unions with funds from both the Japanese armies after the Hunch'un massacre and the Government General of Korea. They offered low-interest loans to destitute farmers to help pay for the purchase of farming tools and land. The credit unions limited the amount of individual loans to 100 won with 0.05 percent daily interest.[22] They set the annual interest rate at 16.2 percent, which was higher than the 8.2 to 10.2 percent charged by the Oriental Development Company but much lower than the 60 to 72 percent charged by usurers. Since the Korean Association's credit unions enrolled borrowers as members, some loan recipients did not even realize they were members of the association.[23]

The Oriental Development Company and the Korean Association serviced a broad range of Koreans. The former served those who owned property and the latter served those without property. As noted earlier, the former financed most of the loans to Korean property owners who could mortgage land or other movable assets. In contrast, the Korean Association made loans to poor Koreans who were in chronic debt. The Government General of Korea acknowledged that the financial capacity of the credit unions was still too small to help all 300,000 Koreans in Kando, yet the Korean Association was a central financial institution that provided loans to the destitute.[24] These loans were often used to repay other loans, including those made by the Oriental Development Company. When the Korean Association, for instance, provided 747,092 won to 14,403 Koreans in 1933, 53 percent of a total amount of loans was spent on paying old debts and only 0.23 percent went toward purchasing land or making agricultural improvements.[25]

Japanese financial apparatuses fashioned the relationships between Japanese power and Koreans into social relations mediated by the exchange of capital. Their social ties warrant a specific understanding beyond their designation as pro-Japanese or colonial. Their relationship was not built solely on racial and political identification with the Japanese empire. Loans made to Korean landowners and poor peasants must be understood as much more than Japanese capital investment. They were a tool of Japan's osmotic politics. Financial institutions advanced the osmotic expansion of the empire hand in hand with the police force and the administrative agents.

Suzerainty over Kando

The consulates extended Japan's social sovereignty from Koreans to Kando. Japanese consular policemen arrested Koreans who had become naturalized as Chinese nationals. Japan's suzerainty is attested by the Koreans' recognition of the consulates as the de facto governing power. For example, when Chinese policemen attempted to arrest Korean violators of a Chinese law that banned the brewing of rice wine, Koreans assaulted the policemen and brought them to the Japanese consulates. When a Korean moneylender filed a suit with the Japanese consulate against a guarantor, consular officials ruled that the guarantor and the debtor must pay the debt by selling their cows and pigs.[26] When Chinese officials in Hunch'un County imprisoned a group of Koreans for smuggling salt from Korea, the Koreans escaped and found refuge in a Japanese consulate.[27] In the late 1920s, Shim Yŏch'u, a promoter of Korean naturalization and self-rule, observed poignantly the idiosyncratic importance of Japanese consulates in the daily lives of Koreans. Koreans confided in Japanese consuls rather than Chinese officials because of the language barrier and their suspicion that they favored Chinese peasants. Chinese county magistrates and police chiefs requested in vain that the Kando Administration negotiate with Japan to terminate the juridical practices of the consuls. According to Shim, the Chinese attempt to ban consuls' judicial activities pleased Korean nationalists, including the communists, but left ordinary Koreans worried about losing a place to file their grievances.[28]

The anti-Japanese activities of Koreans emboldened Japan's use of osmotic politics for establishing sovereignty. The legal rights of Koreans to reside and own land paved the way for exiled Korean politics. Whereas moderate nationalist activities, such as the operation of schools and mutual aid programs for newly arrived Koreans, waned in the mid-1920s, radical communist activities became ascendant. Although the Manchuria General Bureau of the Korean Communist Party was established across Manchuria, its activities yielded the most fruit in Kando. The Kando branch of the Manchuria Bureau organized the East Manchuria Young Men's League of Communist Youth and the Farmers League in early 1920 with several thousand members.[29] Korean Communists engaged in guerrilla activities, assassinating Japanese authorities and destroying strategic buildings and bridges, including Japanese consulates.

The activities of the Korean communists denoted a failure in osmotic transfusion, or "leakage," which Japanese power exploited to advance the osmotic process. In the name of suppressing Korean movements, Japanese police and armies frequently searched houses and organizations and arrested Koreans, many of whom were transported for interrogation and discipline to prisons in northern Korea. In the mid-1920s, Japan had dropped any pre-tense of respecting Chinese authority. It seldom informed Chinese officials of these sweeps until afterward, if at all. It even proclaimed Kando to be part of northern Korea's Hamgyŏng Province. Although some Koreans sought protection against Japanese persecution by becoming naturalized as Chinese, this strategy was ineffective because Japan did not recognize naturalized Koreans as Chinese citizens. Fearing the spread of communism and seeking to preempt further Japanese campaigns, the Chinese officials in the region even collaborated with Japan in subduing the Koreans' nationalist and anti-Japanese activities. Japan asserted that its campaigns against Koreans resulted from its concern that the independence movements in Kando would spread to the Korean Peninsula. Yet Japanese osmotic politics revealed that Japan had broader ambitions.

During the confrontations between the Japanese and Koreans, anticommunism served as a colonial discourse of exclusion, a trope of political difference that defined and disciplined disloyal subjects. Declaring that world politics in the 1930s engaged in wars between communist and anticommunist blocs, Japan lumped itself and its allies, such as Germany and Italy, into an anticommunist bloc, while grouping its enemies in a communist bloc, even portraying the United States, Great Britain, and France as communist. This anticommunism served Japan's ends in Korea and Manchuria. It sought to contain the spread of national movements, especially the alliance of the national liberation movement and the communists who also were exiled in Manchuria before and after the dissolution of the Korean Communist Party in 1928. Japan classified radical resistance groups as communist, who were thought to reject private property, promote violent revolution, and debilitate the Japanese spirit. This helped Japan frame anticolonial resistance as a form of class conflict among Koreans. The Government General of Korea promulgated a series of anticommunist laws, established thousands of anticommunist associations, and mobilized millions of Koreans for numerous police-sponsored gatherings.[30] These anti-Communist campaigns were not confined to Korea but extended to Manchuria, supplying Japan with an excuse to override Chinese authority in Kando.

The strategy of protecting good Koreans from undesirables was productive in this region. Pledging to protect Koreans from radical insurgents, Japan expanded its police force and equipped it to function like an army.[31] Japan rebuked Chinese officials for forcing Koreans to become naturalized and for retaliating against Koreans for associating with Japanese. The Japanese consulates also censured Chinese officials for failing to contain Korean resistance and obstructing Japanese pacification of Koreans. In fact, Japan claimed that the number of policemen stationed in Kando in April 1918 was inadequate to protect the estimated two hundred thousand Koreans living there.[32] Covert strategies for increasing the size of the police force and its scope were adopted to avoid Chinese protests. When new police stations were planned in eighteen places in 1918, the interim consul general proposed a gradual expansion of about four police stations annually. He also suggested calling them consulate substations or police substations instead of police stations. Policemen were directed to wear civilian clothes and only gradually adopt an official uniform.[33] They also were advised to avoid unnecessary conflicts with Chinese officials by asking for assistance from the Chinese police in transporting arrested Koreans or by hiding the arrest of Koreans from them.[34] Accordingly, the size of the Japanese police force increased rapidly in the 1920s from 26 Japanese (and Korean) policemen in Kando in January 1918 to 122 in four police departments and four substations in 1920. There were four police departments and eighteen police substations in the late 1920s and about three hundred policemen in 1930.[35]

Osmotic expansion was not without its flaws, however. It was ensnared by discord between the administrative powers in the region, as in other parts of Manchuria. The most pronounced conflict in Kando developed between the Japanese consulates and the Government General of Korea. While agreeing to prohibit Koreans from becoming naturalized as Chinese citizens, these two apparatuses differed in their basic approach to governance. The Government General of Korea sought to suppress Korean resistance at the risk of bypassing Chinese authorities and inciting tensions between Japan and China. In contrast, the consul general of Kando favored a diplomatic approach, which would compel China to grant extraterritoriality to Japanese subjects and permit Japanese authorities to administer Koreans. He feared that the violent suppression of Korean resistance movements, such as the massacre in Hunch'un, might invite censure from international powers. The two apparatuses engaged in competition over control of the police force. Claiming primary responsibility over Korean affairs, the Government General of Korea declared its sole authority over various important functions, such as the appointment of all consular employees except the consul general and police personnel and preparation of the budget for police operations. In response, the consul general asserted his right to supervise police operations. To resolve the impasse, the Japanese Ministry of Foreign Affairs brokered a compromise. While the Government General of Korea was given the authority to control the police force, the police chief had to follow the rules set out by the consulate general. To restrain its power, the ministry allowed the Government General of Korea to recommend but not appoint consular employees. If disagreements were to occur between the police chiefs and Kando consuls, the former were expected to report to the Government General of Korea and the latter to the ministry. This impetuous division of labor between the Government General of Korea and the Kando consulate general failed to clarify their hierarchical order.

As the consulate general of Kando and the Government General of Korea coordinated the expansion of the police force, tensions arose between them over the issue of recruiting policemen. When the consul general in Kando asked that the Tokyo Cabinet create six new police stations and ten substations, posting 100 additional policemen, he preferred that the Japanese Ministry of Foreign Affairs appoint the policemen rather than the Government General of Korea. He argued that the Government General would not dispatch competent policemen and that circumstances in Kando differed from those in Korea, making policemen from Korea unfit for Kando. But because the administration of Koreans would require policemen capable of communicating in Korean, the Government General of Korea was asked to send policemen to Kando, preferably an equal number of Koreans and Japanese.[36] In June 1918, this proposal was modified to recruit a total 120 policemen, 90 sent by the Government General of Korea (40 Japanese and 50 Koreans), 20 Japanese by the Japanese Ministry of Foreign Affairs, and 10 Koreans by the Kando consulate general.[37] According to many reports from consulates, the tension between the police and the Kando consulate general caused confusion in the operation of the police forces. This instability exposed the shaky ground of the osmotic occupation of Kando, despite the fact that Japan seemed to have established de facto sovereignty over Koreans.[38]

COMPETING CHINESE SOVEREIGNTY

Assimilation

Chinese administrators competed against Japan for control over the Koreans. Within the context of confrontational politics with Japan, the Chinese territorial principle in Kando received distinctive articulations from the 1910s until 1931. While in principle Koreans were excluded from the Chinese community in Fengtian Province, they were not only admitted to reside and own land there but also were forced to assimilate into the Chinese community in Kando. Despite the anxiety over Korean migration, the Kando Administration continued to open its doors to new Korean migrants. Korean migration predated Chinese migration due to the mountain range along Kando, though the latter increased as rapidly as the former in the 1920s.[39] With the increase of Chinese immigrants, the Kando Administration foresaw the need to regulate the naturalization of Koreans and landownership of naturalized Koreans.[40] It repossessed official land given to Koreans as supplements for running educational facilities and distributed it instead to new Chinese immigrants. Chinese landlords revoked tenancy contracts with Koreans and allocated them to new Chinese settlers.[41] But such new restrictions on Korean residence and farming occurred in conjunction with the continued acceptance of Korean migrants.

Behind the panic over Korean settlement was a steadfast approval of Korean farming skills that was never completely overshadowed by increasing Chinese settlement. Only Yŏn'gil and Hwaryong Counties, which were known as the "mixed" region, were designated by the Kando Treaty for residence and landownership by Koreans. But the scope of Korean migration in Hunch'un and Wangch'ŏng Counties was no different. Chinese officials in Wangch'ŏng County noted the difficulty of prohibiting landownership to nonnaturalized Koreans in other counties, observing that the Kando Treaty protected the land and houses of Koreans.[42] The exclusionary policies did not seem to be a viable option since Chinese authorities and Japan competed to integrate Koreans, who comprised the majority of the population.

Signifying land as territory, Chinese authorities saw the cultivation of land by foreigners as an encroachment on "land sovereignty" (t'oji chugwŏn in Korean, tudi zhuquan in Chinese). In close communication with the central Republican and Northeast governments, the Kando Administration aspired to impose Chinese sovereignty over people and land throughout the Kando region, which the Kando Treaty had divided by affirming the vested rights of nonnaturalized Koreans. The introduced measures consisted of the facilitation of Korean naturalization and their assimilation. Promotion of Korean naturalization was a common thrust of nationality policy across Kando, although it was accompanied by sporadic threats to evict nonnaturalized Koreans. Naturalization was enforced especially strongly with the large landowners. In 1922, in Hwaryong County, a new decree required Koreans who owned acreage of more than 1,000 pyŏng to become Chinese citizens or leave the area.[43]

If there was a noteworthy difference between the mixed and nonmixed regions, landownership of nonnaturalized Koreans seems to have been regulated more forcefully in the latter than in the former. In the mixed region (Yŏn'gil and Hwaryong Counties), Korean residents were induced to become naturalized as Chinese nationals, while nonnaturalized Koreans were banned from acquiring land; new settlement by Koreans was also limited. In the nonmixed regions (Wangch'ŏng and Hunch'un Counties), Chinese officials detained new Korean immigrants and forced them to adopt Manchu hairstyles and clothing. According to 1911 decrees in the counties, land owned by nonnaturalized Koreans was to be confiscated by the winter of 1912 and transferred to Chinese tenants. When land cultivated by nonnaturalized Koreans had been subject to tax exemption—five years for state-owned wasteland and three years for privately owned wasteland—it was to be appropriated by the fall of 1913 and distributed to Chinese tenants.⁴⁴

To encourage naturalization, naturalized and nonnaturalized Koreans in 1919 were classified as Kongmin, or "nationalists" (Gongmin in Chinese), and Kanmin, or "cultivators" (Kenmin in Chinese,), respectively.⁴⁵ As the Kando Treaty stipulated, the status of Kanmin entailed specific obligations of Koreans to the Chinese governments (such as payment of taxes and observance of Chinese laws), in return for residence, farming, and even landownership rights in Kando. Chinese officials were instructed to keep records on Kanmin, especially their length of residence, the size of their landholdings, and their economic condition.⁴⁶ Kongmin were promised privileges equivalent to those enjoyed by their Chinese counterparts—the right to vote, tax exemptions, and financial assistance to acquire land and housing. Once naturalized, landless Koreans were to receive wasteland for cultivation for free until they were allowed to buy it at the price of wasteland.⁴⁷ The promise of protection from Japanese arrests at first persuaded many Koreans to become naturalized. But it soon lost its appeal, as Japan disregarded Chinese sovereignty over naturalized Koreans. Addressing this situation in May 1922, the Jilin provincial governor proposed to expand alternative incentives that would improve actual livelihoods, such as easy acquisition of land and cordial relations between Koreans and Chinese.⁴⁸

Local Chinese officials sent policemen to each Korean household to urge at least one person, preferably the head of the household, to become naturalized. Local officials collected applications and submitted them to the provincial government, which in turn obtained certificates of naturalization from the Chinese Ministry of Internal Affairs. Simultaneously, a growing tendency was application on an individual basis. The submissions of multiple applications by one person was prohibited. Application on behalf of others was banned except in the cases of representing the illiterate. Males twenty years of age and older were required to apply for naturalization, submitting forms, including an application form and a letter signed by two people guaranteeing the applicant's qualifications. In 1926, an applicant was required to submit three photographs.[49]

Under the 1914 nationality law of the Republican government, naturalization applications required two guarantors, three years of residence, and the payment of processing fees. Local officials and Korean organizations received applications from individuals and submitted them to county magistrates, who then forwarded them to the Jilin provincial government for final approval from the Chinese Ministry of Internal Affairs in Beijing. The fact that the ministry rejected about one hundred of the six hundred applications because of inadequate documentation suggests the thoroughness of the evaluation process. But soon procedures were simplified to speed up the naturalization of Koreans. For example, Hwaryong County eased the residence requirement. If applicants lived far from the county office, they were permitted to file applications at nearby police stations. Swift processing of applications was ordered to shorten the decision-making period from up to two years to one year. Clandestine counseling of Koreans on naturalization matters was also recommended to forestall Japanese interference.[50]

The requirement that applicants present proof of the annulment of their former nationality (ch'ulchŏk) seemed to impede the process of naturalization far less in Kando than in South Manchuria. This requirement in theory posed an insurmountable challenge to Koreans, since Japan had banned all overseas Koreans from acquiring a foreign nationality. Japan even arrested a number of Koreans who had become naturalized as Chinese nationals or had applied for naturalization. According to the Japanese consul general of Kando, Koreans never lost their nationality as Japanese subjects, and naturalizations of Koreans approved by the Chinese Ministry of Internal Affairs were therefore not only void but also violated the Chinese nationality law, which required applicants to give up their former nationality. The Chinese Ministry of Foreign Affairs countered in 1916, saying that after the annexation of Korea, Koreans had lost their state and lived without nationality, and that Koreans could not lose a nationality that they never had.[51]

A measure to facilitate Korean naturalization included a proposal to establish a government agency in charge of Korean naturalization. While a similar request by naturalized Koreans did not receive any substantive recognition from Chinese officials in other parts of Manchuria, let alone implementation, the Kando Administration saw the merits of establishing a special agency. During the Jilin gubernatorial meeting in 1926, the head of the Kando Administration underscored the importance of this agency for mediating between Koreans and the Chinese government, as well as the appointment of Korean representatives who could persuade fellow Koreans to become naturalized. While it is unclear whether this proposal was ever implemented, it demonstrates the determination of Chinese local authorities to increase Korean naturalization.[52]

When Zhang Xueliang forged an alliance with the Kuomintang government in 1929, the constraints on naturalization of Koreans, which were also imposed in other parts of Manchuria, became effective in Kando. But the new regulations of Korean naturalization coexisted with its continued promotion. On the one hand, the Jilin provincial government canceled various incentives for naturalization on the grounds that naturalized Koreans purchased land on behalf of the Japanese and thus assisted Japan in invading Manchuria. Legal punishment was imposed on naturalized Koreans who purchased land for Japanese, while the application fee was raised to discourage naturalization. When naturalized Koreans did not adopt the Manchu hairstyle and clothing, their naturalization was revoked.[53] On the other hand, the Kando Administration requested that the Jilin government continue to offer incentives for Korean naturalization: "When Japan endeavored to coax Koreans to assist its invasion of Manchuria and Mongolia, our improper response would exacerbate Korean opinion toward China. . . . We must stop oppressing Koreans. If we wish to impair their relations with Japan, it is necessary for us to forcefully encourage Koreans to become naturalized and earn their trust with incentives and benefits."[54] Despite new restrictions on Korean naturalization, in 1930 local officials (hyangsa) decided to establish an office to assist nonnaturalized Koreans, reaffirmed the full privileges of naturalized Koreans, and pledged to protect Koreans from Japanese pacification. They also continued to enroll Koreans in Chinese schools and to oversee the purchase of land by them, while encouraging them to become naturalized.[55]

To assimilate Koreans, Chinese officials endeavored to disband the Korean Association. This effort preceded the attempt to abolish the Japanese police force, which was not enforced until 1929.[56] According to the Kando Administration, Chinese sovereignty was violated by the fact that the Korean Association reported Korean affairs to Japanese consulates and collected a compulsory membership fee, which the Kando Administration considered to be taxes levied by Japan. The administration repeatedly appealed to the Chinese Ministry of Foreign Affairs to negotiate with Japan on the issue of dismantling the Korean Association. In 1921, the Jilin provincial governor tried to replace the Korean Association with the Association for Korean Cultivators (Kanminhoe). He required that Chinese residents report to their nearby police station any branch of the Korean Association.[57] In the same year, the magistrate of Wangch'ŏng County outlawed the Korean Association on the grounds that "Japanese organizations in Chinese territory are not appropriate." One year later, the magistrate of Hwaryong County forbade Koreans to pay membership fees to the Korean Association.[58] In 1926, the Jilin provincial government affirmed various benefits for naturalized Koreans, while calling on nonnaturalized Koreans to abandon their membership in the Korean Association.[59]

Moreover, the Kando Administration sought to eliminate any distinction between Koreans and Chinese. A local government report in Yŏn'gil County states: "The Korean housing style makes it easy for Japan to locate Koreans and to connive some excuses to administer them. . . . Kanmin [nonnaturalized Koreans] in our territory, abiding by our laws, must abandon their own customs. . . . This is an important matter for our state sovereignty [*Kukka chugwon* in Korean, *guojia zhuquan* in Chinese]. The adoption of Chinese housing was required when they built new houses. All Koreans under the age of sixty must follow Ch'ibal yŏkbŏk."[60] Chinese and Manchu customs were imposed on naturalized Koreans. In Wangch'ŏng County, Ch'ibal yŏkbŏk was required of naturalized Koreans "so as to erase the traces of Koreanness."[61] According to the magistrate of Hunch'un County in 1923, this measure was necessary to prevent naturalized Koreans from joining the Korean Association and serving "Japan's opportunistic purposes rather than becoming genuine Chinese nationals."[62] When he promised naturalized Koreans voting rights and other privileges enjoyed by their Chinese counterparts in 1928, the Jilin provincial governor required that naturalized Koreans wear Manchu clothing within six months of naturalization.[63]

The enforcement of Chinese language and education was another key policy of assimilation. A report from Hwaryong County stated that "even longtime residents do not speak Chinese or seek to be naturalized and schools need to be built to educate Koreans in Chinese language and customs."[64] In 1928, the head of the Kando Administration reinforced this approach, saying that "if Koreans would gain knowledge about our country and our language, it would be possible for Chinese and Koreans to communicate with each other." Calling for budget increases for education, he proposed to improve the credentials of teachers, establish new schools, and invite Korean intellectuals to teach Chinese language and customs to their fellow Koreans.[65] These measures were followed by the closure of several hundred Korean schools, most of which were operated by the Korean Association. Additional measures for assimilation discussed in the Jilin gubernatorial meeting included the promotion of collective rice farming among Chinese and Koreans, which was expected to help Koreans to adopt Chinese lifestyles.[66]

The wide-ranging assimilationist measures toward Koreans did not successfully unify the triad of sovereignty over people, land, and territory in Kando. The measures affected a modest increase in naturalization, for instance, from 9 percent (3,538 among 36,900 households) in 1917 to 14 percent (9,144 among 63,479 households) in 1928.[67] The majority of Koreans owned land or worked without becoming naturalized. Administrative incapacity in Kando was not completely responsible for the ineffectiveness of the naturalization policy. The pursuit of capitalist goals by the Northeast government in part thwarted its nationality policy in South Manchuria; it had similar effects in Kando.

Capitalist Integration and Chŏnminje

Codification of nonnaturalized Koreans as Kanmin and the initiative to replace the Korean Association with the Association for Korean Cultivators reveal the extent of institutional recognition of nonnaturalized Koreans by the Chinese authorities. This recognition was in part based on the farming skill of Koreans. For instance, Hwaryong County permitted Koreans to reside there if they intended to cultivate untilled land and had at least two guarantors to verify this intention. The county expected new immigrants to be assisted by acquaintances already settled in the area. The county also provided rentals of houses and land to new immigrants who lacked local contacts to assist them. All newcomers were asked to adopt the Manchu hairstyle and clothing and mark the nameplates of their houses with color to distinguish their houses from those of Chinese. If Koreans were on a short visit or had no specific purpose other than farming, they were ordered to leave.[68]

The growth of the nonnaturalized Korean population and their seditious form of landownership (*chŏnminje* in Korean, *diaminzhi* in Chinese) suggest that the bargaining power of Koreans was based on their importance to agricultural development in the region. Chonminje was originally developed in the late nineteenth century, when local officials in Manchuria divided land into parcels that were too large for most individuals to purchase on their own. Peasants thus put the necessary money together with relatives or village members to purchase land, which was then registered under the name of one person. While the Chinese also practiced this form of landownership, chonminje became a way for Koreans to own land without being naturalized. A naturalized Korean was listed on the title as the nominal owner, called the *chibang chuin*, while the real owners were referred to as *chŏnnong* or *chŏnmin*. For their services, nominal owners received about 10 percent of the total land or its equivalent in cash.[69]

While it appeared to be a practice of collective ownership, chŏnminje had the characteristics of private ownership. The parcel of land was divided according to the amount of money each person contributed. If one's land was washed away by floods or was seized by the government for public use, the others redistributed a portion of their land to compensate the owner. More importantly, the nominal landowner and real landowners produced their own document, called a *masangjo*, which listed the size, price, and location of the land bought collectively and the details of its distribution along with information on taxes. This document was attached to the land title kept by the nominal landowner or the representative of the real landowners. This practice protected the terms of private ownership. It also provided some mutual protection for the real owners, as they collaborated to solve collective problems, such as debt. If a real landowner ran away due to debt or died without naming an heir, the nominal landowner or a representative of all the real landowners reported it to a local office and managed that portion of the land by hiring tenants to cultivate it. The profits made on this land were used to pay debts and other expenses, such as funeral services, while the remaining profits were deposited into a collective fund. Since chŏnminje operated with rules set by the Chinese authorities and individuals, it tended to secure the private property rights of each real landowner.

Chŏnminje had ambiguous implications for Chinese state sovereignty. The arrangement ensured that government taxes would be collected, since the real landowners were expected to take collective responsibility for them. Nominal landowners mediated with Chinese state power and real landowners, collecting from each real owner a share of the tax based on the size of the landholding. When a real owner could not pay his share, others were expected to pay it on his behalf. If someone refused to pay their share, the others could even sell that portion of the land, by force if necessary, in order to pay the taxes. Thus, chŏnminje by no means posed a threat to taxation or the implementation of laws and obligations by individuals. Nevertheless, it undermined Chinese state sovereignty over land and people.

Efforts to reinstate "land sovereignty" called for abolishing chŏnminje, but the ban was inconsistently enforced and had meager results. In the orders to Wangch'ŏng, Hwaryong, Tonhwa, and Hunch'un Counties in the mid-1920s, the Kando Administration barred Koreans from purchasing land under others' names. It proposed that the Chinese government buy back land purchased under chŏnminje, even financing it with bank loans.[70] The ban on chŏnminje was also compromised across Kando. The amount of land owned by nonnaturalized Korean households in Kando (81,413.9 chŏng) was almost equivalent to the amount owned by Chinese (93,303.9) and three times more than the amount owned by naturalized Koreans (28,854 chŏng).[71] As it turned out to be difficult to regulate chŏnminje, the magistrate of Yŏn'gil County approved ownership of land by nonnaturalized Koreans as long as it was reported to local offices. But this decision did not encourage Koreans to abandon the practice of chŏnminje. Instead, it caused suspicion among Koreans that Chinese officials might legalize chŏnminje only to assess the amount of land illegally owned by nonnaturalized Koreans.[72]

The distinction between Kongmin and Kanmin revolved around unequal access to land. In principle, Kongmin were promised full rights of private property ownership and Kanmin were given limited access to landownership and cultivation. These hierarchical categories signify the different value of land under cultivation—the former for productive land and the latter for untilled land. This distinction embodied contradictory logics of capitalist dynamics and national sovereignty. The Kando Administration modified its national principle in order to convert untilled land into arable and productive land. The acceptance of nonnaturalized Koreans reveals an attempt by the Chinese to reconcile its national sovereignty with agricultural development.

DIVIDED KOREAN POLITICS

The structure of colonial and national politics in Kando was not conducive to provoking a clash between Koreans and Chinese, as in the case of the Manbosan Incident. The confrontational relationship between Japan's osmotic expansion and the Kando Administration made the relationship between Korean and Chinese peasants in Kando more amicable than elsewhere. Chinese national and capitalist politics formulated a tiered inclusion of naturalized and nonnaturalized Koreans that enabled Koreans to own land without be-coming naturalized. Access to cultivation and ownership of land by Kore-ans and Chinese were less inequitable in Kando than in South Manchuria. Many Koreans worked for Chinese landlords in this region, and by 1931 the average amount of land owned by Chinese was almost three times that of Koreans. However, Koreans cultivated a sizable amount of land as well. In 1931, when Koreans represented about 75 percent of Kando's population, they held about 59 percent of the total arable land. In 1933, the proportion of landlords to the total population was far higher among Chinese than Kore-ans: landlords constituted 44 percent of the Chinese and 7 percent of the Korean population. About 86 percent of the Chinese and 69 percent of the Koreans were landowners—including landlords, independent farmers, and partly self-cultivators.[73]

Peasant politics in Kando were characterized by a split between Korean support for either Japan or China and by the advocacy of self-rule that de-parted from the nationalist agenda. As explained earlier, the auxiliary Korean organizations of the Japanese consulates grew stronger and more orderly in Kando than elsewhere. Simultaneously anti-Japanese movements gained momentum in Kando, with some support from the Chinese authorities. Some of the exiled Koreans began to cooperate with the Chinese authorities, and they persuaded their fellow Koreans to become naturalized in a show of sup-port for them. In return, the authorities agreed to support the self-rule of Koreans, but this promise was never kept. From around 1910 until 1931, vari-ous efforts to achieve Korean self-rule ebbed and flowed under the auspices of Chinese authorities. A month after the Kando Treaty was announced in 1909, a number of Koreans in Hwaryong County organized the Korean Self-Rule Association (Hanmin Chach'ihoe). This group not only condemned the collaboration of Koreans with Japan. It also vowed to establish self-rule of Koreans in Kando on the grounds that they had their own unique language and customs. In 1910, another group formed the Association for Korean Edu-cation (Kanmin Kyoyukhoe), which established schools across Kando. After the Republican government was formed in China, the founding leaders of the Association for Korean Education appealed to the Chinese government to approve a new organization—the Association for the Self-Rule of Kore-ans (Kanmin Chach'ihoe). On the condition that *Self-Rule* be purged from its name, the Republican government authorized the new Association for Ko-rean Cultivators (Kanminhoe) in 1921.

If the Korean Association assisted Japanese consulates in administering

Koreans, the Association for Korean Cultivators performed similar functions
for Chinese authorities. The Association for Korean Cultivators not only persuaded Koreans to become naturalized as Chinese nationals but also simultaneously pledged its support for Korean self-rule under the protection of
the Chinese authorities. Calling for Koreans to free themselves of Japanese
colonial rule, it mobilized them to meet their obligations to the Chinese government. To offer modern education to Koreans, it aimed to eradicate feudal
customs, operate night schools, and establish a farmers' union to develop
new methods of production and trade and the use of new foodstuffs.[74] Yet
the use of force to coerce Korean naturalization was condemned by the Association for Korean Cultivators and other organizations. For instance, Nongmukye, which opposed modern education and instead sought to maintain
Confucian social values, charged the Association for Korean Cultivators with
burdening Koreans with compulsory membership fees and intimidating nonnaturalized Koreans or Koreans who refused to join with threats of eviction.
As a result, the Republican government outlawed the Association for Korean
Cultivators in 1914.[75]

In 1923, the Korean self-rule movement encompassed different political
camps. When a Chinese soldier killed a Korean bystander, various groups
congregated to denounce both the Chinese authorities and the Japanese consulates for failing to protect Koreans. Whether formerly identified with China
or Japan, these groups declared the launch of the struggle to free Koreans
from double rule of the Chinese and Japanese powers. They not only renounced the nationality of Koreans as Japanese subjects but also pledged to
form defense armies to protect fellow Koreans. This new initiative was supported by the Kando Administration, which promised to appeal to the Beijing government for approval on behalf of Koreans. Denunciations by the
Beijing government and Japanese consulates, however, rendered this effort
futile. After this moment of unity, Korean politics once again became polar-
ized between groups identified with Japan or China. Seeking more protection from Japan, the Korean Association demanded that Japan resolve fundamental Korean issues—their disputed nationality and landownership. Many
new organizations, such as the Organization to Facilitate Self-Rule in Kando,
were formed in the late 1920s with objectives similar to those of their predecessors: inducing Koreans to become naturalized as Chinese, advocating
full rights for naturalized Koreans, and opposing the Korean Association.[76]

The classification of various Korean organizations in terms of their national identification does not fully disclose their capitalist characteristics.

Existing studies ignore the important role of the capitalist order that fore-grounded the divided national politics. Ephemeral yet unrelenting attempts to establish Korean self-rule underscore the fact that Koreans' desires to im-prove their social life were not reducible to the exiled movement to liberate Korea. Self-rule organizations, including the Association for Korean Cultiva-tors, pursued the improvement of social life, with ownership of private prop-erty as the bedrock. Accordingly, it was in the domain of the exchange of land that self-rule organizations developed relations with the Chinese authorities. The promotion of naturalization of Koreans by various self-rule organiza-tions carried with it not just the embrace of the Chinese authorities but also the quest for landownership, whose prerequisite was naturalization as Chi-nese nationals. As elsewhere, the private property system embodied the new relationship between the modern Chinese state—both the Beijing and the Northeast governments—and individuals in Kando. The self-rule movement spread rights to property ownership from Chinese nationals to naturalized Koreans. In other words, the self-rule movement was embedded in the pri-vate property system and its logic of universal rights.

Despite their differences, self-rule organizations and the Korean Asso-ciation both pursued private property rights. Whether supporting Japan or China, Korean politics in Kando hailed the benefits that affordable loans could bring to Koreans. The Korean Association mobilized Koreans with the promise of landownership and low-interest loans. Self-rule organizations in-voked similar rights for Koreans, although they were somewhat vague about them. Led by property-owning Koreans, the Association for Korean Cul-tivators, for instance, postulated "freedom, autonomy, and happiness" as commendable goals for Koreans. The self-rule movement in 1923 endorsed "human equality" and "happiness." Denouncing communism, the Organi-zation to Facilitate Self-Rule in Kando proposed new credit unions as alter-natives to the Korean Association, on which Korean peasants depended to meet their expenses for subsistence and farming.

CONCLUSION

During the reign of Zhang Zuolin, regional variation emerged in Manchuria's national, colonial, and capitalist politics, in which Koreans became the bone of contention between the Chinese and Japanese powers. Chapters 2 and 3 have compared the divergent nature of the relationship between the Chinese and Japanese powers, which resulted in disparate patterns of nationality and landownership for Koreans. A balance of power characterized the triangular relationship among Zhang Zuolin's Northeast government, the Chinese merchant bourgeoisie, and the Japanese in South Manchuria. However, a pattern of confrontational politics between the Japanese and the Kando Administration emerged in Kando without the intercession of the Chinese bourgeoisie. It was in the disparate networks of power that Japanese and Chinese negotiated their territorial and capitalist sovereignty in the two regions, drawing on the different rights of Koreans set forth in unequal treaties.

Japan practiced its osmotic strategy, in which its sovereignty over Koreans and their farmland was equated with its sovereignty over territory. In South Manchuria, Japan applied to Koreans provisions of the 1915 Treaty, which guaranteed the rights of Japanese subjects to lease land and attain extraterritoriality. Claiming Koreans as Japanese subjects, Japanese consulates and the Asia Development Company brought Koreans under Japanese authority. Osmotic expansion in this region was hindered by institutional barriers to landownership by Koreans and the tension between the Government General of Korea and the Japanese consulates over the basic approach to Koreans. The Chinese Northeast government prohibited Koreans from becoming naturalized as Chinese nationals, which in turn made them ineligible to own land.

Japan's osmotic politics matured primarily in Kando. Its expansion was accompanied by the competing ties between Koreans and the Chinese authorities, causing Korean politics to be split between Japan and China. With selective application of the Kando and 1915 Treaties, Japan strove to ensure both landownership and extraterritoriality for Koreans. Japanese consulates and their police forces established de facto sovereignty over Koreans, suppressing resistance movements and allegedly protecting Koreans both from Korean rebels and Chinese oppression. The Oriental Development Company and the Korean Association's credit unions strengthened the ties between Koreans and Japanese. In opposition to Japan's osmotic expansion, the Kando Administration endeavored to sever ties between Koreans and Japanese power. With aims to integrate Koreans into the Chinese national community, the Kando Administration enforced the naturalization of Koreans and assimilation of them regardless of their nationality. When various Korean groups emerged to cooperate with the Chinese authorities in promoting the naturalization of Koreans, their foremost concern was the economic advancement of Korean households in Kando. Whether siding with Japan or China, Korean politics in Kando unfolded within capitalist politics, which prescribed private property ownership as a universal right of Koreans.

Chinese nation formation was predicated on the production of land as national territory and the production of Chinese migrants as property owners. But specific Chinese national policies in Manchuria differed in South Manchuria and Kando. The formation of Chinese national subjects in South Manchuria drew on the binary opposition of Koreans and Chinese in which Chinese migrants were transformed into landowners and guardians of the national territory against Koreans. In contrast, Chinese politics sought to assimilate the Koreans in Kando. Despite the endurance of these opposing policies over the decades, they had little effect in either region. The rate of naturalization of Koreans was as low in Kando as in South Manchuria. Contradicting policies of nationality, nonnaturalized Koreans were permitted to reside and work as tenants and low-wage workers in South Manchuria, while they continued to own land under the names of naturalized Koreans in Kando. The apparent compromise of national policies resulted at least partly from the importance of agricultural development to the Chinese authorities. Because Korean rice farming was crucial for agricultural development, the Northeast government amended their nationality policies to accommodate Koreans.

Chapters 2 and 3 have compared the transformation of migrants into national subjects and of land into national territory, which for both Chinese and Japanese national politics were entwined with capitalist development in the two regions. I have also explicated the overarching tension between the national and capitalist desires of the Northeast government, which circumvented counterstrategies of Chinese power against Japan's osmotic expansion. Chapters 4 and 5 explore the state's governmentality and Korean peasant subjectivity during the Manchukuo period, which demonstrate the historically specific expressions of contradictory national and capitalist dynamics.

CHAPTER FOUR

Multiethnic Agrarian Communities

As we have seen in chapters 2 and 3, by 1931 Manchuria was extensively commercialized by colonial and national forces and had been integrated into the world capitalist market for several decades. As Chinese forces, Japanese power, and Korean migrants shared their capitalist desires yet clashed over national dreams, their simultaneously orderly and capricious negotiations over national membership and property rights both shaped and destabilized social relations of work and exchange. In chapters 4 and 5, I discuss the new integration of Manchuria into the world capitalist network after the Japanese occupation of 1931, which was accompanied by a new national politics and a reconstitution of social relations. The colonization of Manchuria coincided with social crises in Manchuria and the rest of the Japanese empire, especially Korea and Japan, at the moment of the worldwide economic depression. The transformation of Manchuria was therefore driven by an acute sense of overcoming the crises in the empire. National interpretations of social crises, as much as the events themselves, prescribed the social reform of agriculture in Manchuria that reorganized social relations.

Chapters 4 and 5 present agrarian cooperatives as the epitome of new colonial and national dreams that were shaped by the ideas and practices of an alternative capitalism. Historians tend to regard agrarian cooperatives as tools that were employed to pacify enemies within a national territory with enduring feudalistic features in its agricultural relations. Agrarian cooperatives, however, were part of a far broader drive to create an entirely new social system in the colony. The colonial power dreamed that the emigration of Koreans and Japanese and their resettlement in Manchurian cooperatives would resolve social crises in the empire and safeguard Manchuria as a colony.[1] It is important not to conflate territorial and capitalist integration but rather to examine their complex relationship. The projected corporeal unity of the empire, in the form of migration and settlement, gave a new form to the politics of territorial and capitalist integration or the politics of osmosis. The term *osmosis* conjures an image of transnational progression brought about by the bodily movements of individuals across borders. But, as these chapters demonstrate, its actualization was contingent on the process of global expansion that was organized and constructed as internationalization by nation-states with foremost concern for safeguarding national sovereignty in their territories—where multiple national powers in the empire sought to coordinate border crossings and settlement. Inter-nationalization developed a multifaceted relationship with capitalist expansion; when it mediated capitalist expansion, the latter concurrently thrived on and exceeded the former, sowing new seeds of crisis.

The agrarian cooperative was a social program that drew a new boundary between national and antinational and established new social relations. The emergence, forms, and effects of the agrarian cooperative attest to the spatio-temporal relationship between national and capitalist relations during the Manchukuo period. Chapter 4 investigates the social crises in the empire and the strategies for resolving them that were ultimately inflected into national social formations in Manchuria. The historical specificity of the international structure of the Japanese empire will be discussed to account for the agents and subjects of the agrarian cooperative, as well as their hybrid forms. Attending to a different layer of national and capitalist dynamics, chapter 5 examines particular features of Manchurian capitalism that constituted the specific contents of agrarian cooperatives and their constitutive effects on colonial and national governmentality. It also exposes capitalist dynamics that undermined the idea and practices of the cooperative. Taken together, both chapters show paradoxical moments in the arduous process of colonization, in which inadequate national mediations of capitalist crises contributed to a new social relation and a new crisis.

The agrarian cooperative signified a "gemeinschaft capitalism" that was conceived in Japan and elsewhere in the 1920s and 1930s as a response to capitalist experiences. It promised to eliminate social vices wrought by capitalist modernization and envisaged new social relations capable of harmonizing the promises of new technology and modern ideas (e.g., the division of labor, democracy, the people, and the unrelenting desire for stability). Recent studies of capitalist modernity argue that discourses of alternative capitalism laid the foundation for fascism.[2] As the cooperative in Manchuria reflected the metropolitan idea of agrarian communitarianism, I will discuss the implications of the cooperative for fascism in the conclusion of chapter 5.

The deferral of crises from one place to another was an important characteristic of building the empire. Comprehensive accounts of the social crises throughout the Japanese empire exceed the scope of this study. My strategy is to focus on the Korean rice growers, who provided a link in the Japanese colonial chain. From the first moment of colonization, Korean agriculture was organized to supply Japan with rice. The colonial power promoted rice as the dominant cash crop in Manchuria and envisioned Korean migrants as the primary rice growers. As both the colonized and the colonizer in Manchuria, Korean peasants' migration and experience of rice cultivation there embodied the condensation of the capitalist crises in the colony and the repetition of the crises in the empire.

Chapter 4 consists of three parts. First, I discuss the racial riots in Manchuria, under which agrarian communitarianism was grafted onto Manchuria to transform its social relations as a way to resolve the crises in the empire. Then I explore the fantasy of the division of labor in the empire, where the powers of each nation-state represented the welfare of its subjects in the name of benefiting the whole empire. In reality, the fusion and contestation of the nation-state powers produced a dual nationality for Koreans and a hierarchical order among national subjects of the empire. In the last two sections, I examine how the international structure of the empire interacted with capitalist development to shape the formation of agrarian cooperatives in terms of their hybrid practices and the allocation of national subjects to different cooperatives.

RACIAL RIOTS AND COLONIAL LINKS

At the time of the Japanese occupation of Manchuria in 1931, the Chinese unleashed their social and political discontent by attacking Koreans, who the Chinese thought had been assisting the Japanese for decades in penetrating Manchuria. Colonial discourses about and prescriptions for the events prepared the region to become a new nation with a new boundary between national and antinational. Colonial discourses of the racial riots (described in the next section) severed events from the social and historical forces that led up to them. Prescribed as the resolution of the riots, the agrarian cooperative was institutionalized to protect Korean refugees. They were soon expanded as a way to pacify anti-Japanese elements, and separate cooperatives were built for Korean and Chinese residents. The cooperatives were further developed as a means of settlement for new, official Korean and Japanese immigrants. The separate cooperatives further fragmented the social lives of Koreans and Chinese, who had been pitted against each other for decades. The preparation of Manchuria for a new nationhood "naturalized" the old colonial links among Japan, Manchuria, and Koreans in which the racial riots originated. It also obscured the new linkage among them that was constituted by the cooperatives.

Racial Riots

In the aftermath of the Japanese attacks on Manchuria from September 18, 1931, the Chinese unleashed a powerful wave of anti-Japanese sentiment against the Koreans. Although it spread across South and East Manchuria, the violence against Koreans was concentrated less in Kando and other parts of Manchuria than in Fengtian Province, where the conflicts between Chinese and Koreans had been carved out by the Northeast government, the Chinese bourgeoisie, and Japanese power (see chapter 2). The attacks on Koreans in 1931 included assaults, looting, rape, and the destruction of Korean homes. The defeated soldiers were the primary instigators of the riots, but the security armies and civilians also participated. Dozens to hundreds of defeated soldiers looted Korean villages at harvest time, forcing them to leave the crops standing in the fields. When Korean farmers attempted to escape the plunder and travel to cities by train, even railway servicemen were said to have prevented Koreans from boarding. Stories were told repeatedly that Koreans had to hide in the mountains or huddle in reed blinds by day and walk for many nights to reach refuge in the cities. Seeking the protection of the Japanese authorities, thousands of refugees flocked to major stations of the South Manchuria Railway and cities with Japanese consulates.[3]

The scale of the racial riots impelled Koreans within Korea to form an organization—the Committee on the Problem of Korean Compatriots in Manchuria (Manju tongp'o munje hyŏbŭihoe)—to investigate the situation and recommend ways to resolve it to the Government General of Korea. Emergency relief efforts mobilized various Japanese administrative organs, ranging from the Japanese consulates, the Government General of Korea, the South Manchuria Railway Company, and the Kwantung Administration to the Korean Association. Refugees were lodged in schools and factories and were provided employment, for example, on nearby railway construction crews.[4] According to one survey conducted by the Government General of

Korea in December 1931, the total number of refugees was 10,935, with 2,500 of them victims of plunder, assault, arson, and kidnaping or simply missing.[5] Yet, the number of victims must have been far greater, as another survey, in 1932, reported that there were roughly 35,000 refugees in the Kando region alone.[6]

As the riots coincided with harvest time, they intensified the sense of crisis that unexpectedly drew attention to more substantial problems facing Koreans in Manchuria. According to the Committee on the Problems of Korean Compatriots, the actual cause of the crisis was the displacement of Koreans from land in both Korea and Manchuria, which had begun long before the riots. Whether the Koreans returned to Korea or floated in Manchuria as refugees, they would still lack the basic means of survival. According to a Japanese army officer's report, most Koreans were drifting within Manchuria without a home to return to or a place to settle.[7] In a foreign land with different customs and languages, Koreans were said to have survived as temporary tenants of Chinese landlords, enduring various forms of oppression by the Chinese government. The majority of them employed outdated methods of cultivation. Koreans also suffered from excessive rents—up to 60 percent of the harvest—and usury at the hands of the landlords. Elevating the sense of crisis, the report stated that even Koreans' special rice-farming skills were under threat from the increasing migration of Chinese rice growers from South China.

According to colonial discourses, the riots prompted the Japanese authorities to create agrarian cooperatives for both Korean refugees and residents. They feared that if the current refugee conditions were to continue, Koreans might join anti-Japanese forces, including the Korean communists, who had led peasant uprisings in the Kando region and begun to collaborate with the Chinese communists (see chapter 6). The Government General of Korea once again reminded the Japanese government of the looming possibility of Korean communism spilling over from Manchuria to Korea. Since the majority of Koreans were landless, safeguarding their lives was seen to depend on the provision of arable land, which new cooperatives made available. The cooperatives drew on the idea that stabilizing livelihoods was necessary to contain anti-Japanese sentiment because the police and the army alone were not sufficient. Enlarging an initial purpose of "salvaging and protecting" Korean refugees, the cooperatives were further developed as a means of pacifying anti-Japanese forces. More cooperatives were built for Korean residents in areas where guerrilla forces had gained a foothold. In colonial discourses, cooperatives signified paternalistic Japanese power, under which Koreans were expected to live as dutiful Japanese subjects. The new social life created for Koreans through the cooperatives was equated with the pacification of resistance forces, figuring anti-Korean as anti-Japanese.

The Transfer of Crisis

Colonial narratives of the riots and agrarian cooperatives gloss over both the old and new linkages developed among Japan, Manchuria, and Koreans. My discussion of the link between Korea and Japan in this section situates the riots and cooperatives in a historical process in which the expansion of the Japanese empire embodied a transfer of crisis from the metropole to its colonies. The link between Korea and Japan—the initial instance of the transfer of the crisis—momentarily alleviated the crisis in Japan but created a new one in both the metropole and the colony. The crisis in Korea was the historical origin of Korean migration to Manchuria, where they developed triangular relations with Japanese and Chinese. Understanding their origins will prepare us to deconstruct the racial riots, which naturalized the antagonistic relations between Koreans and Chinese.

The initial impetus to turn the Korean countryside into the provider of rice came from a rice shortage in Japan in the aftermath of World War I. During the postwar recession, the countryside experienced a downturn, which discouraged the jobless urban population from returning to rural areas; they instead resorted to various menial and transient jobs such as peddling and day labor. Riots protesting the soaring price of rice in Japanese cities pressured the government to enact reforms in both Japan and Korea. The Rice Law of 1921 established centralized control over the price, supply, and distribution of rice in Japan. In Korea, a policy to expand rice production (*sanmijŭngsik chŏngch'aek*) for export to Japan was vigorously implemented from the first moment of colonization. The infamous cadastral surveys that followed sought to rationalize land measurement and practices of ownership. More explicit measures to further expand rice production throughout the 1920s included improved varieties, transformation of dry fields into rice fields, the use of fertilizer, and the development of irrigation systems. The enforcement of these measures is suggested by the phenomenal expansion of land under cultivation and of rice exports to Japan. In the process, Korean landowners were often forced to give up or sell their land in cases of inadequate documentation of titles. The various policies to expand rice production increased rent and taxes, which Korean peasants were required by law or landlords to pay. To make ends meet, they were compelled to find alternative staple foods and to raise silkworms, horses, and sheep for extra income. Migration to Manchuria was their last resort.

The colonial link between Korea and Japan was formulated by a broader Japanese economic policy aimed at promoting industrialization and turning its colonies into suppliers of resources and capital. It provided temporary relief for the food supply problem and concerns over labor unrest and socialism in Japan. Colonial expansion therefore intensified inequalities within Japan, not just between Japan and Korea. The expansion of rice production in Korea was, for instance, enforced throughout the 1920s, even when Japanese agriculture suffered a severe recession from 1925 onward due to a worldwide surplus of agricultural commodities, a fall in prices, and stagnant productivity. Colonial agricultural policy adversely affected the Japanese countryside. Adapting to such market changes, Japanese farmers switched from their routine production of rice, barley, potatoes, beans, and vegetables to cash crops (silk cocoons, fruit, and livestock) whose prices were higher than those for other commodities.[8] Although it provided some relief, this survival strategy paradoxically made farmers more vulnerable to the business cycle of the world market in Japan and elsewhere in the late 1920s.

The Japanese agrarian calamity of the 1930s transformed the link between Japanese and Korean agriculture. As the prices of major cash crops of Japanese and Korean farmers dropped significantly from the late 1920s on, farm income fell precipitously. Farmers were forced to rely on millet as their staple food, and their debts mounted. Once again, the resolution of the crisis proceeded together in Japan and Korea. In both places, fiscal spending was pledged, if not increased sufficiently, to provide public works projects and low-interest loans for farm villages.[9] Various programs appealed to the peasants to turn to self-help and collective responsibility rather than relying on handouts from the state.[10] At the center of the resolution of this crisis was the ban on Korean rice exports to Japan in 1934. When its rural economy was firmly integrated into the global economy under colonization, Korean peasants were already suffering from plunging prices of rice and other products, including silk cocoons, cotton, and livestock.[11] Given that Korean agriculture had been transformed to export rice to Japan and shipped annually about 40 percent of its total volume of produce, this export ban was a further catastrophe for Koreans.

The ban on rice exports was emblematic of the customary transfer of crisis to the colony. The structure of the Korean national economy prevented a quick absorption of the surplus rice within Korea, whether for private consumption or processing. Food-processing industries in Korea also were designed to export their products, which comprised about 86 percent of all exports in 1929.[12] When Japan ceased to consume Korean products, it deprived Koreans of income, making it even more difficult to consume the surplus products domestically. Reflecting the colonial reorganization of the economy, the proportion of landless peasants increased from 41 percent of the total population in 1922 to 53 percent in 1932.[13] In the late 1920s, the majority of the peasants were forced to survive on usury loans or mountain vegetables. Reflecting the social crisis in Korea, the flow of Koreans to Manchuria soared, expanding from an average of 16,313 annually for the period 1927–30 to 80,712 for the period 1933–36.[14]

The displacement of Koreans under Japanese colonization has long been assumed to prefigure the anti-Japanese nationalism of Koreans in Manchuria and the resultant collaboration of Koreans and Chinese against their common enemy—Japanese imperial power. Such deterministic accounts characterize the national historiographies of Koreans in Manchuria that have been published in Korea and China. They contributed to erasing the racial riots (and the purge of Korean communists by their Chinese counterparts, examined in chapter 6) from the national historiographies. The politics of Chinese nationalism and Japanese colonialism that revolved around Korean rice cultivation in Manchuria served to channel the anticolonialism of the colonized in Manchuria.

Social Characteristics of the Racial Riots

The Chinese expressed their experience of capitalist crisis as racial antagonism within the framework of their national politics which the Northeast government fostered until 1931. This transposition of social experience onto racial politics embedded regional variation that reflected disparate patterns in the negotiation of Chinese nationalism and Japanese colonialism in the regions of Kando (East Manchuria) and Fengtian Province (South Manchuria). Regional variation among the riots was never recognized as significant, although it is documented by the previously mentioned December 1931 survey of the Government General of Korea. The absolute number of Korean victims was far less in Kando than in other parts of Manchuria: 128 refugees, 1,000 missing people, and 342 other victims in Kando; and 10,807 refugees,

884 missing, and 274 other victims in other parts of Manchuria, especially in the south.[15] This regional distribution of Korean victims was skewed, given that Kando comprised about 60 percent of the total population of Koreans in Manchuria.

The regional variation of the riots signifies two significant layers of the social relationship between Koreans and Chinese: regional unevenness and imagined antagonism. This was the product of the disparate politics of Chinese, Japanese, and Korean forces. Chapters 2 and 3 compared the rights of Koreans in South Manchuria, where they lacked the rights to reside, work, and own property, with those that the Koreans in Kando had officially secured, although they were continuously contested. In Kando, Chinese and Japanese forces engaged in confrontational politics, with each competing to include Koreans in its own community. In this region, Koreans had been granted the right to own land. In contrast, in Fengtian Province in South Manchuria, Chinese and Japanese forces had engaged in politics that were at once contentious and conciliatory. Without any legal rights, Koreans had been allowed to reside there only as temporary tenants and low-paid agricultural laborers working for Chinese, who, despite variations within Fengtian Province, tended to be small landowners.[16] The few exceptions worked as middlemen for the Japanese development company. Under such different social structures, the Chinese national community in Kando included far more Koreans than in Fengtian. This history accounts for the greater scale of the riots in Fengtian Province.

The antagonisms between Chinese and Koreans were evoked rather than lived.[17] Chinese rioters transposed their experience of the social crisis into a fascination with "others," that is, with nonnaturalized Koreans. The politics of nationalism and colonialism prior to 1931 laid the groundwork for nationalizing the social crisis. In South Manchuria, where the victims were concentrated, Koreans and Chinese belonged to different socioeconomic groups; the majority of Koreans were illegal laborers, and the majority of Chinese were small landowners. Competition between Koreans and Chinese for land was therefore insignificant. One might infer that the competition between Korean and Chinese tenants occurred due to the preference of Chinese landlords for Korean rice farmers. But if there was a conflict between them it was likely transient, since the provincial government set limits on the number of years Koreans could be employed and their places of residence and wages. Rather, the Chinese experience of landownership was shaped by the politics of nationalism. The provincial government had supplied migrants from North China with financial subsidies and free land. This social program was intended to stabilize their residence in Manchuria, develop farming, and secure territorial sovereignty against the threat of Korean migrants and Japanese power. It enabled the government to integrate them into the Chinese national community.

When the Manchurian economy was shattered by the provincial government's incessant civil wars and the worldwide economic depression, the discontent of Chinese landowners escalated into violence directed against Koreans. Manchuria's economic crisis at the moment of its occupation by the Japanese is documented by the statistical record. In 1932, the harvest of major cash crops (beans, corn, millet, and rice) was at least 17 percent less than the volume prior to 1931. The price of agricultural crops also plummeted in 1931 to less than half the price of the period from 1927 to 1929.[18] At moments of the crisis, Chinese landowners did not launch attacks on the Chinese and Japanese merchants or former provincial government employees who had controlled the market. Nor did they join the movement to create a new state in Manchuria. Through the mediation of national and colonial politics, the social experience of Chinese small landowners expressed itself politically through anti-Korean nationalism.

The racial and regional patterns of the riots indicated their social character: the transposition of the social into racial antagonism. The old colonial link among Japan, Manchuria, and the Koreans gave rise to global and local processes in which the relationship between Koreans and Chinese was imagined and actualized. The institutionalization of agrarian cooperatives—a measure developed to resolve the riots—heralded a new colonial link among the three parties. The efforts to resolve the crisis in Korea and Japan strengthened this emergent link. Before exploring the establishment of cooperatives, which constituted a new linkage between these places, I will discuss the new structure of the empire, which intervened to form the cooperatives.

THE INTER-NATIONAL STRUCTURE OF EMPIRE
AND A NEW ORDERING OF PEOPLE

The osmotic expansion of the empire evoked the organic harmony of the parts, which culminated in the narratives of the East Asian League (Tōa renmei) and the East Asia Co-Prosperity Sphere (Dai tōa kyōeiken) during the Pacific War. However, the division of labor among the parts was incomplete.[19] The historical specificity of the empire hinged on two particular relationships between the parts: hierarchical and overlapping. The dual nationality of Koreans in Manchuria exposed these two facets of the empire, as the Government General of Korea, the Manchukuo state, and the Kwantung Army engaged in negotiations over it. This historically specific structure of the empire shaped nation-states as agents, and national peoples as subjects, of the cooperatives.

Pluralism and Hierarchical Powers

In principle, a division of labor existed among the political powers in which each power represented its own national group in the Japanese empire. The administrative division of labor fragmented the residents of Manchuria into islands of groups, separating them from political representation and, as I later elaborate, residence and farming. The fragmentation of different ethnic and national groups was expressed by the pluralistic ideology of the Manchukuo state: "cooperation and harmony of five ethnic and national groups" (Han Chinese, Manchus, Mongols, Koreans, and Japanese). The Kwantung Army and Japanese consulates not only administered the Japanese population but also placed its rights above those of the colonized. The Government General of Korea continued to oversee the Korean population, despite the termination of the extraterritoriality of most Koreans in early 1935. When extraterritoriality was made effective for Koreans who were enrolled in the family register of Korea—the new nationality system that Japan had implemented in Korea in 1922—most Koreans in Manchuria were not eligible for enrollment. The principle of the ethnic nation laid the groundwork for the persistent claim of the Government General of Korea to represent Manchurian Koreans. The Government General of Korea forbade Koreans to become naturalized as nationals of another state, even those who had left Korea before the foundation of the Government General of Korea or had not been born in Korea. As chapters 2 and 3 demonstrated, this ethnic principle of Korean national membership clashed with Chinese nationalism until 1931. Although the Government General of Korea continued to utilize this principle even after the establishment of Manchukuo in 1932, the principle was at odds with the Manchukuo state, which aspired to become a nation through its fictive independence. Claiming to be the successor of the Qing dynasty, the Manchukuo state pledged to modernize the agricultural and industrial sectors and formed its own national army. It also sought to establish sovereignty over its territory and the people within it.

The order of people was two-tiered in Manchukuo: Manin and Japanese.

Referring to the people of Manchukuo, the category Manin included Han Chinese, Manchus, and Mongols. The category Japanese comprised both Japanese and Koreans. This categorical distinction seemed to be designed to bolster the putative Manchu origin of the Qing and Manchukuo states. However, the Manchukuo state seemed to combine this ethnic principle of nation building with a territorial principle, as it sought to establish its sovereignty over the "Japanese" as well. From 1932 until 1935, the rights and property of the Japanese were protected by extraterritoriality. The right of Japanese subjects to lease land, which was at the heart of the contention between the Chinese and Japanese powers prior to 1931, had been legalized after the Manchukuo state was established in 1932. Japanese consulates validated leasing contracts signed prior to 1932 and administered new ones. With the formal abolition of extraterritoriality in 1935, the Japanese became officially subject to Manchukuo laws and were required to pay taxes.

Lurking behind the categorization of people was a hierarchical order that was produced by the contentious relationships among the political powers in Manchuria. An important dynamic of the Japanese empire was the fictional construct of the whole. While all the constitutive parts were expected to serve the whole, beyond the stated call for unity there might be no such thing as a totality of the empire. The constituent parts might establish political sovereignty in their territories and integrate them with all the other parts. But relations between parts were not necessarily congruous because the parts developed their own immediate national interests. Conflict among the parts threatened the existence of the whole. This dynamic was nothing new for the Japanese empire. The debate on the issue of the naturalization of Koreans as Chinese citizens until 1931 illustrates it and was discussed in chapters 2 and 3. The consul general of Fengtian City, the capital of the Northeast government, advocated the naturalization of the Koreans to expand the occupation of land and spread Japanese influence throughout the region by controlling the Koreans. But the Government General of Korea and the consul general of Kando objected to the naturalization of Koreans, on the grounds that it would divest the Korean state of its legitimacy to regulate the political and social lives of Koreans.

The Japanese occupied the dominant position in this hierarchy. The Kwantung Army defined the Japanese population as model subjects capable of leading the colonization process in Manchuria. In its instructions to Japanese bureaucrats in 1936, the Kwantung Army stated that Japanese immigrants would not only defend the territory from the Soviet Union and participate in war in an emergency but also assume leadership in both its "material and mental" aspects. The Japanese would teach agricultural techniques and management skills to the natives of Manchuria, setting an example for others of a stable and wholesome way of life. In this way, the Japanese settlers would establish an unshakable foundation for Manchukuo and for the East Asia Co-Prosperity Sphere.[20] The modernity of the Japanese would flow from Japan to Manchuria through the example that the immigrants would set.

In his informative study of the Manchukuo state's disciplinary power, Han Suk-Jung delineates the hierarchical order of Japanese, Han Chinese, and Koreans in the political and economic spheres.[21] Using detailed documentation of the ethnic composition of government officials and businessmen, Han demonstrates the structural inequality among these groups. Although Han Chinese were assigned to top ministerial positions to bolster the image of an independent state, their power was nominal. They were commanded by Japanese, who filled posts below the nominal top ranks as vice ministers of departments and provincial governments. The representation of Manin (mainly Han Chinese) was a little larger than that of "Japanese" (including Koreans) in both the central and local governments, and Manin outnumbered Japanese in the police force by almost twenty to one. Japanese also dominated the mining, fishing, and timber industries, while Manin took over medium-sized and small businesses.

Koreans were grouped with Japanese nationals in the Japanese category, although there was undoubtedly an indelible distinction between them. This categorization seems to suggest that Koreans were "in between," situated at the interstices between Chinese and Japanese nationals. It is said that as "second-class" subjects of the Japanese empire, Koreans occupied a middle position between the ethnic Chinese and Japanese populations in Manchuria. According to a Korean journal in Manchuria, the middle position increased the leverage of Koreans vis-à-vis the Chinese, so that a new sense of superiority among Koreans and their contempt for the Chinese aggravated the tensions between them.[22] Yet their status also gave them an unstable standing in Manchurian society, where they were associated with felons, gamblers, opium traders, and bandits.[23] Han Suk-Jung states that Koreans held far fewer government offices than Chinese and Japanese. Koreans were excluded from high-ranking administrative positions of the Manchukuo state. This highlights the fiction of the Manchukuo state's ideology of cooperation and harmony among different ethnic groups. In Kando, which became a province during the Manchukuo period, Koreans comprised about 75 percent of the population but occupied only about 25 percent of the government positions. Koreans did not attain administrative autonomy in Kando, where a Han Chinese was governor. In contrast to the Koreans, Mongols enjoyed greater autonomy in Hsingan Province, which had a Mongolian governor.[24]

Overlapping Powers and the Dual Nationality of Koreans

The elimination of the extraterritoriality of the "Japanese" in 1935 was intended to unify the administration in Manchuria. In the past, Japanese consuls had administered the leasing of land by Koreans and arbitrated their civil disputes. The elimination of extraterritoriality allowed the Manchukuo state to regulate all property contracts and resolve all legal disputes involving Japanese. However, this institutional breakthrough only partially integrated Koreans into the Manchukuo state. Throughout the Manchukuo period, Koreans continued to hold dual nationality (*kukchŏk* in Korean, *guoji* in Chinese) in both Manchukuo and Korea. At the heart of dual nationality was the family register system of Koreans. While Manin were listed on the Manchukuo state's register (*minjŏk* in Korean, *minji* in Chinese), Koreans were expected to enroll on the family register (*hojŏk* in Korean, *huji* in Chinese) of the Government General of Korea. They served not in the Manchukuo army but in the Japanese army run by the Government General of Korea. The abolition of extraterritoriality merely moved the administration of the Korean family register from the Japanese consulates in Manchuria to the Manchukuo state's Department of Police, specifically the Office of Security and Military Conscription. The Manchukuo state levied taxes on Koreans, but the Government General of Korea continued to oversee military conscription, anti-Japanese activities, and social welfare (agriculture, education, and hospitals), the latter two of which were performed through agrarian cooperatives.

Dual nationality represented the incompatibility of national membership in the Korean and Manchukuo states rather than enjoyment of membership in both. Neither the Government General of Korea nor the Manchukuo state exercised sole sovereignty over Koreans. This partial status meant that Koreans had uncertain rights and faced discrimination. Despite being lumped together in the category of Japanese subjects, Koreans and Japanese nationals did not share the same rights, including the right to lease land. Korean membership in the family register of Korea was required for leasing land (*sangjogwon*). When they registered their contracts at the Japanese consulates, they were also obliged to submit a certificate of their family register. Yet the problem was that many Koreans in Manchuria were not enrolled on the family register of Korea. Many had migrated to Manchuria before Japanese power instituted the family register system. As many second- and third-generation Manchurian Koreans did not know where their parents or grandparents came from—often before Japan colonized Korea and the place where they were expected to be enlisted—it was not feasible for them to apply for the family register of Korea. A small number of Manchurian Koreans did not enroll in the family register if they had become naturalized as Chinese prior to 1931.[25]

Their special status rendered Koreans vulnerable to various abuses by administrators, police, and the military. Korean representatives of the Concordia Association (Hyŏphwahoe in Korean, Kyowakai in Japanese), which as I will explore shortly, promoted the official ideologies of the Manchukuo state, and integrated Korean organizations, including the Korean Association, described the types of problems brought about by the separate registration of Koreans, including payment of extra taxes and the lack of legal protections. To facilitate the enrollment of Koreans in the family register, Korean representatives of the Concordia Association, together with the Korean Association, negotiated with the Government General of Korea and Japanese consulates to ease application procedures and reduce various fees. In a proposition to achieve full integration into the Manchukuo state, Korean representatives of the Concordia Association requested in vain that all people of Manchukuo be enlisted in the national register of the state. To end discrimination against Koreans arising from their dual status, the association requested that local officials, police, and soldiers curtail their abuse of Koreans and protect them from Japanese military activities intended to suppress guerrillas. Promoting the inclusion of Koreans in the Manchukuo army, Korean representatives also called for fairer military conscription that did not discriminate according to nationality and economic status and for public works to protect Koreans from floods.[26]

The dual nationality of Koreans captures the incomplete division of labor in nation-states. The ongoing changes in and controversies concerning their rights depict the centripetal force of nation-state formation in the empire, in which the Government General of Korea and Manchukuo state competed for sovereignty over their subjects. As will be seen in chapter 5, the transformation of the development companies that built the Korean cooperatives also demonstrates the competition between the two states.

Effects on Cooperatives

The inter-national structure of the Japanese empire consigned the political powers as agents and national people as subjects of the cooperatives. Each political power administered different cooperatives for its own constitutive group. With funding from the Japanese government, the Kwantung Army oversaw the planning of the cooperatives and directed the Manchuria Development Company to build and operate them for Japanese immigrants. The Government General of Korea emerged as the chief partner of the Kwantung Army and the Southern Manchuria Railway Company in governing the cooperatives for Koreans. It subsidized two development companies—the Oriental Development Company and the Asia Development Company—that built the cooperatives' facilities for Koreans. Modeled after the Korean cooperatives, the Manchukuo state built its own cooperatives mainly for Chinese peasants. The function of the Government General of Korea suggests that the weak administrative and financial position of the Manchukuo state prevented it from governing all the populations residing in its territory. Or it might mean that the Manchukuo state did not have problems with the Korean population, which comprised only 5 to 7 percent of the total. While these factors may have helped the Government General of Korea maintain its presence in Manchukuo, its administration of Korean cooperatives was an effect of the empire's inter-national structure.

The capitalist development of Manchurian agriculture also played a key role in the formation of the cooperatives. The importance of Koreans, Japanese, and Chinese for Manchurian agricultural development altered their order. Rice cultivation enabled Korean peasants to surpass their Chinese counterparts in terms of economic mobility, as the Government General of Korea directed loans to Korean peasants. Tapping the Koreans' skill in rice cultivation, the Government General of Korea increased its leverage against the Kwantung Army in promoting Korean emigration to Manchuria and settlement in the cooperatives. Capitalist development and the international structure of the empire interacted to shape the cooperatives in two major ways: the allocation of Korean and Chinese immigrants to the cooperatives and the hybrid practices of agrarian communitarianism. These are examined in the following two sections.

THE OFFICIAL IMMIGRATION PROJECTS

The Kwantung Army extolled the immigration of Japanese subjects to Manchuria as embodying the ethos of East Asia co-prosperity, in which immigrants served as the principal medium for colonizing Northeast China, other parts of China, and then all of Asia.[27] The official project of sending Koreans and Japanese to Manchuria reformulated the linkages among Manchuria, Korea, and Japan. Korean and Japanese immigrants were expected to grow rice and defend the territory of Manchuria. The crisis in Japan's rural economy and the Japanese occupation of Manchuria renewed its long-held dream of sending its people to its colonies. Japan's continuing desire to secure its staple crops, especially rice, was a motivation underlying the transformation of agriculture in Korea and Manchuria during their colonization by Japan. Although Korean and Manchurian agriculture was envisaged to produce rice and other crops for Japan, the fear of flooding Japan with cheap rice from the colonies propelled concerns for Japanese farmers and incited opposition in Japan at each moment of colonial expansion. These episodes of opposition were brief. Repeatedly invoked fears concerning an anticipated population explosion and the welfare of the urban population often quelled the opposition. Although fears of a population explosion were mostly unfounded, the repeated search for rice producers signified an unfulfilled desire that had driven Japan to establish one colony after another. At the moment of its own economic crisis in the early 1930s, the Government General of Korea also endeavored to relocate its landless peasants in Manchuria.

National politics and capitalist development dictated the process of official immigration of Japanese and Korean peasants. Disputes between the Government General of Korea and the Kwantung Army over the priority of Korean and Japanese immigration hampered the coordination of immigration. The restriction of Korean immigration when the progress of Japanese immigration was sluggish posed an impediment to agricultural development. This economic concern forced the Kwantung Army to intermittently lift restrictions on Koreans. The muddled compromise of national and capitalist politics thwarted the governments in their orderly regulation of immigration and settlement in the cooperatives. As a result, the Government General of Korea enlisted in its official immigration program at best only half of all the Koreans who migrated to Manchuria from 1932 on.

Until 1931, Japanese immigration to Manchuria was concentrated in the Kwantung Peninsula, which Japan officially leased from China, and subsidiary areas along the SMR. The establishment of Manchukuo in 1932 renewed this interest in Japanese migration. The size of Manchuria almost doubled the combined size of Japan, Korea, Taiwan, and Sakhalin, yet its population of about thirty million was only one-sixth of the population of Japan. Manchuria was endowed with bountiful natural resources, and more than half of its arable land was not yet under cultivation. If the arable land were divided equally among Manchuria's population, each household could have an area four times what was available in Japan. As Brazil and other Latin American countries restricted Japanese immigration, Manchuria became an undeniably attractive place for Japan's putative surplus population.

The Kwantung Army subscribed to the idea that Japanese nationals were the key developers and defenders of Manchuria. It outlined a plan to distribute Manchuria's land to 60 percent of the total peasant population of Japan, which would constitute about 25 percent of the total peasant population of Manchuria. At one time, the army hoped to increase the Japanese population in Manchuria up to five million over twenty years, representing 10 percent of Manchuria's projected total population of fifty million.[28] At another time, the Kwantung Army drafted a less ambitious plan to move 100,000 Japanese peasant households to Manchuria for fifteen years, half of which would engage in rice cultivation.[29] In accordance with these plans, Japanese immigrants were brought to three parts of Manchuria: the rice-farming region in Kando; strategic places threatened by anti-Japanese forces in other parts of Manchuria; and locations near cities (along the SMR) important to commerce, transportation, and security. This Japanese dream for Manchuria, however, exceeded the reality. The initial experimental period from 1932 until 1935 brought a total of only 1,785 households from Japan, less than one-fifth of the target number. Immigration increased to 1,000 households in 1936. While the programs of group and free immigration hoped to recruit a total number of 5,000 and 1,000 households in 1937, the actual number was only 4,059 and 473. When the planned figures for group and free immigration reached 100,000 and 5,000 households in 1938, the actual enrollment amounted to just 20 percent of the targets.[30] The number of immigrants fell behind the target as the wartime economy absorbed landless peasants and even generated labor shortages, making immigration to Manchuria unpopular.

The skill of Korean rice farmers brought an initial consensus in the Japanese administration over the official expansion and coordination of Korean immigration to Manchuria. Korean peasants were expected to develop a vast area of uncultivated land, about 55.5 percent of all the arable land in Manchuria. The proponents and opponents took positions similar to those they had held during the debates on the export of Korean rice to Japan. The concern once again emerged that the expansion of rice production in Manchuria and its resultant increase of imports to Japan would cause a drop in the price of crops in Japan and destabilize an already distressed agricultural community. But the need for the rice cultivation in Manchuria was affirmed as a way to prepare for the anticipated population explosion in Japan as well as the growing shortage of rice in Manchuria due to the increased Japanese population of bureaucrats, businessmen, soldiers, and travelers, whose diet consisted mainly of rice.[31]

In January 1932, the SMRC's office on local agriculture prepared a detailed plan to send 100,000 Korean households to Manchuria for twenty years, making them independent farmers. The required qualification for immigration was that each group must consist of five or more households that shared kin relations and/or came from the same village. Half of these would be rice-farming households, which would cultivate two chŏngbo of rice fields and two chŏngbo of dry fields each. Another 20,000 households would cultivate six chŏngbo of dry fields per household in Jilin Province, and the remaining 30,000 would farm ten chŏngbo of (untilled) land per household in North Manchuria. In one of its reports, the "Technique of the Manchuria-Mongolia Immigration Plan," the army in 1932 included not just the Japanese reserve army and youth but also Koreans, and Manin (mainly Han Chinese from North China) in the pool eligible for its official immigration project. In addition, the Asia Development Company proposed that prospective Korean immigrants collectively control credit unions, the cultivation process, and the marketing of crops.[32]

The Government General of Korea also planned to monitor the migration of Koreans more efficiently and to organize their work and everyday lives. Its motivation was derived from the need to contain social crises in Korea in the same way that the Kwantung Army sought to normalize Japanese immigration so as to resolve social crises in Japan. The two land surveys from 1910 to 1918 and the plunging price of crops during the worldwide depression further displaced Koreans from the land and intensified tenancy struggles. Reflecting the social crises in Korea, Korean migration to Manchuria increased dramatically in the 1930s. The annual increase in the Korean population was about 16,313 for the period 1927–30 and about 80,712 for 1933–36.[33] Learning from the examples of Korean refugees in Manchuria, the Government General of Korea attempted to normalize the new flow of Koreans from the start to prevent dislocation from the land. The Government General of Korea hoped to move 150,000 households over the course of fifteen years and doubled this figure in its 1932 planning.[34] It also intended to create a special company to handle Korean immigration to Manchuria. The Government General of Korea insisted to other colonial authorities that neglecting Korean immigration would place colonial rule over Korea at risk, expressing its anxiety over unregulated emigration to Manchuria in the midst of the growing Korean guerrilla movements there.[35]

The Government General of Korea listed a number of benefits that Korean immigration could bring not just to Korea but also to the Japanese empire as a whole. Korean immigration would develop lucrative rice farming in Manchuria. It also would divert the flow of Koreans to Japan, where the influx of cheap Korean labor threatened the employment of unskilled Japanese.[36] Korean immigration also would be more economical than Japanese, since the cost of Korean immigration would be lower.[37] The Government General of Korea gave assurances that Korean farmers had the skills to cultivate rice with simple tools under adverse conditions.

The Kwantung Army showed lukewarm support for implementing the official policy to subsidize Korean migration to Manchuria. In its assessment, rice farming was not a skill unique to Koreans. Japanese farmers also possessed it. It projected that Korean migration to Manchuria would swell even without government sponsorship, since Koreans were now granted legal residency there. The Kwantung Army also feared that the increase in the Korean population would undermine the internal security in Manchuria in the midst of growing anti-Japanese nationalism.[38] In May 1932, the SMRC rescinded its initial support for Korean immigration and urged a laissez-faire approach that would be free of government planning.[39] In an effort to persuade its opponents, the Government General of Korea maintained that after the race riots Koreans had increasingly begun to identify with Japan. He suggested that if Japan provided Koreans with the means to assist them in feeling psychologically and materially secure, rebelliousness among them would disappear.[40] The Kwantung Army and the Government General of Korea agreed in late 1932 that they would first resolve the Korean refugee problem and then prepare for official coordination of the new immigration of Koreans starting in 1935.

It was through the tension with Japanese immigration policy and its ad hoc adjustments that Korean immigration policy was able to pass from an idea to an institution and set of practices. The continuous negotiation between the Government General of Korea and the Kwantung Army classified and reclassified Korean immigration in various contingent ways. The settlement of new Korean immigrants grew in a piecemeal fashion as a substitute for the Japanese immigrants with impromptu restrictive arrangements. In 1936, the Kwantung Army banned the settlement of new Korean immigrants on the border between Manchuria and the Soviet Union and in the areas reserved for Japanese settlers. It also restricted their settlement to the areas along the border with Korea—twenty-three counties in Kando and Tongbyŏndo between Fengtian Province and Korea. In 1938, the Kwantung Army limited the number of new Korean farming immigrants to 10,000 per year. In tandem, a policy was enacted to require Korean residents, some of whom had resided for two or three decades in scattered parts of Kando and South Manchuria, to congregate in sixteen counties within these regions.

The forms of Korean immigration were adjusted over time. Official immigration consisted of group (*chiptan*) and cluster (*chiphap*) programs from 1937 to 1938. While the Government General of Korea financed all the expenses of immigration and settlement under the group program, it contributed only partial funding for free settlement under the cluster program. In 1939, the dispersed (*punsan*) program was added; it issued permits to eligible individuals, who at their own expense could settle freely or join their relatives or acquaintances. The Government General of Korea granted permits to Koreans who demonstrated their political purity, so as to screen prospective immigrants based on their political profiles and further force them to become assimilated into Manchurian society. The Association to Maintain Security in Fengtian and Andong Provinces (near the border between Fengtian Province and Korea) enacted a policy that only accepted new Korean settlers with this permit.

It was mainly the group program that institutionalized agrarian cooperatives as the normative form of settlement. Establishing cooperatives was not the norm in the cluster and dispersed settlement programs. Cooperatives were built for immigrants in the cluster program, under which at least nine households had to negotiate with landowners and ask the development companies to purchase lands for them and distribute them as loans.[41] As a result,

Korean cooperatives included three kinds of villages: safety villages (anjŏn nongch'on), built for the displaced peasants and refugees of southern Manchuria; collective villages (chiptan purak in Korean, jituan buluo in Chinese), built for the residents and displaced persons in Kando; and developers' collective villages (Kaech'ongmin purak) built for new immigrants from 1937 to 1941. From 1933 to 1935, a total of five safety villages were built for 2,620 households or 12,357 individuals, two in Fengtian Province, one in Jilin, and three in Heilongjiang. From 1933 to 1936, a total of twenty-eight collective villages comprised 2,933 households or 16,469 individuals in Kando. From 1937 on, developers' collective villages were built for new immigrants from Korea under the group settlement program. From 1937 to 1941, the total number of households settled under the group, cluster, and dispersed programs amounted to 6,844 (26,714 individuals), 12,562 (65,780 individuals), and 11,869 (133,746 individuals), respectively.[42]

The entire immigration policy was overhauled in 1941. All geographic restrictions for old and new Korean immigrants were discarded to expand Korean immigration beyond South and East Manchuria toward North Manchuria. The operation of the Korean cooperatives and the management of Korean immigration passed from the Government General of Korea to Manchukuo. The Korea-Manchuria Development Company and the Manchuria Development Company were absorbed by the Manchuria Development Corporation (Manju chŏksik hoesa) in 1942, which had been handling Japanese immigration. This restructuring was intended to rationalize and integrate immigration processes that had been divided by ethnicity and nationality. It was taken as a necessary step to end the separation of Koreans and Japanese and encourage a more harmonious relationship. It also signified a substantive change in the administrative division of labor in the Japanese empire. This measure was too ill timed, however, to stimulate the failing immigration policy. Just when the colonial power sought to expand and rationalize Korean immigration to Manchuria, it took a reverse course. More Koreans began to move to Japan than to Manchuria. Although Manchuria and Japan shared an almost equal number of Korean immigrants from 1936 to 1940, a wartime labor shortage in Japan attracted about 90 percent of all Korean immigrants from 1941 to 1944. The conscription of Koreans into the Japanese army also contributed to the declining pool of Koreans heading to Manchuria.

Given the discord between the Kwantung Army and the Government General of Korea, there was neither coherence nor normalization in the move-

TABLE 4. Korean Immigration from 1936 to 1944

	1936–40	1941–44	Total
Japan	249,916	363,327	613,243
Manchuria	255,991	64,887	320,878
China	66,491	13,027	79,518
Total	572,398	441,241	1,013,639

Source: Son Ch'unil, *Manjugugŭi chaeman hanine daehan t'ojichŏngch'aek yŏn'gu*, 317.

ment of the Korean population. The muddled process of balancing Korean and Japanese immigration encumbered the colonial policy of organizing Manchurian agriculture into a new capitalist system. Many Koreans evaded government regulation of immigration and settlement, while a few, especially those in the group immigration program, were chosen to inhabit agrarian cooperatives. The international structure of the empire and capitalist development not only screened the transnational flow of people and their settlement in cooperatives. The two forces also directed disparate nation-state powers to practice agrarian communitarianism in different ways, thus shaping the different contours of cooperatives.

HYBRID FORMS OF AGRARIAN COOPERATIVES

For all their differences in names, subjects, agents, and locations, agrarian cooperatives in Manchuria represented the desire of the colonial power to kill two birds with one stone: to promote both territorial sovereignty and capitalist agricultural reform. They were conflated by the idea that the improvement of social life would be the ultimate means of discouraging peasants from joining anti-Japanese movements. According to a decree promulgated in 1934, the cooperatives were intended to establish security, protect people from bandits, promote orderly collective rule, and provide services such as transportation, communication, and education.[43] However, the relationship between the territorial and capitalist objectives has not yet been carefully investigated. Historical analysis of the cooperatives has routinely characterized them as a measure meant to pacify anti-Japanese forces. Excavating diverse colonial documents, Yoon Hwitak offers perhaps the most insightful account of cooperatives as a security measure aimed at isolating

Koreans from rebels.[44] In the most comprehensive historical analysis of land reforms in Manchuria to date, Son Ch'unil's work is a departure from the customary approach to cooperatives but leaves unexplored the relationship between land reform and the reinvention of the capitalist system, as well as the relationship between the capitalist system and territorial sovereignty.[45]

Building on the historical scholarship, the remainder of this chapter explores the ways in which the territorial powers of the empire practiced the idea of an alternative capitalism in different ways in their cooperatives. Chapter 5 then discusses the historically specific form of capitalism in Manchuria, which constituted the colonial power's territorial sovereignty. The historical specificity of Manchurian cooperatives lies in their practice of the metropolitan idea of agrarian communitarianism. The divergent practices of agrarian communitarianism reflected the different positions of ethnic and national groups in the empire as well as their importance for rice farming. Many of the Japanese settlers became landlords and hired Koreans and Chinese as tenants or laborers. On the opposite end of the spectrum, by building separate cooperatives for different socioeconomic groups of rich, small, and landless peasants, the Chinese cooperatives did not attempt to change the socioeconomic status of tenants.[46] Closest to the ideal of agrarian communitarianism were the Korean cooperatives that transformed the landless into (fictive) small landowners via loan programs. This particular ordering of cooperatives did not correspond to the political order of nationality in Manchuria, where the dual nationality of Koreans made them vulnerable to abuse by Manchukuo officials. The preferential policy of Koreans over Chinese suggests that the Government General of Korea was in a stronger financial position than the Manchukuo state. It also indicates the value that the colonial power placed on rice cultivation in Manchuria, where the majority of the rice farming was done by Koreans.

Agrarian Communitarianism

Group settlement was not without historical precedents.[47] The application of agrarian communitarianism separated Manchurian cooperatives from earlier experiments of group settlement in Japan and elsewhere. Agrarian communitarianism emerged in the 1920s and 1930s in Japan, when the distressed processes of capitalist expansion propelled fleeting fantasies of a new social life yet at the same time were seen as a threat to stability and security. Native ethnologists and communitarian theorists sought to redeem the primordial and communal unity of the past deposited in the memories of village life and folk artifacts. Harry Harootunian observes that fear of alienation and commodification paved the way for communitarianism to forge a partnership with fascism, which itself pledged to insulate society from threats within and without.[48] Stephen Vlastos, among others, presents various discourses of agrarianism that romanticized small farmers in Japan from the late 1800s to the 1930s. Small farmers, who would cultivate an area between 1.5 to 5 cho (1 cho equals to 2.45 acres), were imagined to hold desirable traits of conservatism, loyalty, and obedience. They were also assumed to be immune to "the laws of capitalism" at a time when conflicts over rents between tenant farmers and landlords were escalating. The preservation of small farming was thus expected to defend the Japanese nation from dehumanizing forces of capitalism.[49]

The agricultural proposals of the Concordia Association reflected agrarian communitarianism. The association aimed to implement the cooperation and harmony of five ethnic and national groups as a principle of the kingly way (wangdo in Korean, wangdao in Chinese) of Manchukuo rule, spearheading the extension of this idea throughout Asia. It charged the previous warlord government with diverting popular discontent into antiforeign nationalism and monopolizing assets and market activities. With a pledge to safeguard rights to private property, the association proclaimed the eradication of both monopoly capitalism and communism, promising a fair distribution of the benefits of economic development. When the media in Japan presented a populist image of this organization, describing it as a new institution that would establish a true "representative democracy," this democracy was to be founded on the self-rule of impoverished peasants. As a basis of a new state-controlled economy, self-rule of peasants was expected to be realized through the operation of new collective purchase and sales cooperative unions for farmers, some of which were, as I will examine below, institutionalized by the Farming and Hungnong Cooperatives Companies. Given that the association recruited landlords, merchants, and local elites into neighborhood units responsible for maintaining social order, the efficacy of such proposed reforms remained dubious.[50]

Agrarian communitarianism rendered social relations in an abstract national form. Driven by the dichotomy of city and countryside, cities were condemned as the culprits whose wealth and hedonistic mass culture had ruined the Japanese way of life, while small farmers were regarded as saviors whose culture and morality would not just rejuvenate the countryside but would also build a "truly free, unified, and equal Japan."[51] Village representatives and government bureaucrats promoted the rhetoric of self-reliance and self-help, as well as cooperation and collective effort. Accompanied by these discourses of agrarian communitarianism was the nationwide campaign in Japan to support the official immigration policy.[52] Focusing on the inequalities between city and countryside, these discourses transposed social problems onto society-bound solutions. Among the factors suppressed by communitarian discourses were the colonial links of Japan with its colonies that had transformed industrialization and agricultural reforms in Japan as much as in the colonies.

Manchuria became a "laboratory" that applied agrarian communitarianism to its agriculture. The metropolitan idea influenced Japanese policymakers who were interpreting social relations in Manchuria. An example was a report on land relations compiled by the Ministry of State Affairs of the Manchukuo state.[53] While Japanese and Chinese powers had integrated Manchuria into the capitalist market several decades prior to 1931, the report attributed social problems in Manchuria to the familiar disparity between city and countryside. According to the report, Manchuria had a dual economic system in which the rural sector was feudal and the urban sector capitalist. Peasants were exploited by high rents, taxes, and the monopoly of merchant capital. Ongoing commercialization in cities was expected to ultimately destroy peasant culture, further displacing peasants from the land and swelling their migration to cities, where they would exacerbate the problem of unemployment. The development of the private property system and market competition would render small farmers more vulnerable to merchants and landlords and thus more likely to lose their land. The projection of such a capitalist future in Manchuria was drawn from the European and Japanese experience in the nineteenth century. In the report, it was stated that the Manchurian state must protect small cultivators from the kind of displacement from the land that European peasants had experienced in the early phases of industrialization. Even though land relations in Manchuria were more feudal than those in Japan during the Meiji period (1868–1912), Meiji reform of modernization was taken as the model for the transformation of Manchuria.

This projection of a new Manchuria was based on a national comparison in which Manchuria was homogenized and compared to nations such as France, England, and Japan. The experiences of other national economies were viewed as cautionary examples for the future of Manchuria, whereby it might emulate their positive aspects yet avoid the social disruption that had accompanied capitalist development in Europe and Japan. It was imagined that the independent cultivators' cooperatives would create a new form of capitalism under which Manchurian peasants would be shielded from the rapacious processes of primitive accumulation that characterized the early stages of capitalist development in European and Japanese societies. The cooperatives would become a mechanism to create a new national economy in Manchuria, where the urban and the rural would attain an exceptional balance. The formation of cooperatives would engender harmonious social relations among groups that had previously experienced conflict. In such depictions of Manchuria's future, social relations would be encompassed by a national space under the state's jurisdiction.

Agrarian cooperatives in Manchuria harbored the idea of agrarian communitarianism. But the practices differed according to the agents who built them. In the formation of cooperatives, Koreans were not only accepted as members of Manchukuo but also favored over the Chinese peasants who comprised the majority of Manchuria's population. The comparison of the different cooperatives in the next section is intended to highlight the characteristics of Korean cooperatives, which are further examined in chapter 5.

Chinese and Korean Cooperatives

With its pledge to modernize agriculture in 1933, the Manchukuo state declared agriculture to be the foundation of its economy. Although Japan sought to develop industrial production in Manchuria, agriculture remained the primary sector of the economy. In 1932, the peasant population in Manchuria was about 3.6 million, around 80 percent of the total. Agricultural output constituted about 70 percent of total gross production. In 1934, the Department of Industry, which supervised agricultural matters until 1940, conducted surveys of rural areas and introduced reforms such as irrigation projects, agricultural laboratories, and schools. Distinctive to Manchurian agriculture was the institutionalization of the cooperatives through which the state supervised the processes of production and market exchange—a cost-effective form of agricultural organization. The Manchukuo state's investment in agriculture and the mining industry comprised only about 5 percent of its total investment from 1935 to 1941. Instead of by state subsidy, the operations of the cooperatives were supported by membership fees and their financial and commercial activities.

The cooperatives' market activities were expected to replace the *liangchan* (grain stores), which, because of their predominance, had themselves been called the primary form of merchant capital in the 1920s (see chapter 2). Financed by large landowners and merchants, the liangchan handled wholesale grain dealings and operated stores. They had built political power in Manchuria, collaborating with both the Chinese government and the Japanese authorities. With the political chaos that followed the Japanese invasion of Manchuria and subsequent bandit and guerrilla activities, a considerable portion of this mercantile capital fled to urban areas in Manchuria and China proper. The liangchan's political power and the scale of its economic operations were significantly reduced during the 1930s, although it continued to play an important role on a smaller scale in the market exchange of crops and capital in the 1930s, especially those involving poor tenants.[54] As substitutes for the liangchan, agrarian cooperatives aimed to create a new market system in which peasant producers would sell their own crops in markets that they controlled.

Under the leadership of Fengtian Province, the Manchukuo state established three kinds of cooperatives for different socioeconomic groups of Chinese landowners and peasants: the Financial Cooperative Company for rich peasants (Kŭmyung hapchaksa in Korean, Jingrong hezuoshe in Chinese) in 1934; the Farming Cooperative Company for small farmers (Nongsa hapchaksa in Korean, Nongshi hezuoshe in Chinese) in 1937; and collective villages, which were mainly for tenants, in 1934. From 1934 to 1939, the Financial Cooperative Company established branches in 125 locations and had about 1.3 million members across Manchuria. From 1937 to 1939, the Farming Cooperative Company expanded from 75 to 153 branches, with 666 markets, 366 stores, and 7,765 offices under its jurisdiction.[55] For destitute Chinese peasants (and some Koreans who lived in the same village), the Manchukuo state planned to establish collective villages in 92 areas for three years from 1934 to 1937 to accommodate 9,296 households. By March 1935, the state had integrated 2,534 households into collective villages in Kando.[56] This plan was delayed by various factors, including bandit and guerrilla activities, financial shortages, weather conditions, and residents' opposition to the construction of collective villages.

The Financial Cooperative Company comprised rich landowning farmers who were capable of saving their earnings and holding properties that could be mortgaged to obtain loans from the company. It collected savings from members and lent them to other members. Since it excluded small peasant landowners, the state organized a meeting with researchers and scholars from Japan and Manchuria to help find a way to revitalize agriculture. The proposed alternatives included a series of measures ranging from educating peasants based on the example of the Japanese settlers' village, integrating peasants, improving farming tools and crops, rationalizing the distribution system, improving forest management for the use of firewood, preventing natural disasters, and reforming taxes to reduce the burden on peasants. The distribution system was reformed by the creation of the Farming Cooperative Company.[57] However, the changes necessary to increase productivity, such as changes in the labor process of farming and land reform, were not enacted.

The Farming Cooperative Company consisted of small landowning farmers (and some landless tenants) who lacked assets or savings. A general tenet of the Farming Cooperative Company was that its members would share the profits gained from the collective sale of their produce. In the company, private ownership of land remained intact; individual households controlled their own production processes, deciding for themselves what to grow and how to grow it. As a membership-based organization, the company's collectives controlled decisions over where and to whom products would be sold. This control was thus confined to the relations between individuals and the market, especially contracting out their produce for market sale and purchasing the necessities for daily life and farming. The company's collective assets included storage facilities and stores. While all members were, in principle, granted equal rights to influence decisions regarding the process of sale and purchase, the company operated under the corporatist management of the Manchukuo state. In the name of ensuring rationality and predictability of market transactions, the state set up a bureau that devised and enforced a standard procedure to evaluate the quality and price of crops. One Japanese researcher noted that a major operational problem of the company was this top-down mobilization of landowning peasants, which subverted the collectivist process.[58]

The Developing Cooperative Company (Hŭngan hapchaksa in Korean, Xingan hezuoshe in Chinese) integrated these two companies in 1939. This company promised to facilitate the voluntary participation of members in the kinds of collective market activities that its predecessors had lacked. However, it ended up creating an even more top-down network. As its name (revitalization and security) suggests, the company combined market activities with collective surveillance. Compared to its predecessors, it penetrated further into the daily lives of peasants, requiring that they not only sell their products through its network but also purchase from it almost every essential commodity—salt, oil, matches, farming tools, fertilizer, pesticides, grain bags, and livestock. It also further tightened the relationship between its members and the group defense network called Pogapche, which bound peasant households together as teams in a pyramidal fashion from village to county and assigned its members collective responsibility for political activities. During the war, the Developing Cooperative Company, in cooperation with the Concordia Association, handled the drive to confiscate grain for the war effort.[59]

The Manchukuo state modeled new collectives after Koreans' collective villages. It targeted Chinese refugees, tenants, and dispersed households, although it sometimes included Koreans in collective villages in places where Koreans and Chinese resided together. Although colonial discourses of social crisis in Manchuria mainly focused on the victimization of Koreans by the racial riots, Chinese as well as Koreans faced the problem of displacement of peasants from their land. In the 1920s, the majority of Chinese peasants in Manchuria tended to be small farmers, but in the 1930s they were increasingly becoming tenants due to the economic depression, natural disasters, and the clash between Japanese and anti-Japanese forces. According to a report of Kando Province in 1935, about 40 percent of the total population there was driven out of its villages due to usury, high rents, bad harvests, bandit and guerrilla activities, and Japanese suppression. The Chinese accounted for about 22 percent of all displaced peasants who escaped to cities (10,702 Chinese); the Chinese constituted about 26 percent of the total population in Kando, with only 50 percent of them engaged in farming.[60] In addition, the Manchukuo state's collective villages aimed to integrate peasant households scattered in mountainous areas, especially those with less than twenty households.

Onda Sakubē, in a series of articles published in *Manshū Hyōron* in 1935, offers perhaps the most comprehensive account of the Manchukuo state's collective villages. The collective villages were designed to integrate both tenants and landowners. County officials, on behalf of tenants, negotiated with landlords over relocating tenants and adjusting rent to 30 percent of the harvest. When they joined the collective villages, the landowners were, in principle, expected to receive land of the same value as what they had owned prior to moving into the villages. The amount of land each tenant household received depended on the number of household members: five hectares for a household of less than five people and ten hectares for a household of five or more. In the interest of self-sufficiency, every household was required to use at least one hectare to grow its own subsistence crops such as bar-

ley, potatoes, and corn.[61] Each household in a collective village was provided
with loans—fifty won for house building and twenty for farming expenses—
which it was required to repay within three years. Each collective village was
given 800 won for its collective facilities. These expenses were met using
loans that the Manchukuo state received from the Central Bank of Manchuria at 8.4 percent interest.[62]

Tenants were the main occupants of the Manchukuo state's collective villages, which lacked loan programs capable of transforming the class status
of their members. According to a survey conducted in October 1934, tenants
(including tenants who also cultivated their own land), for instance, constituted about 67 percent of the residents in six collective villages in Hwaryong
County and 52 percent in three collective villages in Wangch'ŏng County in
Kando. Onda Sakubē estimated that there was a larger proportion of tenants
there than in other collective villages, since these villages seemed to have
integrated residents, not just refugees, and thus had a more favorable economic composition.[63] In contrast, Korean cooperatives implemented a loan
program aimed at creating independent cultivators as its main constituents.
With subsidies from the Government General of Korea and the Kwantung
Army, the development companies purchased almost all of their lands from
landlords or acquired them from the Government General of Korea and then
distributed them to Korean peasants as loans.

The largely tenant population of Chinese collective villages, Onda Sakubē
argues, brought about unexpected problems concerning rent. Rent was set
at a maximum of 30 percent of the harvest, although some landlords continued to collect rents of 40 to 50 percent. This new rent was much lower than
prior rents, which had been as high as 50 to 60 percent for dry farming and
70 percent for rice farming. But these reductions fell short of protecting the
lives of the tenants, because the cultivation of lands that had been ravaged
by natural disasters or abandoned yielded meager harvests, especially at the
initial stages of collective villages. Landlords at first tended to embrace the
construction of the collective villages and agreed to the 30 percent rents, because they expected that these villages would protect the areas from bandit
and guerrilla activities and Japanese suppression. Once the stabilization of
farming increased production and the value of farmland, landlords tended to
raise rents and boycotted the further construction of collective villages when
their demands were not met. The living conditions of tenants who cultivated
wasteland or abandoned land were not promising. The exemption from rent

for one to three years on marginal farmland did not benefit tenants either, since the reclamation of such land required more time, especially when the available labor was insufficient.[64] Furthermore, when county officials signed contracts with landlords, tenants had collective responsibility in cases of default. The tenants became like slaves held hostage to debts: regardless of the value of their harvests, they were forced to repay their loans on time.

Onda Sakubē called on the Manchukuo state to distribute land to peasants for free because the domination of landlords, even with reduced rates of rent, inhibited the protection of tenants' rights. He also called for the state to stop demanding the repayment of interest and principal as well as the payment of rent, at least until the tenants had securely established themselves in their collective villages. This was because the success of the collective villages depended on the capacity of members to sustain themselves. He also advocated the practice of collective purchase and sale to insulate members of the villages from the tyranny of the market. He appealed for a formal ban on the operation of merchants in the cooperatives.[65]

The fact that the Manchukuo state's collective villages consisted mainly of tenants reflected at least two factors. First, the socioeconomic composition of the villages embodied the colonial hierarchy. Koreans and Japanese immigrants were expected to engage in agricultural production. Chinese migration from North China to Manchuria was contained, and Chinese residents were expected to migrate to the cities to work in industry. Reduced rail fares for immigrants enacted by the warlord government in the 1920s were abolished in 1932. The provincial authorities were now instructed to prohibit entry to those Chinese without proper passports or adequate funds. In 1933, extremely poor Chinese were prohibited from entering Manchuria. In 1935, the Manchukuo state issued new regulations to screen Chinese immigrants and control the activities of those who were permitted to enter. During 1931–38, about 3.9 million Chinese immigrated to Manchuria and 3.3 million left the area, for a net immigration figure of 600,000. From 1938 onward, the Sino-Japanese War increased the demand for industrial labor in Manchuria, for which Chinese were recruited from North China.[66] Second, the weak financial condition of the Manchukuo state constrained it from enacting programs to turn tenants into independent cultivators in the collective villages. When the state extended loans for housing, farming, and collective facilities in the villages, it required that the applicants report in detail the usage of loans and the methods of repayment and submit this information to the head of the county. In addition, applicants were required to have two guarantors who owned houses or land worth more than 200 won or five guarantors if each owned property worth less than 200 won.⁶⁷

Collective villages built for Chinese tenants differed from those for Korean and Japanese peasants. At the heart of Korean cooperatives was a loan program, which had as its goal the transformation of members from tenants into independent cultivators. It provided members with loans for housing, farm supplies, and collective facilities. Japanese cooperatives also offered loans to their members, and the amounts and terms of them were better than those offered to Korean peasants. Compared to their Korean and Japanese counterparts, Chinese cooperatives lacked substantive mechanisms to improve the living conditions of their members, much less invent a new form of capitalism.

Japanese and Korean Cooperatives

Japanese immigrants resided in collective villages built by the Manchuria Development Company (Manjuch'ŏksikhoesa) under the auspices of the Kwantung Army. Like Koreans, Japanese immigrants were expected to grow rice and staple crops and make themselves self-sufficient. They shared with Korean villagers the ideal of independent cultivators as the pillars of the villages. The privileged position of Japanese in the colonial hierarchy also produced the distinctive dynamics of Japanese collective villages, which differed from Korean ones in terms of the socioeconomic composition of the village, the amount of land owned and under cultivation, and financial subsidies.

Louise Young in her well-received study of the Japanese imaginary of Manchukuo succinctly states that Japanese immigrants by design came from the lowest stratum of village society—the poor, who worked less than 5 tan or 1.25 acres of land and who comprised one-third of all farm households in Japan. Their immigration drew on the policy of rehabilitating poor farmers in Manchuria and middle-class farmers at home. According to surveys of 337 emigrant households in six villages, over half had been tenants in Japan who owned no land. Another 31 percent of emigrating households owned five or fewer tan of land in Japan. This meant that "most emigrants had not been able to survive on cultivation alone and needed to supplement their income through day labor and other side occupations" such as rearing silkworms, making charcoal, vending, carpentry, and tool making.⁶⁸

The formula for transforming the poor into independent cultivators entailed land distribution and loans. Types and areas of cultivation determined the amount of land. In a plan, each rice-farming household would receive 6 chŏngbo of rice fields and 1 chŏngbo of dry fields; each dry farm in South and North Manchuria would receive 12 and 50 chŏngbo of land, respectively; and tobacco farmers and fruit growers would receive 9 and 5 chŏngbo of land, respectively.[69] The actual amount of land distributed to Japanese immigrants was less than planned. Japanese households, which came as part of the second wave of immigration in 1935, received an average of 10 chŏngbo of dry fields and some additional rice fields.[70] Japanese households in the third immigration wave received an average of 1.7 chŏngbo of rice land and 17 chŏngbo of dry fields in North Manchuria.[71] The amount of land distributed to Japanese immigrants was greater than that distributed to Korean immigrants. The South Manchuria Railway Company, for example, proposed that each Korean household would be given 2 chŏngbo of rice fields and 1 chŏngbo of dry fields; in Jilin Province each household would receive 6 chŏngbo of dry fields; and in North Manchuria each household would receive 10 chŏngbo of land.[72] In the group settlement program, Korean households were, in principle, expected to receive on average 2 chŏngbo of rice fields and 4 chŏngbo of dry fields.[73]

The Japanese collective villages appealed to the principles of self-sufficiency, collective management, and family labor based farming. Emigrant households were, in principle, required to minimize monetary exchanges with the outside. Although each household was permitted to hire two farm laborers in the initial period of settlement, this deviation from the ideal of self-sufficiency was expected to end as soon as the children were old enough to help with the farming. New technology and farm equipment were to be introduced to assist family farming.[74] In reality, Japanese farming continued to rely on farm labor. Their collective villages became even more closely integrated into the market as they tried to keep up with rising wages of farm labor, which soared after 1937 due to the demand for workers in the booming industrial sectors. Japanese farm households had significantly less family labor than did the Chinese. Surveys of Japanese immigrants conducted in 1940 show that when the labor power of a male adult was counted as 1 unit a Japanese household on average had about 1.6 units of labor power, 0.5 of annual labor, 1.1 of monthly labor, and 29 of daily labor. An average Chinese household in northern Manchuria had 6.7 units labor power, 0.2 of hired labor, and no annual labor.[75] According to a 1940 report on Japanese immigrants who arrived in a village as part of the third immigration wave, family labor on average accounted for only 31.2 percent of the total amount expended on farming. Households in which family labor constituted more than 90 percent of the total labor comprised only 1.7 percent of the 121 households in this village. The median households, in which family labor comprised about 40 to 50 percent of the total labor, were 25.6 percent of the total number of households.[76]

Japanese immigrants also developed tenancy relations with Chinese and Koreans. When the households in the second immigration wave obtained on average 2 chŏngbo of rice fields and 10 chŏngbo of dry fields, they cultivated all of the rice fields but only 3 chŏngbo of the dry fields using their own family labor and leased the rest to tenants. In the 1940 village report mentioned above, 70 percent of a total of 36 rice-farming households employed tenants, while 30 percent of a total of 64 dry-farming households rented their land to tenants. Korean tenants, in general, were hired for rice farming and Chinese for dry farming.[77] Rent in the Japanese collective village was lower than rent on average in North Manchuria or rent on lands owned by individuals. In a village in 1941, rent was charged at 10 percent for rice farming, 20 percent for dry farming, when the average rent in North Manchuria amounted to 38.8 percent for both rice and dry farming and the rent charged on land owned by individuals, in general, reached about 29.7 percent for rice farming and 36.6 percent for dry farming. The rent was set lower in the Japanese immigrant village because it was difficult to collect higher rents from Chinese and Korean tenants who were discontented, having earlier lost their land to the Manchuria Development Company.[78] As described in the next chapter, Japanese immigrants commonly leased land to Chinese and Koreans farmers.

There was a disparity in loans made to Japanese and Koreans in terms of both principal and interest rates. At first, Japanese immigrants were required to pay only half of the going price for land, though later immigrants were obliged to pay the full amount.[79] In contrast, Korean residents and immigrants were required to repay all loans in full. Furthermore, the average loan made to Koreans amounted to about one-third of the amount loaned to their Japanese counterparts. Each Japanese household received 2,600 won, while the Korean households received 800 to 1,100 won, depending on the type and the duration of farming they practiced and how long they had been doing it. For instance, each Korean household in the cooperative known as the Younggu Safety Village received a total of 1,058 won: 500 for land; 53 for agricultural expenses; 30 for construction of housing; and 475 for other expenses, including transportation, medicine, and education. According to a Japanese study, this disparity in loans to Japanese and Koreans resulted from the calculation of their living expenses based on living standards in Japan and Korea (i.e., middle-level farmers in Japan and tenant households in a southern province of Korea).[80] Furthermore, the interest rate for loans to Koreans was higher than for Japanese. For example, the Manchuria-Korea Development Company provided loans to Koreans at 8.4 percent interest, while the Manchuria Development Company made loans to Japanese at 4.5 percent. This disparity in the interest rate continued even after the Manchuria-Korea Development Company was integrated into the Manchuria Development Corporation in 1941 (the latter had absorbed the Manchuria Development Company in 1937). The corporation rejected the demand by Koreans for equalization of interest rates.[81]

Japanese immigrants, most of whom had been either landless or small landowners in Japan, achieved the greatest economic mobility of all peasant groups in Manchuria. Koreans and Japanese belonged to the same category of "Japanese," but it was only Japanese immigrants who were given land and various other loans. Receiving larger amounts of land and better loans elevated Japanese immigrants to the top position in Manchurian agriculture—that of landlords. While many Japanese immigrants hired Korean and Chinese peasants as tenants and laborers, Koreans in their cooperatives remained independent cultivators who tilled their own land usually with family and some hired labor.

Japanese cooperatives veered away from the ideal form. Japanese dependence on hired laborers and tenants meant the dissolution of the principle of self-cultivation in the Japanese collective villages. Collective management of production, marketing, and debt did not take root either. This was in sharp contrast to the Korean cooperatives, whose collective management was their defining feature, as I will discuss in chapter 5. The deviation of Japanese cooperatives from the prescription of agrarian communitarianism must have been associated with the shortage of labor and the slow adaptation of Japanese immigrants to farming conditions in Manchuria. Japanese immigration to Manchuria was promoted as an option to sons of peasant families whose inheritance of land was precluded by primogeniture. Thus, labor power in Japanese immigrant families tended to be less than in Korean immigrant families. Japanese cooperatives also diverged from the ideal form of cooperative because they were provided with larger amounts of land and they had access to larger loans with better terms. The superior treatment of Japanese immigrants corresponded to their dominant position in the hierarchical order of the empire.

CONCLUSION

In building a new empire, the colonial power aspired to resolve the social crises inherent in capitalism and to expand capital accumulation. A newly envisaged unity of the empire was constituted by the reordering of people through immigration and settlement in agrarian cooperatives. This new osmotic process conjured the image of a transnational process in building the empire. In actuality, the osmotic process developed a new matrix of spatio-temporality, as two forces commanded it: the international structure of empire and capitalist development. Putative nation-state powers administered the immigration of their own national subjects and their settlements. The people therefore did not move in an empty space but crossed territories that were under the jurisdiction of nation-states. The official policy on immigration and resettlement reterritorialized people as subjects of both a nation and the empire. The overlapping and contesting relationship between national powers impeded the orderly nationalization of people. As a result, Koreans in Manchuria, who had been categorized as Japanese, held dual nationality in both Manchukuo and the Government General of Korea, which undermined their rights.

As this chapter explored in terms of the formation of Manchurian cooperatives, this international structure of the empire mediated capitalist development in Manchuria. Practicing the idea of agrarian communitarianism, Manchurian cooperatives emerged as a device that could be used to create an alternative capitalist system, as well as a means of defending the territory of Manchuria. The international structure of the empire homogenized cooperatives by differentiating them according to nationality. For instance, the Government General of Korea, the Kwantung Army, and the Manchukuo state built separate cooperatives for Koreans, Japanese, and Chinese, respectively, buying lands and providing residents with services, loans, and other subsidies. Organized by the national dynamics of the empire, cooperatives concretized the spatial template of the new capitalist system.

These national dynamics of the empire, however, simultaneously fettered the invention of an alternative capitalist system. When agrarian communitarianism figured in independent cultivators as the subjects of the cooperatives, each nation-state constructed cooperatives in different forms. Japanese and Chinese cooperatives deviated from the ideal form in opposite ways, favoring landlords and tenants as constituents, respectively. Closer to the ideal form were the Korean cooperatives, which institutionalized a loan program designed to transform tenants into independent cultivators. The national variation among cooperatives was derived from both the hierarchical order of the nation-states and capitalist dynamics. In the case of Japanese and Korean cooperatives, the different standards of living in Japan and Korea determined the differences in the amount of land and terms of loans that were distributed to Japanese and Korean settlers in Manchuria. For Korean and Chinese cooperatives, Koreans had a better opportunity for upward economic mobility than did their Chinese counterparts, not simply because of the better financial condition of Government General of Korea but also because of their importance in rice farming.

The hybrid forms of cooperatives configured uneven social relations in Manchuria, which replicated the same crisis in a different form that the colonial power was trying to contain in the first place. Although Japanese immigrants were salvaged at least from their own crisis, despite their difficult adjustments to Manchurian farming, Koreans and Chinese were threatened with a new displacement from land. The uneven social relations by nationality and the repetition of the crisis effected a new temporality to the capitalist system in Manchuria. The Japanese resolution of the crisis in Manchuria was no more than a further integration of Manchuria into Korea, Japan, and other parts of the world economy. In other words, it was the reinforcement of the integration of Manchuria into a capitalist chain that had produced the crises in the first place. What was taken to be a resolution, however, produced the opposite effect. This spatio-temporality of capitalist expansion and its implication for territorial power of a nation-state in the empire will be further analyzed in the next chapter.

CHAPTER FIVE

Colonial Governmentality

The agrarian cooperatives embodied a colonial dream of both the colonizer and the colonized, which was brought into being as social practices. The social program of the cooperatives constituted a new technology of governance, with which the colonial power put the idea of communitarianism into practice to redraw the boundary between insider and outsider, reclassify landownership, and transform displaced farmers into productive laborers and fictive property owners. This technology of governance enabled the colonial power to embed itself in the everyday activities of work and exchange and thus, create its social power. The scale of managing corporeal movement within Manchuria and from Korea and Japan to Manchuria and of quarantining the groups in separate cooperatives signified the despotic nature of the colonial power, which was capable of organizing the spatial distribution of people within a colony and across the entire empire.

In this chapter, I examine the ways in which this repressive fascist power was grounded in the social sphere. I focus on the institutional characteristics immanent to the cooperatives themselves rather than on the external forces imposed on them. Although it is important for understanding the new order of people, to attribute the despotic colonial power solely to political and military institutions or the ideology of the imperialization of colonial subjects overlooks the fact that the empire existed only as long as its specific effects were institutionalized in a set of social practices that enabled the colonized to dream their own dreams. The social power implicated the colonized in the immediate social relations of production and exchange. It was through this social power that colonial authorities inserted coercive rule into the dream of the colonized, auto-valorizing the penetration of colonial power into daily life.

The social power of the colonial authorities was mediated by both national politics and capitalist development. The previous chapter focused on
national mediation; the discussion in this chapter centers on the mediation of capitalist development on national and colonial sovereignty. At the
end of this chapter, I explicate the tension in the corporeal process of national and capitalist integration, which I call the politics of osmosis. I also
establish the connection between agrarian cooperatives, osmosis, and fascism in Manchuria. Invested by industrial and finance capital from Japan
and Korea, the cooperatives claimed to liberate peasants from the tyranny of
former (Chinese) landlords and merchants, especially high rents, excessive
rates of usury, and market monopoly. The cooperatives were thus the institutional means through which the colonial power could bring about capitalist modernization without its excesses or without the antagonisms that
caused its structural imbalance. While this fascist dream appeared to nullify
the representational politics of the dominant classes, its new social order
coalesced following the logic of capital. That is, the cooperatives were constituted by three related characteristics of Manchurian capitalism or a historically specific form of capitalist development in Manchuria: the participation of finance capital in Manchurian agriculture, the fictive private property
system, and the communal credit system. The mediation of capital effected
the contradictory processes of homogenizing and differentiating social relations, which therefore both gave rise to and circumvented colonial governmentality.

I focus on Korean cooperatives in order to explore this colonial dream of
social power. As was discussed in chapter 4, Korean cooperatives epitomized
the policy of the cooperatives better than their Chinese and Japanese counterparts in terms of embodying the ideal of agrarian communitarianism. Korean cooperatives consisted of (fictive) self-sustainable small farmers, while
Chinese and Japanese ones had a large proportion of tenants and landlords,
respectively. In Korean cooperatives (the cooperatives hereafter under discussion, if not otherwise specified), the capitalist dynamics within Manchuria homogenized social power in at least three related ways: the economic
rationality of policy planning, the production of colonial subjects as property
owners, and the technique of coercion. Firstly, while invoking premodern
communitarianism, the cooperatives expressed a form of rationality that became a new culture of governmentality. The detailed planning of the cooperatives, involving the investment and distribution of loans and the amount and
terms of them, was an attempt to exercise power at the lowest possible cost

with the greatest possible effect. Second, the cultural, symbolic, and social operations of private property ownership enacted performativity, whereby the colonized imagined their sovereignty within the ongoing commodified process of agricultural production. Third, the credit system inherent in the loan program (the Program to Create Independent Farmers, Chajangnong ch'angjŏng in Korean, Zigengnong chuangding in Chinese) and the Mutual Aid Association (Nongmugye in Korean, Nongwuqi in Chinese) were the institutional metamorphosis of coercion that authorized a new disciplinary subject formation. They transformed the ways in which surplus labor was appropriated from the ground rent system to the credit system. While the credit system imposed a new, socially necessary labor time, the Mutual Aid Association performed everyday discipline in the name of self-rule.

Though it conjured up rationality and the institutionalized coercion of colonial governance, the social program of the cooperatives led to the opposite of the intended policy: the repetition of displacement. Inherent in this homogenization process was the hierarchization of social relations, which was produced by the transfer of land without adequate compensation, together with the disparity in the amount of loans lent to Koreans and Japanese and the unavailability of loans to the Chinese for the purchase of land (see chapter 4). The hierarchy produced another chain of displacement of Koreans and Chinese. Whereas the displacement of the peasants in Korea, Japan, and Manchuria impelled the colonial power to devise the cooperatives in the first place, the cooperatives did not eliminate this crisis of displacement but repeated it on the new frontier of Manchuria. The hierarchy was a necessary precondition and product of an ineffective spatial solution to the capitalist crisis. This solution required maintenance of the comparative advantage of places in the capitalist integration, such as the price of land and living standards being lower in Manchuria than in Korea and lower in Korea than in Japan. Producing the new dynamics of colonial governmentality, the spatial redistribution of people into the cooperatives took the politics of osmosis one step further during the Manchukuo period. But it fell short of harmonizing the two conjoined dreams of territorial and capitalist integration.

SOCIAL POWER AND THE CAPITALIST NETWORK

The preoccupations of the colonial power—racial riots, the displacement of peasants from land, the disruption of agricultural production, and the threat of the anti-Japanese forces—congealed into core elements of a new social order that was made possible by the operation of the cooperatives. In the colonial discourses, the cooperatives eliminated any kind of representation and mediation. While "imperialization" (hwangminhwa) organized a new national identity of colonized subjects, forcing them to adopt Japanese names and proclaim their loyalty to the emperor, the cooperatives engendered a new, transcendental relationship between the colonial power and its subjects. By establishing the cooperatives, the colonial power claimed to have resolved all the problems that had afflicted peasant society and to have overcome political and social antagonism. The loan program of the cooperatives replaced the usury of landlords and merchants that had brought the peasants into an unbreakable cycle of indebtedness. The collective sale of crops and the purchase of necessities were promoted as the means to eradicate the market monopoly of merchants. These economic reforms were expected to stabilize the lives of all members of the Manchukuo state, including Koreans. The elimination of politics debased the political and economic power of the former dominant classes, which had simultaneously collaborated with and opposed Japanese power prior to 1931. The desire to eradicate racial, political, and social antagonism that prefigured the cooperatives laid the groundwork for the fascist power of the colonial authorities. In such colonial discourses, the demarcation of outside and inside was dissolved.

The national historiographies of Koreans in Manchuria, which have been published in China and Korea in recent years, have diametrically challenged this colonial discourse. They subscribe to a view that the cooperatives were nothing but deceptive devices that did not change the fundamental axes of antagonism but deepened the familiar feudal exploitation in the form of rent, unpaid labor, usury, and taxes by landlords and their benefactor, the colonial power. Maximization of profits by the development companies depended largely on lengthening hours of work in cultivation, as well as in the construction of infrastructure such as housing, facilities, and roads and the organization of defense groups. Peasants under such conditions were said to be trapped in a life not much different from that of slavery.[1] According to Son Ch'unil, the loan program never allowed a single Korean to become a landowner, since the repayment of the original loan was set for ten to twenty years and they were liberated from Japan before that time.[2] Even without liberation, landownership was an unrealistic dream, as the loans merely led to more debt. To begin with, Koreans who were relocated in cooperatives possessed almost nothing and had to borrow to purchase everything from food and clothing to seeds and farming tools. They made the required payments on the loans and interest only to borrow more.

In his authoritative critique of the Program to Create Independent Farmers, Pak Ch'angwuk, undoubtedly the most acclaimed historian in China writing about the history of the Korean Chinese community, considers the program to have been a major mechanism of feudal exploitation in the form of usury.[3] He contrasts this feudal mechanism and the capitalist farms to highlight the ways in which the cooperatives fell far short of the promise of modernization. The colonial development companies simply behaved like their predecessors, the former landlords, practicing various forms of exploitation. The development companies distributed land as loans at much higher prices than they had paid. They also appropriated the profits by purchasing crops at low prices from the Mutual Aid Association and selling them at higher prices on the market. The peasants in the cooperatives did not just continue to live as tenants of the development companies, but they were also deprived of the freedom to leave them. If they worked like slaves held in bondage by debt, their counterparts on the capitalist farms were "free" of the land, as they were alienated from the means of production and employed as agricultural laborers.

Reducing the agrarian reforms to the colonizer's desire to create a utopian capitalist development or attributing them to the same old feudalism does not account for the new and specific institutional changes in the relationship between the colonized and the colonizer brought about by the reforms. The cooperatives and their loan program involved a historically specific capitalist dynamic. My question ultimately is not how Japan successfully intensified exploitation and siphoned off the resistance of Koreans through political and military coercion but rather how its social program embedded the sovereignty of the colonial power in the social sphere. The cooperatives must be read as a strategy of the state to shape social experience and discipline colonial subjects.

The utopian project of the cooperatives relied on the state's absolute capacity to insulate the local economy from the global dynamics of capitalism. It provided a context in which communitarianism and the system of private property were imagined to coexist. The system of fictive private property and the credit system constituted colonial governmentality, producing new subjectivities and techniques of discipline. Because of such changes, the lived experience of capitalist transformation manifested far more complexity than is accounted for by notions of capitalist modernization without excess or feudal exploitation. The embedding of colonial power in the social space enables an explication of colonial sovereignty and subjectivity. When production and exchange in the cooperatives were to be carried out independent of the commodification of land and labor power, it shaped a particular sovereignty of the colonial power. Social programs of the cooperatives also fostered a specific form of subjectivity among producers. The discussion of whether these features of cooperatives negated the objectification of peasants' labor power and their social relations must include the institutional network between the colonizer and the colonized mediated by finance capital.

A Pyramidal Institutional Network

Koreans developed their own institutional network with the Government General of Korea and its apparatuses. The financial organizations in Manchuria included banks, the Financial Cooperative Company, pawnshops, and the grain stores called the liangchan. Koreans in Manchuria must have utilized pawnshops and grain stores, which were popular sources of loans among the poor. In addition, Koreans developed a distinctive institutional network with the Government General of Korea, which created a social space for Koreans separate from that of other Manchuria residents. The institutional apparatuses of the Government General of Korea in Manchuria included the development companies, the Korean Association, the Financial Association (kŭmyunghoe in Korean, jinronghui in Chinese), and the Mutual Aid Association. Controlled by their immediate superiors, the apparatuses formed a strict pyramidal order. They advocated the stabilization, modernization, and rationalization of Korean peasant lives. Their actual function for the Government General of Korea and the Japanese empire, however, often digressed from the stated objectives. Even prior to 1931 the financial network had been a primary mechanism through which the Government General of Korea could establish its sovereignty over Korean peasants in the Kando region (chapter 3). After 1932, this financial network continued to strengthen the relationship between the Government General of Korea and the Koreans of Manchuria, with two significant changes. It had expanded beyond the Kando region, and it was also more rationalized than before. I will focus on the effects of the development companies and Mutual Aid Association on colonial sovereignty and subjectivity in the next section. Here I situate them in the pyramidal network.

To begin with, the development companies—the Oriental Development Company in Kando and the Asia Development Company in South Manchuria—had acquired and managed land in Kando and other parts of Manchuria, respectively. The official roles of the development companies included the purchase and management of land and the construction of the cooperatives. Functioning as financial institutions, they also advanced loans to Korean peasants, taking their lands as collateral security. In 1936, the Asia Development Company and the Oriental Development Company transferred their work on Koreans to the Manchuria-Korea Development Company, which itself was incorporated into the Manchuria Development Corporation in 1941.

The Korean Association had been supervised by the Government General of Korea and the Japanese consulate general in Kando since around 1910 (chapter 3). With a subsidy from the Government General of Korea and the Japanese Ministry of Foreign Affairs, the Korean Association expanded from 34 branches in 1931 to 113 (with 128,990 members) in 1935, when the official number of Korean households in Manchuria was estimated at 152,873 (830,601 individuals).[4] Given that only the head of the household joined the association, it enrolled about 84 percent of the total Korean population. While this official figure for the Korean population amounted to only half of the usual estimates of 1.5 million or 2 million by 1945, it suggests the influential power of the association over Koreans.

The Korean Association performed various administrative tasks for the colonial power until all its functions except those concerning education and customs were passed to the Manchukuo state in 1936.[5] Its official functions consisted of education, activities for residents' welfare, for example, firefighting, relocating poor people, accommodating the homeless, operating public facilities (cemeteries and crematoria), controlling contagious disease (vaccinations and quarantine of the infected), and supporting farming (instructions in new farming methods, the operations of markets for crops and livestock, and the construction and management of irrigation systems). It not only informed Koreans of changing policies and laws in Manchuria but also reported on politics, the economy, and culture in Korea. When the extraterritoriality of Koreans was abolished, its publications devoted several issues to the subject and made a variety of policy recommendations. In addition, the management of the cooperatives was a primary task of the association. It searched for proper locations for the cooperatives and selected suitable candidates for them. As the monthly publications of the Korean Association illustrate, it incessantly investigated lands suitable for rice farming and made annual projections of the harvest.

The Korean Association also mediated between financial institutions and

Korean peasants. It screened applicants who requested loans from development companies and oversaw the Financial Association (Kŭmyunghoe). The loans financed by the Financial Association differed from those of the development companies, although both offered peasants financial assistance for the purchase of basic necessities. The development companies were responsible for startup loans, mainly, though not exclusively, for Koreans who were brought into the agrarian cooperatives. They distributed loans for farmland, housing, and collective facilities such as storage buildings and schools, as well as livestock, initial farming expenses, and foodstuffs. In comparison, the Financial Association provided Koreans inside and outside the cooperatives with a variety of regular loans, including funds to meet the payments on loans from the development companies and loans for farming expenses. The Financial Association also differed from the Financial Department (Kŭmyungbu): the former proffered the loans without collateral, while the latter functioned like the regular banks, requiring security or guarantors and thus serving only a few rich farmers.

With the official objective of rationalizing peasant lives, the Financial Association sought to replace the abusive usury system with its loans for the purchase of land and other goods necessary to improve farming, such as oxen and fertilizer, and to finance subsidiary businesses such as cotton growing and weaving. The Financial Association was modeled after the Financial Cooperative (kŭmyung chohap in Korean, jinrongzuhe in Chinese) of Korea, whose real impact on small farmers turned out to be equivocal at best.[6] While the Financial Cooperative pledged to alleviate the suffering of small farmers caused by landlords' usury, they were condemned to become yet another mechanism that renewed familiar forms of exploitation. Their loans expedited the displacement of farmers from land, as the cooperative appropriated the land if debtors defaulted on their loans. Lending capital to landlords at low interest rates, the Financial Cooperative enabled them to make more usurious loans to peasants. With the support of the Government General of Korea and the development companies, the Financial Association quickly spread throughout Manchuria. For example, its twenty-three branches (fifteen main offices and eight subdivisions) in February 1939 grew to twenty-nine in August.[7] The Financial Association was subject to the laws and regulations of the (Chinese) Financial Cooperative Company after 1939.

Once the loans were made to individual Korean peasants, the Mutual Aid Association took charge of repaying the principal and interest to the development companies while furnishing the loans to the peasants. Established under the supervision of the Government General of Korea and the Japanese consulate general in Fengtian, the Mutual Aid Association reinvented the customary Korean mutual support system called kye, in which members mobilized funds or labor in exchange for help with farming, funerals, or other events that required substantial resources. The Government General of Korea was the main source of the capital that the Mutual Aid Association lent to its members.[8] For instance, it subsidized 24,445 won out of a total of 38,000 of expenses of the Mutual Aid Association in the safety villages, leaving the rest to collective finance by its members. The Mutual Aid Association officially vowed to prevent displacement of Koreans from their land by stabilizing their jobs and living conditions. It also performed political functions, and its team members were required to report all villager contact with anti-Japanese forces. Another of its basic functions was the repayment of agricultural loans to the development companies.[9] In the name of promoting self-rule among Koreans inside and outside the cooperatives, the association collected the harvest from its members (less a quantity reserved for domestic consumption), sold the crops on the market, made the required payments on the loans, and returned the balance of cash or crops to each household.[10]

Under different names, the Mutual Aid Association was organized with one representative from each Korean household throughout Manchuria, including the safety villages, collective villages, and other areas where Koreans congregated. After its establishment in the safety villages and cooperatives in Jilin Province in 1935, the Mutual Aid Association spread throughout Manchuria. Within three months of its creation it had 156 branches and lent 236,947 yen to its 3,668 members.[11] By August 1936, there were 319 branches with a total of 10,804 members.[12] Although each branch was expected to consist of less than thirty households and every ten to fourteen branches were grouped into a federation, the actual membership varied. The branches in the safety villages served twenty-five to thirty households, while membership in other areas ranged from seven to seventy.[13] After the extraterritoriality of Koreans was abolished in 1937, the association was subject to the administrative supervision of the Chinese Hungan Cooperative Company, while its functions were monitored and regulated by the Manchuria-Korea Development Company. The Manchuria-Korea Development Company entrusted the Federation of Mutual Aid Associations with the management of the safety villages.[14]

At the bottom of the pyramid of colonial institutions, the Mutual Aid Association enabled the colonial power to actualize the colonial dream and penetrate into the everyday life of peasants. The institutional network of the colonial apparatuses did not, of course, completely serve the colonial power. For example, some leaders of the Mutual Aid Association were Korean nationalists, who used their houses to hide communist guerrillas and plan anti-Japanese activities.[15] It was repeatedly said that Korean peasants risked their lives in delivering some of their crops to anti-Japanese guerrilla armies, hiding their members and providing intelligence on the Japanese military and police. While I do not dispute the Koreans' bravery in the struggle against colonial rule, I seek to examine the ways in which the colonial apparatuses and their institutional network did not merely repress the colonized and conceal their exploitation but also produced the specific forms and content of colonial sovereignty and subjectivity. Before undertaking this analysis, the next section discusses the mediation of finance capital that pervaded the systems of private property and credit among Koreans across Manchuria.

Finance Capital

Finance capital emerged as an important partner of the colonial power as early as 1936. It was through this partnership that the institutional relationship between the colonial power and Koreans was consolidated. Finance capital buttressed the development companies, which had experienced financial difficulties, and enabled them to expand the loan program for Koreans, which previously had been confined to the Kando area. This spatial extension of the credit system signified the increasing infiltration of the colonial power into the social life of Koreans across Manchuria. The participation of finance capital from Korea and Japan in the development of Manchuria coincided with a crucial shift in the seesawing relationship between the Kwantung Army–the de facto supreme power in Manchuria–and Japanese monopoly capital. For the period 1920–29, the Zaibatsu (companies such as Mitsui, Mitsubishi, Sumitonomo, and Yasuda) witnessed an enormous expansion of their wealth and political power, while the Kwantung Army's power waned due to its defeat in the clash with Germany in 1918 and another setback in China and Siberia during 1918–23. The economic depression that began in the late 1920s and the Kwantung Army's invasion of Manchuria in 1931 reversed the dynamics of power between the army and the Zaibatsu. Envisaging a planned economy for Manchuria, the Kwantung Army excluded the Zaibatsu from Manchuria's development.

From 1906 to 1935, the South Manchuria Railway Company had been a main source of the capital needed for the development of Manchuria. Since it was formed with capital of 200 million yen, half of which came from the Japanese government, investment in the SMRC and its subsidiaries reached about 85 percent of all Japanese investment in late 1931 and 68 percent from 1932 to 1935.[16] The SMRC maintained its highly profitable operations at least until the late 1920s. Ramon Myers states that after paying all its annual obligations to bondholders and accounting for other debts and losses, the SMRC still generated significant net revenue each year, rapidly doubling and tripling it in the second and third decades of the century.[17] The unexpected decline in its revenue in the early 1930s can be attributed to two factors. First, many of its economic activities yielded large profits, but retained earnings did not contribute as much to new financial investment as did the issuance of new debt in the forms of bonds and paid-in capital. Although the management and operation of railways were its main activities, the SMRC invested in mines, electricity, and factories in Manchuria, many of which, according to F.C. Jones, included "uneconomic" or "unprofitable" enterprises, such as the Anshan Iron Works, administrative and social services in the railway zones, Japanese colonization settlements in these zones and the Kwantung Leased Territory, and certain "marginal" enterprises such as coal liquefaction at Fushun and the Showa Steel Works.[18] Second, the SMRC was forced by the Japanese state to take over the Chinese Eastern Railway, invest in the construction of new lines, and limit the freight fee so as to facilitate the transportation of soybeans. Such costly changes took place while the market was contracting in the late 1920s, which made it difficult to issue bonds in Japan to raise more funds. During 1932–37, the SMRC retained its principal share in the development of Manchuria, but the Manchukuo state emerged as a competitor that became either a principal or an important shareholder in nineteen key special companies established by it, including the Central Bank, the Manchurian Telegraph and Telephone Company, and an automobile company.[19]

Despite its financial deterioration, the SMRC remained the main stockholder of the development companies. It financed the Asia Development Company, which had acquired and managed land since 1922, and had been constructing cooperatives since 1932 in South Manchuria. The Asia Development Company recorded a dramatic loss in 1932, shrinking the value of its assets by half, from 20 to 10 million won.[20] The functions of the Asia Development Company were absorbed by the new development companies —the Korea-Manchuria Development Company and its auxiliary firm, the Manchuria-Korea Development Company—which the Kwantung Army and the Government General of Korea established to launch the official immigration of Koreans from Korea to Manchuria in 1936. The SMRC, together with the Oriental Development Company, owned almost half of its stock (100,000 and 99,900 shares, respectively, out of 400,000) in the Korea-Manchuria Development Company. The Oriental Development Company experienced sizable financial losses from 1932 to 1935 due to the worldwide economic depression and the subsequent decline in agricultural prices, which reduced its rental income. Starting in the mid-1930s its financial condition improved, due to its expanded investment in mines, shipbuilding, chemical and metal industries, electricity, and transportation.[21]

A new capitalist network involving the colonial power and the Koreans was forged by the growing investment of finance capital in the development companies. Given that the SMRC remained a primary stockholder, industrial capital remained an important partner of the colonial power. But compared to earlier development companies the Korea-Manchuria Development Company was extraordinary in its inclusion of a large proportion of finance capital. A total of eleven insurance companies and six banks in Korea and Japan comprised about 50 percent of the total stock and 74 percent of the stockholders.[22] The investment of finance capital in the Korea-Manchuria Development Company ended a three-decade monopoly by the SMRC in the development of Manchuria, heralding the growing influence of finance capital at least in Manchurian agriculture. From the mid-1930s on, the weakened financial position of the SMRC forced the Kwantung Army to invite new Zaibatsu (in the steel, metal, and chemical industries), as well as existing industrial conglomerates, to invest in Manchuria.[23] While the Zaibatsu did not invest in development companies, the overall restructuring of the relationship between capital and the army was the context in which finance capital emerged as an influential player in Manchurian agriculture.

The scale of the responsibilities assigned to the Korea-Manchuria Development Company was greater than its predecessors. The Korea-Manchuria Development Company oversaw both the old cooperatives outside the Kando region and the new ones built for new immigrants. It also extended the loan program (the Program to Create Independent Farmers) aimed at turning tenants into self-cultivators beyond the Kando region, after years of unfulfilled promises by its predecessor, the Asia Development Company. In addition, the Korea-Manchuria Development Company managed the relocation and settlement of new Korean immigrants, who under the official policy were expected to amount to 200,000 households over fifteen years. In spite of the larger scale of its function, the Korea-Manchuria Development Company's original capital of 20 million won was equal to that of the Asia Development Company, which had been established fifteen years earlier in 1922. In fact, the former's assets were valued at less than those of the latter, if the high inflation of the late 1920s was considered.

The scale of the Korea-Manchuria Development Company was due not so much to the volume of capital investment per se as to its rationalization of the planning and management of the cooperatives. If the cooperatives were anything more than an effective means of containing anti-Japanese forces, it was because of the social relations made possible by the new capitalist network of pyramidal colonial institutions. This new capitalist network promulgated the systems of private property and credit across Manchuria, which homogenized the institutional positions and identities of nationals as prospective property owners and organized the labor process. In other words, the financial network accomplished more than financing the farming and living expenses of Korean peasants. It constituted colonial governmentality.

THE (IN)VISIBLE SPATIAL ORDER OF GOVERNMENTALITY

The architectural apparatus of the agrarian cooperatives gave a visual form to the power relations between colonized and colonizer. The spatial design of each cooperative entailed a self-enclosed village that acted as a type of social quarantine. The gates, roads, identical houses, collective facilities, and checkpoints were arranged in a highly planned spatial order. Yoon Hwitak insightfully describes the architectural design of the cooperatives, drawing on both colonial documents and survivors' testimonies.[24] Each cooperative was circumscribed within a defensive wall built of soil or wood and often topped with barbed wire. The height and width of the wall depended on the strategic importance of the area and the level of threat from anti-Japanese forces. For example, the blueprint of the Manchukuo state's cooperatives in Kando Province, which were modeled after the Korean cooperatives, shows a defensive wall 2.7 meters high and 1 meter wide. In another province, the dimensions were 3 and 2 meters, respectively. A turret was built at each corner of the defensive wall, where as many as five people could fire at enemies outside. Each cooperative, in general, was equipped with four to nine gun batteries. In some cases, barbed wire 2 to 5 meters high was placed around a cooperative, 15 to 20 meters from the wall.

The cooperatives typically had four gates, at least two of which were narrow and short and connected to small passages leading in and out of the vil-

FIGURE 4. A developers' collective village (Kaech'ongmin purak) in Kando in 1941. (From Ryu Eun Kyu, Ich'ojin hŭnjŏk, 48–49.)

lage. For surveillance purposes, a single gate was allotted for everyday use and was closed during the night. The road from the gates to the center of the cooperative was about six meters wide. Just as early American towns were built around a church, according to a description in a Japanese document, each cooperative had a public square at its center, where a police station, self-defense group headquarters, schools, health center, and other public facilities were positioned. Open space in the center was reserved for physical training or assembly in an emergency. A surveillance tower eighteen meters in height was also placed in the center of some cooperatives. Roads were connected to all sides of the village and were used for transporting grain. The roads divided the inner zone of the cooperative into four sectors, each of which was expected to accommodate one communal well and twenty-five households or one-fourth of the total number of households in the village. Each household was allotted 198 to 277 square yards of land. To economize on land use, households were prohibited from having a vegetable garden.

The architectural design of the cooperatives evokes the image of the Panopticon along the lines described by Foucault.[25] A Panopticon is a machine that creates and sustains a visible and verifiable power relation "independent of the person who exercises it."[26] It dissociates "the see/being seen dyad:

in the peripheric ring, one is totally seen, without ever seeing; in the central tower, one sees everything without ever being seen."[27] The imposed spatial order in the agrarian cooperatives in Manchuria produced similar effects, creating the perception by members that they were always being watched. This spatial mechanism might account for the surprising paucity of Koreans' organized protests or clashes with the Japanese forces within the cooperatives. Although the colonial power did not preclude the use of force, the spatial order, combined with the display of police and army personnel, also contributed to displaying the power of the colonizer, which could be internalized by the colonized.

The institutional network of the colonizer and the colonized constituted yet another spatial order of the colonial power. As the architectural landscape of the cooperatives involved built-in mechanisms of panopticism, the institutional network entailed mechanisms immanent to its capitalist characteristics. If the former is visible, the latter is invisible. The external means of power, such as military and police force, relied on negative and punitive measures that repressed the people and excluded them from the social order. The immanent mechanisms of colonial institutions, on the other hand, endowed the colonizer and the colonized with new dreams and desires and thus, produced a new social reality. The interaction of finance capital, the fictive private property system, and the communal credit system produced an economic rationality, the subjectivity of producers, and the everyday regulation of a new labor process.

Economic Rationality

The colonial authorities envisaged the transformation of landless Koreans into small independent farmers. Even before the Japanese invasion of Manchuria, the Asia Development Company considered such a transformation necessary to stabilize the lives of Koreans oppressed by Chinese officials.[28] Immediately following its invasion of Manchuria in 1931, the Kwantung Army also outlined its plan to create 2,500 independent Korean farmers every year: 1,200 in Kando, with loans of 500 won per household; and 1,300 in other places, with loans of 750 won per household.[29] The Korean state pledged to create 7,068 households of Korean property owners in Kando over twenty years from 1933 to 1952, providing an average loan of 800 won per household.

The loan project called the Program to Create Independent Farmers functioned to create fictive small landowners in the following ways. With subsidies from the colonial authorities, the development companies acquired land. The companies leased it in the form of loans to Korean residents (refugees and new settlers) without moratoriums. Koreans were also provided with loans for housing, cultivation, and the other expenses of building the cooperatives. If borrowers paid the interest and a portion of the principal for every year during the term of the loan, usually for ten to twenty years, they would be granted title to the land; it was ruled later that the credit collectives would keep the titles. The number of adults able to farm and the number of livestock were among the criteria that defined eligibility for membership. The loan program was applied to peasants both inside and outside the cooperatives.

Beyond this stated objective, the credit system, which was intrinsic to the loan program, performed another function. It rationalized the implementation of the communitarian ideal, leading the colonial power to plan and regulate the most minor details of production by small landowning farmers. The policy of the Government General of Korea in the Kando region, a modest policy among a range of proposals on loans, demonstrates the breadth and detail of the rationalization of the process. This policy was based on calibrating various expenditures, including the cost of different types of farmland, as well as the costs of livestock, farming, and housing. The interest rate was set at 8.2 percent, which was lower than the 6 to 20 percent rates charged by moneylenders. While the amount of the loans depended in part on the number of household members, each household was expected to receive 800 won in loans on average: 650 won for a total of 6 chŏngbo land (1 chŏngbo of paddy fields and 5 of dry fields); and loans for building a house (40 won), purchasing an ox (50 won), and agricultural expenses (60 won).[30]

The loan repayment schedule was determined by the type of the loan. Interest and principal were repaid in different years for different periods of time. The principal advanced for agricultural expenses was to be repaid within one year, with eligibility to borrow the same amount every year for up to three years. The principal for building a house and purchasing an ox had to be repaid from the second to the fifth year, with annual interest. According to the SMRC's plan, Korean peasants were expected to pay the interest on loans made for land in the first year they harvested; from the second to the fifth year, the company would collect the principal on loans for transportation, irrigation, tools, housing, roads, and storage and other buildings. From the sixth to the twelfth year, all of the principal on loans for land was to be collected, after which the title deeds would be issued.

The reduction of the economic cost of governing was a unique feature of the credit system. Through detailed calculation of the original capital, the distribution of loans, and their annual return over fifteen to twenty years, the colonial authorities determined how many cooperatives were to be built each year and the precise amount of loans to be advanced to the members. The increased predictability of the return on investment permitted the colonial power to design a policy that lasted twenty years. The predictability allowed for the economic use of capital, which maximized its intended effect. The creation of 7,068 households of Korean small landowners over twenty years was based on an investment of 2 million won for five years and its interest, 3.7 million won, for the remaining fifteen years. One-third of the original capital of 2 million won was to be provided by the Government General of Korea and the remainder by the Oriental Development Company. The original capital in the initial five-year period of 1932–36 was expected to create a total of 2,500 independent farming households: 1,000 households in 1933 and 500 annually in 1934, 1935, and 1936. The interest collected from the cooperative members would be used to finance new loans and create an additional 279 households from 1934 through 1936. After 1937, the interest accrued on the original investment would be sufficient to create more landowning households, between 173 and 195 every year until 1952. In other words, the original capital investment was to be recouped by 1936; after that, the repaid principal and interest would be reinvested in the program every year until 1952 (see table 5).[31]

The Program to Create Independent Farmers more or less met its targets. From 1933 to 1935, it produced a total of 2,332 putatively property-owning households in Kando (776 households in the cooperatives and 1,556 outside them), or 111 percent of the target number. These accounted for about 33 percent of all Korean households and 21 percent of all farmland in Kando. Each household in the cooperatives received 2.86 chŏngbo of land, slightly less than planned, while households outside the cooperatives in Kando received 5.1 chŏngbo.[32] The program was extended to cover 2,906 households in Kando until 1937; the actual amount of the loan advanced to each household (577.15 won) was smaller than the planned amount (800 won).[33] A total of 9,224 households enlisted in the program across Manchuria from 1937 to 1940, occupying 41,579 chŏngbo and receiving about 6.1 million won in loans.[34]

The predictability of the return on investment regularized and universalized the technique of governance. The predictability was derived from the credit system, which was a more rationalized and coercive form of risk man-

TABLE 5. Plan for the Program to Create Independent Farmers in Kando, 1933–52

Year	Independent farming households created by the original capital		Repaid capital	Independent farming households created by the repaid capital		Total	
	Capital (in won)	House-hold (number)		Capital (in won)	House-hold (number)	Capital (in won)	House-hold (number)
1933	800,000	1,000				800,000	1,000
1934	400,000	500	14,400	14,400	18	414,400	518
1935	400,000	500	65,192	64,800	81	404,800	581
1936	400,000	500	144,396	144,000	180	544,000	680
1937			156,232	136,000	195	156,000	195
1938			191,366	191,200	239	191,200	259
1939			193,343	192,800	241	192,800	241
1940			177,207	176,800	221	176,800	221
1941			184,202	184,000	230	184,000	230
1942			187,229	187,200	234	187,200	234
1943			196,623	196,000	245	196,000	245
1944			207,876	207,200	239	207,200	239
1945			218,996	218,400	273	218,400	273
1946			251,416	231,200	289	231,200	289
1947			244,387	244,000	305	244,000	305
1948			258,776	258,400	373	258,400	323
1949			273,872	273,600	342	273,600	342
1950			246,394	245,600	307	245,600	307
1951			240,243	240,000	300	240,000	300
1952			229,290	228,800	286	228,800	286
Total	2,000,000	2,500	3,661,640	3,654,400	4,568	5,654,400	7,068

Source: Son Ch'unil, Manjugugui chaeman hanine taehan t'ojichŏngch'aek yŏn'gu, 202.

agement than the ground rent system practiced by development companies before the invention of small landowners. Prior to the implementation of the Program to Create Independent Farmers, the development companies behaved like landlords, hiring Korean farmers as tenants and routinely loaning them money. Under the ground rent system, Korean peasants were required to pay development companies 30 to 40 percent of the harvest. As the size of the harvest varied by year, rental income fluctuated. Such variations rendered the peasants' payments irregular, resulting in an unpredictable return on capital invested in land. The Asia Development Company attributed the loss of half its capital in 1932 to oppression by the Chinese government in the northeast, which in principle banned Koreans and Japanese from landownership and residence until 1931.[35] But the nature of the long-term investment in land and the collection of the interest in the ground rent form also must have compromised the company's ability to manage its investments effectively.

In contrast, the credit system demanded that the peasants or fictive landowners pay a fixed proportion of the principal and interest every year, regardless of the value of the harvest. I will return to a discussion of the credit system as a form of appropriation of surplus labor, but first I will examine its underlying dynamics. The repayment schedules of various loans must have taken into consideration the peasants' capacity to repay them. As the schedules were set for ten to twenty years, however, economic rationality seemed to take precedence over the unpredictability of annual harvests, which was the main factor affecting the ability of peasants to make their loan payments. This rationality in estimating the long-term return on investment enabled the colonial power to develop an appropriate scheme of production for the small landowners.

Colonial Subjectivity

The cooperatives were the emblem of the universal and pluralistic inclusion of Korean and other ethnic and national groups, which had been excluded from Manchurian society in the past. When Koreans were organized in putatively self-sufficient agrarian cooperatives, individuals were transformed into national and imperial subjects. Koreans were expected to live harmoniously with other ethnic and national groups in Manchuria, including the Manchus, Han Chinese, Mongols, and Japanese. As the different types of cooperatives brought Chinese and Koreans into separate social spaces, various groups of Koreans (refugees, residents, the unemployed, residents with or without legal documentation of nationality, and new immigrants, whose experiences in Korea and Manchuria differed) were homogenized as prospective property owners. As I explored in chapter 4, the refugees and residents in different parts of Manchuria had varied experiences of both work and property rights and had suffered during the Chinese riots of 1931. Immigrants coming from Korea from 1936 onward differed not only from the earlier groups but also among themselves in terms of their places of origin in Korea, skill in rice and dry farming, and type of immigration. To normalize such variation among Koreans, the cooperatives drew a new, concrete boundary between displaced and prospective landowners. It was through the loan program of the cooperatives that the Government General of Korea attempted to reterritorialize displaced Koreans in both Manchuria and Korea as prospective landowning producers and to fix their social relations.

The universal desire of Koreans to own land was combined with their aspiration to escape chaos and disorder. Inherent in this production of colonial subjects was the social process of constructing the peasants' consent to colonial rule. The fantasy of landownership compelled colonized Koreans to respond to the calls of colonial authority. The Program to Create Independent Farmers accommodated peasants with loans for various purposes, such as purchasing land, building houses, and the initial expenses of cultivation. In other words, it was the official path to property ownership. Property ownership was a promise that led Korean residents to endure the grueling process of immigrating to Manchuria and relocating in the areas designated for them.[36] In the hope that they could avoid starvation and acquire their own land, Korean immigrants left family members, relatives, and ancestral burial sites. Their hopes were based on propaganda and slogans popularized by the development companies: "Unclaimed and fertile land is everywhere in Manchuria"; "grain and farming seed for the first year, as well as transportation fees, will be loaned"; "by working diligently for only a few years, everyone can be a landowner"; and "we are waiting for you with houses ready."[37]

The promise of landownership became the pedestal on which the colonial power constructed its sovereignty over Korean peasants. This promise enabled the colonial power to intervene in the labor process, as the relocation and immigration of Koreans in groups formed the basis for organization of the collective labor necessary for farming. Irrigation projects were the most essential of the collective tasks. When ice began to melt in early spring, peasants began to work on them in preparation for farming. To divert water to the fields, they moved branches, stones, and bags of soil, working for days in the icy water. Irrigating the fields required digging channels that could run several miles from the nearest river. Fields had to be sown from late May to early June. Some households used ox-drawn plows, while others depended on spades, hoes, and sickles to work the land.[38]

The immigration and relocation policy represents private property ownership as a paternalistic handout from the colonial power. The colonialists provided the capital for the immigration and relocation of Koreans based on a rational estimation of the costs of purchasing land, grain, livestock, farming tools, and other necessities. The fantasy of private property ownership led the colonized work in the present in pursuit of an illusory promise. Colonial sovereignty required that the expectations of the cultivators be met with handouts of land and the products of the allotted fields. Although survivors attested that Korean peasants risked their lives to hide part of their harvests for the anti-Japanese guerrilla armies, daily routines in their collective villages remained governed by the sound prospect of securing their staple grains, paying their debts, and owning land.[39] When this expectation was not met, their protests were met with the power and authority of the Japanese military and police. The migrants demanded new loans for seeds, treatment of the contagious diseases made rampant by the lack of potable water and sanitation, and freedom to travel to the cities. Those who cultivated dry fields demanded relocation to areas where they could engage in rice farming.

Fictive private property ownership bred a new mode of capitalism. The cooperatives were invented as a defense against the ills that capitalist modernization brought to the countryside. They embodied a communitarianism that claimed to negate commodification and by extension colonial capitalism itself—its trade, appropriation of surpluses, and political domination. The cornerstone of commodification, which determines social relations, is production for market exchange. Production exclusively for market exchange, separate from the use value of products generated, is a condition for the alienation of labor and the objectification of social relations. Even if social programs were envisioned as a way to extend the scope of the power of producers over production and distribution of their products, a question key to assessing their sovereignty is: Whose need, feeling, or thought will prevail to shape the relationship?[40] The primary drive of the cooperatives was to expand agricultural production, which was the primary ongoing need of the colonial power. When the state was said to have the "highest" ownership of land, it was not a metaphor for its moral obligation to protect private property ownership but an indication of its control of land, people, and capital.

This moment of colonial desire pointed to a would-be noncapitalist form, yet only in representation. The cooperatives negated capitalism even while they reinforced it. Such negation of capitalism is the process of refiguring capitalism by invoking its opposite. The aura of communal social relations had its clear limit. While the cooperatives promised to foster new social relations beyond the commodity exchange of capital, land, and labor, they merely displaced the unequal relationships between colonizer and colonized and between capital and labor into a financial transaction between creditor and debtor. The cooperatives promised to establish a new social system capable of eliminating the tyranny of landlords and merchants. Instead, they transformed the relationship between the propertyless and the propertied into a relationship between producers, who desired their own land, and the colonial state power, which was primarily interested in the expansion of agricultural production. The communitarian notion of national development of the countryside gave rise to new, unequal relations between the colonial state and colonial subjects. In the conclusion of this chapter, I discuss how this communitarian inversion of social relations laid the groundwork for colonial fascist power.

Techniques of Coercion

The cooperatives institutionalized two mechanisms of coercion through which the colonial power organized a new labor process: the credit system and a communal form of the Mutual Aid Association. The disciplinary power of the credit system was formal and contractual, while the disciplinary power of the Mutual Aid Association was derived from a customary framework. In the credit system, the institutional foundation was the contract between individual households and development companies, which was protected and regulated by law and state policies. In the Mutual Aid Association, customary practices of collective support were devolved to the collective loan payment. The colonial power could have attenuated producers' rights with the direct application of force in the labor process, such as regulating the types of crops to be cultivated and labor schedules. But the colonial power achieved comparable effects or even stricter controls over labor power with the credit system and Mutual Aid Association.

Existing studies have explored the effects of the loan program primarily in terms of the ways in which growing debt reduced prospective landowners to something like slaves. While many survivors saw immigration to Manchuria as an economic opportunity, surveys conducted by the SMRC and the development companies underscored the exploitation by the colonial power.

According to a report of the Government General of Korea, the households in the safety villages complied well with the payment schedule of the loans, paying 64 to 108 percent of the required return in 1934.[41] Other surveys recorded rising debt, as in general the payments on loans and other debts exceeded the average income of households. For instance, when the average income per household ranged between 324 and 586 won in the safety villages in 1937, the required portion of the loan payment in that year (for land, housing, and other costs spent on the construction of the cooperatives) and other debts amounted to 33 percent and 74 to 118 percent of income, respectively.[42] The rate of repayment of loans in the case of the safety villages, where the Program to Create Independent Farmers was implemented in 1937, was very uneven. The amount of the loans repaid in 1938 and 1939 was far below the required amount. The 1940 return exceeded previous returns, even when membership in these safety villages from 1937 to 1940 declined by more than 20 percent.[43] It was said that each year households repaid the required portion of their loans and other debts only to take out new loans to meet their living and agricultural expenses. Son Ch'unil states that debt was widespread across Manchuria. To facilitate the high rates of repayment of loans, Korean farmers were permitted to grow opium. They were also required to save 10 percent of the total harvested crops, 50 percent of opium sales, and 10 percent of supplementary income in the credit unions.[44]

The economic data on households are useful in assessing the peasant economy but inadequate for reaching a comprehensive conclusion. The economic surveys did not explore the correlation between the degree of debt and other factors determining household income and consumption, such as the amount of farmland distributed to each household, the type of land (e.g., rice field, dry field, or wasteland recently converted into arable land), number of laborers, distance between the fields and the cooperatives, and availability of sources of extra income such as firewood and supplementary work. My concern is not so much the actual amount of debt as the stage preceding it—the institutional and communal control of work and the payment of loans. The dual progression of high rates of loan repayment and new debt indicates the effectiveness of the control over household members of the cooperatives. Everyday discipline involved the mechanisms of the credit system and the communal associations.

The cooperatives homogenized the socially necessary time of labor, and nothing could be more emblematic of this than the credit system formulated in the Program to Create Independent Farmers. At the level of politics, the credit system was an inclusive measure that integrated the Koreans as producers and property owners. At the level of economics, the credit system was the market mechanism for the appropriation of surplus labor. Since the harvest proceeds of the farmers' labor were credited to loans, the colonial power's appropriation of their surplus labor came to be seen as legitimate actions necessary to secure the interest on the loans. At the level of society, it enforced the socially necessary labor, compelling individuals to work their hardest, repay their loans, and thus own land. The credit system enabled the colonial apparatuses to intervene through impersonal and bureaucratized forms of expropriation. The interest charged on these loans was similar to the ground rent charged on land in terms of the ways that they appropriated the surplus value created by the farmer. Yet a major difference is that the calculation of the cycle of investment and return came to dictate the amount of labor time of peasants rather than vice versa. While the ground rent system involved an irregular and unpredictable return on investment subject to the annual harvest, the credit system appeared to be legal, rational, and objective. The credit system authorized a form of control even more coercive and punitive than the ground rent system.

Two kinds of ground rents were practiced in Manchuria. One was based on a fixed percentage and the other on a fixed volume of the harvest. The former, called chŏngjo, was widely practiced in Fengtian Province in the 1920s and North Manchuria prior to 1931. The landlords' share was not fixed in a leasehold but depended on the size of the harvest.[45] This meant that landlords benefited from an increase in production but also had to bear some risk. Under the credit system, tenants (or putative property owners) absorbed the risk alone, since, regardless of the size of the harvest, they had to pay a fixed amount of principal and interest. The credit system appeared to be similar to the ground rent system based on the fixed volume of the harvest, because the amount of the payments did not depend on the harvest. However, the credit form was based on calculation of long-term financial investment and its return. The credit system was a means of privatization whereby the predictable installment payments by debtors permitted development companies to plan their reinvestment of profits. The peasants were forced to comply with detailed repayment schedules with different start dates and lengths.

Korean immigrants faced uncertainty by assuming the risk alone, yet they were prohibited from leaving the cooperatives, selling land, or passing it on to others. They therefore had no option but to try to circumvent risk by maximizing the input of their labor in production. The credit system, in combination with the promise of landownership, imposed coercion on the labor process more strongly than ground rent contracts did without moment to moment intervention. Even when rice farming was not required by the colonial power, Korean peasants preferred it, despite its labor-intensiveness, because it yielded a better harvest and larger profits. Although labor was intensified, this form of privatization—the relationship between landlords and putative prospective landowners—cannot be termed semifeudal or an instance of the coexistence of feudalism and capitalism, as historical studies of Korean cooperatives contend. Instead, it was a historically specific form of the private property and credit systems.

Fusing the credit system with communal rule, the Mutual Aid Association was the reinvention of the Korean custom of teamwork, in which peasants provided reciprocal support for farming, funerals, and other events that required a significant expenditure of labor or money. With the official mission to improve Korean's lives, the Mutual Aid Association was built around the need for self-rule, which was believed to be a cure for the displacement of peasants from the land. The reinvented practices of teamwork in Manchuria, combined with the loan program, were said to be intended to support the people and the Korean community as opposed to landlords' usury and merchants' monopoly of the market. It was also promoted as an instrument for collective rule of ethnic and national groups, which was the political ideology of the Manchukuo state.

The private property system and the Mutual Aid Association were two sides of the same coin. One side appealed to those with dreams of individual landownership, while the other appealed to those who valued community. Communal rule was by definition ambiguous. Even previously it was not so much a form of collective empowerment as the last resort for survival of peasants burdened with tenancy rent and other debts. Whatever the essence of the traditional mutual aid, communal rule became abstracted into an anticapitalist strategy in Manchuria. Communal survival strategies, then, were condensed into the essential mechanism of loan payments. Before the Program to Create Independent Farmers was implemented in South and North Manchuria, the Mutual Aid Association educated its members about farming and operated schools and medical facilities. With the establishment of the Manchuria-Korea Development Company, which expanded the program to these areas after 1936, the Mutual Aid Association primarily handled the management of loan repayments.[46] Enforcement of the annual loan repayment did not require external forces like police power. The right to discipline was instead shifted from the police to the peasant collectives. The Mutual Aid Association enforced the collective harvest and sale of crops and the collective payment of loans. Each household in the cooperative was required to submit to its Mutual Aid Association its entire harvest less an amount specified for domestic consumption. The Mutual Aid Association prevented individual households from hoarding their crops. With profits from the collective sale of crops on the market, the Mutual Aid Association paid the portion of loans required of all member households, as well as other collective expenses. Then it distributed the remainder of the profits to each household.[47] The Mutual Aid Association tapped the communal network, becoming a low-cost instrument through which interest payments were collected.

The reinvention of the Mutual Aid Association among the Korean community in Manchuria was similar to what occurred in Korea. During the days of the agricultural revitalization movement in the 1930s in Korea, a peasant community organization called the Hyangyak was installed in villages. Like the Mutual Aid Association in Manchuria, the Hyangyak promoted self-rule of the peasant community in the form of collective farming, collective sale and purchase, and sharing of facilities. In both cases, the idea of communal collectives shaped the coercive dynamics as mutual aids and collective rule. They sought to transform the conflictual relationship between landlords and tenants into a harmonious one. But the Mutual Aid Association and Hyangyak differed. The former in principle consisted of small independent farmers, while the latter comprised tenants, and the former attempted to re-create peasant culture, while the latter, inspired by the Confucian tradition, stressed patriotism and loyalty to the state and ruler.[48]

Embraced in the guise of communal self-rule, the Mutual Aid Association became identified with the management of loan payments. Those who failed to make the required payments were saved from the threat of losing their land but were exposed to collective surveillance over their everyday lives and the processes of production and consumption. Communal self-rule in the cooperatives was a recourse to a classic form of mandatory compulsion, inverting coercion into collective voluntarism. The Mutual Aid Association performed a new collective disciplining of cooperative members. Its loan management activities exposed the meaning of private property ownership, rationality, and self-rule, which heightened the desire of the colonized. Its explicitly expressed objectives were inconsistent with its function.

In sum, colonial sovereignty and subjectivity rested on two simultaneous inversions. One was the communitarian inversion, in which the property relations of small landowners were organized by the principle of collective rule. Its invisible mechanisms of fictive private property ownership, the credit system, and communal associations enabled the colonizer to appropriate the surplus labor of Koreans in the cooperatives. Beyond this function of capital accumulation, these mechanisms, in the name of the utopian ideal of collective rule, organized the everyday lives of producers so that the cooperatives themselves assumed responsibility for the loan payments, even without direct, moment to moment intervention. The formation of colonial subjects was less about instilling entrepreneurship in small farmers than about creating responsible producers capable of paying off loans on schedule. Cooperatives were no longer the utopian ideal of the communitarianism coined by intellectuals. Instead, the utopian ideal was distilled into the essential embodiment of colonial governmentality. The other inversion was the translation of the relationship between the colonizer and the colonized into a financial relationship between creditor and debtor—a transformation that substantiates colonial domination in a capitalist form. Their credit relationship embodied an inversion of this relationship, creating the appearance that the development companies' collection of principal and interest was a legitimate return on their investment. The financial relationship between the colonizer and the colonized socially validated the domination of the colonizer over the labor power of the colonized.

A REPETITION OF THE SOCIAL CRISES

Colonial governmentality encountered its own uncanny reverse. Driven by the machines of finance capital—the fictive private property system and the communal credit system—the colonial policy of the cooperatives promised to install a new regime of production and consumption. The machines instated a new subjectivity and power for both colonizer and colonized; the lived experience of them negotiated the demand to homogenize social relations at the same time as it reinforced hierarchy. When the colonizer and the colonized aspired to create a new spatial configuration of social relations, the hierarchy exposed the ineffectiveness of colonial governmentality. The hierarchy reveals that the cooperatives fostered a repetition of the very social antagonism that communitarian cooperatives were expected to resolve. The supposed resolution in fact produced discontent and exclusion. Displacement of people from land was paradoxically integral to the antinomadic techniques of the cooperatives. This repetition of displacement discloses the temporal dimension of capitalist modernity.

The Axes of Hierarchy

The axes of hierarchy among ethnic and national members were determined by the transfer of land from one group to another, as well as unequal access to loans and different types of loans for the different groups. Loan-making practices were discussed in chapter 4. Here the discussion concentrates on the inequitable transfer of land from Chinese and Korean residents to Japanese and Korean refugees and new immigrants. The preferred sites for the cooperatives were, in principle, state-owned land and wasteland outside of the security areas, land that could be easily acquired and could contribute to agricultural development. However, in the name of enforcing security the development companies dispossessed many owners of their land, sometimes without compensation or with the declaration that the owners could not be identified.[49] The two land surveys conducted by the Manchukuo state in 1932 and 1936 divested many landlords of their lands, as they did in Korea from 1910 to 1918. When landowners were required to present their titles for registration, many of them had no title or multiple landowners had deeds to the same land. It was not unusual for the owners of large tracts to be unknown.[50] In many cases when landowners did not have proper deeds the Manchukuo state pressured them to sell or lease their land rather than establish ownership. Even when compensation was offered, it was so inadequate that landowners equated it with plunder or armed invasion. When cash compensation was offered, the price of the land was set much lower than the market price and payment was often delayed.

For example, the Asia Development Company acquired arable land at 2 won and wasteland at 1 won per ssang in 1935 in Jilin Province, where the market price ranged from 58.4 to 121.4 and 41.4 to 60.7 won, respectively. In 1936, the company paid 8.2 and 2 won for arable and wasteland per ssang, while the market prices were 120 and 40 won each. In the face of this extreme devaluation in the price of land, some owners refused to sell and hid their titles inside the walls of their houses. The Kwantung Army soldiers often used force to complete land transactions, breaking into houses to search for property documents. In one case, the soldiers shot to death all eight members of a family that disobeyed the order to sell its land. In a well-known riot in Tor-yongsan Village in Ŭiran County in March 1934, a group of Chinese peasants attacked a contingent of soldiers to put a stop to land transactions.[51] When the Asia Development Company purchased land in Heilongjiang Province in 1933, it ordered the owners to pick up their payments at a police substation in distant Harbin. The compensation reportedly did not amount to much after the deduction of travel expenses and lodging in Harbin, where the owners had to wait weeks for their payments.[52]

Some Korean refugees and new immigrants were sent to areas where the land had never been farmed. But some of them also settled in areas where Chinese had lived and farmed. Whereas this reversed the previous relationship between the Chinese and Koreans, the groups remained opposed to each other. Prior to the establishment of the Manchukuo state, Koreans' land had been appropriated by the Chinese government and landlords under a nationalist policy that barred foreigners from owning land. During the Manchukuo period, the relationship was reversed, as old and new Korean immigrants were often relocated in areas that the Chinese (and sometimes Koreans) had formerly inhabited. Popular memory recalls that Korean settlers arriving at their assigned land and houses found that rooms and kitchen stoves were still warm, indicating how recently and quickly the former occupants had been driven out. For example, in Hwinam County in Tongbyŏndo in 1938 the Manchuria-Korea Development Company removed Chinese peasants from their land with little compensation and leased it to 210 Korean households that had immigrated from the Cholla Province of Korea. It was said that this process of displacement was like a stone rolling from its place, dislodging other stones from theirs.[53]

Although some Koreans benefited from the settlement policy, others lost their land to Japanese settlers and were displaced. If untilled land with unproven productivity was unsuitable for new Japanese immigrants, whose reaction to the immigration policy was lukewarm, rice fields owned by Koreans were distributed to them. Some Koreans drifted away. Some remained, working as tenants and agricultural laborers for the new Japanese settlers. For instance, when 186 Japanese households settled in Ohinata Village from 1937 to 1941, the Manchuria Development Corporation bought about half of the total rice fields in the village to distribute to the Japanese settlers. This village was widely reported as a model farm in the Japanese media; its Japanese settlers leased to tenants about 60 percent of the land they had been granted, charging rent on the basis of three grades of land quality. Tenants were required to pay taxes and irrigation expenses. Some Koreans were also hired as laborers for rice farming and received monthly wages and in-kind payments such as rubber shoes, tobacco, clothing, and grain.[54] In another village, Japanese settlers rented more than half of the land they had received to the Chinese and Koreans who formerly had owned or cultivated it.[55]

The policy of agrarian cooperatives, in principle, prevented members from subleasing land. Infringement on this principle can be attributed to contingencies in the implementation process, such as Japanese immigrants being fewer than planned, a shortage of farm labor, and the fact that Manchuria's farming conditions (land quality, irrigation, and weather) were unfamiliar to Japanese settlers. But a comparison of the areas that Korean and Japanese immigrants settled suggests that the practice of subleasing may not have been inadvertent. Jones explains that the zone chosen by the Manchuria-Korea Development Company from 1936 to 1939 for the settlement of Korean immigrants overlapped the zone of Japanese settlement.[56] Jones attributed this overlap to the skill of both Koreans and Japanese in rice farming and to the assistance the Koreans provided to the Japanese. According to him, "Koreans were utilized to pave the way for the Japanese colonists by undertaking the initial clearing of the land and preparing the rice fields, while after the arrival of the Japanese, the Koreans served as intermediaries with the Chinese authorities, as labourers and in some cases as tenants of the Japanese. Without Koreans in these roles, the Japanese subsidized agricultural settlements probably never would have taken root."[57] It would seem that as the declared leaders in developing Manchuria the Japanese immigrants benefited most from the chain of settlement and property transfer.

Displacement

In tandem with differences in the size of loans advanced to Koreans and Japanese and the unavailability of loans to Chinese, the transfer of land from one ethnic group to another created a hierarchy among them. This hierarchy exposed the ineffectiveness of colonial governmentality, which sought to rationalize, homogenize, and legalize the social relations of production and exchange. It furthered the displacement of peasants from land in Manchuria—exactly what the colonial power purportedly had sought to eliminate. The relocation of refugees and new immigrants displaced others from land. This chain effect led to the downward mobility of Chinese and some Korean residents. Although it is hard to assess the full impact of displacement, it can be inferred from statistics and anecdotes. Chinese historiography states that tenants and agricultural laborers at the beginning of the Manchukuo period constituted about 26 and 30.3 percent, respectively, of the total rural population, while they increased to 34 and 49 percent in the late Manchukuo period.[58] The burden on tenants also increased, as landlords transferred the cost of land and other taxes to tenants.[59] According to survivors' accounts, they were forced to leave immediately when their land was appropriated for the settlement of immigrants. When they lost their land, they were dispossessed of their homes, which were used to house the new settlers. The only options for the displaced were to become tenants elsewhere, find employment, live in the wilderness, or move to the mountains.

The new chain of displacement was a primary problem for the Korean community as well. The Korean representatives of the Concordia Association perceived displacement as a threat to the political principles of the Manchukuo state. During the national meeting of the Concordia Association in Sinkyŏng (Harbin) from September 30 to October 10, 1939, sixteen Korean representatives argued that the new immigration policy had been undertaken at the expense of Korean residents.[60] The primary cause of social instability was the loss of land to new immigrants. When an area settled by Koreans was chosen as a place for new settlement, Koreans had no choice but to leave the land that they had made productive. A representative at an annual meeting of the Concordia Association outlined the dilemma: if the Chinese could insist on keeping their land, Koreans could not afford to refuse to sell theirs because of their insecure status. While government officials told Koreans to stay until new immigrants arrived, they tended to leave since they had no prospects of regaining their land. In one example, this situation created apprehension among the 560 Korean households in an area, as well as about 70 households who lost their land. Although the official policy was to purchase uncultivated land for new immigrants, county officials did not follow these rulings. Another representative contended that the immigration project should use uncultivated land or offer sufficient compensation if arable land already worked by Koreans was to be purchased. The representatives also appealed to the colonial power to expedite negotiations with landowners so that displaced peasants could farm on wasteland or uncultivated land. In addition, the Korean representatives wished to reduce this displacement by teaching the virtue of saving and patience so peasants would become bound to place, job, and land.

The failure to address the tenancy issues also denotes the ineffectiveness of cooperatives in serving as the national resolution of the social crises in the empire. In 1939, the Korean representatives of the Concordia Association identified the insecure tenancy contract as another major source of displacement. Even when the contract stated a five- or six-year tenancy period, it was not rare for landlords to change tenants after two or three years, contracting with whomever would pay the most rent. The increase in prospective tenants, with more Koreans arriving in Manchuria under the "free" immigration policy or the dispersed program, aggravated this perennial problem. The representatives pointed out the tension between landlords and tenants, with the former possessing legal ownership of land and the latter having some rights to irrigation facilities.

As landlords usually refused to provide any assistance, the tenants themselves paid for the labor and expenses of irrigation and thus kept the rights to it. This allowed them to exercise certain powers, even without the consent of landlords, over the transfer of tenancy. It was said that whoever acquired the water rights would become the real tenants, even without the landlords' approval. Moreover, in some situations landlords did not know who their actual tenants were because the original ones often traded their tenancy along with the water rights. When the colonial power tried to resolve this tenancy conflict with a law extending tenancy contracts to more than five years, the Korean representatives asked that the colonial power move the jurisdiction of tenancy conflicts from civil to criminal law. Although the insecurity of property rights was at the heart of the capitalist system, the Korean representatives did not postulate it as a crisis of capitalism. They articulated these concerns within the ideological domain of the association as problems threatening the unity of Manchukuo and thus the Japanese empire. They believed that if these problems were not adequately addressed they would become a crisis for the Japanese empire and would disrupt the harmonious existence of the community.

Capitalist Politics

The disparity among Koreans precludes attribution of the axes of the hierarchy to national politics. As this chapter has explored, the Manchukuo state, the Government General of Korea, and the Kwantung Army claimed to represent Chinese, Koreans, and Japanese, respectively. These putative nation-state powers competed against one another in pursuing their own interests and claimed to speak for the identities and interests of their national subjects. As a result, the policies designed for Japanese settlement took precedence over those for Korean settlement. The hierarchical transfer of land and the disparity among Chinese, Koreans, and Japanese in terms of the benefits associated with their cooperatives might reflect the unequal power among

TABLE 6. Land Acquired by the Manchukuo State and the Manchuria Development
Corporation (in ching)

	Total land	Paid land	Unpaid land
Manchukuo State	8,306,000	4,875,754	3,430,246
Manchuria Development Corporation	11,720,000	5,925,176	5,794,824
Total	20,026,000 (100%)	10,800,930 (54%)	9,225,070 (46%)

Source: *Kunan douzheng shisinian*, 2:251.

the nation-state powers. However, the hierarchical transfer of land, which
pitted some Korean residents against other Korean residents and new immigrants, demonstrates that the hierarchy did not result exclusively from national politics.

The hierarchy must be situated within the context of the process of capitalist expansion. Although the development companies sold land to borrowers at prices higher than the original purchase price, capitalist dynamics exceeded this profit-making strategy. Capitalist dynamics are instead marked
by a structural contradiction in which capital expansion simultaneously
homogenizes and differentiates social relations. Japanese policymakers
pledged to end the displacement of peasants in Korea, Japan, and Manchuria
through the rational allocation of people and land. This spatial reorganization of the economies required that the price of land, wages, and living expenses in Manchuria be substantially less than in Korea and Japan. In other
words, it was because of Manchuria's comparative advantage that destitute
peasants from Korea and Japan would become productive labor in Manchuria, living and farming more cheaply there than in Korea and Japan. This formula, which David Harvey calls the outward "spatial fix" of a capitalist crisis,
required that regional disparities between Korea, Japan, and Manchuria be
created and reproduced.

The colonial policy of the cooperatives did not, in fact, increase the price
of land in Manchuria during this period of agricultural development. Instead, the policy dramatically devalued land through forceful appropriation
and inadequate compensation. For instance, the proportions of paid and unpaid land were almost equivalent for land acquired by the Manchukuo state
and the Manchuria Development Corporation (see table 6). The process of

capital accumulation by means of devaluation of assets authorized a colonial mode of capitalist expansion. Farming and household costs in Manchuria were kept lower than in Korea and Japan by maintaining cheaper prices for land and crops and eliminating usury and the merchants' monopoly of markets. The hierarchical transfer of land was a condition for capitalist expansion. And the disparity between loans made to Japanese and Korean settlers in Manchuria resulted from the practice of making larger loans to Japanese on the grounds that they had higher and more expensive standards of living.

CONCLUSION: A PARADOX OF OSMOSIS
AND COLONIAL FASCISM

The formation of the agricultural cooperatives was a new mechanism in the politics of osmosis or the corporeal process in which the movement of people across borders engendered the national and capitalist expansion of the Japanese empire. The colonial power saw redistribution of the peasant population as a way to resolve social crises in Japan, Korea, and Manchuria and cultivate the organic unity of these places. Two distinct logics characterize this politics of osmosis: the logic of nation-state formation, which utilized nation-states as building blocks of the empire; and the logic of capital, which simultaneously homogenized and differentiated national economies within the empire. Although the colonial discourse of osmosis posits the homology of national and capitalist integration, the politics of osmosis was caught in a paradox. Chapters 4 and 5 explicated this paradox in terms of the tension between the two processes.

Chapter 4 tracked the limits of capitalist development in Manchuria imposed by the dynamics of nation-state formation. Colonial authorities (the Government General of Korea, the Kwantung Army, and the Manchukuo state) rationalized the immigration process through detailed planning of the relocation of residents and new immigrants. Yet their competing national interests compromised the effectiveness of such policies. Chapter 5 traced the other process of osmotic politics — the ways in which capitalist development simultaneously facilitated and constrained nation-state formation in Manchuria. Contradictory forces were central to the process of capitalist development. On the one hand, the cooperatives homogenized the social lives of Koreans, Chinese, and Japanese. The institutional means of finance capital, fictive private property ownership, and the communal credit system rationalized governmentality, constructed national subjects, and regulated the processes of production and consumption. This homogenization corresponded to the Manchukuo state's ideology of harmony and cooperation among various ethnic and national groups and the Japanese colonial ideology of a unified empire. On the other hand, the hierarchy among Koreans and between ethnic and national groups in terms of the benefits of the cooperatives was a spectacular manifestation of the capitalist mechanism that differentiated them. In accordance with the requirements of capitalist expansion, the Government General of Korea, the Manchukuo state, and the Kwantung Army created and maintained differences among Koreans, Chinese, and Japanese in terms of the costs of living, farming, and relocating.

The politics of osmosis during the Manchukuo period stood in dialectical relation to national and colonial dreams of capitalist expansion. The colonial dream was twofold: the colonizer imagined pacifying all social crises in Korea, Japan, and Manchuria simultaneously through the spatial relocation of the peasants into the cooperatives; and the colonized imagined that they would establish their sovereignty over their own labor. Within the framework of this dream, cooperatives remained as a social alternative to the capitalist model exemplified by the putative Western experience. Accompanying the colonial dream was a national dream. Envisaging the cooperatives as an alternative capitalism was based on the problematic assumption that the national economy (Japanese, Korean or Manchurian) could be insulated from the world capitalist economy and that capitalist modernization could develop independent of mediation.

In actuality, the colonial and national dream of an unmediated economy was transmuted into an instance of control by the fascist state, which equipped itself with new coercive mechanisms that produced new forms of subjectivity. The relocation of peasants in the cooperatives—the spatial fix—did not resolve the crises but merely deferred them by transferring the problem of the displacement of producers to a new frontier. The colonized were driven into a newly invented communal regime of production and exchange, where the credit system and communal associations determined their socially necessary labor. The communitarian inversion of fascist power was accomplished through this historically specific form of capitalism (finance capital, the fictive property system, and the communal credit system).

Agrarian communitarianism entered a partnership with fascist state powers in Japan and elsewhere in the first half of the twentieth century, which sought to offer a new capitalist future. This alternative capitalism was invented as a resolution of the crises and claimed to eliminate all contradictions in the capitalist system. As intellectuals and policymakers sought to overcome the commodification and alienation that accompanied industrialization, communitarianism as a negation of commodification and alienation emerged as an alternative. Collective rule by small cultivators was the main thrust of the agrarian communitarianism that emerged as a political discourse in Japan and Korea. This form of alternative capitalism was imposed in the new colony of Manchuria to resolve the crises in Japan and Korea. Agrarian cooperatives embodied the desire to overcome the indeterminate effects of global capitalism and thus imagined a communal life in a form compatible with colonial capitalism. The cooperatives combined two contradictory goals of colonial capitalism: to sustain the basis of capital accumulation and to animate the support of these very producers through social programs, invoking their new national and social consciousness as would-be property owners. Peasants from Korea and Japan, as well as Korean residents in Manchuria, were offered the momentary promise of landownership, which would establish their sovereignty over their labor. Colonial power embedded its fascist power in the construction of this new social relation.

The agrarian cooperatives situated the osmotic process and colonial fascism within a politics of time. When cooperatives were provided with a rationale to modernize the process of production and market exchange and create safeguards from commodity markets, they reformulated the concepts of premodern and modern. They refuted the linear conception of history that understood social change in terms of the progression from feudalism to capitalism and the diffusion of modernity from city to countryside. Instead, the cooperatives were vested in a utopian future of capitalism without primitive accumulation. At the same time that it fed on this national and colonial dream, the accelerated capitalist transformation of Manchuria repeated the displacement of peasants from land. Bewildered by dreams intertwined with actuality, the lived experience of the repetition was as much phantasmagoric as historically specific.

CHAPTER SIX

The Specter of the Social:

Socialist Internationalism,

the Minsaengdan,

and North Korea

As discussed in the preceding chapters, the logic of capital and the logic of nation converged as two distinct yet intertwined principles to fashion uneven social relations in different regions of Manchuria. The Zhang Zuolin government, the Government General of Korea, and the Manchukuo government each inscribed its national power in the social sphere. In each case, the production of national subjects embodied the desire of migrant peasants to own land and improve their social lives. Nation formation was predicated on the promise of alternative social relations of production and market exchange. The private property system was the bastion of national politics within both the Japanese and Chinese political frameworks. The resulting social relations were fragmented and led to regional and national disparities. Prior to 1932, Koreans were divided over national identification and self-rule in Kando; in other parts of Manchuria, they were pitted against the Chinese. Through their integration into agricultural cooperatives after 1932, Koreans, Japanese, and Chinese developed a new hierarchy, which structured the exchange and distribution of land.

If socialist politics were to succeed in mobilizing the masses, it would have to provide alternative arrangements of social relations that would be capable of severing the ties between peasants and the different national and colonial powers. The viability of new social relations hinged on the simultaneous critique of the intertwined logics of capital and nation that had organized social relations. The unity of Korean and Chinese peasants would arise only through discrete struggles capable of addressing their own fragmented and antagonistic relations. The unity would not be predetermined but was forged during the struggle. The resulting types of revolutionary subjects should have remained largely indeterminate. However, Korean and Chinese communists conceived revolutionary subjects in Manchuria as national and class subjects whose experiences were presumed to be essentially homogeneous. As the communists espoused nationalism, socialist internationalism in Manchuria became an aggregation of national politics rather than a global politics capable of challenging the capitalist relations of production and exchange. When Korean and Chinese communists undertook standard forms of class or anti-Japanese struggle, they construed social classes of peasants as national subjects bound to a nation-state. For instance, Korean migrants, regardless of their origins and relations with the Northeast government and Japan, were defined either as Korean nationals whose a priori concern was the liberation of Korea or as a minority that was expected to share the interests of the Chinese majority in engaging in an anti-Japanese revolutionary struggle. This conception of socialist internationalism was not equipped to tackle the disparate social relations within and between Korean and Chinese peasant groups, which required diverse and fragmented struggles.

Framed as spies of the Minsaengdan, a pro-Japanese organization, between 1931 and 1936 Korean communists were purged from the Eastern Manchurian Special Committee of the Chinese Communist Party (CCP) and its organizations. Existing historical studies attribute the purge to scapegoating and discrimination against Korean communists by Chinese communists and to a Chinese nationalism that subordinated the tasks of the Korean revolution to those of the Chinese revolution.[1] According to a recent study, the scapegoating of Koreans occurred in a context in which not just Korean communists were increasingly skeptical of the swiftness of making revolution but also the Korean masses were disenchanted with the radical reforms enforced in the liberated guerrilla bases.[2] My contribution to the literature lies in the double claim that Korean nationalism is just as liable as Chinese nationalism and that the purge signified a new production of the social. I explore both Chinese and Korean nationalism and, more importantly, their constitutive effects on the reorganization of peasants' social relations. The victimization of Koreans in the purge was the product of a particular conception of the social that was formulated by socialist internationalism and shared by Korean and Chinese communists. The purge can be understood as an attempt to create homogeneous subjects and a singular direction for the socialist revolution, when ontological unity was impossible. The purge was a futile attempt to reconcile the vastly uneven character of Manchuria and the illusory prospect of a unitary collective social. When Minsaengdan spies were condemned as pursuers of Korean self-rule in Manchuria, the politics of self-rule was grounded in local social conditions in Manchuria that were irreducible to the larger objectives of national socialist liberation in China and Korea.

The specter of the Minsaengdan in the purge suggests that the surplus of social relations could not be contained by the nationalist prescription for the social. The specter did not necessarily refer to the Koreans' assistance to Japanese imperialism and the mounting threats from Japanese armies. It was, rather, social antagonism that continued to haunt those who were perplexed by the persistent gap between their nationalist programs and the actual social conditions of the people they represented. The purge occurred mainly in Kando, where anticolonial revolutionary movements involved the masses (mainly Korean peasants) beyond guerrilla actions. It took place when the expansion of the revolutionary forces was at its peak. The spatio-temporality of the purge suggests that it concerned not merely the nationalist conflicts among communists but also the revolutionary tasks of mobilizing the masses and transforming social relations. In some ways, alleged Minsaengdan spies were comparable to "wandering Jews," an external enemy of society in the sense that both Jews and Minsaengdan members were "the ulti-mate guarantee" of social unity. According to Žižek, "what happens in the passage from the position of strict class struggle to Fascist anti-Semitism is not just a simple replacement of one figure of the enemy (the bourgeoi-sie, the ruling class) with another (the Jews), but the shift from the logic of antagonism which makes Society impossible to the logic of external Enemy which guarantees Society's consistency." [3] Similarly the drive to purge Kore-ans did not simply replace the class and national struggle of Koreans against the landlords, bourgeoisie, and Japanese with a new enemy, the Minsaeng-dan. It instead naturalized the seamless unity of Korean and Chinese com-munists, Korean peasants and the CCP, and Korean and Chinese peasants.

This chapter begins by exploring the development of the Minsaengdan and the anti-Minsaengdan struggle. It then situates Manchuria and Koreans within the disparate national politics of the CCP and Korean communists and delineates the significance of the anti-Minsaengdan struggle for the revo-lutionary politics of constructing new social relations. Finally, I explore the implications of the purge for the North Korean revolution during the post-colonial period, which invoked the Manchurian struggle as its origin.

THE MINSAENGDAN

The Minsaengdan (Minshengtuan in Chinese) existed from January to July of 1932.[4] Following the initiatives of a few visitors from Korea, who observed the vulnerable conditions of Koreans in Manchuria, about one thousand people joined together to form the Minsaengdan. It existed in an interstitial moment between the Manchuria Incident in September 1931 and the establishment of the Manchukuo state in March 1932. Like other Korean self-rule movements in Kando, it also saw the acquisition of national membership and the improvement of the social lives of peasants as the foundation of self-rule for Koreans. The Minsaengdan replaced the Association to Facilitate Self-Rule (Chach'i ch'okchin wiwŏnhoe), which had abandoned its support for the Northeast government as local governments submitted to Japanese power after the Manchuria Incident.[5] At its inaugural meeting on February 15, 1932, the Minsaengdan declared its main objectives: the acquisition of national membership (kongmin'gwŏn in Korean, gongminqun in Chinese) in the imminent state in Manchuria and Mongolia; the establishment of an autonomous area for Koreans; and the promotion of plans for economic development, including the creation of independent farmers, the operation of farmers' unions, and the expansion of credit and financial organizations. The Minsaengdan fruitlessly requested of the Manchukuo state that the Kando Administration be placed under the jurisdiction of the Manchukuo state, not the Jilin provincial government; that Koreans be appointed to serve in the Kando Administration, reflecting the fact that Koreans were the largest ethnic group in Kando; and that local residents run administrative units below the county level.

The genealogy of the Minsaengdan demonstrates that Korean self-rule was at the heart of the issue. At first, it received support from the Japanese Ministry of Foreign Affairs, the Japanese consulates in Manchuria, and the Government General of Korea. This momentary support was in alignment with the Japanese policy adopted in the aftermath of the Manchuria Incident. Japan bolstered the self-determination movements of the Mongols and Chinese in order to separate them from both the Nanjing government and the Northeast government headed by Zhang Xueliang. Japan's support for self-determination for Koreans was a colonial strategy meant to separate them from the competing national powers in Manchuria. The most ardent supporter of the Korean self-rule movement in Manchuria was the Government General of Korea. In an unsolicited article in the *Kandosinbo*, a Kando newspaper published in both Korean and Japanese, the Government General of Korea declared Kando to be part of Korea and asserted its right to defend the interests of Koreans. The head of the police department of the Government General of Korea expressed his enthusiasm: "As an extension of Korea, Kando should be designated as a special administrative area with a governmental organization similar to that of Korea, and it would suit both the emergent state of Manchuria-Mongolia and the Government General of Korea if an administration similar to that of Korea were to be established in Kando."[6] The Government General of Korea planned to organize a Committee on Manchuria-Mongolia to establish administrative units, dispatch Korean officials, and support the emigration of Koreans to Manchuria. It expected to rule over the Koreans in Kando rather than placing them under the sovereignty of the prospective state of Manchuria and Mongolia. Upon the objection of the Kwantung Army, however, the Government General of Korea quickly withdrew its support for Korean self-rule.

The Japanese consul general in Kando was more cautious than the Government General of Korea about the idea that Kando would be part of Korea. The Japanese consul general registered his reservations about the initial proposal of the Minsaengdan organizers, especially their promotion of a "free world for Koreans," which implied advocacy for the independence of Korea and Kando. The consul general gave his approval to the Minsaengdan only after its founders twice revised its statements on self-rule. In the latest measure, the idea of Kando and Manchuria as part of Korea was dropped, while such catchphrases as *self-defense, independence,* and *autonomy* continued to be emblematic. Emphasis was added to the promotion by the Minsaengdan of the "industrialization" of Korean life and the restriction of such activities to Kando. The stated objectives of the Minsaengdan underwent further revision in March 1932. This time the Japanese Ministry of Foreign Affairs opposed Korean self-rule in Kando. It feared that the creation of a special government for Korean self-rule in Kando would separate it from the newly created Manchukuo state. In response, the Minsaengdan organizers changed their goals from the promotion of "a special administrative organization led by 400,000 Koreans in Kando," to "a specific district for self-rule" (*t'ukpyŏl chach'i kuyŏk* in Korean, *tebie zizhi quyu sheding* in Chinese), to "a special area for self-rule" (*chach'iryŏng* in Korean, *zizhiling* in Chinese), and finally to a "special administrative unit" (t'ukpyŏl haengjŏnggu in Korean, tebie xingzhengqu in Chinese) under the jurisdiction of the Manchukuo state. To allay Manchukuo's misgivings, the proposal underscored the harmonious relations between Koreans and Chinese.

The issue of Korean self-rule received intermittent endorsement from Japan until it was finally rejected in May 1932. The guidelines of the Kwantung Army on the security and governing of Kando that were issued on April 3, 1932, emphasized a division of labor between the Kwantung Army and the Government General of Korea and its Korean Army. The Kwantung Army would oversee administration and appoint officials and advisers, taking recommendations from the Government General of Korea. The Government General of Korea would maintain security and supervise local officials and associations. The guidelines neither mentioned self-rule of Koreans nor included any plan to create a special administrative unit in Kando. On April 7, 1932, the head of the Japanese Ministry of Foreign Affairs delegated the issue of Korean self-rule to the jurisdiction of the Jilin Province of the Manchukuo state and not to the Government General of Korea. However, a month later it ordered the Minsaengdan to terminate the self-rule movement. Until it closed its offices in July 1932, the Minsaengdan's main activities were limited to welcoming Japanese armies to Manchuria and training Koreans for the self-defense corps. Even the latter lasted only ten days, as the Manchukuo took over the supervision of the local defense corps. But even after its formal dissolution in October 1932, the Minsaengdan wreaked havoc in communist politics in Kando.

THE ANTI-MINSAENGDAN STRUGGLE

Over time, tension developed between the Minsaengdan and the CCP. The Minsaengdan mobilized conservative Koreans in opposition to communism, while the CCP launched critiques of the Minsaengdan. The CCP asserted that the Minsaengdan was led by Korean landlords, rich peasants, usurers, and merchants. Under the instructions of the Manchuria Provincial Committee of the CCP, the Eastern Manchurian Special Committee of the CCP, which comprised four counties in Kando and two others (Ando and Tonhwa), engaged in a struggle against the infiltrated remnants of the Minsaengdan from October 1932 to February 1936. The Manchurian Provincial Committee (MPC) translated the anti-Minsaengdan struggle (hereafter "the struggle") into a total war against members of its own party and its anti-Japanese organizations. As the MPC traced the Minsaengdan's infiltration into every unit of the CCP in Kando, it implicated almost everyone as Minsaengdan spies. A party member dispatched by the MPC to the Eastern Manchurian Special Committee in 1934 observed:

> The Minsaengdan organization has used our [CCP] organization to develop its own organization, appropriated our communications systems to develop their own communication systems, and exploited our own patrol system to detect our struggle against them. Therefore, our committee has become their committee. Our county committees, district committees, and branches have become their county committees, district committees, and their branches, respectively. The Minsaengdan members in East Manchuria [Kando] comprise at least 50 or 60 percent of all our party, party organizations, people's revolutionary armies, and various mass organizations.[7]

As the CCP turned the struggle into a mass movement, the investigation and prosecution spread from top cadres to rank and file members of the Eastern Manchurian Special Committee and from commanders of guerrilla armies to almost everyone, including the elderly, women, and children in guerrilla bases. In late 1934, a representative from the MPC observed that the guerrilla bases of the CCP continued to serve as breeding grounds for the Minsaengdan, even after one year of successful anti-Minsaengdan struggle. In his estimate, on average Minsaengdan members had infiltrated about 70 percent of the party and its mass organizations and about 50 percent of the youth corps.[8] It took almost two years for the MPC to recognize the farce in such an uncanny assessment: In mid-1935, a member of the MPC pointed out the great exaggeration of the anti-Minsaengdan struggle, saying that if Minsaengdan members constituted more than 60 or 70 percent of people in guerrilla bases in Kando, Japan must have already destroyed them.[9]

The three-year struggle against the Minsaengdan spies curtailed the representation of Koreans in the Eastern Manchurian Special Committee of the CCP. Before the struggle in April 1931, the Eastern Manchurian Special Committee in Kando had 636 members, all but 18 of whom were Korean.[10] When the membership of the Eastern Manchurian Special Committee expanded to 965 members in September 1933, the representation of Koreans also increased from 96.5 to 97.9 percent. This tendency also prevailed in other communist organizations, such as the Communist Youth Organization, in which Koreans comprised the majority. Estimates of the number of Koreans purged during the struggle range from several hundred to thousands. Fear induced more than 2,000 (all Korean except for 47) to defect to the Japanese armies between September 1934 and March 1936. When the Eastern Manchurian Special Committee regrouped its revolutionary army in May 1935, the number of enlisted Koreans had shrunk significantly at the levels of both the leadership and the rank and file. Only two Koreans, including Kim Il Sung, who emerged as the leader of North Korea in the postliberation period, remained in the leadership in a total of eight army units. Koreans comprised only 50 to 60 percent of the total of 1,200 rank and file members.[11]

The purge of Koreans was equivalent to the CCP's destruction of its own organization in Kando. The weakening of the revolutionary struggle in Kando threatened the CCP's capacity in Manchuria as a whole because Koreans constituted the backbone of the Eastern Manchurian Special Committee, the best-organized unit in Kando. The three-year witch-hunt against the Minsaengdan, together with Japan's pacification program and the establishment of agrarian cooperatives, dissolved the guerrilla bases in Kando. Lacking help from Korean peasants, the guerrilla armies could not purchase clothing, food, or other necessities. One witness dramatized the effects of the struggle: "Before it was easy for us to purchase anything, but we did not have enough money; now, we have money but lack places to purchase goods. Before, we had plenty of people but not guns; now we have a lot of guns without people. Before, we usually stayed in villages, but now we are always moving in the mountains [to escape the Japanese]. Before, we easily knew the whereabouts of our enemies, but now our enemies easily learn of our activities."[12]

The struggle battled with the specter of the Minsaengdan after its formal dissolution. Lee Chong Sik attributes the struggle to the scapegoating of Koreans for the failure of mass mobilization. When the Eastern Manchurian Special Committee organized a red army and created soviet governments in 1932, it sought to recruit Chinese soldiers that had deserted pro-Manchukuo leaders and to mobilize the masses. But many Chinese were estranged from the radical policies of the Chinese communists toward landlords and the predominantly Korean makeup of the committee. When Japanese pacification forced the communists to retreat into the hinterlands in Yon'gil, Wangch'ong, and Hunch'un Counties, they organized five soviet districts, encompassing 4,100 persons, between November 1932 and February 1933. But the soviet districts served little more than refugees from Japanese suppression and deserters from the agricultural cooperatives. The soviet governments also suffered from the increasing desertion of its members. In these contexts,

Korean communists were accused of being Minsaengdan spies and faction-alists, whose senseless infighting and secessions undermined organizational unity and weakened its defense against Japanese infiltration.[13]

In perhaps the most comprehensive study of the struggle to date, Kim Songho, a Korean Chinese scholar, explores two important features of the struggle: its concentration in East Manchuria and the participation of Kore-ans. Kim credits these features to characteristics of the Chinese communist leadership, the ethnic and national composition of the pro-Japanese group, and, more importantly, the ethnic and national prejudices of Koreans and Chinese toward each other. The struggle did not take place in South Man-churia, not only because Koreans were too few to be suspected of being pro-Japanese. It was because the Chinese communist leadership espoused more internationalism than in East Manchuria and integrated the Koreans more closely.[14] In East Manchuria, Koreans were in the majority and had long been suspected of spearheading Japanese imperialism. Furthermore, even where Korean communists and the revolutionary masses constituted the backbone of Chinese communist organizations, their Chinese comrades discriminated against them. National differences, such as those of language and customs, inhibited communication between Koreans and Chinese in the revolution-ary forces. The difficulty of translating Chinese documents into Korean de-layed the execution of MPC orders by Koreans and fueled suspicions about their loyalty. The inability of Korean revolutionaries to speak fluent Chinese and their everyday customs, including their eating habits, discouraged them from working closely with their Chinese comrades in guerrilla armies, where they lived, slept, and ate in close proximity. When the penetration of the Min-saengdan members into communist organizations was feared, the customs of Koreans fanned the mistrust of them. In order to shed their inferior posi-tion as foreigners, Korean revolutionaries earnestly took part in the struggle.

South Korean scholars Lee Chongsŏk and Shin Chubaek contend that the struggle originated with Chinese nationalism, which is a more profound and less circumstantial origin than scapegoating and cultural prejudices. Chi-nese nationalism pitted the goal of a Chinese revolution against the goal of liberating Korea and making a revolution there. According to Lee Chongsŏk, nationalism led Chinese communists to interpret the initiative of Koreans for self-rule as a move intended to estrange Koreans from the Chinese revo-lution.[15] For Shin Chubaek, Chinese nationalism prompted Chinese commu-nists to regard Korean communists' desire to liberate Korea as an illustration of Korean nationalism and thus a violation of socialist internationalism.[16]

The following discussion further explores the Chinese and Korean forms of nationalism, particularly their composition and the pitfalls they encountered in prescribing new social relations for Manchuria.

When the Chinese communists censured the Minsaengdan infiltrators for promoting Korean self-rule, self-rule epitomized the concerns for the local social conditions of Korean peasants. Various self-rule movements in Kando, including the one promoted by the Minsaengdan, promised secure landownership and alternative models of production and market exchange. In other words, social concerns of cultivation and landownership shaped the politics of Korean peasants. The initiatives for self-rule differed from the Wilsonian notion of self-determination endorsed by the CCP and the MPC. While the Korean self-rule movement tackled the social conditions of Korean peasants, the Chinese communists merely pursued political independence. The Chinese communists' policy of Korean self-determination pledged to join the struggle for the construction of an independent Korean state. This policy of Korean self-determination portrayed Koreans of Manchuria as ethnic minorities or exiles under the Japanese thumb. It obscured the enduring social ties between Korean peasants and Japanese capital, which produced complex social relations between Koreans and Chinese.

In the CCP's anti-Minsaengdan struggle, self-rule became a signifier of the social that both Chinese and Korean communists could not articulate. The approaches of Chinese and Korean communists were inseparable from their disparate nationalisms, which cast Manchuria as an extension of Korea and part of China, respectively. Their approaches prevented them from understanding the regional and national disparities in social relations in Manchuria. Condemnation of self-rule externalized the inability of the communists to address the social reality of Kando. The purge allowed both the Chinese and Korean communists to impose homogeneity on Chinese and Korean peasants, whose experiences were fragmented by their differing ties with the Northeast government and Japanese power.

CHINESE COMMUNIST NATIONALISM

Five years after the Chinese Communist Party was formed, it established the Manchurian Provincial Committee in October 1927 in Shenyang in South Manchuria. The MPC oversaw Chinese communist organizations and activities in Manchuria. The creation of the MPC marked an attempt by the CCP to facilitate communications with local cadres and strengthen communist organizations in Manchuria. However, it was not until Korean communists in Manchuria joined the CCP in early 1930 that the communist forces experienced a concrete expansion. In 1927, the Chinese communist forces in Manchuria amounted to a mere 173 cadres; they had a limited capacity to organize and enlist support from workers and peasants. According to one Japanese estimate, CCP members in Kando numbered 3,800 Koreans and 150 Chinese.[17] The admission of Korean communists enhanced the mass basis of the CCP. Korean communists, who comprised more than 90 percent of the communist constituency, led peasant riots in the cities and launched attacks on Japanese facilities.

This large component of Koreans in the Chinese communist forces in Manchuria posed problems for the MPC, whose Chinese nationalism came into focus in the late 1920s. A main component of the MPC's nationalism included the assimilation of Manchuria and Koreans into the Chinese nation. Historical studies of communist activities in Manchuria have mainly focused on the link between Manchuria and China, taking it as the indicator of the shifting hierarchy of the MPC, the CCP, and the Comintern.[18] Prior to 1933, a radical policy of class struggle, called the Li Li-san line, refuted the previous position of the CCP, which, in the Sixth Congress of the Comintern in June 1928, for example, accepted conditions in China such as the putatively underdeveloped economy and the advance of Japanese imperialism in Manchuria. A directive of the CCP in January 1933 replaced class struggle with the anti-Japanese struggle in order to address the specific conditions in Manchuria. I situate the variant representations of Manchuria within the formations of Chinese nationalism, which shaped the relations of Korean and Chinese communists.

China, Manchuria, and Koreans Prior to 1933

The Li Li-san line of the CCP policies promulgated a uniform policy of anticapitalist class struggle across China, especially after October 1929. It identified the Kuomintang landlords and rich peasants as the enemies of the revolution and vowed to abolish private property. After attacks by the Kuomintang, the CCP's Central Committee in Shanghai prioritized the anti-Kuomintang struggle over anti-Japanese actions. This policy was in accord with the Comintern's policy not to provoke Japan. Before Japan's occupation of Manchuria in 1931, the Comintern pursued compliant diplomatic relations with Japan in order to maintain Japanese recognition of the Soviet Union and retain Soviet control over the Chinese Eastern Railway. The Li Li-san line was soon criticized for its failure to accommodate both the anti-Japanese struggle and the desire of peasants for landownership. Even after the CCP formally repudiated the Li Li-san line in January 1931, class struggle remained the primary focus of the CCP until 1932.

The literature on communism in Manchuria describes the recurring tensions between the CCP and the MPC over the policy on Manchuria.[19] The standard revolutionary policy led the CCP to suppress the historical specificity of Manchuria. As the MPC failed to receive the support of the CCP in accommodating the critique of Japanese imperialism in its revolutionary struggle, it tended to take sides with the Comintern, which increasingly clashed with Japanese imperial power in the late 1920s. However, such a view of communist politics in Manchuria ignores the MPC's specific understanding of advanced Japanese imperialism as a unique feature in Manchuria. In actuality, the MPC representatives continued to reflect on Manchurian conditions but without developing acute tension over the CCP's policy. For the MPC comprehended Manchurian conditions within the framework of class struggle. In its opinion, class contradictions coincided with national contradictions in Manchuria. Japanese imperialism had furthered a catastrophic capitalist crisis in Manchuria, teaming up with the Chinese bourgeoisie and the warlords to exploit peasants and workers. Zhang Zuolin and his close associates were the largest landlords and the most powerful merchants. The official capital owned by the Northeast government constituted the dominant capital in Manchuria. This portrayal of Manchuria lumped together all landlords, warlords, the national bourgeoisie, and Japanese imperialists as the common enemies of workers, tenants, and farm laborers.

In particular, the MPC identified the worldwide capitalist economic depression as the primary cause of the economic crisis in Manchuria. The value of currencies plummeted, while the export of agricultural products, including crops and processed foods, also plunged, reducing peasant incomes. Railway companies and other transportation industries also experienced a slump, which led to layoffs and wage cuts for workers. Peasants suffered under the burden of various taxes and exploitation by landlords, such as increased rents and high interest on loans. Warlords, the national bourgeoisie, and Japanese imperialism compounded the misery of the masses. The Northeast government, which was under the control of warlords, had a variety of methods for stealing land from cultivators, such as intentionally mismeasuring it and setting unrealistic requirements for documenting ownership. The Northeast government and the national bourgeoisie also collaborated with Japanese imperial powers in exploiting peasants, workers, and small merchants. Japanese merchants controlled about 60 percent of all retail stores. Japanese also operated the South Manchuria Railway, mines, and various factories, while continuing to amass agricultural lands.[20] With this assessment of Manchuria's economic conditions, the MPC lumped capitalists, landlords, and bourgeoisie into the category of class enemies of the peasants and workers.

This MPC evaluation of Manchuria converged with the CCP policy of class struggle but with differences on the prognosis of the vanguard of the revolution. For the CCP, workers in North Manchuria, especially those in and near Harbin, should be the vanguard, because North Manchuria employed more workers in railways, mines, and factories than anywhere else. For the MPC, as its April 1930 meeting report suggests, workers on the South Manchuria Railway and in the ports, mines, and artillery factories of South Manchuria had the greatest capacity to lead the revolution in Manchuria. The MPC diagnosis is derived from the observation that workers in North Manchuria concentrated on economic struggle rather than political mobilization, while those in South Manchuria experienced more oppression due to the fact that South Manchuria was the stronghold of warlords and the Japanese.[21]

Both the CCP and the MPC glossed over the fact that Koreans in East Manchuria were leading the revolutionary struggle. Organized by the Comintern principle of one party in one country, the CCP directed the Koreans of Manchuria to join the CCP. While Korean communists had led various organizations before joining the CCP, the CCP refused to enlist them as a group that could hold representative power within it. The MPC demanded that the Korean communists abandon their struggle to liberate Korea and instead commit to the Chinese revolution. This clearly demonstrates the homogenizing force of the Chinese nationalism adopted by the MPC and CCP.

The MPC attempted to address the unequal social relations of Korean and Chinese peasants within Chinese nationalism. This attempt was lodged in a particular comparative framework that recognized distinctions between Korean and Chinese peasants only in terms of their quantitative differences. Compared to their Chinese counterparts, Korean peasants were seen to be suffering more oppression from landlords, the warlord government, and Japanese imperialism. Koreans were also said to be exploited by pro-Japanese organizations such as the Korean Association and the Association to Protect Koreans. The MPC thus called on Koreans to join the class struggle, which sought to seize land from the landlords and pro-Japanese landowners. Appropriated land was distributed to the families of guerrillas, tenants, and farm laborers based on the amount of labor power per household (men between fifteen and fifty years of age and women between fifteen and forty counted as one point). The soviet governments in liberated zones owned the confiscated land and outlawed land transactions and other market trading.

Other qualitative differences between Koreans and Chinese identified by the MPC included types of farming, cultural differences, and relations with the Northeast government. According to the reports of the MPC, Korean peasants congregated along rivers because rice farming requires a good water supply, while Chinese peasants engaged in dry farming. Koreans and Chinese lacked a common means of communication due to their different languages. In addition, the hostility between Koreans and Chinese ran more deeply than cultural differences. The Northeast government had long accused Koreans of acting as the vanguard for Japanese encroachment. The Kuomingtang's attack on Koreans in the aftermath of the Manchuria Incident reflected this sentiment. Japanese tactics further aggravated the antagonism between Koreans and Chinese. For instance, some Japanese forces wore Korean-style clothing during the occupation of Manchuria in 1931.[22] When the Northeast government in most parts of Manchuria banned Korean residence and landownership in its effort to stop Japanese encroachment, the MPC pledged to protect Koreans from the threat of eviction.[23]

This series of MPC assessments on ethnic relations fell short of understanding the historical specificity of Manchuria. While the MPC presupposed a priori class identities that Korean peasants shared with Chinese counterparts, each Korean and Chinese peasant was, in reality, tied to the Japanese and the Northeast government, respectively, through similar social programs. With the promise of improving the social lives of Koreans, Japanese colonizers mobilized Korean peasants by offering loans and other economic subsidies. Similarly, the Northeast warlord government and the Chinese bourgeoisie provided similar services to Chinese peasants to obtain their support. These practices of the imperialists and the Northeast warlord government blurred the boundary between landowners and poor peasants. The class struggle, which aimed to abolish private property, was unlikely to attract the support of poor peasants. The class struggle alone would not break the peasants' ties to the enemies of the Chinese revolution. Unless they could offer alternatives to loans and other social provisions, the Chinese communists could not appeal to Korean peasants.

The MPC constructed Koreans as a "minority" and advocated their right to pursue self-determination. As this policy was similar to the Leninist strategy that supported the self-determination of ethnic groups in the Russian empire so as to facilitate its disintegration, this MPC policy served the similar purpose of separating Koreans from the Japanese. In February 1932, the Eastern Manchurian Special Committee under the MPC presented self-determination as an alternative to the national self-rule (*minzu zizhi* in Chinese) long pursued by Koreans, including the Minsaengdan movement: "How could the Minsaengdan secure freedom and housing for people by promising self-defense, autonomy, and independence? It is absurd to rescue millions of the unemployed in capitalist society with an economic security program (*chanye quebaohui* in Chinese). . . . Together with the Chinese revolution, the CCP's policy of self-determination of the minorities will provide freedom and equality to all Koreans in Manchuria."[24]

Understanding the national question as a political question, the MPC policy of promoting self-determination supported the construction of a new independent state in Korea. A problem was that there was no intrinsic link between self-determination of ethnic groups and their support for socialist revolution: the self-determination of each ethnic group would not guarantee the class unity of different ethnic and national groups that could bring them to the socialist revolution. Recognizing a similar gulf between ethnic nationalism and socialism in the Russian revolution, Luxemburg unleashed a critique of self-determination, noting that this "nothing but hollow, pettybourgeoisie," nationalistic demand threatened the very heart of the Russian revolution, since the basic principle of revolution would be the opposition of all oppression, including that practiced by nationalists.[25]

Chinese communists tried to bridge this gulf by fixing Korean peasants as class subjects whose interests were thought to be identical to those of the Chinese peasants. The construction of Koreans as a minority harbored ambiguous meanings for the relationship of Koreans with the Chinese revolution. Although the categorization of Koreans as a minority referred to their status under Japanese rule, it also came to denote their relations with the Chinese nation-state, represented by Chinese communists. While the notion of Korean self-determination implies the right of Koreans to create their own nation-state, the concept of the minority assimilated Koreans' politics into the making of the Chinese revolution. The term *minority* was a territorially based concept that considered the Chinese (presumably the Han Chinese) to be the majority and subordinated other ethnic groups. Despite their cultural differences, Koreans and Chinese in this framework were supposed to have an identical subjectivity in support of the Chinese revolution.

These policies about Koreans failed to account for the intertwined relationship of nationalism, capitalism, and Japanese imperialism. In both the politics of the Northeast warlord government and Japanese imperialism, nationalism had organized the capitalist relations of production and market exchange, producing the uneven relations of Koreans and Chinese. Both the Northeast warlord government and Japanese imperialism had therefore embedded their powers in social relations. The supposition of nationalism as intrinsic only to the nation-state system prevented the Chinese communists from comprehending the unique conditions in Manchuria. The nationalist Chinese communist policy on the Korean minority further escalated from 1933 to 1935, when its anti-imperialist struggle was accompanied by the anti-Minsaengdan struggle.

Socialist Internationalism from 1933 to 1935

The CCP's adoption of the anti-Japanese national struggle in January 1933 was hailed as a major move toward finally acknowledging the distinctive local conditions of Manchuria. The cross-class alliance was taken as a political strategy to expand the mass base of the national struggle. The national struggle heralded changes in land reform and the policy on Koreans. The new land reform acknowledged the private property system. While the previous policy of class struggle called for confiscation of land from all landlords, the new policy of anti-Japanese struggle aimed to seize land only from pro-Japanese landlords. The new policy allowed the exchange of land and market activities, focusing on the reduction of rent rather than abolition of the landlord system.

Historians have debated the issue of whether land reform or anti-imperialist nationalism galvanized peasant support for communists in the Chinese revolution. Mark Selden accepts both, while Chalmers Johnson identifies nationalism as the main source of the support.[26] In the case of Manchuria, Lee Chong Sik observed that moderate land reform expanded the guerrilla bases. While the soviets enlisted only 4,500 persons in East Manchuria, about one-fifth of the peasant mobilization during the Harvest and Spring uprisings, which had involved more than 20,000, the thirteen people's governments had more than 30,000 adherents by the end of 1933.[27] Peasants and communists also built defense walls, developed emergency communication networks among themselves and in other villages, and drafted escape plans such as digging tunnels into the mountains. They also operated weapons-making facilities and sewing centers to supply clothing to the guerrillas.

The new land reform policy broadened the support for communist activities. But it was too flawed to resolve social antagonism. It did not enable the Chinese communists to account for the ways in which the Northeast government and Japanese imperialism drew on nationalist politics, anchoring it in social relations. Like the previous land reform policy, it bound nationalism only within the nation-state system, without grounding it in the social sphere. The policies pertaining to the Korean minority prolonged this political and cultural approach to nationalism. After receiving the CCP's order to commence the anti-Japanese struggle in June 1933, the MPC formulated a resolution aimed at integrating "minority nationalities" (shaoshu minzu in Chinese) into the united front against Japanese imperialism: "We must integrate minority nationalities in Manchuria so as to launch together the anti-Japanese struggle. . . . We need to instruct the working people of China and Korea to oppose the strategy of Japan, Manchukuo, and the Kuomintang, which has sought to divide the united front of the people of China and Korea."[28] In the same resolution, the MPC equated its organizational expansion with the task of making Chinese the majority in the CCP: "Although the CCP has incessantly expanded its influence, its organization still remains too small to execute its political tasks. One of the most important tasks is to expand its organization, steadfastly increase the collection of taxes, and turn it into a mass party. Before August 1, 1933, we must at least triple the membership of the party to increase the representation of Chinese to no less than two-thirds of the membership and the representation of workers to at least one-fifth."[29]

The MPC's aspiration for organizational hegemony reinvented social relations. All Chinese peasants, regardless of the time and duration of their migration, their origins, and their place of residence, were homogenized as unified national subjects. All Korean peasants in Manchuria were to be singularized and incorporated as a minority. Their experiences of oppression and subsequent revolutionary objectives were identical to those of Chinese peasants. This singularization of Korean and Chinese subjectivities elided the fact that the social relations of Koreans and Chinese were organized not just by the dynamics of the nation-state system but also by capitalist dynamics. Japanese imperialists, the Northeast warlord government, the Chinese bourgeoisie, and the Manchukuo state instigated conflicts and undertook negotiations in their competing pursuit of the territorial occupation of Manchuria. They simultaneously collaborated and contended for the capitalist development of the region. With the exchange of capital and trade, capitalist dynamics bound the Manchurian market to other parts of the Japanese empire and the world economy. Assuming the essentialist national identities of the revolutionary masses, the MPC misrecognized the global social experiences of peasants as *societal* experiences within the territory of an imagined nation-state. This tendency was manifest in the ways the CCP built its mass organizations as territorial and societal units of the nation-state. Examples include the Married Women's Society, Children's Corps, Youth Corps, peasant associations, and workers' unions. The national practices of the MPC obscured the fact that, although they did not preclude their social unity in the struggle for socialist revolution, the disparate social relations of Korean and Chinese peasants required that they engage in related yet discrete social struggles.

KOREAN COMMUNIST NATIONALISM

The approach of Korean communists to revolutionary struggle in Manchuria is fraught with the same symptoms that afflicted Chinese communists —the nationalist abstraction of the social. They operated within the nation-state framework, in which they vacillated between pursuit of Korean independence and participation in the Chinese revolution. Korean communists thus shared with their Chinese counterparts a nationalist perspective that assimilated Manchuria into the nation-state they advocated. Korean communists in general oscillated between two struggles—to liberate Korea and to make the Chinese revolution—struggles they viewed as incompatible. Their brief advocacy of Korean self-rule was only a moment in their attempt to confront the unique conditions in Manchuria. I examine three instances of Korean communist activity when Korean communists modified their conceptualization of Manchuria within the nation-state framework: the struggle to re-create the Korean Communist Party (KCP) in Manchuria from 1923 to 1928, the united front with Korean noncommunist nationalists from 1929 to 1930, and the party's entry into the Chinese Communist Party in 1930. The conceptualizations of Manchuria in these periods embodied their social consciousness of Korean peasant conditions. Each moment was marked by a distinctive organizational reconfiguration of the Korean communists.

Korea and Manchuria

Korean communist activities dated from the early 1920s. Korean communist youth organizations were formed across Manchuria in 1923. After the Korean Communist Party was founded in Seoul in May 1925, its Manchurian General Bureau (Manju Ch'ongguk, hereafter referred to as "the bureau") was established in May 1926. Kando was the center of the activities of the bureau, which concentrated on organizing peasants and youth. Following a large-scale demonstration led by the bureau in October 1927, the arrests of Korean communists by Japanese consular police left the bureau in disarray. The Tuesday group of Korean communists, which had directed the bureau until 1927, reconstructed it with its own members in February 1928.[30] In a power struggle, the rival Marxist-Leninist (ML) group and Seoul-Shanghai group established bureaus in the same year.[31]

Until they joined the CCP in 1930, various Korean communists shared the goal of Korean independence and class struggle in Manchuria and Korea. They represented Korean peasants as national and class subjects, both of which presupposed their a priori interests. As national subjects, Korean peasants were said to have a vested interest in liberating Korea from Japanese rule. As class subjects, they presumedly shared identical interests with Chinese peasants. The Tuesday group's bureau vowed to abolish Japanese imperialism while engaging in class struggle to fight the Kuomintang and warlords and confiscate all land owned by landlords. Peasant federations formed by the Tuesday group aimed to liberate Korea from Japanese rule and nationalize the land. The ML group's bureau also declared class warfare while calling for a united front with the national bourgeoisie against feudal oppression.[32] Their main activities included organizing protests, such as the labor protests that took place on May Day in 1928, and staging attacks on Japanese consulates and other facilities.

This representation did not bear on Koreans' specific experiences and concerns, which resulted from the warlord politics and Japanese imperialism that organized landownership, tenancy, and employment of Korean peasants in ways different from their Chinese counterparts. When Korean communists focused on conditions in Manchuria, they did not attend to the social relations of production and exchange. Instead, they focused on Japanese imperialism and the corruption of Chinese officials. For instance, in 1927 the bureau opposed the construction of railways by Japan, a well-known anti-Japanese action. In order to preempt the allied actions of Japanese and Korean merchants to defend their monopoly on foreign trade, the bureau also protested against the Northeast government's increase in tariff rates. In addition, the bureau called for a democratic transformation of the Northeast government, proposing to end the abusive power of the Hyangyak, the village administrative unit. Since it oversaw the registration of households and the collection of taxes, the Hyangyak discriminated against Koreans, assigning higher and special kinds of taxes and dues to Koreans, but not to Chinese, and forcing Koreans to become naturalized.[33] The Youth Federation of Koreans in China (Chaechungguk Hanin ch'ŏngnyŏn tongmaeng), which was established by the ML group in 1928 and became the largest organization in Manchuria, also urged Koreans in Manchuria to remove corrupt Chinese officials and end discrimination against Koreans.[34]

It was the united front with Korean nationalists that brought the attention of Korean communists to the specific social conditions of Koreans in Manchuria. Encouraged by the united front of the CCP and the GMD in China and the coalition of communists and the national bourgeoisie in Korea, Korean communists in Manchuria joined other nationalists to create a unified national party (Minjok yuiltang) in 1928. Key noncommunist nationalist groups in the united front included the Ch'amŭibu, Chungŭibu, and Sinminbu, which were formed in the mid-1920s in South and North Manchuria. Before the formation of the united front, they had concentrated on launching attacks on pro-Japanese Koreans and Japanese facilities. Representing themselves as Koreans' self-government, the noncommunist nationalist groups also promised to stabilize the lives of Korean peasants, operate collective farms, and provide education. As they collected compulsory membership fees and other financial contributions from Korean residents, however, the communists had condemned them for exploiting Koreans, who already were oppressed and impoverished.[35]

In 1928, Korean communists began to cooperate with noncommunist nationalists to create two coalition groups of the Korean united front: the Hyŏbŭihoe and Ch'oksŏnghoe. Still torn by ideological conflicts over the format of the coalitions, the Korean united front underwent a series of intense organizational restructurings—a phenomenon called factionalism. The Hyŏbŭihoe was comprised of the Chŏngŭibu and two communist groups—the Tuesday group and the Seoul-Shanghai group—while the Ch'oksŏnghoe was comprised of the Ch'amŭibu and youth organizations led by the ML group. The Hyŏbŭihoe created the League of Koreans (Kungminbu) in April 1929, which soon split into civil and military departments. The civil department retained the name to focus on self-rule in Manchuria, and the military department was reorganized into the Korean Revolutionary Party (Chosŏn Hyŏngmyŏngdang). Ch'oksŏnghoe was renamed the Revolutionary Assembly (Hyŏksin ŭihoe) in December 1928 and formed the Ch'aekchinhoe one year later. With the dissolution of the Sinminbu in 1928, the Revolutionary Assembly incorporated its military group, while the League of Koreans absorbed the civil group. Some members of the Sinminbu collaborated with anarchists to organize the Korean Federation (Hanjok ch'ong yŏnhaphoe) in July 1929.[36]

As Korean noncommunist nationalists, especially the Chŏngŭibu, had invoked Korean self-rule, the united front in Manchuria adopted Korean self-rule as one of its important declarations. Both the Hyŏbŭihoe and Ch'oksŏnghoe supported the naturalization of Koreans. Under the slogan of self-rule, the League of Koreans elected representatives in Korean residential areas. In order to obtain the right to cultivation for Koreans, it pledged to negotiate with Chinese officials on a number of measures, including restricting the monopoly of landlords, guaranteeing a specific time period for Korean cultivation, reducing rent, and assisting with irrigation facilities. The Revolutionary Assembly also vowed to create a self-rule administration.[37] The League of Koreans ran several mills and stores to alleviate the condition of the Korean peasants, as they had depended on mills owned by Chinese landlords and merchants, who charged high fees and operated stores in the cities.[38] The Korean Federation also combined the goals of liberating Korea and establishing Korean self-rule in Manchuria. While training guerrilla armies, it formed its organizations on the basis of self-rule units in the villages. Its social measures for Koreans in Manchuria were similar to those adopted by the Manchukuo state and the Government General of Korea in 1933. Defining itself as an independent, self-governing, cooperative organization, the Korean Federation pledged to thwart Korean displacement from land, establish collective farms, operate farmers' cooperative unions, oversee instruction about new agricultural methods and innovations, and institute the collective purchase of daily essentials and collective sale of crops.[39]

As much as the united front was a political strategy to expand the anti-Japanese struggle, sponsorship of self-rule came to coexist with the class struggle pursued by the communists, who joined the united front. During the formation of the unified national party, key Korean organizations reached a consensus on self-rule, despite some differences. The Hyŏbuihoe foresaw the Korean self-rule organization as being part of the Chinese administrative unit. The ML group sought to create Korean self-rule in cooperation with the

Chinese under the leadership of naturalized Koreans. The League of Koreans favored more autonomy for the Korean self-rule movement, objecting to the idea that the Korean self-rule organization would submit to the Chinese administration.[40] The Youth Federation of Koreans in China announced as its primary objectives Korean self-rule, acquisition of Chinese national membership, and pursuit of the right to buy and sell land.[41] The issue of Korean self-rule signified the social consciousness about Korean peasants' conditions. Even though their advocacy of self-rule did not fully encompass the complex social relations between Koreans and Chinese, at least it demonstrated the attempt to address the conditions under which Koreans were deprived of landownership and residency. The promotion of self-rule by the united front indicates a revision in its earlier nation-state approach, which regarded Manchuria "as an extension of Korea" (Chosŏn yŏnjang chuŭi). It helped them to recognize that Korean conditions in Manchuria could not be addressed solely by a national struggle for Korean independence or by class struggle.

But there was tension in the marriage of the self-rule movement and the class struggle. While the class struggle of the communists at that time condemned the private property system, the Korean self-rule movement in Manchuria aspired to attain the right for Koreans to cultivate and own land. Korean communists also disputed the naturalization of Koreans as Chinese nationals, which the Northeast warlord government enforced as a prerequisite for landownership and secure residency. While the ML group's youth organizations accepted the naturalization of Koreans, the Korean Communist Youth Association opposed it on the grounds that the naturalization fees would increase the revenue of the warlord government, which was allied with the Kuomintang. The disjuncture between the objectives of the Korean communists and the goal of self-rule suggests a crucial limit to their local social consciousness.

The Korean communists' attention to local conditions in Manchuria was momentary. They soon adopted a different nation-state perspective, one that subsumed Manchuria into the goal of establishing a new Chinese state. If the united front modified the territorial nationalism of Korean communists, joining the CCP again reconfigured it. In March 1930, the ML group announced its entrance into the Chinese Communist Party, which was followed by the Tuesday group a few months later. Korean communists now denounced their earlier commitment to the liberation of Korea and Korean self-rule in Manchuria. Instead, they pledged to make the Chinese revolution.

Appealing to other Korean communists to abandon their struggle to liberate Korea, the ML group offered a self-critique for pursuing Korean nationalism, competing against the CCP and its Chinese revolution. The ML group also united the Korean masses with the Chinese revolution, postulating that the Korean masses were class subjects whose interests were identical to those of the Chinese masses. This drastic change showed Korean communists a new nation-state perspective that posited the revolutions in Korea and China as irreconcilably antagonistic. The declaration in which the ML group dissolved its organization in March 1930 encapsulates this perspective:

> Korean communists have extended the organization of the Korean Communist Party to Manchuria, thereby sustaining national organizations rivaling the CCP. . . . Their [the Korean workers and peasants] calamitous experiences of oppression and exploitation did not arise from their condition as Koreans but from their condition as workers and peasants. Furthermore, their wretched conditions are not confined to Korean peasants but shared by Chinese workers and peasants. Under these conditions, it is now apparent that the struggle to liberate Korea will not bring about the liberation of the Koreans of Manchuria from capitalist and feudal oppression and exploitation. . . . Korean workers and peasants in Manchuria must unite with their Chinese counterparts [to make the Chinese revolution]. . . . Various factions of the Korean communists in Manchuria must therefore abandon their idea of Manchuria as an extension of Korea.[42]

The Korean communists' nationalism and their united front overshadowed their cooperation with Chinese communists in the 1930s. When the Chinese communists accused their Korean comrades of pursuing nationalism and factionalism, they cited the constant reorganization of Korean communist groups during the 1920s. Prior to 1930, as the word *factionalism* suggests, Korean communists were denounced for their power struggles accompanied by capricious organizational restructuring. A primary focus of the existing literature on Korean communism is the genealogy of its numerous organizations, especially the power struggles among communists and their conflicts with noncommunist nationalists. Yet this factionalism was not completely attributable to power struggles; it was exacerbated by participation in the united front, which strove to tackle the social conditions of Manchuria. As mentioned earlier, the Hyŏbŭihoe coalition of the united front, for instance, broke into two separate organizations and pursued goals perceived to be incompatible—movements to realize Korean self-reliance and independence. As far as the united front supplied Korean communists with an opportunity, though fleeting, to attend to the historically specific conditions of Manchuria, this perspective of the Hyŏbŭihoe on the relationship between Manchuria and Korea exposed Korean communists to the unique social conditions of Koreans in Manchuria.

THE CONSTRUCTION OF SOCIAL UNITY

Chinese and Korean nationalisms prescribed the anti-Japanese national struggle, which became an increasingly irrelevant tool for challenging the colonial establishment and envisaging sensible struggles to organize social relations. In Manchuria, the tendency toward fragmentation and antagonism between Korean and Chinese peasants was inscribed in the very social relations organized by colonial and national politics before and after the founding of the Manchukuo state. In the MPC's politics, the social unity of Korean and Chinese peasants was imposed by its political project of assimilation rather than by the resolution of social relations. The specter of the Minsaengdan in the purge was, in fact, social antagonism in Kando that could not be completely domesticated by the political project. Minsaengdan members constituted an external enemy of a newly envisaged social whole; their purge was "the ultimate guarantee" of the social unity. The drive to purge Koreans did not simply replace their class and national struggle against landlords, the bourgeoisie, and Japanese with a new enemy—Minsaengdan members. Rather it naturalized the unity of Korean peasants and the CCP, as well as the unity of Korean and Chinese peasants. The purge was the process of formulating the unity of the society. In other words, the anti-Minsaengdan struggle was an attempt to realize unity in the social realm by constructing Korean revolutionaries as "others," social elements of the "counterrevolution" (panhyŏngmyŏng in Korean, fangeming in Chinese). Describing Korean revolutionaries as factionalists and nationalists pinpoints an essential feature in the formation of Chinese nationalism: the CCP obscured its own nationalism by representing itself as the defender of universal revolution (ridding itself of any ethnic or national character) and casting Korean communists as the other of the revolutionary struggle. The purge turned the elimination of Koreans into the elimination of counterrevolutionary elements. The excesses of the purge alone signify the ways in which the CCP attempted to deny its own nationalism and act of self-cleansing while forcefully pursuing national goals. This act of sterilization was the social process used by the CCP to construct social relations as a homogeneous entity, displacing the uneven integration of Koreans and Chinese and their hierarchical property relations.

The purge was a traumatic manifestation of the contradiction between the Chinese communists' nationalist project and an ideal socialist internationalism. The unbridled cruelty against their ever-present enemies points to the impossibility of displacing such contradictions. Even slender deviations from norms, such as the short haircuts of women in the revolutionary forces, were regarded as signs of a Minsaengdan influence that would alienate would-be supporters and weaken the revolutionary forces.[43] Inadvertent accidents, ranging from the accidental firing of a gun and spelling errors in reports to an oversight in transporting grain or cooking a meal, were treated as acts of counterrevolution and signs of support for the Minsaengdan. Even the slightest suggestion of criticism of the party, such as expressing apprehension concerning the hardships and homelessness of refugees living in the mountains with winter approaching, was suspected as a Minsaengdan behavior.[44] This series of bizarre allegations suggests that when the CCP refused to recognize its nationalism, its nationalism came to be embodied only in the phantom construction of its enemy. The excessive terror and violence of the purge paradoxically denotes the impossibility of homogenizing the social space. It is for this reason that, despite the prevalence of nationalism in the CCP across Manchuria, the purge took place only in Kando, where the revolutionary struggle actually progressed with Korean participation.

During the anti-Minsaengdan struggle, the CCP described its enemy as having three heads: nationalism, factionalism, and Minsaengdan. The real enemy was Korean self-rule, since it was a common denominator of the three heads.[45] The CCP identified Korean communists as "factionalists," defining them as "nationalists masked as communists." Appealing to the Korean masses in December 1933, the Eastern Manchurian Special Committee reproached Korean communist factionalists for supporting Korean self-rule.[46] In late 1933, a representative of the MPC declared that more than half the Minsaengdan members were the leaders of "factionalist organizations" who had penetrated CCP organizations and that the Minsaengdan stood for counterrevolution.[47] In the May 1933 edition of its official bulletin, *Liangtiao zhangxian* (in Chinese), the Eastern Manchurian Special Committee disclosed its extensive position on the Minsaengdan. It was comprised of Korean landlords, rich peasants, usurers, and merchant capitalists, who under the auspices of the Manchukuo state and Japan were resisting the revolution; it also recruited various Korean nationalists, factionalists, and religious groups to its leadership positions. According to the Eastern Manchurian Special Committee, the Minsaengdan threatened the communist insurgency in Kando, confounding the Korean masses of laborers, middle-level peasants, and poor peasants with the idea of self-rule.[48]

Korean revolutionaries were defenseless during the struggle. Moreover, the struggle progressed with the quasi-spontaneous participation of Koreans in the very act that condemned them. This double trauma of Korean revolutionaries as victims and appellants in erroneous allegations in part harbored its own misrecognition of the social conditions of Koreans in Manchuria. The inability of Korean communists to defend their stance on Korean self-rule in part stemmed from their own nationalism, which conflated the nation with the territorial state. Like their Chinese counterparts, the territorializing nationalism of Korean communists was to be blamed for their inadequate recognition of the social conditions of Koreans in Manchuria. As the Chinese and Korean communists presumed a homogeneous national subjectivity of Chinese and Korean revolutionary peasants, respectively, the issue of Korean self-rule symbolized the undesirable disunity of revolutionary subjects. On the one hand, as they ascribed Korean distinctiveness merely to ethnic customs, Korean self-rule came to denote the ontological difference between Koreans and Chinese that would disturb the territorial unity of the Chinese revolution. On the other hand, Korean communists adopted a similar nationalist approach to the question of Koreans in Manchuria. Combining the struggle to liberate Korea with the class struggle in Manchuria, Korean communists assumed uniformity in the national and class subjectivity of Koreans in both Korea and Manchuria. Although the united front of Korean communists and Korean nationalists provided a significant opportunity to suspend the nationalism that had subordinated Manchuria to Korea, Korean communists combined the social issues of Manchuria and the national issue of Korea without exploring their relationship. Both Chinese and Korean communists attempted to reduce the distinctive concerns of Koreans to a homogeneous revolutionary task. The issue of Korean self-rule represented an insupportable separation of Koreans from putatively unified subjects.

Their nationalist approaches obscured the Manchurian characteristics that interlaced national and capitalist relations between Koreans and Chinese before and after 1932. Japanese imperialism, capitalist dynamics, and the Northeast government in Manchuria integrated Korea and Manchuria into the capitalist world market while reproducing differences in terms of institutional property systems and the relations of production and exchange. Whether it was the Northeast government, the Government General of Korea, or the Manchukuo, national power was embedded in the social sphere. Prior to 1932, national policies of the Northeast government, which had outlawed landownership by nonnaturalized Koreans and denied them material assistance, organized capitalist relations between landlords and tenants. After the establishment of the Manchukuo state in 1932, a new nationalist dynamics of the Government General of Korea and the Manchukuo state reversed the property relations of Koreans and Chinese, reinforcing the uneven national and capitalist relations between them.

In other words, the opposition of Koreans and Chinese had been rooted not just in different ethnic and cultural customs but also in their antagonistic property relations. If it were to tackle Manchurian conditions, the anti-Japanese revolutionary movement would have to forge separate struggles for the Koreans and Chinese. The social experiences and subjectivities of Koreans and Chinese were not to be homogenized with those of Korea or China. The unity of the struggle in Manchuria, Korea, and China would not be presupposed. Instead, it would be formed through the process of struggle itself. Yet the Korean and Chinese communists failed to adequately recognize differences among Korean conditions within Manchuria, as well as between conditions in Manchuria and those in Korea or China.

The ideological figuration of the anti-Minsaengdan struggle enabled Korean and Chinese communists to suture their nationalism, social consciousness of local conditions, and socialist internationalism. The struggle was shaped by national prescriptions for social life that obscured the historical specificities of social life in Manchuria. It signified the attempt of Chinese and Korean communists to elude the tension between their desire to create a new nation-state and their commitment to resolve social contradictions in Manchuria. The struggle attempted to create a new social order—one characterized by homogeneous social relations within the space of essential national and class imaginaries. The tasks of overcoming the oppression of Korean peasants and establishing a new independent state were subordinated to the supreme goal of making the Chinese revolution. The purge personified this national desire in the ghostly body of the Minsaengdan. Korean and Chinese communists envisaged their socialist internationalism in terms of the aggregation of two incompatible revolutionary struggles to construct new nation-states in Korea and China. This particular socialist internationalism understood social relations in national terms. It suspended the indeterminate dialectics that could have combined the separate social struggles in a unified struggle for revolution on a world scale.

The outcome of the revolutionary struggle in Kando during the anti-Minsaengdan struggle was double-edged. On the one hand, the Eastern Manchurian Special Committee and its revolutionary units undertook an impressive amount of anti-Japanese activity despite its harrowing internal struggles. According to one Japanese report, guerrillas had launched 954 skirmishes in 1934 in which about 201,025 guerrillas had engaged in 184 confrontations with the Japanese and Manchukuo armies, for which they printed as many as 11,040 propaganda leaflets.[49] On the other hand, the CCP paradoxically crafted its organizational hegemony at the expense of its own revolutionary base in Kando. Although the number of MPC members increased from 636 in April 1931 to 11,000 in late 1931, it shrank to 965 in September 1933 and 131 in May 1935. If Koreans comprised the majority of the membership in 1931, the Chinese members increased by 10 to 20 percent during this general decline in membership. The drastic reduction in Korean membership resulted more from the anti-Minsaengdan struggle than Japanese pacification.[50] The substantial decrease in CCP membership in Kando meant its imminent dissolution in the whole of Manchuria because its best-organized and most active units were in Kando.

With the disarray of the revolutionary forces and the dwindling support of the Korean constituency, the MPC reassessed the struggle in the middle of 1935. Unnecessary brutality, demoralization of the revolutionary forces, and alienation of the Korean masses were condemned. Moreover, critics within the MPC began to rebuke the Eastern Manchurian Special Committee for ignoring two concerns of the Korean masses—the liberation of Korea and Korean self-rule in Manchuria. Although the nationalist codification of Koreans as the minority continued to prevail, the establishment of a special district for self-rule by Koreans in Kando was now proposed. The education of the masses on the difference between the policy of the CCP on Korean self-rule and a similar policy of Japan and exiled Koreans was also recommended.[51]

In 1936, the MPC issued a new resolution that terminated the anti-Minsaengdan struggle, though without authorizing a new social consciousness. The resolution reconfigured the nature of the coalition between Korean and Chinese communists. But the issue of self-rule of Koreans in Kando was not elaborated. The resolution reshuffled the Chinese revolutionary armies, separating units in charge of the Chinese revolution and the liberation of

FIGURE 5. Korean and Chinese members of the anti-Japanese united forces in the Soviet Union in the early 1940s. Kim Il Sung and Zhou Baozhong are second and third from the right in the front row. (From Ryu Eun Kyu, *Ich'ojin hŭnjŏk*, 102.)

Korea. As the MPC gave up guerrilla bases in Kando, its People's Liberation Armies moved to South and North Manchuria in 1936. Moreover, the MPC organized a special unit devoted to the struggle to liberate Korea, consisting exclusively of Koreans. This Second Eastern Manchuria Revolutionary Army was later renamed the Second Army of the First Route Army of the Anti-Japanese United Forces. The CCP reorganized its revolutionary armies, permitting Korean communists and guerrilla forces to attend to the task of liberating Korea. Although there was some discussion about organizing the armies along ethnic lines, this proposal was opposed by some sections of the MPC, especially the Northern Manchurian Committee.[52] Instead, the Sixth Division of the Second Army of the First Route Army of the Anti-Japanese United Forces, which under the leadership of Kim Il Sung was comprised mainly of Koreans, was given permission to concentrate its efforts on liberating Korea in the Tongbyŏndo area—the border area between Fengtian Province and northern Korea—and launching attacks on the Japanese in Korea. Kim Il Sung and his Korean and Chinese comrades retreated to the Soviet Union in the early 1940s.

The reformation of the CCP revolutionary armies signified an overdue rapprochement between the Korean struggle for the independence of Korea and the general task of the Chinese revolution. But the rapprochement was limited by continued Chinese nationalism. If the anti-Minsaengdan struggle was driven by the territorializing nationalism of Korean and Chinese communists in conflict, the termination of the struggle did not end but only bolstered the nationalist approach to socialist internationalism. For instance, Wu, one of the most outspoken critics of the struggle within the MPC, who was sent to observe the situation in Manchuria by the Manchurian Provincial Committee of the CCP, charged the struggle with positing class struggle in opposition to the struggle to liberate Korea.[53] Bypassed in this self-criticism were the two faces of the CCP: the supposition of class struggle as a universal interest and the adoption of nationalism. Reinvoking Chinese nationalism, the secretary of the Eastern Manchurian Special Committee asserted that "unless the Chinese become the main constituents of the people's liberation armies, there will be no major improvement."[54] He identified areas where the Chinese population was concentrated but agrarian cooperatives had not been established as ideal for guerrilla bases. When he suggested abandoning the guerrilla bases of Kando, as they no longer had any "people," he must have been indicating that the Koreans had deserted. Yet the "people" might have also meant the "Chinese," who were largely absent or voiceless in the Kando bases.

A pitfall of Chinese or Korean nationalism in Manchuria was the loss of space for critiques of capitalism. Nationalism supplied an optic through which Korean and Chinese communists interpreted the social conditions of people in Manchuria. In the refracted vision of nationalism, historical specificity was emptied at the moment of revolutionary time. For instance, Korean communists' understanding of the social experiences of the Korean peasants of Kando was at best frozen in the seemingly timeless bourgeois idea of self-rule, if it was not absorbed into an imagined national entity. Korean communists' ambiguous endorsement of self-rule was tangled up with the issues of universal rights of property ownership and individual freedom. Obscured was the regional and national disparity in social relations, which could not be swept away by the appeal for class struggle or the anti-Japanese united front.

In sum, the national optics of the communists contrived the singularity of people as both class and national subjects. The formation of class subjects was embedded in nation-state formation, which obliterated the ethnic, national, and social heterogeneity of peasant groups in different places and times. The national narratives of the Korean and Chinese communists invoked the peasants, who were presumed, regardless of their ethnic and national identities, to share a litany of oppression, ranging from unbearable rents, exploitative usury, taxes, and market monopoly to the intensifying domination of the imperialists. In turn, the codification of majority and minority conceived Chinese and Korean peasants as national subjects, integrating them into a collective dream of anti-imperialist struggle.

Social relations in Manchuria were a global problem mediated by national dynamics. While capitalist dynamics spearheaded by Japanese imperialism integrated Manchuria with Korea and the world, they also drew on national uniqueness to exploit disparities among Manchuria, Korea, and other parts of the world in levels of wages, skills, labor power, and resources. Such unevenness demanded a specific struggle in Manchuria different from those in Korea or China. Although it would not preclude the recognition of unity with others, such unity must not be presupposed but forged through the process of struggle. However, the struggle in Kando was subsumed either to the struggle to liberate Korea by invoking ethnic identities of Koreans, or to the struggle to make the Chinese revolution by appealing to Korean's minority status in Manchuria and China. When Korean communists conjured Manchuria as a space of the Korean nation, they perceived the Manchurian struggle to be mutually exclusive to the making of the Chinese revolution. When they joined the CCP and denounced their struggle to liberate Korea, they reversed their position to conflate the Manchurian struggle with the formation of the Chinese revolution. Socialist internationalism in Manchuria was thus reduced to the amalgamation of two separate national revolutions at best or the absorption of one by the other.

THE ORIGINS OF THE NORTH KOREAN REVOLUTION

After liberation from Japanese rule, the Korean communist experience in Manchuria turned into a most peculiar spectacle: the origin of the North Korean revolution. According to Kim Il Sung and his comrades, who governed North Korea for at least four decades, their Manchurian experience laid the foundation for their revolution. After liberation, Kim Il Sung's group joined other exiled groups that returned to Korea, including the Soviet and Yenan groups, which had engaged in communist activities in the Soviet Union and China proper. After seizing power in the late 1950s, Kim Il Sung's group elevated the experience of the Manchurian struggle of the 1930s to the North

Korean state's official ideology of *juch'e* (self-reliance). Since then, the memory of the Manchurian struggle has been lodged in the heart of the political culture of North Korea, exerting its influence in all aspects of economic, political, and cultural activities. Various memoirs and recollections of the armed struggle were taught in schools, workplaces, communities, and political units of North Korean society.[55] Given the ubiquitous presence of Manchuria in North Korean politics and culture, an understanding of North Korea requires comprehension of the linkages between Manchuria and the North Korean revolution.

A primary focus of the study of the North Korean revolution has been the veracity of the claim of anti-Japanese struggle in Manchuria. The whereabouts of Kim Il Sung have been of especially keen interest for historians, as conservatives, including the authoritarian states in South Korea, have discounted his claims as false. Quelling most of the doubts, Wada Haruki has provided one of the most comprehensive chronologies of Kim Il Sung. After graduating from a middle school operated by the Chŏngŭibu, he participated in the Korean Communist Youth Association (Chosŏn kongsan ch'ŏngnyŏn-hoe) in 1929, which supported the Chonguibu and the League of Koreans. He joined the Korean Revolutionary Army (Chosŏn Hyŏngmyŏnggun). After joining the CCP, he and his guerrilla army joined the unit of the Wangch'ong guerrilla army of the Eastern Manchurian Special Committee of the CCP in 1933. He was appointed as a member of the Committee for Political Affairs (Chŏngch'i wiwŏn) of the army.

During the anti-Minsaengdan struggle, Kim Il Sung was once charged with being a Minsaengdan spy. According to Kim Songho's analysis, the release of Kim is attributable to his close relations with Chinese communist leaders and his fluency in Chinese.[56] Contributing to ending the struggle, Kim burned documents that framed about one hundred new members of this army as Minsaengdan members. During the struggle, his army launched two expeditions to North Manchuria between October 1934 and the end of 1935. In 1936, when the CCP transformed the Second Army of the Northeast People's Revolutionary Army into the Northeast Anti-Japanese United Army, Kim was appointed the leader of its Third Unit. In late 1936, he dispatched communists to Korea to organize the Federation to Liberate the Fatherland (Choguk kwangbokhoe). Until his escape to the Soviet Union in the early 1940s, he continued to engage in skirmishes with the Japanese police and armies in both Manchuria and Korea.[57]

Lee Chongsok's thesis, the first South Korean study of the Manchurian experience and the North Korean state, identifies three major constitutive effects of the former on the latter: the national united front that encompassed diverse political camps so as to create a unified state in the postliberation period, the land reforms that distributed land to peasants, and the priority given to mobilizing and benefiting the masses.[58] In North Korean politics, the relationship between the party and the masses is compared to the relationship between fish and water. The masses are regarded as indispensable elements in the truth of the Manchurian struggle. The analysis of nationalism and social relations in this book suggests that the historical legacy of mass politics entailed its own limits. The national united front among Koreans and socialist internationalism in China was caught up in territorializing nationalism, which for both Korean and Chinese communists presented barriers to understanding the social conditions of the masses.

The multifaceted Korean history in Manchuria shows that Korean politics and anti-Japanese revolutionary movements were anything but unified in terms of their objectives, leadership, and constituencies. Korean peasants experienced social relations that differed by region and over time, developing complex relationships with their Chinese counterparts. The socialist internationalism of the Korean and Chinese communists deviated from the ideal of global unity. The memory of the Manchurian experience embodies the unfulfilled unity of the Korean masses and communists for national and socialist causes. Excised from the memory of the Manchurian struggle is the irreducible gap between the masses' social life and socialist national politics. The analysis of the purge and the subsequent reorganization of the anti-Japanese struggle in Manchuria shed light on the national history of mass politics, which has been deeply repressed in the historiography of North Korean nationalism. This book attempts to situate the North Korean construction of the Manchurian struggle within the complex history of nationalism, imperialism, capitalism, and a particular form of socialist internationalism.

EPILOGUE

The moment of liberation from the Japanese in 1945 was overshadowed by violence on a scale comparable to the 1931 riots. Assaults, lootings, and a new round of displacement once again exposed the dream of Koreans for a stable social life as unsustainable. The violence signified the arbitrary nature of the social relations that were consolidated through a patchwork of colonial laws and policies but instantly vanished when the forces sustaining them disappeared. The riots in both eras discharged Chinese antagonism toward the Japanese and Koreans, whom Chinese perceived as the medium of Japanese imperialism. As explored in this book, this national antagonism is foregrounded in its fragmented and antagonistic social relations, since the politics of nationality mediated and was shaped by market transactions of land and labor.

Set on the day of liberation, "Dual Nationality" (Ijung kukchŏk), a short story by Kim Mansŏn published in 1948, encapsulates the colonial order lodged in social space.[1] The story's depiction of the abrupt dissolution of colonial rule exposes the operations of social institutions of nationality and private property through which colonial power domesticated the desires of the colonized. At a glance, the story represents adaptation as a survival strategy of a colonized subject living in the interstitial space between Chinese nationalism and Japanese colonialism—a subject devoid of loyalty to any nation. The protagonist, Elder Pak, appears to be an exceptional opportunist, who, in order to improve his economic prospects, switches back and forth between Chinese and Korean nationality (a pandoin, or "person" of the peninsula by which Japan referred to Koreans). But, more importantly, the story signifies Elder Pak's arduous struggle to safeguard his sovereignty over his own labor, which is embodied in his land.

For Elder Pak, nationality is a tool for accumulating wealth. Before the

Manchukuo state was established, he was naturalized as a Chinese national in order to secure ownership of his land. During the Manchukuo period, he hid the certificate of naturalization in a safe box, since it was more advantageous to be identified as a Korean. On the eve of the Japanese surrender, he again began to carry his certificate of Chinese naturalization in the inside pocket of his jacket. While cultivating his own land, he also mediated land transactions between Japanese and "Manin" (people of Manchukuo). Using his networks with the Japanese, he introduced Chinese landowners to Japanese buyers. In his mind, this service for his Chinese neighbors, together with his impeccable Chinese lifestyle, proved his Chineseness. He had spoken Chinese for more than thirty years, wore Manchu-style clothes, and even acquired a Manchurian concubine, who would soon replace his dead Korean wife. This frame of mind explains why, despite rumors of bombing by the Allied forces and riots by the Chinese, Elder Pak did not join other Koreans in seeking refuge in Korean agricultural cooperatives or cities, if not at Japanese consulates. Should all his markers of assimilation into Chinese society fail to affirm his Chinese identity, he is certain that the certificate will authenticate his Chinese identity once and for all.

The story locates Elder Pak's true essence in his sovereignty over his own labor. Disapproving of his son's desire to return to Korea, he states that "any place is a good place if one can live well."[2] Elder Pak's celebration of liberation is accompanied by a compulsion to find a friend who fled without repaying a debt. Even when looters attack his house, his attachment to his belongings almost fatally delays his escape. When he finally goes into hiding at the house of a Chinese friend, Mr. Wang, he consoles himself by recalling that his money is hidden inside his belt and by counting the bills every night. Although he envies Mr. Wang and the other looters, the money with which he identifies is not abstract wealth but the asset that he has hoarded during his years in Manchuria. When Elder Pak ventures into the street, risking his life, he neither joins the looters nor returns to his home. Instead, he makes several trips to the house of Mr. Kim, who owes him money; Elder Pak takes Mr. Kim's household property, including a dresser, desk, radio, and record player. In terms of their number and value, the objects that Elder Pak takes from Mr. Kim's home and carries back to Mr. Wang's house amount to everything that a respectable household might own. In other words, Elder Pak's loot differs from Mr. Wang's. It consists of large and bulky items that cannot be safely hidden and are worth less than Mr. Wang's booty. In Mr. Wang's baffled assessment, the combined value of everything taken by Elder Pak is less than a few bundles of cotton fabric. However, what matters to Elder Pak is claiming what he regards as his own property rather than stealing that of others.

Elder Pak's fixation on his money and property discloses the bewildered subjectivity of the colonized. His wealth represents the value of his labor as a farmer and middleman who also assisted Chinese in selling their land to the Japanese. Protecting his own property is equivalent to defending his sovereignty over his labor of the past thirty years. At the same time, his fearless defense of his property reveals a colonial subjectivity invented by the colonial power. As has been noted throughout this book, the colonizer appealed to the desire of the colonized to acquire private property and improve the social relations of farming and market exchange. Ownership of private property was a mechanism through which the colonizer embedded its power in social relations.

Elder Pak's attempt to protect his private property results in the final rejection of his Chineseness and subsequently his death. This story's denouement overturns the colonial ideology of private property. The certificate and money operate as fetishes; both rob Elder Pak of common sense and confuse the distinction between him and "others." The large items taken from Mr. Kim's house attract the lethal attention of a Chinese army squad. Observing the array of Korean household goods in the yard, a Chinese soldier asks whether Elder Pak is Korean. Rejecting the answer that he is Chinese, the soldier asks again why a Chinese would stockpile Korean household goods. Elder Pak thinks that this is finally the moment when he can use the certificate of naturalization to prove his nationality. Without asking about the identity of the army squad, he hands the certificate to the soldier. Yet for this soldier the certificate conclusively proves that he is not Chinese. Elder Pak does not grasp that his certificate of naturalization is valid only under a particular regime and can be rejected by some Chinese authorities. Mr. Wang speculates that Elder Pak's life might be spared if the squad belongs to the Kuomintang, although it does not seem to have arrived in Manchuria. The squad's ragged uniforms resemble those of the fleeing Manchukuo army, which had incited the riots against Koreans. The deadly tribulation of Elder Pak at the hands of the retreating Manchukuo army attests to the breakdown of a colonial order that had enjoined pluralistic inclusion of all ethnic and national groups. This story also reveals that Elder Pak's dream was a fragile emanation of the colonial order, a dream that was shattered when this order came to an abrupt end.

Decolonization in the form of repatriation of overseas Koreans (Chaeoe

Tongp'o) to the home country (from Japan and its former colonies) was short-lived. After their liberation from Japanese rule, the former colonies concentrated on establishing independent nation-states. Although Japanese rule had prompted the emigration of about 20 percent of the total Korean population, neither Korea nor China concluded international treaties or passed national resolutions to make it possible or easier for former immigrants to return to Korea. Of the 1.5 million Koreans in Manchuria, about half returned; some were driven off by violence, and others yearned to return to family and neighbors in Korea. Many of the Koreans who remained in Northeast China were mobilized by the Chinese revolution. Some were brought home to assist the North Korean army during the Korean War. During the cold war, Koreans in Northeast China discontinued their relations with South Korea while remaining North Korea's closest allies.

The post–cold war era has provided a new opportunity for decolonization. Koreans in China (known as Korean Chinese), as well as Koreans in former socialist countries, have developed new economic and cultural relations with South Korea. It is apt here to consider a thesis of this book: colonialism is not simply a process of imposing a new military, political, and cultural rule on the colonized, all the while representing it as a process of enlightenment. Colonialism also integrates the colonized into a global capitalist economy, inducing the commodification of land and labor in the colonies. Decolonization, therefore, requires a substantial change in the global capitalist system. If the cold war era is to be understood as an American project for establishing capitalist hegemony, the post–cold war period does not negate the goals of the cold war establishment. The post–cold war era reconfigures a capitalist order marked by an unprecedented transnational flow of capital and labor and neoliberal economic principles.

The drive for economic and cultural globalization in South Korea that began in the early 1990s has transformed the Korean nation from a territorial to a deterritorialized nation. Departing from the previous focus on territorial disputes with North Korea, South Korea in the post–cold war era construes the Korean diaspora as an enormous asset capable of advancing Korea on the global stage. South Korea's new relationship with the Korean Chinese community surpasses its relations with other members of the Korean diaspora, including Korean Russians and some Korean Japanese, who used to embrace North Korea. South Korean overseas investment in China has drawn on the invocation of ethnic ties with Korean Chinese, who have provided various services including translating, networking, buying property, and supplying labor. Fanning the Korean dream among Korean Chinese, this capitalist investment has brought them to South Korea, though it denies them any substantial rights as ethnic members. In early 2004, around 300,000 Korean Chinese constituted 60 percent of the foreign workforce in South Korea.

The versatile institutional status of the Korean Chinese demonstrates the unstable temporality of the new Korean nation, which stems from the inherent paradoxical relation between capital and nation formation. The disputes over the rights of Korean Chinese are marked by the disparity between law and state policy. On the one hand, the Law on Overseas Koreans, which passed in 1999 in South Korea has become an emblem of the inclusive ethnic Korean nation, grants overseas Koreans the right to invest capital, own property, and be employed in the private and public sectors. The controversy is over the definition of *overseas Koreans*, as the 1999 law categorizes them as persons that once lived within South Korea as citizens and the descendants of such persons. This definition excludes Koreans in China, as well as other members of the colonial diaspora in Russia, Sakhalin, and Japan.

On the other hand, the state's policies recognize Korean Chinese as ethnic Koreans, allowing family visitation. In an attempt to broaden family visitation, the Ministry of Justice lowered the age restriction from fifty-five years of age and older in the late 1980s to thirty years of age and older in 2003. The modification of this rule does not benefit most Korean Chinese, who lost contact with their relatives during the colonial and cold war periods or whose relatives are in North Korea. The training program for factory employment, another legal form of migration, is also too restrictive, with limits on the annual number of trainees and wages only 60 to 70 percent of a domestic worker's. Korean Chinese have therefore come illegally, paying brokers to purchase legal invitations to work in South Korea, like any other foreign worker.

History repeats itself for the Korean Chinese. A revision of the Law on Overseas Koreans proposed by the Ministry of Justice in September 2003 parallels the practice of national membership during the Manchukuo period that was explored in chapter 4. The proposal establishes the family register (hojŏk) as a new criterion for national membership. It also assigns the rights to only two generations—those who left Korea and their children. The Ministry of Justice presents this as an inclusive measure that will endow Korean Chinese with the right to free visitation and employment in South Korea. However, this new criterion of family registration, let alone the generational restriction, has backfired. Institutionalized in 1922 under Japanese colonialism, the system of family registration has negative historical associations. Furthermore, the majority of Korean Chinese do not enroll in the family register in South Korea. This replicates the thorny predicament of Koreans seventy years ago in Manchuria. When the Koreans held dual nationality during the Manchukuo period as members of Korea and Manchukuo, their Korean membership was based on their enrollment in the family register in Korea. Many Koreans in Manchuria could not prove their membership because they had migrated to Manchuria prior to the institutionalization of the family register system in Korea. This problem posed a barrier for Koreans who wished to exercise rights of private property ownership in Manchuria, since proof of registration was required for filing a land title.

The fact that Korean Chinese were subject to similar discriminatory practices in Manchuria and South Korea at different historical moments suggests that the illegality of migrant labor is not a historical anomaly. Instead, it is produced by the incomplete national mediation of capitalist expansion. As argued in this book, national mediation does not denote a functional affinity between nationalism and capitalism but rather an intrinsic tension. For some critics, the Law on Overseas Koreans and its proposed revisions aim to sustain conditions advantageous for South Korea's economy such as the utilization of Korean Chinese as illegal laborers and the protection of the domestic market from abrupt changes in labor demand. However, the exclusion of Korean Chinese from the new Korean nation exceeds its functional effects for the South Korean economy. While employers with small factories, construction companies, and restaurants have demanded the expansion of the migrant workforce in order to alleviate labor shortages, policymakers have not yet fulfilled their expectations. Rather, the coexistence of the appeal for a new, deterritorialized, ethnic nation and the continued discrimination against Korean Chinese points to the elusive practices of South Korean capital, which have simultaneously postulated borderless capitalist expansion and re-created the ethnic nation, utilizing the Korean diaspora for its purposes.

In an attempt to obtain the right to visit and work in South Korea, Korean Chinese have inserted themselves into national politics, representing themselves as "returnees." Their politics draws on their colonial Manchurian history. Their representation of the Manchurian experience is dichotomous: they are seen as colonial victims and heroes of the anti-Japanese struggle. They claim that South Korea has the responsibility to embrace Korean Chinese who were forced by the colonizer to migrate to Manchuria. This representation counters the way Manchurian history has been incorporated into Chinese national history. Since 1951, when an autonomous prefecture for Koreans was established by the Chinese government in Yanbian (previously Kando), the history of the Korean minority has incorporated the anti-imperialist struggles of Koreans in Manchuria into the process of the Chinese revolution, not the liberation of Korea.

This national politics has progressed without exploring Koreans' social experiences as migrant laborers. This tendency has obscured the position of Korean Chinese in the South Korean economy as guest workers, separating them from other foreign workers. Their national politics also confounds subjectivities and entraps Korean Chinese migrants in the opposition of Korean and Chinese nationalism. When their ethnic identity is superimposed in both South Korea and China, Korean Chinese find it impossible to be legitimate Koreans. The more they endeavor to represent themselves as ethnic Koreans, the more they find it impossible to be equal to South Koreans in all aspects of history, institutional status, and culture. Their subjectivities therefore oscillate between their yearning to be recognized as Koreans and their desire to renounce their Korean identity. Moreover, their close identification with South Korea has prompted the Chinese state to reprimand them. The Chinese state has downgraded Korean Chinese from their high status as a model minority with a hoary revolutionary past to one of the recalcitrant minority groups that threaten the unity of the Chinese nation.

Recognition by Korean Chinese of their social conditions in South Korea and China will be necessary if they are to envisage new relations with their home and host countries, as well as with other migrant workers. This prospect depends on an understanding of global capitalist dynamics that integrates the Chinese and South Korean economies. What has led the Korean Chinese to interact with South Korea is an exchange of capital and labor that reinforces ethnic nationalism but simultaneously transcends it. As examined in this book, the contradictory dynamics of global capitalism renders the nationality of migrant workers unstable, even when the home and host countries impose it. The resolution of their ethnic predicaments must involve a simultaneous critique of nationalism and capitalism. Embedding nationalism in the process of global capitalism is vital for Korean Chinese if they are to articulate their distinctive experiences of nationality and work in both South Korea and China.

This prospective politics will take place in new terrains of cultural politics and historical conditions of global capitalism in the contemporary period. While a unitary national or class identity was taken for granted in the early twentieth century, the notion of a fragmented identity and an appeal to dual nationality marks new terrains of representation. In addition to the economic restructuring of Korea and China, new conditions in Asia encompass the growing interest in formulating an Asian economic bloc and the imminent market transition of North Korea. Furthermore, power relations among Asian countries are being transformed from the previous ideological divides into economic cooperation and rivalry, as the Koreas, China, Russia, and Japan negotiate to create an Asian economic bloc.

The spate of new forces and conditions may engender a new life for Manchurian history. The Manchurian experience illustrates the complex relationship between nationalism and capitalism, which still directs the dynamic processes of transnational migration, citizenship, and sovereignty over one's own body and labor. Naturalized as national memory, the Manchurian experience has so far entered the politics of nationalism articulated by different groups of Koreans during and after the cold war. It remains to be seen whether the politics of the Korean Chinese will be coupled with the South Korean movement to overcome the colonial and cold war legacies. The relationship between Korean Chinese and South Koreans would be transformed by the imminent North Korean reform and the expected migration of more North Koreans to neighboring countries, including China and South Korea. The different memories of the colonial history of Manchuria, which are shared by North Koreans and Korean Chinese, can mediate their new relations with each other, as well as with South Koreans and other members of the Korean diaspora.

The contemporary dynamics of global capitalism can also compel Korean Chinese to renegotiate their relations with other foreign workers beyond national and transnational frameworks. This impending possibility coalesces with the emergent interest in forming an Asian community. Various Asian imaginaries have appeared in parts of Asia, as Russia, China, Japan, and the two Koreas explore the possibilities for creating a single currency and developing their border regions and border-crossing infrastructures. As observed in the first Asian community—the East Asia Co-Prosperity Sphere—promoted by Japan during the colonial period, a new Asian bloc is also predicated on differences between countries, at least in terms of economic conditions, wages, skills of workers, and infrastructures. Competition among Asian countries as much as cooperation drives regional development in Asia. It remains to be seen in what ways this emergent formulation of an Asian bloc will invoke the memory of the colonial Asian community, in which Manchuria occupied center stage.

NOTES

PREFACE

1 Prasenjit Duara, *Sovereignty and Authenticity* (Oxford: Rowman and Littlefield, 2003); Rana Mitter, *The Manchurian Myth: Nationalism, Resistance, and Collaboration in Modern China* (Berkeley: University of California Press, 2000); Louise Young, *Japan's Total Empire* (Berkeley: University of California Press, 1998); Yoshihisa Tak Matsusaka, *The Making of Japanese Manchuria, 1904–1932* (Cambridge: Harvard University Asia Center, 2001).

2 Benedict Anderson, *Imagined Communities* (London: Verso, 1991). Partha Chatterjee, *The Nation and Its Fragments* (Princeton: Princeton University Press, 1993); Ranajit Guha, *Dominance Without Hegemony: History and Power in Colonial India* (Cambridge: Harvard University Press, 1998).

3 Han-Chinese from China proper were also considered colonialists in Manchuria.

4 Duara, *Sovereignty and Authenticity*; Mitter, *The Manchurian Myth*; Young, *Japan's Total Empire*; Shin Chubaek, *Manju chiyŏk haninŭi minjok undongsa (1920–45)* (Korean National Movement in Manchuria) (Seoul: Aseamunhwasa, 1999); Yoon Hwitak, *Ilchjeha Manjuguk Yŏn'gu* (A Study of the Manchukuo State under the Japanese Rule) (Seoul: Iljogak, 1996); Kim Cheŏl, "Mollakhanŭn sinsaeng: 'Manjuŭi kkumkwa Nonggunŭi odok" (Collapsing Rebirth: Dream of Manchuria and Misreading of Nonggun) in *Sangho Hakpo* 9 (2002): 123–58; and Lee Kyŏnghun, "Harbinŭi purŭn hanŭl: 'Pyŏkkongmuhan' gwa taedonga kongyŏng" (Blue Sky in Harbin: 'Pyŏkkongmuhan' and the East-Asia Co-Prosperity Sphere), in Kim Incheol and Sin Hyŏnggi (eds.), *Munhak sogŭi Fascism* (Fascism in Korean Literature) (Seoul: Samin, 2001), 190–234.

5 The name Kando was first used by Koreans. It is said that the Chinese Qing government (1644–1911) came to recognize this name in 1904, when Lee Pomyun, a Korean official who was dispatched by the Korean Chosŏn government (1392–1910) to protect Koreans and organize armies in this region, referred to this region as Kando in his letter to the magistrate of the Chinese Dunhua county. In the letter, Lee Pomyun criticized the Chinese landlords for oppressing Korean peasants in the region.

The age-old territorial disputes between Korea and China over Kando played a key role in the formation of Japanese imperialism. In 1712, Korea and China erected a boundary stone, on which the Tomun and the Yalu (Amnok in Korean) rivers were engraved as their border. In the late nineteenth century, the disagreement over the names and locations of the two rivers reopened the territorial disputes. China claimed Kando as part of its territory on the grounds that the Tomun river referred to the Tuman (Tumen in Chinese) river running between Kando and northern Korea. In Korea's view, the Tomun river denoted not the Tuman river but the upper stream of the Songhua river that divided China from Russia, rendering Kando part of Korean territory. The increasing settlement of Koreans in Kando in the nineteenth century intensified the territorial disputes over the region. During the Qing period, the Chinese government designated Manchuria as the sacred birthplace of the Manchu and thus as imperial ground, prohibiting the settlement of people except a few government officials, Manchu and Mongol bannermen, and exiled officials. Yet Korean farmers began to migrate to Kando during political and economic crises in the Korean peninsula. In response, the Chinese government legalized the settlement of Chinese in Manchuria including Kando. In 1909, Japan represented Korea in settling the territorial disputes over Kando, signing the Kando Treaty. Though formally stating Chinese sovereignty over Kando, the treaty never completely resolved the disputes. Instead it encouraged Japan's strategy of osmotic expansion of Japanese power from Kando to the rest of Manchuria and beyond. Although the Protectorate Treaty signed in 1905 authorized Japan to represent Korea in international affairs (and thus authorized the signing of the Kando Treaty), the absence of the required signature of the Korean emperor Kojong on the Protectorate Treaty has generated disputes over the validity of both the Protectorate Treaty and the Kando Treaty ever since.

Kando in general refers to four counties: Yŏn'gil (Yanji in Chinese), Hwaryong (Helong in Chinese), Hunch'un (Hunchun in Chinese); and Wangch'ŏng (Wangqing in Chinese). But the precise geographic and administrative boundary of Kando in China has been transformed by political changes over centuries. A brief genealogy of the chief Chinese administration in Kando is as follows. The first Chinese administration in Kando was Hunchunxieling (Hunchun military office), which was established in 1714 and replaced by Hunchunfudutong (Hunchun vice metropolitan governor's office) in 1881. After being founded in 1907, the Jilin provincial government in Manchuria in 1909 reconstituted Kando as Dongnanlu xunbeingbeidao (or Dongnanlu beingbeidao, the east-south district imperial patrol troops office), one of its five administrative districts. During the Republican period (1912–1931), Jilin province renamed Kando: in 1913 as Jilinsheng Dongnanludao (the east-south district of Jilin province), one of its newly constituted four administrative districts; in 1914 as Yanjidao (Yanji district), with Daoyin as the head administrative position.

The genealogy of Chinese counties in Kando is as follows. During the Qing period, Kando comprised six counties that were set up over time: Dunhua (1881); Yanji (established in 1902); Helong (1902); Hunchun (1909); Wangqing (established in 1909); and Ando (1910). During the Republican period, Kando included only four counties, leaving out Dunhua and Ando. In 1934 during the Manchukuo period (1932–1945), Ando was reintegrated into Kando region, which was then constituted as Kandosheng (Kando province). In 1958, Dunhua was incorporated into the Yanbian Autonomous Prefecture. Tian Zhihe and Pan Jinglong, *Jilin jianzhimogegaishe* (An Outline of the Establishment of Jilin Province) (Changchun: Jilin renmin chubanshe, 1990).

6 For representative studies of Manchuria in South Korea that link Manchuria with the North Korean state, see Shin Chubaek (ed.), *1930 Nyŏndae minjok haebang undongron yŏn'gu II* (Seoul: Saekil, 1990); Lee Chaehwa, *Han'guk kŭnhyŏndae minjok haebang undongsa* (Seoul: Paeksansŏdang, 1988); and Lee Chongsŏk, "Pukhan chido chipdangwa hangil mujang t'ujaeng" (The North Korean Leadership and the Anti-Japanese Armed Struggle), in *Haebang chŏnhusaŭi insik 5* (A Study of History Before and After the Liberation 5) (Seoul: Han'gilsa 1989), 35–154. For the North Korean publications, see *Choguk kwangbokhoe undongsa*, vols. 1–2 (The History of the Korean Liberation Federation) (P'yongyang: Chosŏn nodongdang ch'ulp'ansa, 1986); Sahoe kwahak ch'ulp'ansa, *Hangil mujang t'ujaengsa* (The History of the Anti-Japanese Armed Struggle) (P'yongyang: Sahoe kwahak ch'ulp'ansa, 1980); and Sahoe kwahagwŏn yŏksa yŏn'guso, *Choson kŭndae hyŏngmyŏng undongsa* (The History of the Modern Revolutionary Movement) (Reprinted in Seoul: Hanmadang, 1988).

INTRODUCTION

1 Franz Fanon, *The Wretched of the Earth* (New York: Grove Press, 1963), 204.

2 Ibid., 148–205.

3 For a discussion of the dichotomy of rural and urban, see Ato Seki-Otu, *Fanon's Dialectic of Experience* (Cambridge: Harvard University Press, 1996), 113.

4 Benedict Anderson, *Imagined Communities: Reflections on the Origin and Spread of Nationalism* (London: Verso, 1991). Anderson's initial conception of the original and the copy remains largely unchanged in his later work. In *The Spectre of Comparisons: Nationalism, Southeast Asia, and the World* (London: Verso, 1998), he explores a bewildering vision of the modernity conceived by colonized elites who cannot see their own societies without the specter of Western images and meanings. Even when he analyzes democratic developments among newly independent nation-states after World War II, Anderson relies on his reified notion of Western liberal democracy and the role of the bourgeoisie in it as a measure of the progress of democratization in former colonies.

5 Harry Harootunian, "Ghostly Comparisons: Anderson's Telescope," *Diacritics* 29:4 (2004): 135–49.

6 Partha Chatterjee, *The Nation and Its Fragments: Colonial and Postcolonial Histories; Rana-*

jit Guha, *Dominance without Hegemony: History and Power in Colonial India* (Cambridge: Harvard University Press, 1998).

7 For an insightful discussion of the written word and social practices, see Henri Lefebvre, *The Production of Space* (Oxford: Blackwell, 1991).

8 Karl Marx, *Grundrisse* (New York: Vintage, 1973), 458.

9 For an elaboration of the nation as a system of closure, see Rogers Brubaker, *Citizenship and Nationhood in France and Germany* (Cambridge: Harvard University Press, 1992).

10 For discussions of people, land, and culture, see Harry Harootunian, *Things Seen and Unseen* (Chicago: University of Chicago Press, 1988).

11 On ground rent, see Karl Marx, *Capital* vol. 3 (New York: Vintage, 1981), 917–52.

12 A primary thesis that links nationalism and capitalism concerns the formation of a domestic market. In an internal market, individuals are presumed to act as private and "free" commodity owners abiding by judicial laws in the economic unit of the internal market. Such market activities obscure the unequal relations that result from the exchange of capital and labor. See Etienne Balibar, "The Nation Form: History and Ideology," in Etienne Balibar and Immanuel Wallerstein, *Race, Nation, Classes* (London: Verso, 1991).

13 Ernesto Laclau, Judith Butler, and Slavoj Žižek, *Contingency, Hegemony, Universality: Contemporary Dialogues on the Left* (London: Verso, 2000), 50.

14 Michele Barrett, *The Politics of Truth: From Marx to Foucault* (Stanford: Stanford University Press, 1991), 241–42.

15 Ernesto Laclau, *Politics and Ideology in Marxist Theory* (London: Verso, 1977), 167.

16 Barry Smart, *Foucault, Marxism and Critique* (London: Routledge, 1983); Barrett, *The Politics of Truth*, 140.

17 For discussions of the analytical terrain of hegemony, see Michele Barrett, "Ideology, Politics, Hegemony: From Gramsci to Laclau and Mouffe," in *Mapping Ideology*, ed. Slavoj Žižek (London: Verso, 1994); Aijaz Ahmad, *In Theory: Classes, Nations, Literatures* (London: Verso, 1992); and Anna Marie Smith, *Laclau and Mouffe: The Radical Democratic Imaginary* (New York: Routledge, 1998).

18 Nicos Poulantzas, *State, Power, and Socialism* (London: Verso, 1980), 107.

19 Ibid., 104–15; Nicos Poulantzas, *Classes in Contemporary Capitalism* (London: Verso, 1975), 70–84. Poulantzas does not fully overcome the critique that because the nation is removed from social relations of production and circulation national consciousness engenders an illusion or fictional subjectivity. Even though he situates the nation in social relations, he is preoccupied with the integrating function that the nation is expected to perform. There is a fundamental tension within Poulantzas's framework between an attempt to situate the nation in a social formation and the conceptualization of social relations and the nation as separately given and fixed. It is not clear whether ideology simply unifies fractured and segmented relations among people so that they will perform the tasks of the division of labor as a unit, whether ideology articulates with material practices to constitute new

social relations and subjectivity, or whether the nation transforms itself as a result of its articulation with social relations. The tension between the nationalization of frontiers and the transnational expansion of capital also needs to be examined.

20 Laclau, *Politics and Ideology in Marxist Theory*, 167.

21 Neil Smith and Cindi Katz, "Grounding Metaphor: Towards a Spatialized Politics," in *Place and the Politics of Identity*, ed. Michael Keith and Steve Pile (New York: Routledge, 1993).

22 Studies of gender and race tackle this problem when they expose unequal gender or racial representations in state institutions, including institutionalized racism, which are built into the system. An example is the seniority system, which inadvertently discriminates against newly included groups such as African Americans, women, and new immigrants.

23 David Harvey, *The Limits to Capital* (London: Verso, 1999), 418.

24 Ernesto Laclau (with Chantal Mouffe), "Post-Marxism without Apologies," in Ernesto Laclau, *New Reflections of the Revolution of Our Time* (London: Verso, 1990).

25 Barrett, *The Politics of Truth*, 140.

26 Michel Foucault, *Power and Knowledge* (New York: Pantheon Books, 1972), 116-20.

27 Ibid., 125-42.

28 Ibid., 159-60. On other occasions, Foucault uses *production* in the broad sense of the creation of an army, the invention of the prison, and circulation of the population. For this reason, when he mentions the term *labor* he often refers to people "situated outside the circuits of productive labor." See the conversation with Foucault in ibid., 160-61.

29 Michel Foucault, *Discipline and Punish* (New York: Vintage, 1979), 208.

30 Karl Marx, *Critique of Hegel's "Philosophy of Right"* (London: Cambridge University Press, 1970).

31 For discussions of primitive accumulation, see Rosa Luxemberg, *The Accumulation of Capital* (New York: Monthly Review Press, 1973); Etienne Balibar, "Elements for a Theory of Transition," in Louis Althusser and Etienne Balibar, *Reading Capital* (London: Verso, 1970); Michael Hardt and Antonio Negri, *Empire* (Cambridge: Harvard University Press, 2000), 258; Michael Perelman, *The Invention of Capitalism* (Durham: Duke University Press, 2000); Jason Read, "Primitive Accumulation: The Aleatory Foundation of Capitalism," *Rethinking Marxism* 14:2 (Summer 2002): 24-40; and Keith Tribe, *Genealogies of Capitalism* (London: Macmillan, 1981).

32 For one of the few studies of Korean-Chinese relations in Manchuria that takes capitalism into account, see Kwon Hyang Suk, "Chūgoku niokeru 'chōsenzoku' no kenkyu josetsu" (An Introduction to the Study of the Korean-Chinese Community: Methodological Consideration), *Aziya Kenkyu* 47:3 (2001): 81-105.

33 Karl Marx, *Capital* vol. 1 (New York, Vintage, 1981), especially 935-36.

34 The analysis in this book draws on three sets of data published in China, Japan, and Korea. The first consists of reports compiled by the Chinese central and local administrations (those of Republican China and the Manchukuo state), the Japa-

nese Ministry of Foreign Affairs, and the Government General of Korea. The second consists of diverse documents dealing with agricultural relations, including economic surveys conducted by the South Manchuria Railway Company and reports of colonial development companies and the Chinese government. The first and second sets contain primary sources, while the third contains secondary publications such as memoirs, compiled histories of Manchuria, and scholarly studies.

Three related representations in the sources run counter to the analytical themes of this book: the separation of nationalist and agricultural relations, the separation of nationalist and economic subjects, and the dyadic schema of the national and colonial powers. Whether primary or secondary, the sources describe nationalist or agricultural relations but rarely both. The Chinese and Japanese government reports mainly concern disputes over territory, sovereignty, and national membership. The Chinese reports frequently equate the Japanese invasion and illegal Korean migration with the occupation of land as both territory and an agricultural resource. But the primary and secondary sources on agricultural relations rarely link national and agricultural policies in systematic ways. Furthermore, whether prepared by Chinese, Koreans, or Japanese, the sources on agricultural relations categorize individuals as class subjects: landlords, independent cultivators, tenants, or laborers. The distinction between Chinese, Koreans, and Japanese is rarely made in the agricultural records.

These two depictions in the sources are the problematic representations of national and colonial politics. As I noted earlier, landownership was contentiously marked as a right reserved for nationals and was implemented as a nationalist policy in complex ways from the second decade of the century to 1945. These representations coalesced with another tendency in the sources, which pairs colonial and national politics in an oppositional relation. Under colonial rule, Koreans in both Japanese and Chinese sources are categorized as Japanese and therefore pitted against the Chinese. Japanese police reports distinguish Koreans only in terms of whether they are pro- and anti-Japan. The triangular relationship among Japanese, Chinese, and Koreans does not principally register in either the Chinese or Japanese sources. Korean (and Chinese) communists and activists grouped the Koreans and Chinese in Manchuria together in an effort to mobilize them to form a united front against the Japanese. Their political writings often gloss over the conflicts between Koreans and Chinese over national membership and property ownership, as well as differences between Koreans of Manchuria and Koreans of Korea.

My method of interpreting data has simulated an ethnographic approach that advocates a participant role for the researcher in interactions with the subjects and events under observation. Of course, archival historical research precludes direct physical contact with subjects or events. However, my interaction has been guided by two practices that have helped me immerse myself in history: a deconstructive reading of texts and an analytic focus on social practices. My reading of the data has interacted with the theoretical approaches to colonialism, nationalism, and capitalism that I outlined earlier. Theoretical debates have helped me make the links between things, events, and categories that are not apparent in archival and contemporary texts. My theoretical and historical approach is the result of my new readings of the sources.

Moreover, observing patterns of social practices has made it possible to glimpse the social lives of the people of Manchuria. Irregular and incoherent practices of landownership and national membership, which persistently deviated from laws and policies, convey the ways in which people interpreted events, assigned meanings to their labor and property, and interacted with others. Just as an ethnographer participates in daily lives of people and thus shapes their interactions with one another and the course of events under observation, I have adopted strategies of reading and analysis that can help us comprehend the complex social reality of Manchuria. My uncovering of what is not evident in the sources suggests that my explanation provides not so much a discovery of objective reality as an interpretation of structural forces and social practices.

ONE   *The Politics of Osmosis*

1   An Sugil, Pukkando (Northern Kando), vol. 1 (reprint; Seoul: Samjungdang, 1993).
2   For a collection of prominent writers' accounts of travel in Manchuria, see *Kando Yurang 40 nyŏn* (Forty Years of Travel in Kando), ed. So Chaeyoung (Seoul: Chosŏnilbosa, 1989). Writers who moved to North Korea following the Japanese defeat included Kang Kyŏngae, Lee Taejun, and Lee Kiyŏung. For a South Korean collection of colonial writings on Manchuria, see Oh Yangho, *Han'guk munhakkwa Kando* (Korean Literature and Kando) (Seoul: Munye chulp'ansa, 1988).
3   Carter Eckert et al., *Korea: Old and New* (Cambridge: Korea Institute, Harvard University, 1990), 221–24.
4   An Sugil, Pukkando, 1–64.
5   Ibid., 65.
6   Ibid.
7   Ibid., 84.
8   Ibid., 158; Eckert et al., *Korea*, 236–541; Mark Peattie, "The Japanese Colonial Empire, 1895–1945," in *The Cambridge History of Japan*, vol. 6, ed. Peter Duus (Cambridge: Cambridge University Press, 1988), 6:226.
9   An Sugil, Pukkando, 190.
10   Ibid., 195.
11   Ibid., 220.
12   Ibid., 222.
13   Ibid., 226.
14   Ibid., 321.
15   Ibid., 319.
16   Ibid., 321.

17 Ibid., 322.

18 Ibid., 374–75.

19 For comprehensive accounts of routes of Korean migration and settlement, see Hyŏn Kyuhwan, Han'guk Yuiminsa I (The History of the Migration of Koreans) (Seoul: Ŏmungak, 1967), 145–647. The estimates of the Korean population varied. Son Ch'unil compares various statistics as follows: "In 1929, the Japanese consulate estimated the Korean population of Manchuria to be 589,990; in 1926, the SMRC reported it as 783,187; and in 1925, the Chosŏn newspaper of Korea announced it to be 1.2 million," cited from Son Ch'unil, Haebangjŏn tongbuk Chosŏnjok t'oji kwan'gaesa yŏn'gu vol. 1 (A Study of Land Relations of Koreans in Northeast China Before Liberation) (Jilin, China: Jilin Inmin ch'ulp'ansa, 2001), 129.

20 Koreans also migrated to Russia, Japan and its other colonies, especially Sakhalin. But it was mainly the Korean migration to Manchuria that served the osmotic expansion of the Japanese empire.

21 Peter Duus, Ramon Myers, and Mark Peattie, eds., The Japanese Informal Empire in China, 1895–1937 (Princeton: Princeton University Press 1989).

22 Japan encouraged the migration of Japanese to Korea and Manchuria, though it never met the government's expectations. Japanese in Taiwan and Korea numbered 5.8 and 2.9 percent of the total population of Taiwan and Korea, respectively, in 1945. For more information, see Peattie, "The Japanese Colonial Empire, 1895–1945," 262.

23 Quoted from Premier Tanaka, The Tanaka Memorial (San Francisco, n.p., n.d.), 3. The authenticity of this report, presented by Tanaka to the Japanese emperor on July 25, 1927, is controversial. The controversy over authenticity obscures the fact that the report succinctly epitomizes Japanese territorial ambitions from the late nineteenth century on. For the most recent debates over the authenticity of the document, see Zhengxie Shenyangshi weiyuanhui wenshi ziliao yanjiu weiyuanhui bian (Department of the Archives of the Committee of the Politics and Negotiation, Shenyang), Shenyangwenshi ziliao (Shenyang Archives), vol. II, Zhang Xueliang jiangjun shiliao xuanji (Collected Histories of General Zhang Xueliang) (Shenyang: Zhengxie Shenyangshi weiyuanhi wenshi ziliao yanjiu weiyuanhui bangongshi chuban, 1986), 47–56.

24 Chungmoo Choi, "The Discourse of Decolonization and Popular Memory: South Korea," in The Politics of Culture in the Shadow of Capital, ed. Lisa Lowe and David Lloyd (Durham: Duke University Press, 1997), 468.

25 See Peattie, "The Japanese Colonial Empire, 1895–1945," 238–41; and Choi, "The Discourse of Decolonization and Popular Memory."

26 See Harry Harootunian, Overcome by Modernity: History, Culture and Community in Interwar Japan (Princeton: Princeton University Press, 2000), especially chapter 5 on the communal body, which includes his discussion of Jean Luc Nancy's concept of immanentism.

27 Stefan Tanaka, Japan's Orient: Rendering Pasts into History (Berkeley: University of Cali-

fornia Press, 1993). This cultural construction of inclusion is not unique to Japanese colonialism. Thomas R. Trautmann, in his recent study of British India, argues that the British in the mid–eighteenth century evoked the linguistic affinity of Europe and India and kinship relations between Indians and Britons. With a historical study of Aryans, he also traces how this view came to be contested by race science and orientalism in the nineteenth century. See Thomas R. Trautmann, *Aryans and British India* (Berkeley: University of California Press, 1997).

28 Tanaka, *Japan's Orient*, 70.

29 For the resolution on Korean nationality that was passed in a Cabinet meeting in Tokyo, see Yamabe Kentaro, *Ilche gangjŏmhaŭi han'guk kŭndaesa* (The Modern History of Korea under Japanese Occupation), trans. Lee Hyŏnhee (Seoul: Samkwang, 1988), 11–13. In this book, I prefer the term *national membership* to citizenship to refer to membership in a state, though I use both. This is because, although *national membership* and *citizenship* tended to correspond to each other in the twentieth century, especially prior to the current neoliberal capitalist expansion (when citizenship was usually restricted to nationals), Koreans in Korea and Manchuria were not endowed with the rights to vote and free association during the colonial period. The unprecedented surge of transnational migration that began in the 1980s has engendered a new politics of citizenship in which foreign migrants have demanded their rights to public education, to vote in local elections, and to receive other benefits. For the uncoupling of *national membership* and *citizenship*, especially in Japan, see Chikako Kashiwazaki, "The Politics of Legal Status: The Equation of Nationality with Ethnonational Identity," in *Koreans in Japan*, ed. Sonia Ryang (New York: Routledge, 2000); and Alexander Aleinkoff and Douglas Klusmeyer, eds., *From Migrants to Citizens* (Washington, D.C.: Brookings Institution, 2000).

30 For more on the adoption of foreign nationality by exiled Korean nationalists, see Yamabe, *Ilche gangjŏmhaŭi han'guk kŭndaesa*, 13; and chapter 3 in this volume.

31 *Kunan douzheng shisinian* (Struggles and Hardship for Fourteen Years), vol. 2 (Beijing: Zhongguo dabeike quanji chubanshe, 1995).

32 The SMRC was established to operate the South Manchuria Railway, but it came to oversee various colonial projects, such as the research on agriculture and the immigration of Japanese subjects. See also Ito Takeo, *Life along the South Manchurian Railway: The Memoirs of Ito Takeo*, trans. with an introduction by Joshua Fogel (Armonk, N.Y.: M. E. Sharpe, 1988), vii.

33 *Gaimushō Keisatsushi* (The Police History of the Japanese Ministry of Foreign Affairs) vol. 19, SP 205-5, 162–91 (Tokyo: Fuji Shuppan, 1998), 42–50, esp. 42–43.

34 Lim Yŏngsŏ, "1910–20 nyŏndae Kando hanine daehan chunggugŭi chŏngch'aekwa minhoe" (Chinese Policies on Koreans of Kan-do and Min-hwe from the 1920s until the 1930s), M.A. thesis, Seoul National University, 1933, 22. For the interpretation by Chinese officials of the relationship between Koreans and Japanese power, see Ch'u Hŏnsu, ed., *Han'guk tongnip undong* (Korean Independence Movements), vol. 4, *Haewoe ijumin'gwa tongnip undong I* (Overseas Immigrants and the

Liberation Movement) (Seoul: Yonsei University Press, 1975), esp. "Part III: Man-chu Munjewa Chungil Kwankye" (The Manchuria Question and the Relationship between China and Japan), 809–39.

35 Pak Ch'angwuk, "Chimnyage riyong haryŏnŭn ilcheŭi Chosŏnin imin chŏng-ch'aek" (The Japanese Immigration Policy Used in the Invasion), in *Chungguk Chosŏn minjok palchach'wi ch'ongsŏ* (History of the Korean Chinese in China), vol. 2, *Pulssi* (Kindling) (Beijing: Minjok Ch'ulp'ansa, 1995), 4–12, quotation on 7. This quota-tion originally came from a report of the Tōa Kangyō Kabushiki Gaisha (Asia De-velopment Company).

36 Duus, *The Cambridge History of Japan*, 6:1–13; Ikuhiko Hata, "Continental Expan-sion, 1905–1941," in Duus, *The Cambridge History of Japan*, 6:287–89. Hata cautioned against oversimplifying the comparison between the Manchurian policies of the Shidehara and Tanaka Cabinets.

37 Peattie, "The Japanese Colonial Empire, 1895–1945," 245.

38 My discussion of the three periods is derived from "Ilbonŭi chaeman kikwanŭi tongil munje" (The Problem of the Integration of Japanese Institutions in Manchu-ria), *Manju Ilbo* (September 1934), in Ch'u Hŏnsu, *Han'guk tongnip undong*, 4:991–98.

39 Peattie, "The Japanese Colonial Empire, 1895–1945," 244. The Ministry of Colo-nial Affairs was replaced by the Greater East Asia Ministry when the Pacific War began in 1940.

40 The Oriental Development Company also promoted the migration of Japanese peasants to Korea, sending 9,096 households between 1910 and 1926.

41 Yamame, *Ilche kangjŏmhaŭi han'guk kŭndaesa*, 34.

42 On the practice of accumulating land, especially by the Oriental Development Company, see ibid., 34.

43 On Japanese recollections of this deception, see ibid., 45.

44 *Tōyō Takushoku Kabushiki Gaisha Sanjūnenshi* (The Thirty-Year History of the Oriental Development Company) (Tokyo: Tōyō Takushoku Kabushiki Gaisha, 1939), 235–43.

45 The financial subsidies provided by the Korean colonial state and the Kwantung Administration varied from 150,000 to 400,000 yen and 50,000 to 200,000 yen, re-spectively, in 1927 and 1931. For more details, see *Tōa Kangyō Kabushiki Gaisha Jūnen-shi* (The Ten-Year History of the Asia Development Company) (Tokyo: Tōa Kangyō Kabushiki Gaisha, 1933), 21–30.

46 *Senman Takushoku Kabushiki Gaisha Mansen Takushoku Kabushiki Gaisha Gonenshi* (The Five-Year History of the Korea-Manchuria Development Company and the Man-churia-Korea Development Company) (Changchun: Senman Takushoku Kabushiki Gaisha Mansen Takushoku Kabushiki Gaisha, 1941), 12–43.

47 Aihwa Ong, *Flexible Citizenship: The Cultural Logics of Transnationality* (Durham: Duke University Press, 1999); Arjun Appadurai, *Modernity at Large: Cultural Dimensions of Globalization* (Minneapolis: University of Minnesota Press, 1996).

TWO Between Nation and Market

1 On the transformation of the Manchus in Manchuria, see Dan Shao, "From Homeland to Borderland: Manchus and Manchuria in the Early Twentieth Century," paper presented at the workshop "Manchuria's Borderland: History, Culture, and Identity in a Colonial Space," April 30–May 1, 2004, Fairbank Center for East Asian Research, Harvard University.

2 For biographical notes and recollections of Zhang Zuolin and Zhang Xueliang by former friends and officials, see Zhengxie Shenyangshi weiyuanhui wenshi ziliao yanjiu weiyuanhui bian, Shenyang wenshi ziliao (Shenyang Archives), vol. 11, Zhang Xueliang jianjun, esp. 191–94, on a secret agreement between Zhang Zuolin and the Kuomintang on the united front against Japan just before his death; and Zhengxie Shenyangshi weiyuanhui wenshi ziliao yanjiu weiyuanhui bian, Shenyang wenshi ziliao (Shenyang Archives), vol. 12, Zhang Zuolin (Collected Histories of Zhang Zuolin) (Shenyang: Zhengxie Shenyangshi weiyuanhui wenshi zilia yanjiu weiyuanhui bangonshi chuban, 1986). On Zhang Xueliang's anti-Japanese positions and opposition to civil wars, see especially Zhang Deliang and Zhou Yi, Dongbei junshi (The Military History of Northeast China) (Shenyang: Liaoning daxue chubanshe, 1987), 186–97, 647–62.

3 Hsi-sheng Ch'i, Warlord Politics in China, 1916–1928 (Stanford: Stanford University Press, 1976); Jerome Ch'en, "Defining Chinese Warlords and Their Factions," Bulletin of the School of Oriental and African Studies 31 (1968): 563–600; Diana Lary, "Warlord Studies," Modern China 6:4 (1980): 439–70; Henry McAleary, "China under the War-Lords, Part I," China Today 12:4 (1962): 227–33; Henry McAleary, "China under the War-Lords, Part II," China Today 12:5 (1962): 303–11; Gavan McCormack, Chang Tso-lin in Northeast China, 1911–1928 (Stanford: Stanford University Press, 1977).

4 Zhang Zuolin financed at least two former military advisers who won seats in the Japanese Diet. For details on his relations with the Japanese military advisers, see Zhengxie Shenyang shiweiyuanhui wenshi ziliao yanjiu weiyuanhui bian, Shenyang wenshi ziliao, 11:195–99. The Manchuria Incident in 1931 paved the way for Japan to create a puppet government in Manchuria. When a bomb exploded on the SMR near Shenyang (then known as Mukden), the Kwantung Army seized the incident as a pretext to occupy major cities in Manchuria.

5 Dongbei jingjishi (The Economic History of Northeast China) (Chengdu: Sichuan renmin chubanshe, 1986), 92, 389–91.

6 Ronald Suleski, Civil Government in Warlord China: Tradition, Modernization and Manchuria (New York: Peter Lang, 2002), 113–14.

7 McCormack, Chang Tso-lin in Northeast China, 1911–1928; Suleski, Civil Government in Warlord China. On innovative methods to increase revenue, see Li Hongwen, Chang Cheng, and Zhu Jianhua, Xiandai Dongbeishi (The Modern History of Northeast China) (Harbin: Heilongjiang jiaoyu chubanshe, 1986), 12–52.

8 See Kang Chao, The Economic Development of Manchuria: The Rise of a Frontier Economy

(Ann Arbor: University of Michigan Center for Chinese Studies, 1982); Ramon Myers, "Japanese Imperialism in Manchuria: The South Manchurian Railway Company, 1906–1933," in *The Japanese Informal Empire in China, 1895–1937*, ed. Peter Duus, Ramon Myers, and Mark Peattie (Princeton: Princeton University Press, 1989); and Ronald Suleski, "The Rise and Fall of the Fengtien Dollar, 1917–1928: Currency Reform in Warlord China," *Modern Asian Studies* 13:4 (1979): 643–60.

9   Li Hongwen, Chang Cheng, and Zhu Jianhua, *Xiandai Dongbeishi*, 57.

10 On the boycott of Japanese currency in 1915, see *Fengtiansheng yihui ziliao* JC 10-1695 (Records of the Parliament of Fengtian Province), 2378–2386 (Reserved in Shenyang: Liaoningsheng danganguan).

11 Li Hongwen, Chang Cheng, and Zhu Jianhua, *Xiandai Dongbeishi*, 116–18.

12 Dongbei jingjishixuehui, ed., *Dongbei jingjishi lunwenji Xia* (Collected Works on the Economic History in Northeast China) (Harbin: Yajing Heilongjiang chubanshe, 1984), 194–95.

13 *Dongbei jingjishi*.

14 Herbert Bix, "Japanese Imperialism and the Manchurian Economy, 1900–1931," *China Quarterly* 51 (1972): 425–43.

15 Owen Lattimore, *Manchuria: Cradle of Conflict* (New York: Macmillan, 1935).

16 McCormack, *Chang Tso-lin in Northeast China, 1911–1928*, 14.

17 *Dongbei jingjishi*.

18 Ibid., 285. For a detailed list of the personal properties of Zhang and his close associates, see Li Hongwen, Chang Cheng, and Zhu Jianhua, *Xiandai Dongbeishi*, 60. Zhang Zuolin's personal property included 151,500 *ssang* of land, two houses, silver worth five thousand yuan; savings in banks; and investments in grain stores, pawnshops, mines, railways, textiles, banks, and joint ventures between the Northeast government and merchants. His associates invested in pawnshops, farms, electricity companies, textile factories, banks, steel factories, mines, and railways. For information on Zhang Zuolin's investment in Sino-Japanese joint ventures in coal and steel factories, see Kim Kibong et al., *Ilbon cheguk chuŭiŭi tongbuk ch'imnyaksa* (The History of the Japanese Invasion of Northeast China) (Yanji: Yanbian People's Publishing Company, 1987), 92.

19 *Dongbei jingjishi*, 136–50, 178–390.

20 For histories of the official banks, see *Dongbei jingjishi*, 278–309. See also Suleski, *Civil Government in Warlord China*, chapter 6.

21 *Contemporary Manchuria* 2:4 (1938): 59.

22 For more information on joint ventures prior to the treaty, see *Fengtiansheng yihui ziliao* JC 10–1695 (Records of the Parliament of Fengtian Province), 2378–2386; and Dux Uncheng, *Riben zaijiu zhongguode touzi* (Japanese Investment in China) (Shanghai: Shanghai shehui kexueyuan chubanshe, 1986), 401–8. The proportion of Japanese investment in joint ventures in Northeast China increased from 63.7 percent of the total capital in 1907 to 90 percent in 1925.

23 McCormack, *Chang Tso-lin in Northeast China, 1911–1928*.

24 For more on these attempts to separate Manchuria from China proper, see Kim Kibong et al., *Ilbon chegukchuŭiŭi tongbuk ch'imnyaksa*, 50–89.

25 For a recent compilation of Korean history in Manchuria, see *Chungguk Chosŏn minjok palchach'wi ch'ongsŏ*, vol. 2, *Pulssi*.

26 For historical studies that focus on the leasing of railways and the peninsula, see Duus, Myers, and Peattie, *The Japanese Informal Empire in China, 1895–1937*.

27 Liaoningsheng danganguan bian (Archives of Liaoning Province), *Zhonghua minguo shizi liaoconggao diangao fenzi junfa mi dian* (Collections of Historical Documents of the Chinese People's Republic, Feudal Warlord Secret Telegrams), vol. 1, 1919 (Shenyang: Zhonghwa shuju, 1987) (Reserved in the Liaoning Provincial Archives in Shenyang, China). This volume contains official and confidential documents exchanged between China and Japan, as well as between central and various local government officials, during and after the negotiations. I draw on these documents to explore the contestation of landownership discussed in this section. A brief report on the land leasing and dual nationality of Koreans can be found in the *Lytton Report* (Seoul: Tamgudang, 1986), 372–92.

28 Chapter 3 examines the issue of the geographic application of the Treaty. For an excellent summary of the disputes over sangjo, also see Son Ch'unil, *Manjugugŭi chaeman hanine daehan t'oji chŏngch'aek yŏn'gu* (A Study of the Manchukuo Policy on the Land Rights of the Koreans in Manchuria) (Seoul: Paesan Charyowŏn, 1999), 55–56.

29 The Japanese view is suggested in "The Reality of Modern Mongolia," in *Han'guk tongnip undong*, ed. Ch'u Hŏnsu (The Liberation Movement of Korea), vol. 4, *Haeoe ijumin'gwa tongnip undong I* (Overseas Immigrants and the Liberation Movement) (Seoul: Yŏnsei taehak ch'ulp'ansa, 1975). This book maintains that in Mongolia the Japanese term sangjogwon refers to the right to lease permanently. In his account, "although the contract of *sangjo* restricts the leasing of land up to 30 years, it equals permanent leasing since those who leased land would have to pay the fee to landowners" (1146–47).

30 Son Ch'unil, *Manjugug'ŭi chaeman hanine taehan t'oji chŏngch'aek yŏn'gu*, 56.

31 Ch'u Hŏnsu, *Han'guk tongnip undong*, 4:1156.

32 Liaoning sheng danganguan bian (Archives of Liaoning Province), *Zhonghua minguo shizi liaoconggao diangao fenzi junfa mi dian* (Collections of Historical Documents of the Chinese People's Republic, Feudal Warlord Secret Telegrams), vol. 1, 1919, 76.

33 On the Fengtian provincial government's policy for rice cultivation, see *Chungguk Chosŏn minjok palchachw'i ch'ongsŏ*, vol. 2, *Pulssi*, 147. Population estimates varied. In one estimate, Koreans in Tongbyŏndo alone, which was the border region of the Fengtian Province and Korea, amounted to 250,000 in 1920. See *Gaimushō Keisatsushi* (The Police History of the Japanese Ministry of Foreign Affairs), vol. 10, SP 205-4, 5180–81, (Tokyo: Fuji Shuppan, 1997), p. 104. In another estimate, the Korean population increased from 96,235 to 169,514 in Fengtian Province, including Tongbyŏndo. See Hyŏn Kyuhwan, *Han'guk yuiminsa I*, 165.

34 For reports on Korean living conditions, see *Gaimushō Keisatsushi*, vol. 10, SP 205-
    4, 4910–25, pp. 38–40; and *Chōsen Sōtokufu Teikoku Kaigi Setsumei Shiryō* (Documents
    Prepared by the Government General of Korea for the 51st Imperial Assembly,
    1926), vol. 16 (Tokyo: Fuji Shuppan, 1926), 66–70.

35 My discussion of the consul meeting draws on Hyŏn Ch'unch'u, "Iljeŭi 'che ilch'a
    yŏngsahoeŭi' wa Chosŏnjogŭi ogurhan 'ijung kukchŏk' munje" (The First Consul
    Meeting and the Undeserved Dual Nationality of Koreans), in *Chungguk Chosŏn min-
    jok palchach'wi ch'ongsŏ*, vol. 2, *Pulssi*, 13–33.

36 For a recent study of the disputes over Korean naturalization, see Barbara Brooks,
    "Peopling in the Japanese Empire: The Koreans in Manchuria and the Rhetoric of
    Inclusion," in *Japan's Competing Modernities: Issues in Culture and Democracy, 1900–1930*,
    ed. Sharon Minichiello (Honolulu: University of Hawai'i Press, 1998), 25–44.

37 For detailed discussion of this requirement of the nationality law, see Son Ch'unil,
    Manjugugŭi chaeman hanine taehan t'oji chŏngch'aek yŏn'gu, 156–57. The requirement
    was eliminated in 1929.

38 Hyŏn Ch'unchu, "Iljeŭi 'che ilch'a yŏngsahoeŭi' wa Chosŏnjogŭi ogurhan 'ichung
    kukjŏk' munje," 19–20.

39 For a discussion of this new Japanese stand on Korean naturalization, see Son
    Ch'unil, *Manjugugŭi chaeman hanine taehan t'oji chŏngch'aek yŏn'gu*, 158–59.

40 *Gaimushō Keisatsushi*, vol. 7, SP 205-4, 885–91 (Tokyo: Fuji Shuppan, 1996), pp. 227–
    28.

41 Ibid., SP 205-4, 960–63, p. 246.

42 The precarious state of Korean nationality contradicted the claim by Japan of Kore-
    ans as Japanese subjects. Some Koreans possessed dual nationality by becoming
    naturalized as Chinese nationals without giving up their original nationality, while
    some Koreans born in Manchuria did not hold any identification as Japanese sub-
    jects; however, the status of Korean naturalization did not seem to matter, since
    the relations between Koreans of Manchuria and Korea still seemed inseparable
    whether the former were naturalized or not.

43 *Chōsen Sōtokufu Teikoku Kaigi Setsumei Shiryō*, vol. 15, 1925 (Tokyo: Fuji Shuppan, 1998)
    260–67. Rice cultivation was highly valued in Manchuria, especially after World
    War I, when prices surged in international markets. However, soybeans were the
    primary cash crop. Soybeans comprised about 42 percent of total agricultural pro-
    duction in 1923 and 51 percent in 1928. They constituted about 30 percent of the
    total value of exports until 1930. For more details, see *Dongbei jingjishi* II, 30; and
    Kim Kibong et al., *Ilbon chegukchuŭiŭi tongbuk ch'imnyaksa*, 53–54, 95–96.

44 *Tōa Kangyō Kabushiki Gaisha Jūnenshi*, 53–63. For examples of the annulment of leas-
    ing in 1922 and 1925 and Chinese protests against Japanese reclamation, see Pak
    Ch'angwuk, "Simyang, Musun chiguesŏ" (In the Shenyang and Musun Regions),
    in *Chungguk Chosŏn minjok palchach'wi ch'ongso*, vol. 2, *Pulssi*, 146–49.

45 Ibid.; and *Tōa Kangyō Kabushiki Gaisha Jūnenshi*, 85–137.

46 *Chōsen Sōtokufu Teikoku Kaigi Setsumei Shiryō*, vol. 15, 260–67.

47 Ibid.; and Pak Ch'angwuk, "Simyang, Musun chikuesŏ," 148. According to Pak, the area under rice cultivation did not increase much, despite the emphasis on its expansion. In some regions, it actually decreased in the late 1920s due to heightened tension between Japan and China over land.

48 *Chōsen Sōtokufu Teikoku Kaigi Setsumei Shiryō*, vol. 15, 260–67; and *Tōa Kangyō Kabushiki Gaisha Jūnenshi*, 161–70.

49 *Gaimushō Keisatsushi*, vol. 11, SP 205-4, 7552–7555, pp. 328–29; and *Gaimushō Keisatsushi*, vol. 12, SP 205-4, 7963–7969 (Tokyo: Fuji Shuppan, 1997), pp. 7–11.

50 This figure on Japanese forces is from Zhongyang danganguan (Chinese Central Archives) et al., eds., "Jiangyu gei Zhongyang de baogao-guanyu Manzhou de yiban ginzhi, dangde fanzhan zhuang kuang deng Wenti (1931.5.11)" (Jiangyu's Report to the Central Chinese Communist Party on General Conditions in Manchuria and the Development of the Party [1931.5.11]), in Jia 31, in *Dongbei diqu geming lishi wenjian huiji* (Archives of Revolutionary History in Northeast China), ed. Zhongyang danganguan (The Chinese Central Archives) (Harbin: Harbin hulan yinshuachang, 1989), 53–85. According to another Chinese source based on an official survey in 1931, Japanese police and military forces numbered 24,677, including 5,400 guards defending the South Manchuria Railway, 1,860 air force soldiers, 1,937 military policemen, 720 private uniformed policemen, and 14,760 regular military personnel. The number of Japanese police and military forces increased five times from 1922 to 1931. For the details, see Ch'u Hŏnsu, *Han'guk tongnip undong*, 4:875–76. For more on the illicit expeditions of Japanese forces, see Ch'u Hŏnsu, *Han'guk tongnip undong*, 4:875–905.

51 *Gaimushō Keisatsushi*, vol. 8, SP 205-4, 1493–1507 (Tokyo: Fuji Shuppan, 1996), pp. 3–6.

52 My discussion of the Association for the Protection of People draws on ibid., SP 205-4, 1493–1538, pp. 3–14; 1559–1604, pp. 19–30; 1819–34, pp. 72–73; 1996–2024, pp. 124–36.

53 For a discussion of the major Korean independence organizations, especially in the Tongbyŏndo region, including the Hanjokhoe, Tongnipdan, and Kunbidan, see ibid., vol. 10, SP 205-4, 5177–86 (Tokyo: Fuji Shuppan, 1997), pp. 103.

54 Japanese consulates also supported other farmers' organizations. For instance, financial assistance from a consulate enabled one farmer's organization, Haerim Kwonnoghoe (Haerim Farmer's Union), to pay the interest on loans from the Asia Development Company. For details, see ibid., vol. 15, SP 205-4, 12622–37, pp. 6–10.

55 *Gaimushō Keisatsushi*, vol. 4, SP 205-3, 290–93 (Tokyo: Fuji Shuppan, 1996), pp. 75–76.

56 In 1911, the magistrate of Wangch'ŏng County requested that Dongnanlu bingbeidao formulate policies to address the swelling migration of Koreans and the Japanese claims on them. See Dongnanlu bingbeidao "Wangqingxiancheng ganmin ruji geqingxing bingfeng daocheng jiegan jiebao jiege liubai zhangyou" (Wangqing

County's Report on Various Circumstances of the Naturalization of Koreans and the Submission of Six Hundred Official Documents, Oaths, and Letters of Guarantee), 1910, 10.22–1911, 9.24. anjuanhao 22, 1.1-1.

57 *Wangqing xian zhengzhi baoguoshu* (Wangqing County Political Reports). vol. 1, 38.

58 "Guanyu guanli hanqiao fangfa de zhiling" (Instructions on Supervising Koreans), Jilin Yanjidao Daoyin gongshu zhiling de 20 hao, ling Dunhuaxian zhishi 1928 (The Decree of the Head of Yanji District of Jilin, Number 20, the Order to the Magistrate of Dunhua County in 1928).

59 Dongnanlu bingbeidao, "Wangqingxian cheng ganmin ruji geqingxing bingfeng daocheng jiegan jiebao jiege liubaizhang you."

60 On the Colonization and Development Plan, see Suleski, *Civil Government in Warlord China,* 91–96. The population of Manchuria increased from approximately 24 million in 1900 to 31 million in 1920, 37 million in 1930, and 47 million in 1942. For a comprehensive study of Chinese migration in the twentieth century, see Thomas R. Gottschang and Diana Lary, *Swallows and Settlers: The Great Migration from North China to Manchuria* (Ann Arbor: Center for Chinese Studies, University of Michigan, 2000).

61 *Contemporary Manchuria* 2:4.

62 Ramon H. Myers, *The Japanese Economic Development of Manchuria 1932 to 1945* (New York: Garland Publishing Inc., 1982), 88.

63 Chōsen Sōtokufu Keimukyoku, *Zaiman Senjin to Shina Kanken* (Koreans and Chinese Officials in Manchuria) (Keijyō: Gyōsei Gakkai Insatsujo, 1930), 272.

64 Ibid., 243.

65 Ibid., 278. On various anti-Japanese protests in this period, see Li Hongwen, Chang Cheng, and Zhu Jianhua, *Xiandai Dongbeishi,* 89–127.

66 The revised nationality law in Northeast China in 1931 stipulated such penalties on leasing land to foreigners as a maximum of five years' imprisonment and arrest of landlords. For more details, see Lee Hun'gu, *Manjuwa Chosŏnin* (Manchuria and Koreans) (Kyongsŏng: Hansŏngdosŏ chusikhoesa, 1932), 252–54.

67 Chōsen Sōtokufu Keimukyoku, *Zaiman Senjin to Shina Kanken,* 274.

68 For more on the prohibition of leasing land to Japanese, see *Tōhoku Kankensho Hatsu Hainichi Hōrei Shū* (Collection of Chinese Laws against Japan in Northeast China) (Minami Manshū Tetsudō Kabushiki Gaisha, 1931), 1–47.

69 On these customs, see Son Ch'unil, *Manjugug'ŭi chaeman hanine taehan t'oji chŏngch'aek yŏn'gu,* 38; Pak Ilcho, "Yŏnbyŏnesŏ sŏnghaengdoen 'Chŏnminjedo'" (A Popular Practice, Chŏnminje, in Kando), in *Chungguk Chosŏn minjok palchach'wi ch'ongsŏ,* vol. 2, *Pulssi,* 110–15.

70 On Korean oppression by Chinese officials and cases of Koreans returning to Korea, see *Zaiman Senjin Appaku Jijō* (The Conditions of Korean Oppression in Manchuria) (Minami Manshū Tetsudō Kabushiki Gaisha, 1928), 17–22; and *Tōhoku Kankensho Hatsu Hainichi Hōrei Shū,* 48–56.

71 Chōsen Sōtokufu Keimukyoku, *Zaiman Senjin to Shina Kanken,* 201. According to Lee

Hun'gu, there were 181 cases of oppression of Koreans by Chinese officials in 1927, with 42 cases of forced naturalization and 7 cases of the confiscation of the residence permit. Although Lee does not specify where the oppression occurred, there was great regional variation in Chinese policies on Korean naturalization (discussed in chapters 2 and 3). Though vague, Lee's figures suggest inconsistency in the Chinese policies on Korean naturalization in southern Manchuria (Lee Hun'gu, Manjuwa Chosŏnin, 241–45).

72 For details on the three required forms of naturalization, the application form, the form that verified applicants' qualifications, and the form documenting the renunciation of their original citizenship, see Yang Zhaoquan and Li Tiehuan, eds., Dongbei diqu manxianren geming douzhe ziliao xuanji (Archives of the Revolutionary Struggle of Koreans in Northeast China) (Shengyang: Liaoningsheng minzu chubanshe, 1992), 63–65.

73 Li Hongwen, Chang Cheng, and Zhu Jianhua, Xiandai Dongbeishi, 89–127. The eviction of Koreans was extended beyond southern Manchuria to Jilin (Lee Hun'gu, Manjuwa Chosŏnin, 244–51).

74 Chōsen Sōtokufu Teikoku Kaigi Setsumei Shiryō, 14:12.

75 Gaimushō Keisatsushi, vol. 11, SP 205-4, 6729–44, pp. 135–39.

76 Yang Zhaoquan and Li Tiehuan, eds., Dongbei diqu manxianren geming douzheng ziliao xuanji, 94–96.

77 Chōsen Sōtokufu Keimukyoku, Zaiman Senjin to Shina Kanken, 159.

78 Contemporary Manchuria 3 (1939): 26. The productivity of Korean rice farmers on average was 3.7 times higher than the Chinese, as can be inferred from statistics of 1934. For instance, the average yield of rice per chŏngbo under Korean and Chinese cultivation was 27.4 and 8.6 sok, respectively, in Fengtian Province; 5.6 and 2.7 sok in Andong Province (part of the earlier Tongbyŏndo region of Fengtian Province); and 26.4 and 14.9 sok in Jilin Province. An exception was the Kando region, with 25.9 and 35.0 sok for the average yield of rice per chŏngbo under Korean and Chinese cultivation. For more details, see Zaiman Nihon Teikoku Taishikan Hensan, Zaiman Chōsenjin Gaikyō (The General Condition of Koreans in Manchuria), 1934, 541.

79 Estimates of rice fields cultivated by Koreans and Chinese varied by region. Rice fields cultivated by Koreans amount to on average 84 percent of the total area under rice cultivation in Manchuria in 1925 and 85 percent in the Fengtian region (Fengtian Province minus the Tongbyŏndo region), 70 percent in the Andong region (part of Tongbyŏndo), and 100 percent in Jilin and Heilongjiang Provinces. The estimated proportion of rice fields to the total area of land cultivated by Koreans suggests the degree of risk and the number of failed attempts at rice cultivation, since Koreans resorted to farming other crops only when soil conditions were unsuitable for rice. Although discourses portrayed Koreans as engaged primarily in rice farming, the proportion of rice fields to the total area of land that they cultivated was 31 percent on average, with wide regional variations: 34 percent in

southern Manchuria, 8 percent in Kando, and 100 percent in northern Manchuria (Lee Hun'gu, *Manjuwa Chosŏnin*). In a different estimate, rice fields constituted about 26 percent of the total land reclaimed by Koreans (Hyŏn Kyuhwan, *H an'guk Yuiminsa* I, 266). Yet, these statistics are only suggestive and perhaps underrepresent the proportion of rice fields under Korean cultivation, since they do not specify the probable transfer of rice fields from Koreans to Chinese.

80 Chōsen Sōtokufu Keimukyoku, *Zaiman Senjin to Shina Kanken*, 242–47. The exclusionary policy toward Koreans encouraged landlords to increase rents when they hired them (Lee Hun'gu, *Manjuwa Chosŏnin*, 254–57).

81 Although there were many attempts by landlords and Koreans to experiment with rice farming in Tongbyŏndo, because this region is mountainous, the proportion of rice fields to the total area of land cultivated by Koreans was about 4 percent, much lower than the average of 26 percent (Hyŏn Kyuhwan, *Han'guk Yuiminsa* I, 266). Examples of partial inclusion in this region, which was least appropriate for rice farming, suggests that the Northeast government may have been more lenient in places where Koreans engaged in more rice farming.

82 Chōsen Sōtokufu Keimukyoku, *Zaiman Senjin to Shina Kanken*, 167.

83 Ibid., 247.

84 Ibid., 248.

85 For details on the Manbosan Incident, see Makoto Nukaga, "The Koreans in Manchuria," M.A. thesis, University of California, Berkeley, 1931. For a compilation of various Chinese sources on this event, see Liaoningsheng danganguan, *Wanbaoshan shijian* (The Wanbaoshan Incident) (Jilin: Jilin renmin chubanshe, 1990). For news reports in the United States, see the *New York Times*, July 17, 1931, and August 3, 1931. For a study renowned in South Korea, see Pak Yŏngsok, *Manbosan sagŏn yŏn'gu* (A Study of the Manbosan Incident) (Seoul: Asea munhwasa, 1978).

THREE *Agency of Japanese Imperialism*

1 Kando (Jiandao in Chinese) also means "reclaimed island" ("kan" means "cultivation and reclamation" and "do" means "island"). See Shim Yŏch'u, *Yŏnbyŏn chosa sillok* (The Research History of Yanbian) (reprint; Yanbian: Yanbian University Press, [1930] 1987), 11–12.

2 For the full text of the Kando Treaty, see *Gaimushō Keisatsushi*, vol. 4, SP 205–3, 176–80, pp. 47–48.

3 Ibid., vol. 19, SP 205–5, 546–64, pp. 142–46; and Lee Hongsŏk, "Kando hyŏbyage taehan yuhyorongwa muhyoron" (The Validity and Annulment of the Kando Treaty), in *Chungguk Chosŏn minjok palchach'wi ch'ongsŏ* (The History of the Korean Chinese in China), vol. 1, *Kaech'ŏk* (Reclamation) (Beijing: Minzu chubanshe, 1999), 241–48.

4 Herbert Bix, "Japanese Imperialism and the Manchurian Economy, 1900–1931," *China Quarterly* 51 (1972): 425–43.

5 Yŏnbyŏn Chosŏnjok yaksa p'yŏnch'anjo, *Chosŏnjok Yaksa* (A Short History of the Koreans) (reprint; Seoul: Nonjang Press, 1989), 37–43; Shim Yŏch'u, *Yŏnbyŏn chosa sillok*, 33–34.

6 The amount of paper notes (Jilin yonghung kwanch'op) issued by the Jilin provincial bank, for instance, increased 59 times from 10,040,000 in 1917 to 559,000,000 in 1910. See Yŏnbyŏn Chosŏnjok yaksa p'yŏnch'anjo, *Chosŏnjok Yaksa*, 40.

7 The consul general in Fengtian Province reported to the Japanese Ministry of Foreign Affairs on September 27, 1920, that there were about ten Korean independence armies in Yŏn'gil and Wangch'ŏng County had ten armies, each of which comprised 60 to 450 members. For details, see *Gaimushō Keisatsushi*, vol. 20, SP 205-5, 1557–60 (Tokyo: Fuji Shuppan, 1998), pp. 187–88.

8 Ibid., SP 205-5, 1770–71, p. 240.

9 Hyŏn Ch'onch'u, "Ponggŏn kunbŏrhaŭi kwajunghan pudamgwa roryage modaegin Chosonjok inmindŭl" (Heavy Burden on and Oppression of Koreans under Feudal Warlords), in *Chungguk Chosŏn minjok palchach'wi ch'ongsŏ*, vol. 2, *Pulssi*, 135–36. The principal financial institutions in Kando were the Kando Hungŏphoesa, the Kukchaka Trading Compay, and the Tudogu Siksan Company.

10 Shim Yŏch'u, *Yŏnbyŏn chosa sillok*, 63–64. The Jilin provincial government prohibited Chinese landowners from mortgaging land as security for loans. For an example, see "Jilin Wangqingxian gongshu xunling di 368 hao minguo 8 nian" (1919).

11 On various Korean organizations and the Korean Association, see Oh Sech'ang, "Cheman Chosŏnin Minhoe yŏn'gu" (A Study of the Korean Association in Manchuria), *Paeksanhakpo* 25 (1979): 117–54; and Lim Yŏngsŏ, "1910–20 nyŏndae kando hanine taehan chunggugŭi chŏngch'aekkwa Minhoe."

12 Quoted in Lim Yŏng-sŏ, "1910–20 nyŏndae kando hanine taehan chunggugŭi chŏngch'aekkwa Minhoe," 55; originally from *Ilbonŭi Han'guk ch'imnyak saryo chongsŏ*, 26–30.

13 The statistics are cited in Lim Yŏngsŏ, "1910–20 nyŏndae kando hanine taehan chunggugŭi chŏngch'aekkwa Minhoe," 57.

14 *Gaimushō Keisatsushi*, vol. 20, SP 205-5, 1067–1100, pp. 64–73, especially p. 68.

15 Shim Yŏch'u, *Yŏnbyŏn chosa sillok*, 55.

16 Ibid., 77.

17 For Chinese officials' criticism of the Korean Association, see *Gaimushō Keisatsushi*, vol. 21, SP 205-5, 3291–97 (Tokyo: Fuji Shuppan, 1998), pp. 298–99.

18 On the characterization of the Korean Association as pro-Japanese, see Oh Sech'ang, "Chaeman Chosŏnin Minhoe yŏn'gu."

19 Lim Yŏngsŏ, "1910–20 nyŏndae kando hanine taehan chunggugŭi chŏngch'aekkwa Minhoe."

20 For this letter submitted by Choi Chongkyu, the adviser of the Association for the Protection of Koreans, to the head of the Japanese Ministry of Foreign Affairs on October 17, 1923, see *Gaimushō Keisatsushi*, vol. 8, SP 205-4, 1830–34, pp. 87–88.

21 Ibid., SP 205-4, 1869–1910, pp. 97–107.

22 *Chōsen Sōtokufu Teikoku Kaigi Setsumei Shiryō*, 17:103–17.

23 Hyŏn Ch'onch'u, "Ponggŏn kunbŏrhaŭi kwajunghan pudamgwa roryake modaegin Chosŏnjok inmindŭl."

24 *Chōsen Sōtokufu Teikoku Kaigi Setsumei Shiryō*, vol. 17 (Tokyo: Fuji Shuppan, 1998), 103–17. According to the report of the Government General of Korea, there were eight financial institutions in Kando. Only three—the Korean Association's credit unions, the Kando Relief Association, and the Kando Sint'ak Company—offered loans to the poor.

25 Hyŏn Ch'onch'u, "Ponggŏn kunbŏrhaŭi kwajunghan pudamkwa roryake modaegin Chosŏnjok inmindŭl."

26 See "Xiangwei rijing zaimaoshanqian chuanxun kenmin Zhang Guowu sanming qingchahe" (The Investigation of the Matter in Which Japanese Policemen Arrested and Interrogated Three Koreans, Including Zhang Guowu, at the Mao Mountain), Yanbianzhou danganguan (Archives of the Yanbian Autonomous Prefecture), 21-6-29, 1915.

27 *Gaimushō Keisatsushi*, vol. 19, SP 205–5, 619–32, pp. 160–63. For more information on the conflicts between Chinese officials and Japanese consulates over administering Koreans, see *Gaimushō Keisatsushi*, vol. 20, SP 205–5, 1067–1100, pp. 64–73. The head of the Kando government and local officials developed detailed communications over the issue of Japanese consulates and police forces that exercised sovereignty over Koreans, such as the arrests of Koreans who applied for naturalization as Chinese citizens. As examples, see "Xiangwei rijing zaimaoshanqian chuanxun kenmin Zhang Guowu sanming qingchahe"; "Liudaoju shangbujuzhang xianghoubao bunei ruji hanmin renshu ji xingming kaixue qing jianyou" (The report by the head of the Department of Commerce on the number and names of Koreans who became naturalized in Liudaoju and his request for a review) and "Toudaoju shangbujuzhang xiangcha ming ruji hanmin xingming houbao qingjian you" (The report by the head of the Department of Commerce on the number and names of Koreans who became naturalized in Toudaoju), Jilin yanjidao daoyin gongshu minguo sinian 114 hao anjuan, 1915 (The head of Yanji district in Jilin Province, number 114, 1915); "Wangqing zhishi xiangbao hanqiao guihua shishi jianming biaoyou" (The magistrate's report on the naturalization of Koreans in Wangqing county), Jilin Yanjidao daoyin gongshu minguo wunian 60 hao anjuan, 1916 (The head of Yanji district in Jilin Province, number 60, 1916); and "Jilinsheng gongshu zhiling di 9 hao, ling Yanji daoyin Taobin, minguo wunian, 1916" (Jilin Province, order number 9, the order to Taobin, the head of Yanji district in 1916).

28 Shim Yŏch'u, *Yŏnbyŏn chosa sillok*, 56–57.

29 Nym Wales and Kim San, *Song of Ariran: A Korean Communist in the Chinese Revolution* (San Francisco: Ramparts, 1941), 233. See also Hyŏn Ryongsun, *Chosŏnjok paengnyŏn sahwa*, (One Hundred Years of Korean History in China), vol. 2 (reprint; Seoul: Korŭm Publishers, 1989).

30 For a rare study of anticommunism in this period, see Chŏng Yŏngt'ae, "Ilchemal migunjŏnggi pan'gong ideologiŭi hyŏngsŏng" (The Formation of Anticommunist Ideology during the Late Colonial Rule and the American Military Government), Yŏksa pip'yŏng 16 (Spring 1992): 126–38.

31 Following the March First Movement and subsequent nationwide protests in 1919 in Korea, exiled Koreans transferred their resistance to Kando, which led Japanese forces to attempt to pacify Korean rebels and commit the massacre in Hunch'un County in 1920.

32 Gaimushō Keisatsushi, vol. 19, SP 205–5, 692–735, pp. 178–89.

33 Ibid., SP 205–3, 740–50, pp. 190–93.

34 Ibid., vol. 5, SP 205–3, 2302–16 (Tokyo: Fuji Shuppan, 1996), pp. 198–202.

35 On the construction of police stations and the recruitment of policemen in the 1920s, see ibid., vol. 19, SP 205–5, 692–735, pp. 178–89; and vol. 21, 205–5, 2539–78, pp. 110–20. For the Chinese appraisal of Japanese police forces in 1930, see vol. 5, SP 205–3, 2314–16, pp. 201–2. According to another Chinese source, Japanese police forces in Kando consisted of five departments and thirteen police substations in 1928. Several dozen additional policemen were routinely dispatched by the Japanese Ministry of Foreign Affairs (Ch'u Hŏnsu, Han'guk tongnip undong, vol. 4, Haeoe ijumin'gwa tongnip undong I, 885–86).

36 Gaimushō Keisatsushi, vol. 19, SP 205–5, 692–735, pp. 178–89.

37 Ibid., vol. 5, SP 205–3, 2067–68, pp. 139.

38 Ibid., vol. 20, SP 205–5, 1067–1100, pp. 64–73; vol. 21, 205–5, 2539–578, pp. 110–20.

39 The Chinese population expanded from 49,000 in 1912 to 73,748 in 1923 and 116,666 in 1929, while Koreans swelled from 163,000 in 1912 to 307,806 in 1921 and 381,561 in 1929.

40 Chōsen Sōtokufu Keimukyoku, Zaiman Senjin to Shina Kanken, 216.

41 Cited from Lim Yŏngsŏ, "1910–20 nyŏndae kando hanine taehan chunggugŭi chŏngch'aekkwa Minhoe," 40.

42 Wangqing xian xhengzhi baoguoshi (Wangqing County Political Reports), 2:25–27, 56–61.

43 Chōsen Sōtokufu Keimukyoku, Zaiman Senjin to Shina Kanken, 205.

44 I draw on Pak Kŭmhae's excellent summary of the complex policies in these two areas of Kando. See Pak Kŭmhae, "Chaeman Chosŏnjoge taehan Min'guk chŏngbuŭi kibon chŏngch'aek (The Republican Government's Basic Policy Toward Koreans), in Chungguk Chosŏn minjok palchach'wi ch'ongsŏ, Vol. Kaech'ŏk, 285–93, especially 290–91.

45 "Jilin Wangqingxian gongshu xunling di 8007 hao, minguo 8 nian" (Decree of Wangqing County in Jilin Province, Number 8007), Archives of the Yanbian Autonomous Prefecture, 39 quanzong 2 hao anjuan 67; "Jilinshengzhang gongshu xunling di 39 hao, 1923" (Decree of the Jilin Provincial Governor, Number 39, 1923); "Wei ruji hanmin bujia kenmin mingchen" (An Order Not to Call Natural-

262   Notes to Chapter 3

ized Koreans Kanmin), Archives of the Yanbian Autonomous Prefecture, 36 hao quanzong 2 hao anjuan 661, 1919.

46 "Jilinshengzhang gongshu xunling di 39 hao, 1923."

47 Ibid.

48 Chōsen Sōtokufu Keimukyoku, *Zaiman Senjin to Shina Kanken*, 204.

49 Jilin xunanshi gongshu michi di 167 hao, 1916 (Secret order of Jilin Xunanshi, 1916); Chōsen Sōtokufu Keimukyoku, *Zaiman Senjin to Shina Kanken*, 211.

50 For details on the processes of naturalization for Koreans, see "Xunanshi chizhi hanmin qingqiu ruji yifaban lizhuan xing daozhao you" (On the Implementation of the Law on the Koreans' Applications for Naturalization), Jilin xunanshi gong-shuchi di 48 hao minguo sinian (Jilin xunanshi, order number 48, 1915); "Xunanshi chizhi teding qiaomin shishi jianming chazhao you" (Instructions on the Investigation of the Naturalization of Special Koreans), Jilin xunanshi gongshu michi di 142 hao minguo sinian (Secret order of Jilin Xunanshi, Number 142, 1915); "Jilin xunanshi chizhi hanmin chengqing ruji xunsu zhaozhang xiangqing heban gejie-you" (Order on the Processing of the Applications of Koreans for Naturalization), Jilin xunanshi gongshuchi de 4724 hao minguo si nian (Decree of Xuanshi in Jilin Province, Number 4724, 1915); "Wangqing zhishi xiangbao hanqiao guihua shi-shi jianmingbiaoyou" (Magistrate's Report on the Naturalization of Koreans in Wangqing County), Jilin Yanjidao daoyin gongshu minguo wu nian 60 hao anjuan (Decree of Yanji District in Jilin Province, Number 60, 1916); "Shengzhang miling hanmin guihua anchaosong rishi zhaohui ji neiwubu zifu weijiaobu wengao qing-chao zhaoyou" (The Objection of Japanese Consuls to the Naturalization of Kore-ans and the Order to Follow the Policy of the Chinese Ministry of Foreign Affairs), Jilinsheng gongshu mixunling di 67 hao, ling Jilin Yanji daoyin, minguo wu nian, 9, 19 (Decree of Jilin Province, Number 67, the Order to the Head of Yanji District in 1916, September 19).

51 As Japanese consulates claimed Koreans as Japanese subjects, county magistrates requested that the Kando administration and the Jilin provincial government clar-ify their nationality status. See "Jilinsheng gongshu zhiling di 9 hao, ling Yanji daoyin Taobin minguo wu nian" (Decree of Jilin Province, Number 9, the Order to Taobin, the Magistrate of Yanji County, in 1916); "Shengzhang miling hanmin gui-hua anchaosong rishi zhaohui ji neiwubu zifu weijiaobu wengao qingchao zhao-you" (The Objection of Japanese Consuls to the Naturalization of Koreans and the Order to Follow the Policy of the Chinese Ministry of Foreign Affairs), "Jilinsheng gongshu mixunling di 67 hao, ling Jilin Yanji daoyin, minguo wu nian, 9, 19" (De-cree of Jilin Province, Number 67, the Order to the Head of Yanji District in 1916, September 19); and "Hunchun zhishi xiangfu riling fandui hanqiao ruji zunchi dafu qingjian heyou" (Yanji District's Response to the Inquiry by the Magistrate of Hunchun County on the Japanese Consul's Objection to the Naturalization of Koreans), Yanji daoyin gongshu minguo wu nian 51 hao anjuan (Decree of Yanji District, Number 51, 1916).

52 Chōsen Sōtokufu Keimukyoku, *Zaiman Senjin to Shina Kanken*, 210.

53 Ibid., 219–20, 225.

54 Ibid., 163.

55 Ibid., 223.

56 When the alliance of Zhang Xueliang and Kuomintang forces launched anti-Japanese movements, it inspired the Chinese movements to demand that Japan dissolve its consulates, withdraw its police forces, and cede its rights to rule on court cases (Yŏngsa chaep'ankwŏn).

57 *Gaimushō Keisatsushi*, vol. 21, SP 205–5, 3377, p. 319.

58 Chōsen Sōtokufu Keimukyoku, *Zaiman Senjin to Shina Kanken*, 195–96.

59 Ibid., 209.

60 "Jilin Bianwuchu Xuantong yuannian 5 hao quanzong 4 hao an juan" (Bianwuchu of Jilin Province, 5 hao quanzong 4 hao). Available at the Institute of Ethnology, Yanbian University, Yanji, China.

61 "Jilin Wangqingxian gongshu xunling di 8007 hao minguo 8 nian" (Decree of Wangqing County, Number 8007, August 6, 1919), Archives of the Yanbian Autonomous Prefecture, 39 hao quanzong 2 hao anjuan 67.

62 Chōsen Sōtokufu Keimukyoku, *Zaiman Senjin to Shina Kanken*, 205.

63 Ibid., 215.

64 "Helonggu Fenfangting Xuantong 2 nian 3 hao quanzong 340 hao anjuan" (Helong County, 3 hao quanzong 340 hao). Available at the Institute of Ethnology, Yanbian University, Yanji, China.

65 Chōsen Sōtokufu Keimukyoku, *Zaiman Senjin to Shina Kanken*, 161.

66 Ibid., 210.

67 This 1917 figure did not include Hunch'un County. According to Pak Ilcho, there were 68,200 Korean households in 1930 but only 5,000 of naturalized Koreans. See Pak Ilcho, "Yŏnbyŏneso sŏnghaengdoen 'Chŏnminjedo,'" 115; and Hyŏn Kyuhwan, *Han'guk Yuiminsa* I, 240.

68 "Guanyu guanli hanqiao fangfa de zhiling" (Instructions on Supervising Koreans), Jilin Yanjidao Daoyin gongshu zhiling de 20 hao, ling Dunhuaxian zhishi 1928 (Decree of the Head of Yanji District of Jilin, Number 20, the Order to the Magistrate of Dunhua County in 1928).

69 My discussion of Chŏnminje draws from Pak Ilcho, "Yŏnbyŏneso sŏnghaengdoen 'Chŏnminjedo,'" 110–15.

70 It was issued as a decree of the Jilin provincial government: Jilinsheng zhengfu xunling (Decree of the Jilin Provincial Government), "Xoanzhi hanmin dingming maidi" (The Prohibition of the Koreans to Purchase Land Using Others' Names) 1108 hao, quanzong 46 hao 1 hao (Archives of the Yanbian Autonomous Prefecture, number 1108, 46–1). See also Chōsen Sōtokufu Keimukyoku, *Zaiman Senjin to Shina Kanken*, 207–8.

71 "Kando, Hunchun kaewhang," Saito Document 11:96, cited in Lim Yŏngsŏ, "1910–20 nyŏndae kando hanine taehan chunggugŭi chŏngch'aekkwa Minhoe," 35.

72 Chōsen Sōtokufu Keimukyoku, *Zaiman Senjin to Shina Kanken*, 210.

73 The statistics are from Lee Hyŏngch'an, "1920–1930 nyŏndae Han'guginŭi manju imin yŏn'gu" (A Study of Korean Emigration to Manchuria in the 1920s–1930s Period)," 237–39. *Chinese* refers mainly to Han Chinese, though Manchus were included.

74 Chŏn Sinja, "'Kanmin kyoyukhoe' wa 'Kanminhoe'" (Kanmin Kyoyukhoe and Kanminhoe), in *Chungguk Chosŏn minjok palchach'wi ch'ongsŏ*, vol. 1, *Kaech'ŏk*, 356–62.

75 Kim Ch'unsŏn, "'Kanminhoe' wa 'Nongmugye'" (Kanminhoe and Nongmugye), in *Chungguk Chosŏn minjok palchach'wi ch'ongs*, vol. 1, *Kaech'ŏk*, 365–69.

76 Il Mok, "'Choi Ch'angho sagon'gwa kando chumindaehoe'" (The Choi Ch'angho Incident and Residents' Rally in Kando), in *Chungguk Chosŏn minjok palchach'wi ch'ongsŏ*, vol. 2, *Pulssi*, 135–36; Pak Ilcho, "Yŏnbyŏneso sŏnghaengdoen 'Chŏnminjedo'" (A Popular Practice, Chŏnminje, in Kando), in *Chungguk Chosŏn minjok palchach'wi ch'ongsŏ*, vol. 2, *Pulssi*.

FOUR Multiethnic Agrarian Communities

1 I use the term *colonial power* in the singular not to suggest a seamless unified power but to refer to the abstract power of the Japanese empire, which was created through coordination among administrative authorities, notwithstanding the tension and conflict among them.

2 Harootunian, *Overcome by Modernity*.

3 For descriptions of various incidents, see Manju tongp'o munje hŏbŭihoe (Committee on the Problem of Korean Compatriots in Manchuria), *Manju tongp'o sanghwang chosa pogo* (Investigation Report on the Situations of Korean Patriots in Manchuria) (Kyŏngsŏng, Korea: Misongsa 1931), 11–8, 49–77.

4 For details on the emergency relief efforts, see Son Ch'unil, *Manjugugŭi chaeman hanine taehan t'oji chŏngch'aek yŏn'gu*, 152–53.

5 Manju tongp'o munje hŏbŭihoe, *Manju tongp'o sanghwang chosa pogo*, 28.

6 Nakatani Kyūji, "Kanhun Chihō ni Okeru Sennō Shūdan Buraku" (Korean Collective Villages in Kando and Hunchun), *Chosen* 5:15 (January 1934), cited in Son Ch'unil, *Manjugugŭi chaeman hanine taehan t'ochi chŏngch'aek yŏn'gu*, 152.

7 This report is included in Manju tongp'o munje hŏbŭihhoe, *Manju tongp'o sanghwang chosa pogo*, 34–36.

8 Takafusa Nakamura, *Economic Growth in Prewar Japan* (Senzenki Nihon keizai seicho no bunseki), trans. Robert Feldman (New Haven: Yale University Press, 1983).

9 Takafusa Nakamura, *A History of Showa Japan* (Showa shi), trans. Edwin Whenmouth (Tokyo: University of Tokyo Press, 1998), 105.

10 For a thorough study of various collective movements, see Yutaka Nagahara, *Tennōsei Kokka to Nōmin: Gōi Keisei no Soshikiron* (The Emperor State and Peasants: On Consent-Based Organization) (Tokyo: Nishon Keizai Hyōronsha, 1989), esp. chaps. 3 and 4. In Korea, the Agricultural Development movement, which was

organized in the provinces, districts, and villages in 1933, similarly called for reforming such everyday practices of Korean farm households as excessive consumption and inefficient work habits. See Han Tohyŏn, "1930 nyŏndae nongch'on chinhŭng undongŭi sŏnggyŏk" (The Characteristics of the Agricultural Development Movement in the 1930s), in Han'guk sahoesa yŏn'guhoe, ed., *Han'guk kŭndae nongch'on sahoewa ilbon chegukchuŭi* (Rural Society and Japanese Imperialism in Modern Korea) (Seoul: Muhakkwa chisongsa, 1986), 233–77; and Yamabe, *Ilche kangjŏm haŭi Han'guk kŭndaesa*.

11 For instance, the price of Korean rice per 100 kun (1 kun equals 0.6 kilograms) dropped from 11.4 won in 1925 to 4.63 in 1931. See Pak Hyŏnch'ae, *Minjok kyŏngje ron: Pak Hyŏnch'ae p'yongnonsŏn* (On the National Economy: Selected Works of Pak Hyonch'ae) (Seoul: Han'gilsa, 1978), 75.

12 Pak Hyŏnch'ae, *Minjok kyŏngjeron*, 91–94.

13 Han Tohyon, "1930 nyŏndae nongch'on chinhŭng undongŭi sŏnggyok," 234.

14 The statistics are from *Senman Takushoku Kabushiki Gaisha Mansen Takushoku Kabushiki Gaisha Gonenshi*, 3.

15 *Manju tongp'o munje hŏbŭihoe, Manju tongp'o sangwhang chosa pogo*.

16 Most Chinese peasants owned land in the southern half of Fengtian Province; their landholdings were small, averaging less than 6.5 acres per household. In the northern half of the province and in Jilin, more Chinese were tenants, with 40 percent of the Chinese peasants owning little or no land. On the uneven patterns of landownership across Manchuria, see Ramon H. Myers, *Japanese Economic Development of Manchuria, 1932 to 1945*; and "Socioeconomic Changes in Villages of Manchuria during the Ch'ing and Republican Period: Some Preliminary Findings," *Modern Asian Studies* 19:4 (1976): 591–620.

17 A well-known example is the Manbosan Incident, which occurred in 1931 in a village about eighteen miles north of Changchun City in Jilin Province. The incident offers some insight into this imagined, mediated antagonism. It began as a dispute over the use of water and land ruined by irrigation work, which might have been solved through a prior agreement with the Chinese peasants or economic compensation, an option that might have prevented the intervention of both Chinese and Japanese policemen. Instead, it became a national issue in Manchuria, as well as in Korea. It became a contest in disguise between the Japanese and Chinese governments. Disputes around the incident offer an outstanding example of the way local economic conflicts can become politicized as national issues.

18 For detailed statistical documentation of the capitalist crisis (the price index of major crops from 1921 to 1933, the area of cultivated land and volume of production from 1929 to 1937, and the rapidly declining number of animals owned by farmers from 1931 to 1936), see *Kunan douzheng shisinian* (Struggles and Hardship for Fourteen Years), vol. 1 (Beijing: Zhongguo dabeike quanji chubanshe, 1995), 452–53.

19 For various discourses of pan-Asianism in Manchuria, see Prasenjit Duara, *Sovereignty and Authenticity: Manchukuo and the East Asian Modern* (Oxford: Rowman and

Littlefield, 2003), esp. the chapter entitled "Asianism and the New Discourse of Civilization."

20 *Kunan douzheng shisinian*, 2:81.

21 For statistical documentation and analysis, see Han Suk-Jung, *Manjuguk kŏn'gugŭi chaehaesŏk* (A Reinterpretation of the Construction of the Manchukuo State) (Pusan: Tonga University Press, 1999), chap. 5.

22 Pongch'ŏn Hunga hyŏphoe, *Chaeman Chonsŏnin t'ongsin* (Korean Communication in Manchuria), vol. 72 (November 1939), 14.

23 Han Suk-Jung, *Manjuguk kŏn'gugŭi chaehaesŏk*, 167–70. For an example of the literary representation of images of Koreans narrated in short stories during the colonial period, see Lee Kyŏnghun, "Harbinŭi p'urŭn hanŭl: 'Pyŏkkongmuhan' kwa taedonga kongyŏng" (Blue Sky in Harbin: "Pyŏkkongmuhan" and the East-Asia Co-Prosperity Sphere), in *Munhak sogŭi Fascism* (Fascism in Korean Literature), ed. Kim Cheol and Sin Hyŏnggi (Seoul: Samin, 2001).

24 Ibid., 171–72.

25 For discussion of the problems of the Korean family register and their implications for landownership, see *Zenman Chōsen Jinminkai Rengōkai Kaihō* (The Official Magazine of the Federation of the Korean Association in Manchuria), 39 (February 1936) and 54 (August 1937). When the right to lease land was abolished in 1935, property transactions by Koreans and Japanese became subject to the laws of the Manchukuo state.

26 Under the auspices of the Kwantung Army, the Concordia Association was established in Tokyo, with its headquarters in Xinjang and branches and local units throughout Manchuria, in 1932. See Pongch'ŏn Hunga hyŏphoe, *Chaeman Chonsŏnin t'ongsin*, 72 (November 1939), which offered several fora during and after the annual meeting of the Concordia Association and published the details of the proposals that the Korean representatives made. Of the sixteen Korean representatives, five were drawn from in the area of agriculture; two each from education, local functionaries, and public companies; and one each from the state bureaucracy, commerce, law, private companies, and credit unions.

27 This claim was made in a 1938 proposal by the Kwantung Army. See *Kunan douzheng shisinian*, 2:165–66.

28 Ibid., 231–32. According to a Japanese estimate, the composition of the population at the beginning of Manchukuo period was 28 million Han Chinese, 4 million Manchus, 1.1 million Mongols, 0.85 million Koreans, 0.6 million Japanese, and 0.1 million Russians. Koreans were usually considered to number at least one million.

29 Asada Kyōji, "Manshū Nōgyō Imin Seisaku no Ritsuan Katei" (The Formation of the Policies on Korean Emigration to Manchuria), in *Nihon Teikokushugika no Manshū Imin* (Emigration to Manchuria during Japanese Imperialism), ed. Manshū Iminshi Kenkyūkai (Tokyo: Ryūkei Shosha, 1976), 17.

30 Son Ch'unil, *Manjugug'ŭi chaeman hanine taehan t'oji chŏngch'aek yŏn'gu*, 266.

31 For a discussion about the discourse of population explosion, see Germaine Hoston, *Marxism and the Crisis of Development in Prewar Japan* (Princeton: Princeton University Press, 1987), Chapter 8, 223–50, cited from 227.

32 For the plans for Korean immigration that these various Japanese powers proposed, see Son Ch'unil, *Manjugug'ŭi chaeman hanine taehan t'oji chŏngch'aek yŏn'gu*, 238–57.

33 This statistic is from *Senman Takushoku Kabushiki Gaisha Mansen Takushoku Kabushiki Gaisha Gonenshi*, 3.

34 Ryu Byongho, "Samsim nyŏndae Chosŏnjok imin" (Korean Immigrants in the 1930s), in *Chungguk Chosŏn minjok palchach'wi ch'ongsŏ* (History of the Korean Chinese in China), vol. 3, *Ponghwa* (Beacon) (Beijing, Minzu chubanshe, 1989), 190.

35 Korean guerrilla movements are discussed in chapter 6.

36 In Japan, only about 17 percent of Koreans worked in factories, mines, and agriculture, with the rest unemployed. For a comprehensive study of the employment and politics of Koreans in Japan, see Ken Kawashima, "Contingent Commodifications: Micropolitics of Recession and the Colonial Conditions of Korean Labor Power in Japan between the Two World Wars." Ph.D. diss., Department of History, New York University, 2003.

37 For the positions of the Government General of Korea, see Son Ch'unil, *Manjugug'ŭi chaeman hanine taehan t'oji chŏngch'aek yŏn'gu*, 390–93.

38 Ibid., 245.

39 The SMRC functioned as a semicolonial government. Its conflicts with the Kwantung government and the Kwantung Army is a well-studied subject. With the colonization of Manchuria in 1931, Japan made an effort to integrate these administrations, with limited success. With respect to immigration policy, the SMRC aligned with the Kwantung Army in prioritizing Japanese over Korean immigration.

40 Son Ch'unil, *Manjugug'ŭi chaeman hanine taehan t'oji chŏngch'aek yŏn'gu*, 285.

41 Piao Changyu (Pak Ch'angwuk in Korean), "Riben diguo zhuyi zaidongbei zhimin tongzhi shiqi chaoxianzu nongmin suo xingde 'zigengnong chuangding' shilun" (A Study of the Program to Create Independent Farmers that Was Practiced for Koreans in Northeast China during Colonial Rule), in *Zhongguo chaoxianzu lishi yanju* (A Study of the History of the Korean Chinese in China) (Yanbian: Yanbian University Press, 1995), 425.

42 For the statistics, see Son Ch'unil, *Manjugug'ŭi chaeman hanine taehan t'oji chŏngch'aek yŏn'gu*, 181; and *Senman Takushoku Kabushiki Gaisha Mansen Takushoku Kabushiki Gaisha Gonenshi*, 81–82.

43 "Shūdan Buraku Kensetsu ni Kansuru Ken" (On the Construction of Collective Villages), December 3, 1934, Minseibu Kunrei, no. 969, cited in Yoon Hwitak, *Ilcheha Manjuguk Yŏn'gu*, 269.

44 Yoon Hwitak. *Ilcheha Manjuguk Yŏng'u*. For an earlier study of cooperatives in Manchuria as a security strategy, see Lee Chong Sik, *Revolutionary Struggle in Manchuria*.

45   Son Ch'unil, *Manjugug'ŭi chaeman hanine taehan t'oji chŏngch'aek yŏn'gu*.

46   The cooperatives built by the Manchukuo state were mainly for the Chinese, though Koreans were sometimes included.

47   In Japan this practice began in Hokkaido in the 1870s, where a number of Japanese mainlanders were sent to colonize the island and cultivate land formerly inhabited by natives. In the early twentieth century, the Japanese state encouraged its citizens to migrate to Hawaii, the United States, Canada, South America, Australia, and New Zealand, although Japan never reproduced the success of the Hokkaido settlement in other places. On this settlement policy, see Young, *Japan's Total Empire*, 311–12. After World War II, Jewish settlement took this form in the West Bank and Gaza, which were seized from the Palestinians after the 1967 war. The United States also engaged in group settlement of Vietnamese refugees during the Vietnam War.

48   Harootunian, *Overcome by Modernity*, esp. chap. 5.

49   Stephen Vlastos, "Agrarianism without Tradition," in *Mirror of Modernity: Invented Traditions of Modern Japan*, ed. Stephen Vlastos (Berkeley: University of California Press, 1998), 79–94. Around the same time in Korea, a similar agrarianism combined with neo-Confucianism to produce a critique against colonial modernity. Rescuing this Korean agrarianism from nationalist narratives, Gi-Wook Shin documents variant utopian discussions of rural life that attempted to reinvent the Korean nation with traditional natural villages as a model. For agrarianism in Korea at that time, see Gi-Wook Shin, "Agrarianism: A Critique of Colonial Modernity in Korea," *Comparative Studies in Society and History* 41:4 (1999): 784–804.

50   See Yim Sŏng-mo, "Manjuguk Hyŏphwahoeŭi ch'ongnyŏkchŏn ch'eje kusang yŏn'gu: 'Kungminundong' nosŏnui mosaekkwa kŭ songgyŏk" (The Planning of Total War System in Manchukuo: The Search for the 'National Movement without Nation' of the MCA), Ph.D. diss., Department of History, Yonsei University, 1997, 108–11. He compares the agrarian reforms proposed by the Concordia Association in Manchuria with those advocated in Korea and Japan, the former seeking to eliminate landlordism and the latter upholding it.

51   Vlastos, "Agrarianism without Tradition," 92.

52   Young, *Japan's Total Empire*. For a discussion of Marxist discourses of agrarianism, see Hoston, *Marxism and the Crisis of Development in Prewar Japan*, 223–50.

53   My account of this comparative analysis is drawn from a policy report by Fukushima Miyoshi, "Manshūkoku Tochi Seido no Genjō to Tochi Seisaku" (Conditions of Land System and Land Policy in the Manchukuo State), Kokumuin Chiseki Seirikyoku (Department of the Reorganization of Land Ownership in the Ministry of State Affairs), 1937, no. 45, esp. 53–131.

54   In 1937, there were 1,600 grain stores with 39 million won of capital. With pawnshops, the liangchan were the most prevalent financial organizations among destitute peasants, who had to borrow money in the spring for farming and in the fall for purchasing essential goods. Pawnshops also offered short-term loans for farming, taking in exchange clothing, farm tools, and carts. An average loan amounted

to 3 or 4 won with 2.5–15 percent monthly interest for about ten months. Pawnshops numbered 1,057 in 1938 and 980 in 1941, serving 1.12 million and 0.88 million individuals, respectively. Those operated by the Manchuria Central Bank comprised about 37.4 percent of all pawnshops in Manchuria and charged the lowest interest rates, from 0.6 to 2.5 percent monthly. For more on pawnshops and the reorganization of banks, see *Manzhuguoshi* (The History of the Manchukuo), vol. 1: Dongbei shitan daxuexiao yin shuachang, 1990), 746–89.

55 *Kunan douzheng shisinian*, vol. 2, 200.

56 Onda Sakubē, "Tōman Chihō ni Okeru Nōson no Genjō: Shūdan Buraku Kensetsu no Jūyōsei, (Chū no Ni), (Ni Zoku)" (The rural condition in Northeast China: The importance of constructing collective villages), *Manshū Hyōron* 9:8 (1935): 23–30, cited from 28.

57 *Manzhuguoshi*, 2:224–30.

58 Ibid., 230–42.

59 The company assigned a minimum quota for the sale of produce per household (and later per company) and collected the harvested produce to be sold at prices often considered much lower than the market price. Before the harvest, the company signed a contract with county magistrates to decide the amount of a "sale," with a partial (nominal) prepayment. In this compulsory collectivization, the notion of a sale meant the confiscation of produce (ibid., 242–55).

60 Onda Sakubē, "Tōman Chihō ni Okeru Nōson no Genjō: Shūdan Buraku Kensetsu no Jūyōsei, (Chū no Yon), San (Zoku)," *Manshū Hyōron* 9:10 (1935): 24–28, quoted on 24–25.

61 Ibid., 22.

62 Onda Sakubē, "Tōman Chihō ni Okeru Nōson no Genjō: Shūdan Buraku Kensetsu no Jūyōsei, (Chū no Ni), (Ni Zoku)," 26–27.

63 Onda Sakubē, "Tōman Chihō ni Okeru Nōson no Genjō: Shūdan Buraku Kensetsu no Jūyōsei (Ge), San (Zoku)." *Manshū Hyōron* 9:11 (1935): 22–26.

64 Onda Sakubē, "Tōman Chihō ni Okeru Nōson no Genjō: Shūdan Buraku Kensetsu no Jūyōsei (Kan), San (Zoku)." *Manshū Hyōron* 9:12 (1935): 23–27.

65 Ibid., 25–27.

66 On the migration of Chinese from North China, see F. C. Jones, *Manchuria since 1931* (Toronto: Oxford University Press, 1949), 168.

67 Yoon Hwitak, *Ilcheha Manjuguk Yŏn'gu*, 303.

68 Young, *Japan's Total Empire*, 399–400.

69 Asada Kyōji, "Manshū Nōgyō Imin Seisaku no Ritsuan Katei," 3–110, esp. 9.

70 Kobayashi Hideo, "Manshū Nōgyō Imin no Einō Jittai" (The Management of the Peasant Emigration to Manchuria), in *Nihon Teikokushugika no Manshū Imin* (Emigration to Manchuria during Japanese Imperialism), ed. Manshū Iminshi Kenkyūkai (Tokyo: Ryūkei Shosha, 1976), 387–490, esp. 428–31.

71 Ibid., 460.

72 Son Ch'unil, *Manjugug'ŭi chaeman hanine taehan t'oji chŏngch'aek yŏn'gu*, 240.

73 Ibid., 292–93.
74 Kobayashi Hideo, "Manshū Nōgyō Imin no Einō Jittai," 394.
75 Ibid., 449.
76 Ibid., 451–52.
77 Ibid., 461.
78 Ibid., 462.
79 Asada Kyōji, "Manshū Nōgyō Imin Seisaku no Ritsuan Katei," 10.
80 Son Ch'unil, Manjugug'ŭi chaeman hanine taehan t'oji chŏngch'aek yŏn'gu, 211.
81 Ibid., 382.

FIVE Colonial Governmentality

1 For the recollections of survivors, see Chungguk Chosŏn minjok palchach'wi ch'ongsŏ (History of the Korean Chinese in China), vol. 3, Ponghwa (Beacon) (Beijing: Minzu chubanshe, 1989); and Chungguk Chosŏn minjok palchach'wi ch'ongsŏ (History of the Korean Chinese in China), vol. 4, Kyŏlchŏn (Final War) (Beijing: Minzu chubanshe, 1991).

2 Son Ch'unil, Manjugug'ŭi chaeman hanine taehan t'oji chŏngch'aek yŏn'gu; Yoon Hwitak. Ilcheha Manjuguk Yŏn'gu.

3 Piao Changyu (Pak Ch'angwuk in Korean), "Riben diguo zhuyi zaidongbei zhimin tongzhi shiqi chaoxianzu nongmin suo xingde 'zigengnong chuangding' shilun," 425–28.

4 For this statistic, see Oh Sech'ang, "Chaeman Chosŏnin Minhoe yŏn'gu" (A Study of the Korean Association in Manchuria," Paesanhakpo 25 (1979): 118–54, 135.

5 The functions of Korean Association were significantly reduced in 1936 on the grounds that its administrative work defied the Manchukuo state's political principle of cooperation and harmony. For more on this transformation, see Zenman Chōsen Jinminkai Rengōkai Kaihō 4:10 (October 1936): 67–81; Son Ch'unil, Manjugug'ŭi chaeman hanine taehan t'oji chŏngch'aek yŏn'gu, 133–36.

6 For the kŭmyung chohap in Korea, see Zenman Chōsen Jinminkai Rengōkai Kaihō 8 (October 1933); 9 (November 1933); 11 (January 1934). See also Lee Kyŏngran, Ilcheha kŭmyung chohap yŏn'gu (A Study of the Financial Cooperatives) (Seoul: Hean, 2002); and Han Tohyŏn, "1930 nyŏndae nongch'on chinhung undongŭi sŏng-gyŏk," 237.

7 Zenman Chōsen Jinminkai Rengōkai Kaihō 42 (August 1936); 36 (February 1936).

8 Tōa Kangyō Kabushiki Gaisha Jūnenshi, 307–8.

9 Senman Takushoku Kabushiki Gaisha Mansen Takushoku Kabushiki Gaisha Gonenshi, 128–30.

10 Piao Changyu, "Riben diguo zhuyi zaidongbei zhimin tongzhi shiqi chaoxianzu nongmin suo xingde 'zigengnong chuangding' shilun," 426–27.

11 Tōa Kangyō Kabushiki Gaisha Jūnenshi, 307–8.

12 *Zenman Chōsen Jinminkai Rengōkai Kaihō* 6 (August 1933), 26; 7 (September 1933), 18.

13 Ibid., 6 (August 1933), 25. For more on the *Nongmukye*, see *Tōa Kangyō Kabushiki Gaisha Jūnenshi*, 307; and *Senman Takushoku Kabushiki Gaisha Mansen Takushoku Kabushiki Gaisha Gonenshi*, 128–30.

14 *Senman Takushoku Kabushiki Gaisha Mansen Takushoku Kabushiki Gaisha Gonenshi*, 128–30.

15 Hungnyonggangsŏng palchach'wi py'ŏnch'ansil (The Publication Committee in Heilongjiang Province), "Hadong nongjang (Hadong Farm)," in *Chungguk Chosŏn minjok palchach'wi ch'ongsŏ*, vol. 3, *Ponghwa* (Beacon), 186–89.

16 Jones, *Manchuria since 1931*, 146–47.

17 According to Myers, "the SMR's first-year net earnings of 2.0 million yen more than trebled by 1913–1914, doubled again by 1917–1918, and almost doubled again by 1920–1921 in nominal terms. Those net earnings continued to rise during the 1920s until 1931–1932, when they sharply tumbled but then rose the very next year. . . . The total revenue produced by the SMR in 1923 came to 185 million yen, compared to the same year's ordinary budget for Korea of 101 million yen and for Formosa of 100 million yen." Myers, "Japanese Imperialism in Manchuria," 111–13.

18 Jones, *Manchuria since 1931*, 145–47.

19 Ibid., 146.

20 See *Tōa Kangyō Kabushiki Gaisha Jūnenshi*, 18.

21 Kim Sŏkjun, "Tongyangch'oksik hoesa saŏp chŏn'gae kwajŏng (the Development Process of the Oriental Development Company), in *Han'guk sahoesa yŏn'guhoe, Han'guk kŭndae nongch'on sahoewa ilbon chegukchuŭi* (The Modern Agricultural Society and Japanese Imperialism) (Seoul: Munhakkwa chisŏng, 1986), 134.

22 *Senman Takushoku Kabushiki Gaisha Mansen Takushoku Kabushiki Gaisha Gonenshi*, 1941, 29–31.

23 On the changing relationship between the Zaibatsu and the army, see Jones, *Manchuria since 1931*, 145–46.

24 Yoon Whitak, *Ilcheha Manjuguk Yŏn'gu*, 304–9.

25 Foucault, *Discipline and Punish*, 200.

26 Ibid., 201.

27 Ibid., 202.

28 *Tōa Kangyō Kabushiki Gaisha Jūnenshi*, 312.

29 For more information, see Manju tongp'o munje hyŏbŭihoe, *Manchu tongp'o sanghwang chosa pogo*, 79. The SMRC estimated the necessary amount of loans a bit higher, setting it at 820 won per household. For more details, see Son Ch'unil, *Manjugugŭi chaeman hanine taehan t'oji chŏngch'aek yŏn'gu*, 193–94.

30 "Chōsen Sōtokufu Sandai Jigyō: Anzun nōson, Shūdan Buraku, jisaku nōsōtei" (Three tasks of the Government General of Korea: Safe Village, Collective Village, and the Policy to Create Independent Farmers), *Zenman Chōsen Jinminkai Rengōkai Kaihō* 27:3–5 (May 1935), 106–14; Yoda Yoshiie, "Manshū ni Okeru Chōsenjin Imin"

272 Notes to Chapter 5

(The Korean Emigration to Manchuria), in *Nihon Teikokushugika no Manshū Imin* (Emigration to Manchuria during the Japanese Imperialism), ed. Manshū Iminshi Kenkyūkai (Ryūkei Shosha, 1976), 582.

31 Son Ch'unil, *Manjugugŭi chaeman hanine taehan t'oji chŏngch'aek yŏn'gu*, 201–3.

32 The figure for 1935 is from Chōsen Sōtokufu Kanbō Gaijika, "Kantō Chihō ni Okeru Shūdan Buraku no" (The Conditions of Collective Villages in Kando), in *Zenman Chōsen Jinminkai Rengōkai Kaihō* 4:6 (June 1936): 30–31. One Chŏngbo equals 10 pan; 1 ssang—a unit of Chinese measurement equals 6 pan, 1 mu, 20 p'yŏng.

33 Son Ch'unil, *Manjugugŭi chaeman hanine taehan t'oji chŏngch'aek yŏn'gu*, 204.

34 *Senman Takushoku Kabushiki Gaisha Mansen Takushoku Kabushiki Gaisha Gonenshi*, 1941, 87.

35 On the political causes of the loss of the Asia Development Company's assets, see *Tōa Kangyō Kabushiki Gaisha Jūnenshi*, 13.

36 Immigration and relocation took place between late fall and late winter, after the harvest and before planting. This means that Korean immigrants traveled to Manchuria without warm clothing to protect them from its harsh winter. For the recollections of Kim Yŏngsong and Ro Chŏngsuk on the process of relocation, see Lee Chŏngsu, "Ryangjach'on nongmindŭrŭi kangbak iju" (The Forced Migration of Peasants in Ryangja Village), in *Chungguk Chosŏn minjok palchach'wi ch'ongsŏ*, vol. 4, *Kyŏlchŏn*, 5–8. When the Japanese army relocated one hundred Korean households from five villages in Tongnyŏng County (southeast of Heilongjiang Province and adjacent to Kando and Fengtian Provinces) in 1935, the peasants were given five days to pack their belongings—pots, bowls, farming tools, grain, and blankets. They were required to assemble at a Japanese army base located seven to fifteen kilometers from their villages. Their village was burned after they left. After three days' travel by train and on foot, they arrived at their newly designated settlement and slept on the concrete floor of millhouses or storage rooms until their houses were built. They even had to procure their own building materials, cutting and transporting wood from the forest to make house frames and then applying a mixture of tree branches, earth, and water to the roof and floor. For similar recollections collected in the same volume, see Ch'ae Tosik and Ch'ae Sŏnae, "Rajaguesoŭi iminsari" (A Life as Immigrants in Rajagu), in ibid., 19–23. According to these recollections, new houses were erected in their collective in four or five days. Built with such shabby materials, the houses developed frost inside the walls. It was not uncommon for the head of Korean villages to cheat immigrants of money that the development companies had provided to pay for the expenses of moving and building houses. See Sŏk Chŏngsong, "Ilbonimindanŭi t'oji yakt'al" (The Plundering of Land by the Japanese), in ibid., 24–26.

37 Choi Kansik, "Hwinam Chosŏn ijuminŭi nunmulgyŏwun saenghwal" (The Wretched Life of Korean Settlers in Whinam)," in ibid., 9–12. Although this series of promises was based on accounts of Korean immigrants from Cholla Province to Hwinam County in the Tongbyŏndo area, such promises were commonly made

by the Manchuria-Korea Development Company and the Asia Development Company.

38 *Chungguk Chosŏn minjok palchach'wi ch'ongsŏ*, vol. 4, *Kyŏlchŏn*. This volume of an anthology on the history of Koreans in China offers various recollections of the experience of moving and farming in new places. For instance, Kim Yongmu remembers that, when his family and 99 other households settled in Sangjihyon County in Heilongjiang Province in 1939 the land was so fertile that it was like a dream harvest that only required weeding, sowing, and bringing water to the rice fields. Even dry farming yielded a bountiful harvest of millet, corn, beans, and potatoes, as well as watermelon and other fruits. With this promise of a rich reward, they worked strenuously and practically lived in the fields. Kim recalls that the joy and hope continued until Japan confiscated their harvest, imposing a mandatory minimum quota in 1941. See Hwang Hyŏngu, "Manggungnoŭi sŏrwum" (Sorrows of People without Nation), 40–46; and Kim Yongmu, "Sangjihyŏn Ojihyangesoŭi iminsari" (Life as Immigrants in Ojihyang Sangji County), 13–18.

39 For the recollections of survivors, see ibid., 1–24.

40 Alfred Sohn-Rethel, *Intellectual and Manual Labour: A Critique of Epistemology*, trans. Martin Sohn-Rethel (London: Macmillan, 1978), 41.

41 Son Ch'unil, *Manjugugŭi chaeman hanine taehan t'oji chŏngch'aek yŏn'gu*, 343.

42 Pio Changyu, "Riben diguo zhuyi zaidongbei zhimin tongzhi shiqi chaoxianzu nongmin suo xingde 'zigengnong chuangding' shilun," 434–35.

43 *Senman Takushoku Kabushiki Gaisha Mansen Takushoku Kabushiki Gaisha Gonenshi*, 89. Membership in the Ch'olryŏng and Hadong villages declined from 384 households in 1937 to 283 in 1940 in Ch'olryŏng, and from 683 to 378 in Hadong. The 1937 figure is from Piao Changyu, "Riben diguo zhuyi zaidongbei zhimin tongzhi shiqi chaoxianzu nongmin suo xingde 'zigengnong chuangding' shilun," 433; and the 1940 figure is from *Senman Takushoku Kabushiki Gaisha Mansen Takushoku Kabushiki Gaisha Gonenshi*, 88.

44 Son Ch'unil, *Manjugugŭi chaeman hanine taehan t'oji chŏngch'aek yŏn'gu*, 204–5.

45 Ibid., 78. A fixed amount of rent paid in kind and cash, called *choja*, was also practiced in Fengtian Province prior to 1920s.

46 *Senman Takushoku Kabushiki Gaisha Mansen Takushoku Kabushiki Gaisha Gonenshi*, 128–30, 214–32.

47 On the role of the Mutual Aid Association, see Piao Changyu, "Riben diguo zhuyi zaidongbei zhimin tongzhi shiqi chaoxianzu nongmin suo xingde 'zigengnong chuangding' shilun," 426.

48 Han Tohyŏn, "1930 nyŏndae nongch'on chinhung undongŭi sŏnggyŏk," 244–55.

49 *Kunan douzheng shisinian*, vol. 1 (Struggles of Hardship for 14 Years), 450. In another statistic on the amount of "purchased" land (10,678,247 ching), North Manchuria (Hukha, Pukan, and Samgang Provinces) and Central Manchuria (Pingan, Jilin, and Kang Provinces) accounted for about 83 percent (approximately 44 and 39 percent, respectively). East Manchuria (Tongan, Kando, and Pokdangang Provinces),

South Manchuria (Fengtian, Kumju, and Tongan Provinces), and West Manchuria (Hungantong and Hunannam Provinces) accounted for about 14, 1.9, and 1.6 percent. For more on these statistics, see *Kunan douzheng shisinian*, 2:251–52.

50 Jones, *Manchuria since 1931*, 169–71; *Contemporary Manchuria* 2:5 (September 1938): 131.

51 *Kunan douzheng shisinian*, 2:450.

52 *Kunan douzheng shisinian*, 3:302.

53 Ibid.

54 *Kunan douzheng shisinian*, 2:2558.

55 Ibid., 256.

56 Jones, *Manchuria since 1931*, 96–97.

57 Ibid., 73.

58 *Kunan douzheng shisinian*, 2:197. In the early days of the Manchukuo state, they occupied about 32.5 percent of the land in eastern and southern Manchuria, 48.9 percent in central Manchuria, and about 3.2 percent in northern Manchuria.

59 Ibid., 198. The land tax increased from 29.1 percent of its value in 1934 to 40.1 percent in 1938.

60 My discussion draws on an article in a Korean magazine, Pongch'on Hŭnga hyŏphoe, *Chaeman chosŏnin t'ongsin*, vol. 72 (November 1939): 3–12, which reported on the annual meeting of the Concordia Association.

six *The Specter of the Social*

1 For the thesis of scapegoating and national discrimination, see Kim Sŏngho, *1930 nyŏndae Yŏnbyŏn Minsaengdan sagŏn yŏn'gu* (The Minsaengdan Incident in Yanbian in the 1930s) (Seoul: Paeksan Charyowŏn, 1999). For the argument that the purge originated in Chinese nationalism, see Lee Chongsŏk, "Pukhan chido chiptankwa hangil mujang t'ujaeng," 35–154; and Shin Chubaek, *Manju chiyŏk Haninŭi minjok undongsa (1920–45)*. For the history of the Korean Communist Party in English, see Robert Scalapino and Lee Chong Sik, *Communism in Korea, Part I* (Berkeley: University of California Press, 1972); and Suh, Dae-sook, *The Korean Communist Movement, 1918–1948* (Princeton: Princeton University Press, 1967).

2 Han, Hongkoo, *Wounded Nationalism*, 151–75.

3 For Žižek's discussion of the Jews as the external enemy of society in fascist anti-Semitism, see Slavoj Žižek, "Class Struggle or Postmodernism? Yes, please!" in Judith Butler, Ernesto Laclau, and Slavoj Žižek, *Contingency, Hegemony, Universality: Contemporary Dialogues on the Left* (London: Verso, 2000), 121.

4 My discussion of the Minsaengdan in this section draws from Kim Sŏngho, *1930 nyŏndae Yŏnbyŏn Minsaengdan sagŏn yŏn'gu*, esp. 26–113.

5 The Minsaengdan was influenced by the self-rule movement in Korea, which aspired to modernize the country and create a form of autonomy comparable to

what Canada had realized under British rule. In Korea, the movement for self-rule emerged in the 1930s as a controversial nationalist project. According to its proponents, it was a nationalist movement modeled after colonies in the European empire that had gained some autonomy.

6   Kim Sŏngho, *1930 nyŏndae Yŏnbyŏn Minsaengdan sagŏn yŏn'gu*, 64.

7   "Hurengei zhonggong ningan xianwei, di wu dangwei de xin—guanyu kangri jundui gaijian dongbei fanri lianhejun zongzhihuibu, Minshengtuan jiduijiu guojun celue deng wenti (1935, 3.17)" (Report of the Niang County Committee of the Chinese Communist Party regarding the Minsaengdan and the National Salvation Army [1935, 3.17])," in *Dongbei diqu geming lishi wenjian huiji*, Jia 44 (The Archives of Revolutionary History in Northeast China), ed. Zhongyang danganguan (The Chinese Central Archives) et al. (Jilin: Jilinsheng gongshanglian yinshuachang, 1990), 415–23.

8   "Tuanshengwei tepaiyuan Zhong guanyu dongman fanri douzheng qingkuang de baogao (1934, 12. 4)" (Report concerning the Anti-Japanese Struggle in East Manchuria [1934, 12.4]), in *Dongbei diqu geming lishi wenjian huiji*, Jia 20, ed. Zhongyang danganguan et al. (Harbin: Harbin hulan yinshuachang, 1990), 285–350.

9   "Zhonggong Manzhoushengwei jidong xunshiyuan (wu) zhi dongman tewei de xin-guanyu dongman fanri youji yundong, tongyi zhanxian, fan Minshengtuan douzheng decelue ji danghevqunzhong kongzuo deng wenti (1935, 2. 10)" (Report from Wu concerning the Anti-Japanese Movement, its Unified Strategy, the Anti-Minsaengdan Struggle, and the Mass Mobilization [1935, 2. 10]), in *Dongbei diqu geming lishi wenjian huiji*, Jia 21 ed. Zhongyang danganguan et al. (Jilin: Jilin gongshanglian yinshuachang, 1988), 41–63.

10   The Southern Manchurian Committee of the CCP had 200 members, all but seven of whom were Korean. An exception was the Liaoning Committee in Yonggu, a major port in southern Manchuria, which had a total of thirty members, all of whom were Chinese. See "Zhonggong Manzhoushengwei gei zhonggong de baogao-guanyu Manzhou zhengzhi jingji zhuangkuang ji jixiang juti kongzuo wenti (1931, 4. 24)" (Report of the Manchurian Provincial Committee Submitted to the CCP: The Political Economic Conditions of Manchuria and the Concerned Specific Tasks of the Party [1931, 4. 24]), in *Dongbei diqu geming lishi wenjian huiji*, Jia 8, ed. Zhongyang danganguan et al. (Jilin: Jilinsheng gongshanglian yinshuachang, 1988), 1–77.

11   Kim Sŏngho, *1930 nyŏndae Yŏnbyŏn Minsaengdan sakŏn yŏn'gu*, 169–70.

12   "Wang Runcheng gei zhongyang daibiaotuan de baogao—guanyu 1935 nian—1936 nian dongman dongbu gongzuo qingkuang (1937, 1. 17)" (Report from Wang Runcheng Submitted to the Central Representative Committee [1937, 1. 17]), in *Dongbei diqu geming lishi wenjian huiji*, Jia 28 ed. Zhongyang danganguan et al. (Jilin: Jilinsheng gongshanglian yinshuachang, 1989), 336.

13   Lee Chong Sik, *Revolutionary Struggle in Manchuria*, 108.

14 In exploring the regional variation in communist activities, Lee Chong Sik noted that the Eastern Manchurian Special Committee practiced highly ideological programs, such as land reform, while its counterparts in South Manchuria, such as the Panshih Committee, emphasized the anti-Japanese struggle. See ibid., 212–13.

15 Lee Chongsŏk, "Pukhan chido chipdankwa hangil mujang t'ujaeng," 75–80.

16 Shin Chubaek, *Manju chiyŏk Haninŭi minjok undongsa (1920–45)*, 408–9.

17 Lee Chong Sik, *Revolutionary Struggle in Manchuria*, 111.

18 The Comintern, Third International was an international Communist organization that Lenin and the Russian Communist Party established in March 1919. For a study of the triangular relationship among the CCP, the MPC, and the Comintern, see Lee Chong Sik, *Revolutionary Struggle in Manchuria*, 62–188; and Pak Sunyoung, "The Relationship between the Chinese Communist Party and the Comintern with Regard to the Manchurian Provincial Committee (1930s)," manuscript.

19 Ibid.

20 For general assessments of these economic conditions, see "Tuan Manzhoushengwei gongzuo dagang (1931, 1. 16)" (The Major Tasks of the Manchuria Committee of the CCP [1931, 1. 16]), in *Dongbei diqu geming lishi wenjian huiji, Jia 7*, ed. Zhongyang danganguan et al. (Jilin: Jilinsheng gongshanglian yinshuachang, 1988), 243–64; "Diguozhuyi jianta xia de Manzhou de jingji weiji [xx] zai 'Gongren tongxun'di liu qi shangfa biaode wenzhang (1931, 1, 19)" (The Economic Crisis in Manchuria under Imperialism [xx] in Workers' Communication [1931, 1, 19]), in *Dongbei diqu geming lishi wenjian huiji, Jia 7*, ed. Zhongyang danganguan et al. (Jilin: Jilinsheng gongshanglian yinshuachang, 1988), 299–307; and "Zhonggong Manzhoushengwei guanyu chunhuang douzheng de jueyi (1933, 2. 28)" (The Manchurian Provincial Committee of the CCP on the Strategy on the Spring Struggle [1933, 2. 28]), in *Dongbei diqu geming lishi wenjian huiji, Jia 12*, ed. Zhongyang danganguan et al. (Harbin: Harbin hulan yinshuachang, 1988), 183–97.

On warlords and Japanese imperialism, see especially "Zhonggong Jichang quwei shiyi yuefen gongzuo baogao (1927, 12. 1)" (Report of the Jichang Committee of the CCP on November Tasks [1927, 12. 1]), in *Dongbei diqu geming lishi wenjian huiji, Jia 1*, ed. Zhongyang danganguan et al. (Liaoning: Liaoning meishu yinshuachang fenchang, 1988), 194–98; "Zhonggong Manzhousheng linwei guanyu muqian gongzuo jihua jueyian (1927, 12. 24)" (Resolution on the Immediate Tasks of the Manchurian Provincial Committee of the CCP [1927, 12. 24]), in *Dongbei diqu geming lishi wenjian huiji, Jia 1*, ed. Zhongyang danganguan et al. (Liaoning: Liaoning meishu yinshuachang fenchang, 1988), 217–30; "Zhonggong Manzhousheng linwei zhengzhi dangwu baogao-Manzhou de zhengzhi jingji xingshi ji dang de gongzuo qingkuang (1928, 2. 12)" (Reporting the Manchurian Provincial Committee—Political Economic Conditions in Manchuria and the Situations of the Tasks of the Party [1928, 2. 12]), in *Dongbei diqu geming lishi wenjian huiji, Jia 1*, ed. Zhongyang danganguan et al. (Liaoning: Liaoning meishu yinshuachang fenchang, 1988), 323–29; and "Zhonggong Manzhoushengwei gei zhonggong de baogao: Guanyu Manzhou zhengzhi jingji zhuangkuang ji jixiang juti kongzuo wenti (1931, 4. 24)," in *Dongbei diqu geming lishi wenjian huiji*, Jia 8, esp. 1–2.

21 "Zhonggong Manzhousheng weiyuanhui huiyijilu–guanyu zhongdonglu douzheng, fandi yundong, dang de zu zhi deng wenti (1930, 4. 2)" (Meeting Report of the Manchuria Provincial Committee of the CCP–on the Struggle in Zhongdonglu, the Anti-imperialist movement, and the Party's Concerns [1930, 4. 2]), in *Dongbei diqu geming lishi wenjian huiji*, Jia 4, ed. Zhongyang danganguan et al. (Liaoning: Liaoning meishu yinshuachang fenchang, 1989), 289–322.

22 "Zhonggong Manzhoushengwei tepaiyuan Ji Zi baogao di yi hao: Gguanyu Jilin, Changchun de zhengzhi jingji xingshi, dangqun gongzuo ji jin hou de gongzuo buzhi (1931 10.2)" (First Report from Ji Zi, an Agent Sent from the Manchurian Special Committee of the CCP, concerning the Political and Economic Conditions in Jilin and Changchun [1931 10.2]), in *Dongbei diqu geming lishi wenjian huiji*, Jia 9, ed. Zhongyang danganguan et al. (Jilin: Jilinsheng gongshanglian jinshuachang, 1988), 77–85; "Tuanmanzhoushengwei xiaohe xunshi nanman gongzuo baogao-guanyu nanman zhengzhi jingji zhuangkuang, geming xingshi ji jinhou de yijian, banfadeng (1931, 11. 17)" (Report on South Manchuria: The Political and Economic Conditions in Manchuria and Assessments of Revolutionary Conditions [1931, 11. 17]), in *Dongbei diqu geming lishi wenjian huiji*, Jia 9, ed. Zhongyang danganguan et al. (Jilin: Jilinsheng gongshanglian jinshuachang, 1988), 249–73.

23 "Zhonggong Manzhoushengwei guanyu Manzhou Hanguo minzu wenti jueyian (1931. 5. 26)" (The Manchurian Provincial Committee's Resolution on Koreans in Manchuria [1931. 5. 26]), in *Dongbei diqu geming lishi wenjian huiji*, Jia 8, ed. Zhongyang danganguan et al. (Jilin: Jilinsheng gongshanglian yinshuachang, 1988), 133–43.

24 Kim Sŏngho, *1930 nyŏndae Yŏnbyŏn Minsaengdan sagŏn yŏn'gu*, 94–95.

25 Rosa Luxemburg, *The Russian Revolution and Leninism or Marxism?* (Ann Arbor: University of Michigan Press, 1970), 49.

26 Mark Selden, *China in Revolution* (New York: M. E. Sharpe, 1995); Chalmers Johnson, *Peasant Nationalism and Communist Power* (Stanford: Stanford University Press, 1962).

27 Lee Chong Sik, *Revolutionary Struggle in Manchuria*, 204.

28 Manjusŏngwi wiwŏnhoe (The Manchuria Provincial Committee of the CCP), "Chungguk Manjusŏngwiŭi panje t'ongilchŏnsŏn chiphaengkwa musan kegŭp yŏngdogwŏn chaengch'wie kwanhan kyŏrui" (Resolution of the Manchurian Provincial Committee of the Chinese Communist Party on the Practice of the Anti-imperialist United Front and the Acquisition of the Leadership of the Propertyless upon Receipt of the January 26 Letter from the Central Committee of the CCP), May 15, 1933, translated in Shin Chubaek, *1930 nyŏndae minjok haebang undongron yŏn'gu II*, 96–97.

29 Ibid., 103.

30 The Tuesday group consisted of Korean communists who continued to develop close relations with Moscow and carried out their activities as they circulated in

Moscow, Korea, and Manchuria to gather resources to reconstitute the KCP. See
Ko Chunsŏk, Chosŏn kongsandanggwa Comintern (The Korean Communist Party and
the Comintern), trans. Kim Yŏngchŏl (Seoul: Kongdongch'e, 1989), 101–2.

31 The Tuesday group also absorbed the Shanghai group in North Manchuria in the
mid-1920s. For the formation of the Tuesday and other Korean communist groups,
see Shin Chubaek, Manju chiyŏk haninŭi minjok undongsa (1920–45), 63–76, 128–46.

32 Ko Chunsŏk, Chosŏn kongsandanggwa Comintern, 100–104.

33 Kim Taeguk, "Wigie jingmyŏnhan Chosŏn kongsandang Manju ch'onggukkwa che
2 ch'a Kando kongsandang sagŏn," in Chungguk Chosŏn minjok palchach'wi ch'ongsŏ,
vol. 2, Pulssi, 449–56.

34 Kim Taeguk, "Chaechungguk hanin ch'ŏngnyun dongmaeng" (The Youth Federation of Koreans in China), in Pak Ch'ang-wuk Chungguk Chosŏn minjok palchach'wi
chongsŏ, vol. 2, Pulssi, 433–42.

35 Kim Ch'unsŏn, "Sinminbuŭi haech'e" (The Dissolution of the Sinminbu), in Chungguk Chosŏn minjok palchach'wi ch'ongsŏ, vol. 2, Pulssi, 218–23; Ryu Pyŏngho, "Ch'amŭibuŭi panil kŭn'gŏji" (The Anti-Japanese Base of the Ch'amŭibu)," in ibid., 302–7;
and Ryu Pyŏngho, "Chongŭibuŭi panil kŭn'gŏji" (The Anti-Japanese Base of the
Chŏngŭibu), in ibid., 323–30.

36 For Korean noncommunist groups and their alliances with Korean communists
in forging the united front, see Shin Chubaek, Manju chiyŏk Haninŭi minjok undongsa (1920–45), 76–96. For various organizations such as the Tamuldang, Koryŏ
hyŏngmyŏngdang, and Han'guk nodongdang, see 108–28. For the conflicts between communists and the Sinminbu, see Kim Ch'unsŏn, "Sinminbuŭi haech'e"
(The Dissolution of the Sinminbu), in Chungguk Chosŏn minjok palchach'wi ch'ongsŏ,
vol. 2, Pulssi, 222; and Lee Kanghun, "Kongsandange amsaltanghan Kim Chwajin
changgunuŭi ch'oehu" (The Last of General Kim Chwajin, Assassinated by Communists), Pukhan (North Korea) (1984): 198–207. The Japanese general consul
claimed that the Sinminbu extorted money from Koreans through threats and
violence in the name of Korean national liberation. For a discussion of the Sinminbu, see Kim Ch'unsŏn, " Hanjok ch'ong yŏnhaphoe" (The Korean Federation),
in Chungguk Chosŏn minjok palchach'wi ch'ongsŏ, vol. 2, Pulssi, 232–40.

37 Lim Hŭijun, "Hyŏksinŭihoewa chaeman ch'aekchinhoe" (The Revolutionary Assembly and Chaekchinhoe in Manchuria), in Chungguk Chosŏn minjok palchach'wi
ch'ongsŏ, vol. 2, Pulssi, 349–51.

38 Ryu Pyŏngho, "Namman chigu panil t'ongil tanch'e: Kungminbuŭi ch'angnip"
(The Anti-Japanese Organization in South Manchuria: The Establishment of Kungminbu)," in Chungguk Chosŏn minjok palchach'wi ch'ongsŏ, vol. 2, Pulssi, 356–61.

39 Kim Ch'unsŏn, "Hanjok ch'ong yŏnhaphoe," 232–40.

40 Shin Chubaek, Manju chiyŏk Haninŭi minjok undongsa (1920–45), 216.

41 Kim Taeguk, "Chaechungguk hanin ch'ŏngnyŏn tongmaeng."

42 For the full text translated into Korean, see Ko Chunsŏk, Chosŏn kongsandanggwa
Comintern, 107–10.

43 Hyŏn Ryongsun, *Chosŏnjok paengnyŏn sahwa*, 3:108–9. Kim Sŏngho (*1930 nyŏndae Yŏnbyŏn Minsaengdan sagŏn yŏn'gu*) also documents valuable recollections of survivors.

44 In his comprehensive study of the Minsaengdan, Kim Sŏngho collected the experiences of those who were charged with being Minsaengdan members. See Kim Sŏngho, *1930 nyŏndae Yŏnbyŏn Minsaengdan sagŏn yŏn'gu*, 172–80.

45 A cartoon that depicted a body with three heads—nationalism, factionalism, and Minsaengdan—was widely circulated within the CCP organizations in Manchuria.

46 Kim Sŏngho, *1930 nyŏndae Yŏnbyŏn Minsaengdan sagŏn yŏn'gu*, 138.

47 "Zhonggong dongman dangtuan tewei gongzuo baogao: Muqian yiban zhuangkuang, jieshou zhongyang luxian yianhou de qingxing (1933, 10. 25)" (Report of the Eastern Manchuria Special Committee on the General Conditions and Situations before and after the Receipt of the CCP Policy), in *Dongbei diqu geming lishi wenjian huiji, Jia 30*, ed. Zhongyang danganguan et al. (Jilin: Jilinsheng gongshanglian yinshuachang, 1989), 1–48.

48 The original was translated in Kim Sŏngho, *1930 nyŏndae Yŏnbyŏn Minsaengdan sagŏn yŏn'gu*, 126–27.

49 This figure is from ibid., 265.

50 Shin Chubaek, *Manju chiyŏk Haninŭi minjok undongsa (1920–45)*, 398–99.

51 For excellent documentation of the series of critiques within the CCP, including the role of Kim Il Sung, see Han Hongkoo, *Wounded Nationalism*; Kim Sŏngho, *1930 nyŏndae Yŏnbyŏn Minsaengdan sagŏn yŏn'gu*, 144–99; and Shin Chubaek, *Manju chiyŏk Haninŭi minjok undongsa (1920–45)*, 391–97.

52 Shin Chubaek, *Manju chiyŏk Haninŭi minjok undongsa (1920–45)*, 442.

53 "Zhonggong Manzhoushengwei jidong xunshiyuan (Wu) zhi dongman tewei de xin: Guanyu dongman fanri youji yundong, tongyi zhanxian, fan Minshengtuan douzheng decelue ji danghevqunzhong kongzuo deng wenti (1935, 2. 10)" in *Dongbei diqu geming lishi wenjian huiji, Jia 21*, 48–56.

54 Kim Sŏngho, *1930 nyŏndae Yŏnbyŏn Minsaengdan sakŏn yŏn'gu*, 197–99.

55 As key examples of memoirs and recollections of the Manchurian struggle, see Lim Ch'unch'u, *Hangil mujang t'ujaeng sigirŭl hoesang hamyŏ* (Remembering the Anti-Japanese Armed Struggle) (P'yŏngyang: Chosŏn nodongdang, 1960); *Hoesanggi* (Recollections), vols. 1–7 (P'yŏngyang, Chosŏn nodongdang ch'ulp'ansa, 1961); *Hangil ppalch'isan ch'amgajadurŭi hoesanggi* (Memoirs on the Anti-Japanese Armed Struggle) (P'yŏngyang: Chosŏn nodongdang ch'ulp'ansa, 1968); *Hangil mujang t'ujaeng kyŏnghŏm*, vols. 1–3 (Experience of the Anti-Japanese Armed Struggle) (P'yŏngyang: Chosŏn nodongdang ch'ulp'ansa, 1983); and Yomaeng p'yŏnjip wiwŏnhoe (Publications Committee of the Women's Federation), *Suryŏngkke ch'ungjikhan yugyŏk kŭngŏji yŏsŏngdŭl* (Women in Guerrilla Bases Who Were Loyal to the Great Leader), vols. 1–4 (P'yŏngyang: Women's Federation, 1969). For general historical accounts of the Manchurian struggle, see *Choguk kwangbokhoe undongsa* (The History of the Korean Liberation Federation), vols. 1–2 (P'yŏngyang: Chosŏn no-

dongdang ch'ulp'ansa, 1986); Sahoe Kwahak Ch'ulp'ansa, *Hangil mujang t'ujaengsa* (The History of the Anti-Japanese Armed Struggle) (P'yŏngyang: Sahoe Kwahak Ch'ulp'ansa, 1980); Sahoe Kwahagwŏn yŏksa yŏn'guso, *Chosŏn kŭndae hyŏngmyŏng undongsa* (The History of the Modern Revolutionary Movement) (reprint; Seoul: Hanmadang, 1988); and Sahoe Kwahagwŏn yŏksa yŏn'guso, *1926–1945 nyŏn chosŏn munhaksa* (The History of Korean Literature, 1926–1945) (reprint; Seoul: Yŏlsaram Press, 1981).

56 Kim Sŏngho, *1930 nyŏndae Yŏnbyŏn Minsaengdan sagŏn yŏn'gu.*

57 See Wada Haruki, *Kim Il Sung kwa Manju Hangil chŏnjaeng* (Kim Il Sung and the Anti-Japanese War in Manchuria) (Seoul: Changjakkwa Pip'yŏng, 1992) 42–43, 127; and Dae-Sook Suh, *Kim Il Sung: The North Korean Leader* (New York: Columbia University Press, 1988).

58 Lee Chongsŏk, "Pukhan chido chipdan'gwa hangil mujang t'ujaeng," 125–34. See also Armstrong, *The North Korean Revolution, 1945–1950.*

EPILOGUE

1 Kim Mansŏn, "Ijung kukjŏk" (Dual Nationality), in *Han'guk iimin sosŏl sŏnjip* (Selections of the Novels on Korean Migrants) (Seoul: Kyemyŏng University Press, 1989). From 1941 until 1945, Kim Mansŏn worked as a reporter for the *Mansŏn* newspaper in Manchuria. He returned to Seoul in 1945 and moved to North Korea in October 1950 during the Korean War. Even in South Korea, he is considered one of the key literary critics in North Korea. It is said that he moved back to China during the political purge in North Korea in late 1950s and early 1960s and that he currently works at a publishing company in Beijing. "Ijung kukjŏk" was originally published in a collection, *Amnokkang* (The Amnok River) (Seoul: Tongjisa, 1948).

2 Kim Mansŏn, "Ijung kukjŏk," 500.

GLOSSARY

Asia Development Company (Tongakwŏnop hoesa in Korean, Tōa kangyō kabushiki geisha in Japanese, 東亞勸業株式會社)

Association to Facilitate Self-Rule (Chach'i ch'okchin wiwŏnhoe in Korean, 自治促進委員會)

Association for Korean Cultivators (Kanminhoe in Korean, 墾民會)

Association for Naturalized Koreans (Kwihwa hanin tonghyanghoe in Korean, 歸化韓人動向會)

Association for the Protection of People (Pominhoe in Korean, 保民會)

Association for Self-Rule of Koreans (Kanmin Chach'ihoe in Korean, 墾民自治會)

Chambers of commerce (Sanghoe in Korean, shanghui in Chinese, 商會)

Chinese local government (hyangsa in Korean, 鄉事)

Chinese nationality (kongmin in Korean, gongmin in Chinese, 公民)

Chinese wholesale grain stores (liangchan in Korean, liangzhan in Chinese, 糧棧)

Cluster immigration (chiphap imin in Korean, 集合移民)

Collective villages (chiptan purak in Korean, jituan buluo in Chinese, 集團部落)

Committee for Political Affairs (Chongch'i wiwŏnhoe in Korean, 政治委員會)

Committee on the Problem of Korean Compatriots in Manchuria (Manchu tongp'o munje hyŏpŭihoe in Korean, 滿洲同胞問題協議會)

Counterrevolution (panhyŏngmyŏng in Korean, fangeming in Chinese, 反革命)

Developing Cooperative Company (Hŭngan hapchaksa in Korean, Xingan hezuoshe in Chinese, 興安合作社)

Dispersed immigration (punsan imin in Korean, 分散移民)

Dual nationality (ijung kukchŏk in Korean, 二重國籍)

East Asia Co-Prosperity Sphere (Tae tonga kongyŏngkwŏn in Korean, Dai Tōa kyō eiken in Japanese, 大東亞共榮圈)

East Asian League (Tonga yŏnmaeng in Korean, Tōa renmei in Japanese, 東亞聯盟)

Eastern border or the border area of Fengtian Province (Tongbyŏndo in Korean, 東邊道)

Ethnic principle of nationality (Sogin chuŭi in Korean, Shuren zhuyi in Chinese, 屬人主意)

Family Register of Korea (Hojŏk in Korean, Huji in Chinese, 戶籍)

Farming Cooperative Company (Nongŏp hapchaksa in Korean, Nongshi hezuoshe in
 Chinese, 農事合作社)
Federation to Liberate the Fatherland (Choguk kwangbokhoe in Korean,
 祖國光復會)
Financial Association (Kŭmyunghoe in Korean, 金融會)
Financial Cooperative (Kŭmyung chohap in Korean, 金融組合)
Financial Cooperative Company (Kŭmyung hapchaksa in Korean, Jingrong hezuoshe
 in Chinese, 金融合作社)
Financial Department (Kŭmyungbu in Korean, 金融部)
Group defense network (Pogapche in Korean, 保甲制)
Group immigration (chiptan imin in Korean, 集團移民)
Hunch'un (Hunchun in Chinese 暈春)
Hwaryong (Helong in Chinese, 和龍)
Imperial nationality (cheguk kukchŏk in Korean, 帝國國籍)
Imperialization (hwangminhwa in Korean, 皇民化)
Kando Relief Association (Kando kujehoe in Korean, 間島救濟會)
Korea-Manchuria Development Company, Manchuria-Korea Development Company
 (Sŏnman ch'ŏksik chusik hoesa, Mansŏn ch'ŏksik chusik hoesa in Korean,
 Senman Takushoku Kabushiki Gaisha Mansen Takushoku Kabushiki Gaisha in
 Japanese, 鮮滿拓殖株式會社 滿鮮拓殖株式會社)
Korean Association (Chosŏnin minhoe in Korean, 朝鮮人民會)
Korean Communist Youth Association (Chosŏn kongsan ch'ŏngnyŏnhoe in Korean,
 朝鮮共產靑年會)
Korean Federation (Hanjok ch'ongyŏnhaphoe in Korean, 韓族總聯合會)
Korean Residents' Association (Chosŏnin kŏryuminhoe in Korean,
 朝鮮人居留民會)
Korean Revolutionary Army (Chosŏn Hyŏngmyŏnggun in Korean, 朝鮮革命軍)
Korean Self-Rule Association (Hanmin Chach'ihoe in Korean, 韓民自治會)
Koreans without Chinese nationality (Kanmin in Korean, Kenmin in Chinese, 墾民)
Kwantung Administration (Kwantongch'ŏng in Korean, 關東廳)
Land sovereignty (t'oji chugwŏn in Korean, tudi zhuquan in Chinese, 土地主權)
League of Koreans (Kungminbu in Korean, 國民部)
Leasing (sangjo in Korean, shangzu in Chinese, 商租)
Manchu clothing and hairstyle (hŭkpok pyŏnbal in Korean, 黑服辮髮;
 ch'ibalyŏkpok in Korean, 薙髮易服)
Manchu p'yongron (Manshū Hyōron in Japanese, 滿洲評論)
Manchuria Development Company (Manchuch'ŏksik kongsa in Korean,
 滿洲拓殖公社)
Manchurian General Bureau of the Korean Communist Party (Manju Ch'ongguk,
 滿洲總局)
Ministry of Colonial Affairs (Takumusho in Japanese, 拓務省)
Mixed residential region (chapkŏ chiyŏk in Korean, zayudiyu in Chinese, 雜居地域)

Mutual Aid Associations (Nongmugye in Korean, 農務契)

Nation (minjok in Korean, minji in Chinese, 民籍)

National membership (kongmingwŏn in Korean, gongminqun in Chinese 公民權)

National Punishment Law (Kukchŏk chingbŏl chore in Korean, 國籍懲罰條例)

National self-rule (minjok chach'i in Korean, minzu zizhi in Chinese, 民族自治)

Nationality (kukchŏk in Korean, guoij in Chinese, 國籍)

Oriental Development Company (Tongyang ch'ŏksik chusik hoesa in Korean, Tōyō
  takushoku kabushiki gaisha in Japanese, 東洋拓殖株式會社)

Pandoin (半島人)

People's Livelihood Corps (Minsaengdan in Korean, Minshengtuan in Chinese,
  民生團)

Policy to increase rice production (Sanmijŭngsan chŏngch'aek in Korean,
  産米増産政策)

Policy of protecting good Koreans and repressing rebellious Koreans (Pohoch'wich'e
  in Korean, 保護取締)

Principle that regards Manchuria as an extension of Korea (Chosŏn yŏnjang chuŭi,
  朝鮮延長主意)

Program to Create Independent Farmers (Chajangnong ch'angjong in Korean,
  Zigengnong chuangding in Chinese, 自作農創定)

Renouncing registration as Japanese subjects (ch'ulchŏk in Korean, 出籍)

Revolutionary Assembly (Hyŏksin ŭihoe in Korean, 革新議會)

Rule of the kingly way (wangdo in Korean, wangdao in Chinese, 王道)

Safety villages (Anjŏn nongch'on in Korean, 安全農村)

Self-determination of the Korean minority (sosu minjok chagyŏl in Korean, shaoshu
  minzu zijue in Chinese, 少數民族自決)

Self-reliance (Juch'e in Korean, 主體)

Special administrative unit (t'ukpyŏl haengjŏnggu sŏljŏng in Korean, tebie
  xingzhengqu sheding in Chinese, 特別行政區設定)

Special area for self-rule (chach'iryŏng sŏljŏng in Korean, zizhiling sheding in
  Chinese, 自治領設定)

Specific district for self-rule (t'ukpyŏl chach'i kuyŏk sŏljŏng in Korean, tebie zizhi
  quyu sheding in Chinese 特別自治區域設定)

State sovereignty (kukka chugwŏn in Korean, guojia zhuquan in Chinese,
  國家主權)

Territorial principle of nationality (Sokchi chuŭi in Korean, Shudi zhuyi in Chinese,
  屬地主意)

Tonhwa (敦化)

Two dreams in one bed (tongsang imong in Korean, tongchuang yimeng in Chinese,
  Dōshō imu in Japanese, 同床異夢)

Type of collective landownership (Chŏnminje in Korea, Diaminzhi in Chinese,
  田民制)

Unified national party (minjok yuiltang in Korean, 民族唯一黨)

Wangch'ong (Wangqing in Chinese, 汪清)

Yangdo Chŏnsŏn (Liangtiao zhangxian in Chinese, 兩條戰線)

Yon'gil (Yanji in Chinese, 延吉)

Youth Federation of Koreans in China (Chaechungguk Hanin chŏngnyŏn tongmaeng in Korean, 在中國 朝鮮人靑年同盟)

BIBLIOGRAPHY

Ahmad, Aijaz. *In Theory: Classes, Nations, Literatures*. London: Verso, 1992.

Aleinkoff, Alexander, and Douglas Klusmeyer. *From Migrants to Citizens*. Washington, D.C.: Brookings Institution, 2000.

An Sugil. *Pukkando* (Northern Kando). Vol. 1. Seoul: Samjungdang, 1993.

Anderson, Benedict. *Imagined Communities: Reflections on the Origin and Spread of Nationalism*. London: Verso, 1991.

———. *The Spectre of Comparisons: Nationalism, Southeast Asia, and the World*. London: Verso, 1998.

Appadurai, Arjun. *Modernity at Large: Cultural Dimensions of Globalization*. Minneapolis: University of Minnesota Press, 1996.

Armstrong, Charles. *The North Korean Revolution, 1945–1950*. Ithaca: Cornell University Press, 2003.

Asada Kyōji. "Manshū Nōgyō Imin Seisaku no Ritsuan Katei" (The Formation of the Policies on Korean Emigration to Manchuria). In *Nihon Teikokushugika no Mansh Imin* (Emigration to Manchuria during the Japanese Imperialism), ed. Manshū Iminshi Kenkyūkai. Tokyo: Ryūkei Shosha, 1976.

Balibar, Etienne. "Elements for a Theory of Transition." In Louis Althusser and Etienne Balibar, *Reading Capital*. London: Verso, 1970.

———. "The Nation Form: History and Ideology." In Etienne Balibar and Immanuel Wallerstein, *Race, Nation, Classes*. London: Verso, 1991.

Barrett, Michele. *The Politics of Truth: From Marx to Foucault*. Stanford: Stanford University Press, 1991.

———. "Ideology, Politics, Hegemony: From Gramsci to Laclau and Mouffe." In *Mapping Ideology*, ed. Slavoj Žižek. London: Verso, 1994.

Bix, Herbert. "Japanese Imperialism and the Manchurian Economy, 1900–1931." *China Quarterly* 51 (1972): 425–43.

Brooks, Barbara. "Peopling in the Japanese Empire: The Koreans in Manchuria and the Rhetoric of Inclusion." In *Japan's Competing Modernities: Issues in Culture and Democracy, 1900–1930*, ed. Sharon Minichiello. Honolulu: University of Hawai'i Press, 1998.

Brubaker, Rogers. *Citizenship and Nationhood in France and Germany*. Cambridge: Harvard University Press, 1992.

Butler, Judith, Ernesto Laclau, and Slavoj Žižek. *Contingency, Hegemony, Universality: Contemporary Dialogues on the Left.* London: Verso, 2000.

Ch'ae Tosik and Ch'ae Sŏnae. "Rajaguesoŭi iminsari" (A Life as Immigrants in Rajagu). In *Chungguk Chosŏn minjok palchach'wi ch'ongsŏ* (History of the Korean Chinese in China). Vol. 4, *Kyŏlchŏn* (Final War). Beijing: Minzu chubanshe, 1991.

Chao, Kang. *The Economic Development of Manchuria: The Rise of a Frontier Economy.* Ann Arbor: University of Michigan Center for Chinese Studies, 1982.

Chatterjee, Partha. *The Nation and Its Fragments: Colonial and Postcolonial Histories.* Princeton: Princeton University Press, 1993.

Ch'en, Jerome. "Defining Chinese Warlords and Their Factions." *Bulletin of the School of Oriental and African Studies* 31 (1968): 563–600.

Ch'i, Hsi-sheng. *Warlord Politics in China, 1916–1928.* Stanford: Stanford University Press, 1976.

Choguk kwangbokhoe undongsa (The History of the Korean Liberation Federation). Vols. 1–2. P'yŏngyang: Chosŏn nodongdang ch'ulp'ansa, 1986.

Choi, Chungmoo. "The Discourse of Decolonization and Popular Memory: South Korea." In *The Politics of Culture in the Shadow of Capital*, ed. Lisa Lowe and David Lloyd. Durham: Duke University Press, 1997.

Choi Kansik. "Hwinam Chosŏn ijuminŭi nunmulgyŏwun saenghwal" (The Wretched Life of Korean Settlers in Hwhinam). In *Chungguk Chosŏn minjok palchach'wi ch'ongsŏ* (History of the Korean Chinese in China). Vol. 4, *Kyŏlchŏn* (Final War). Beijing: Minzu chubanshe, 1991.

Chŏng Yŏngt'ae. "Ilchemal migunjŏnggi pan'gong ideologiŭi hyŏngsŏng" (The Formation of Anti-communist Ideology during the Late Colonial Rule and the American Military Government). *Yŏksa pip'yŏng* 16 (Spring 1992): 126–38.

Chōsen Sōtokufu Kanbō Gaijika. "Kantō Chihō ni Okeru Shūdan Buraku no" (The Conditions of Collective Villages in Kando), in *Zenman Chōsen Jinminkai Rengōkai Kaihō* 4:6 (June 1936): 30–31.

Chōsen Sōtokufu Keimukyoku. *Zaiman Senjin to Shina Kanken* (Koreans and Chinese Officials in Manchuria). Keijyō: Gyōsei Gakkai Insatsujo, 1930.

"Chōsen Sōtokufu Sandai Jigyō: Anzun nōson, Shūdan Buraku, jisaku nōsōtei" (Three Tasks of the Government General of Korea: Safe Village, Collective Village, and the Policy to Create Independent Farmers). *Zenman Chōsen Jinminkai Rengōkai Kaihō* 27:3–5 (May 1935): 106–14.

Chōsen Sōtokufu Teikoku Kaigi Setsumei Shiryō (Documents Prepared by the Government General of Korea for the Imperial Assembly). Vols. 14–17 (1924–27). Tokyo: Fujishuppansha, 1998.

Chŏn Sinja. "'Kanmin kyoyukhoe' wa 'Kanminhoe'" (Kanmin Kyoyukhoe and Kanminhoe). In *Chungguk Chosŏn minjok palchach'wi ch'ongsŏ* (History of Korean Chinese in China). Vol.1, *Kaech'ŏk* (Reclamation). Beijing: Minzu chubanshe, 1999.

Ch'u Hŏnsu. *Han'guk toknip undong* (Korean Independence Movements). Vol. 4, *Haeoe* ijumin'gwa tongnip undong I (Overseas Immigrants and the Liberation Movement). Seoul: Yonsei University Press, 1975.

Chungguk Chosŏn minjok palchach'wi ch'ongsŏ (History of Korean Chinese in China) Vols. 1–4. Beijing: Minzu chubanshe, 1991–1999.

"Diguozhuyi jianta xia de Manzhou de jingji weiji—zai 'gongren tongxun' di liu qi shangfa biaode wenzhang (1931, 1. 19)" (The economic crisis of Manchuria under imperialism—xx in 'Workers' Communication' 1931, 1. 19), in Dongbei diqu geming lishi wenjian huiji (Archives of Revolutionary History in Northeast China), Jia 7, ed. Zhongyang danganguan (The Chinese Central Archives), Liaoningsheng danganguan (Liaoning Provincial Archives), Jilinsheng danganguan (Jilin Provincial Archives), and Hilongjiang danganguan (Heilongjiang Provincial Archives). Jilin: Jilinsheng gongshanglian yinshuachang, 1988.

Dongbei jingjishi. (The Economic History of Northeast China). Chengdu: Sichuan renmin chubanshe, 1986.

Dongbei Jingjishixuehui. Dongbei jingjishi lunwenji xia (Collected Works on the Economic History in Northeast China). Harbin: Yajing Heilongjiang chubanshe, 1984.

Dongnanlu bingbeidao. "Wangqingxiancheng ganmin ruji geqingxing bingfeng daocheng jiegan jiebao jiege liubai zhangyou" (Wangqing County's Report on Various Circumstances of the Naturalization of Koreans and Submission of Six Hundred Official Documents, Oaths, and Letters of Guarantee), 1910, 10.22–1911, 9.24. anjuanhao 22, 1.1-1.

Duara, Prasenjit. Sovereignty and Authenticity: Manchukuo and the East Asian Modern. Oxford: Rowman and Littlefield, 2003.

Duus, Peter, ed. The Cambridge History of Japan. Vol. 6. New York: Cambridge University Press, 1988.

Duus, Peter, Ramon Myers, and Mark Peattie, eds. The Japanese Informal Empire in China, 1895–1937. Princeton: Princeton University Press, 1989.

Dux, Uncheng. Riben zaijiu zhongguode touzi (Japanese Investment in China). Shanghai: Shanghai shehui kexueyuan chubanshe, 1986.

Eckert, Carter, et al. Korea: Old and New. Cambridge: Korea Institute, Harvard University, 1990.

Fanon, Frantz. The Wretched of the Earth. New York: Grove, 1963.

Fengtiansheng yihui ziliao JC 10–1695 (Records of the Parliament of Fengtian Province). Shenyang: Liaoningsheng danganguan.

Foucault, Michel. Power and Knowledge. New York: Pantheon, 1972.

———. Discipline and Punish. New York: Vintage, 1979.

Gaimushō Keisatsushi (The Police History of the Japanese Ministry of Foreign Affairs), Vols. 4, 5, 7, 8, 10, 15, 19, 20, 21. Tokyo: Fuji Shuppan, 1996–1998.

Gottschang, Thomas, and Diana Lary. Swallows and Settlers: The Great Migration from North China to Manchuria. Ann Arbor: Center for Chinese Studies, University of Michigan, 2000.

"Guanyu guanli hanqiao fangfa de zhiling" (Instructions on Supervising Koreans). Jilin Yanjidao Daoyin gongshu zhiling de 20 hao, ling Dunhuaxian zhishi 1928 (Decree of the Head of Yanji District of Jilin, Number 20, Order to the Magistrate of Dunhua County in 1928). Yanji: Institute of Ethnology, Yanbian University.

Guha, Ranajit. *Without Hegemony: History and Power in Colonial India*. Cambridge: Harvard University Press, 1998.

Han, Hongkoo. "Wounded Nationalism: The Minsaengdan Incident and Kim Il Sung in Eastern Manchuria." PhD diss., University of Washington, 1999.

Han Suk-Jung. *Manjuguk kŏn'gugŭi chaehaesŏk* (A Reinterpretation of the Construction of the Manchukuo State). Pusan: Tonga University Press, 1999.

Han Tohyŏn. "1930 nyŏndae nongch'on chinhŭng undongŭi sŏnggyŏk" (The Characteristics of the Agricultural Development Movement in the 1930s). In *Han'guk kŭndae nongch'on sahoewa ilbon chegukchuŭi* (Rural Society and Japanese Imperialism in Modern Korea), ed. Han'guk sahoesa yŏn'guhoe. Seoul: Muhakkwa chisŏngsa, 1986.

Hangil mujang t'ujaeng kyŏnghŏm (The Experience of the Anti-Japanese Armed Struggle). Vols. 1–3. P'yŏngyang, Chosŏn nodongdang ch'ulp'ansa, 1983.

Hangil ppalch'isan ch'amgajadŭrŭi hoesanggi (Memoirs on the Anti-Japanese Armed Struggle). P'yŏngyang: Chosŏn nodongdang ch'ulp'ansa, 1968.

Hardt, Michael, and Antonio Negri. *Empire*. Cambridge: Harvard University Press, 2000.

Harootunian, Harry. *Things Seen and Unseen*. Chicago: University of Chicago Press, 1988.

———. *Overcome by Modernity: History, Culture and Community in Interwar Japan*. Princeton: Princeton University Press, 2000.

———. "Ghostly Comparisons: Anderson's Telescope." *Diacritics* 29 (2004): 135–49.

Harvey, David. *The Limits to Capital*. London: Verso, 1999.

Hata, Ikuhiko. "Continental Expansion, 1905–1941." In *The Cambridge History of Japan* vol. 6, ed. Peter Duus et. al. New York: Cambridge University Press, 1988.

"Helonggu Fenfangting Xuantong 2 nian 3 hao quanzong 340 hao anjuan Fenfanting of Helong, 3 hao quanzong 340 hao" (The Department of Helong County, 3–340, 1909). Yanji: Institute of Ethnology, Yanbian University.

Hoesanggi (Recollections). Vols. 1–7. P'yŏngyang: Chosŏn nodongdang ch'ulp'ansa, 1961.

Hoston, Germaine. *Marxism and the Crisis of Development in Prewar Japan*. Princeton: Princeton University Press, 1987.

Hungnryonggangsŏng palchach'ŭwi py'ŏnch'ansil (The Publication Committee in Heilongjiang Province). "Hadong nongjang" (Hadong Farm). In *Chungguk Chosŏn minjok palchach'wi ch'ongsŏ* (History of the Korean Chinese in China). Vol. 3, *Ponghwa* (Beacon). Beijing: Minzu chubanshe, 1989, 186–89.

"Hunchun zhishi xiangfu riling fandui hanqiao ruji zunchi dafu qingjian heyou" (The Yanji District's Response to the Inquiry by the Magistrate of Hunchun County on the Japanese Consul's Objection to the Naturalization of Koreans). Yanji daoyin gongshu minguo wu nian 51 hao anjuan (The decree of Yanji district, number 51, 1916). Yanji: Institute of Ethnology, Yanbian University.

Hwang Hyŏngu. "Manggungnoŭi sŏrum" (Sorrows of People without a Nation). In *Chungguk Chosŏn minjok palchach'wi ch'ongsŏ* (History of the Korean Chinese in China). Vol. 4, *Kyŏlchŏn* (Final War). Beijing: Minzu chubanshe, 1991.

"Hurengei zhonggong ningan xianwei, di wu dangwei de xin—guanyu kangri jundui gaijian dongbei fanri lianhejun zongzhihuibu, Minshengtuan jiduijiu guojun celue deng wenti (1935, 3.17)" (Report of the Niang County Committee of the Chinese Communist Party regarding the Minsaengdan and the National Salvation Army, 1935, 3. 17), in *Dongbei diqu geming lishi wenjian huiji, Jia 44*, ed. Zhongyang danganguan et al. Jilin: Jilinsheng gongshanglian yinshuachang, 1990.

Hyŏn Ch'onch'u. "Iljeŭi 'che ilch'a yŏngsahoeŭi' wa Chosŏnjogŭi ogurhan 'ijung kukchŏk' munje" (The First Consul Meeting and the Undeserved Dual Nationality of Koreans). In *Chungguk Chosŏn minjok palchach'wi ch'ongsŏ* (History of the Korean Chinese in China). Vol. 2, *Pulssi* (Kindling). Beijing: Minzu chubanshe, 1995.

———. "Ponggŏn kunborhaŭi kwajunghan pudamgwa royake modaegin Chosŏnjok inmindŭl" (The Heavy Burden on and Oppression of Koreans under Feudal Warlords). In *Chungguk Chosŏn minjok palchach'wi ch'ongsŏ* (History of the Korean Chinese in China). Vol. 2, *Pulssi* (Kindling). Beijing: Minzu chubanshe, 1995.

Hyŏn, Kyuhwan. *Han'guk Yuiminsa I* (The History of the Migration of Koreans). Seoul: Ŏmungak, 1967.

Hyŏn Ryongsun. *Chosŏnjok paengnyŏn sahwa* (One Hundred Years of Korean History in China). Vols. 1–3. Reprint; Seoul: Korŭm, 1989.

"Ilbonŭi chaeman kigwanŭi t'ongil munje" (The Problem of Integrating Japanese Institutions into Manchuria). *Manju Ilbo* (September 1934). In *Han'guk toknip undong* (Korean Independence Movements) Vol. 4, *Haeoe ijumingwa tongnip undong I* (Overseas Immigrants and the Liberation Movement I), ed. Ch'u Hŏnsu. Seoul: Yonsei University Press, 1975.

Il Mok. "Choi Ch'angho sagŏn'wa Kando chumindaehoe" (The Choi Ch'angho Incident and Residents' Rally in Kando). In *Chungguk Chosŏn minjok palchach'wi ch'ongsŏ* (History of the Korean Chinese in China). Vol. 2, *Pulssi* (Kindling). Beijing: Minzu chubanshe, 1995.

Ito Takeo. *Life along the South Manchurian Railway: The Memoirs of Ito Kakeo*. Translated by Joshua Fogel. Armonk, N.Y.: M. E. Sharpe, 1988.

"Jiangyu gei zhongyang de baogao—guanyu Manzhou de yibian qinzhi, dangde fanzhang zhuang kuang deng wenti (1935, 5.11) (Jiangyu's Report to the Central Chinese Communist Party—on general conditions in Manchuria and the development of the Party, 1935, 5. 11), in *Dongbei diqu geming lishi wenjian huiji Jia 31*, ed. Zhongyang danganguan et al. Harbin: Harbin hulan yinshuachang, 1989.

"Jilin Bianwuchu Xuantong yuannian 5 hao quanzong 4 hao anjuan" (Bianwuchu of Jilin Province, 5 Hao Quanzong, 4 Hao). Yanji: Institute of Ethnology, Yanbian University.

"Jilinsheng gongshu zhiling di 9 hao, ling Yanji daoyin Taobin, minguo wunian, 1916" (Jilin Province, Order Number 9, the Order to Taobin, the Head of Yanji District in 1916). Yanji: Institute of Ethnology, Yanbian University.

"Jilinsheng zhengfu xunling" (The Decree of the Jilin Provincial Government), "Xianzhi Hanmin dingming maidi" (The Prohibition of the Koreans to Purchase Land Using Others' Names) 1108 hao, quanzong, 46 hao 1 hao. Archives of the Kanbian Autonomous Prefecture, 1108, 46-1.

"Jilin Wangqingxian gongshu xunling di 368 hao minguo 8 nian, 1919" (The Decree of Wangqing County in Jilin Province, Number 368). Yanji: Institute of Ethnology, Yanbian University.

"Jilin Wangqingxian gongshu xunling di 8007 hao, minguo 8 nian" (The Decree of Wangqing County in Jilin Province, Number 8007, 1919). Archives of the Yanbian Autonomous Prefecture, 39 quanzong 2 hao anjuan 67.

"Jilin xunanshi chizhi hanmin chengqing ruji xunsu zhaozhang xiangqing heban gejieyou" (The Order on the Processing of the Application of Koreans for Naturalization). Jilin xunanshi gongshuchi de 4724 hao minguo si nian (The Decree of Xuanshi in Jilin Province, Number 4724, 1915). Yanji: Institute of Ethnology, Yanbian University.

Jinlin xunanshi gongshu michi di 167 hao, 1916 (The Secret Order of Jilin Xunanshi, 1916). Yanji: Institute of Ethnology, Yanbian University.

Johnson, Chalmers. Peasant Nationalism and Communist Power. Stanford: Stanford University Press, 1962.

Jones, F. C. Manchuria since 1931. Toronto: Oxford University Press, 1949.

Kashiwazaki, Chikako. "The Politics of Legal Status: The Equation of Nationality with Ethnonational Identity." In Koreans in Japan, ed. Sonia Ryang. New York: Routledge, 2000.

Kawashima, Ken. "Contingent Commodifications: Micropolitics of Recession and the Colonial Conditions of Korean Labor Power in Japan between the Two World Wars." Ph.D. diss., Department of History, New York University, 2003.

Kim Cheol. "Mollakhanŭn sinsaeng: Manjuŭi kkumkwa 'Nonggun'ŭi odok" (Collapsing Rebirth: The Dream of Manchuria and the Misreading of "Nonggun"). Sangho Hakpo 9 (2002): 123–58.

Kim Chongmi, Chūgoku Tōhokubu ni okeru Kōnichi Chōsen: Chūgoku Minshūshi Josetsu (Introduction to the History of the Anti-Japanese People in Northeast China). Tokyo: Gendai Kikakushitsu, 1992.

Kim Ch'unsŏn. " Hanjok ch'ong yŏnhaphoe" (The Korean Federation). In Chungguk Chosŏn minjok palchach'wi ch'ongsŏ (History of the Korean Chinese in China). Vol. 2, Pulssi (Kindling). Beijing: Minzu chubanshe, 1995.

———. "Sinminbuŭi haech'e (The Dissolution of the Sinminbu). In Chungguk Chosŏn minjok palchach'wi ch'ongsŏ (History of the Korean Chinese in China). Vol. 2, Pulssi (Kindling). Beijing: Minzu chubanshe, 1995.

———. " 'Kanminhoe' wa 'Nongmugye' " (Kanminhoe and Nongmugye). In Chungguk

Chosŏn Chungguk Chosŏn minjok palchach'wi ch'ongsŏ (History of the Korean Chinese in China). Vol. 1, *Kaech'ŏk* (Reclamation). Beijing: Minzu chubanshe, 1999.

Kim, Kipong. *Ilbon chegukchuŭiŭi tongbuk ch'imnyaksa* (History of the Japanese Invasion of Northeast China). Yanji: Yanbian People's Publishing Company, 1987.

Kim Mansŏn. *Amnokkang* (The Amnok River). Seoul: Tongjisa, 1948.

———. "Ijung kukjŏk" (Double Nationality). In *Han'guk iimin sosŏl sŏnjip* (Selections from the Novels of Korean Migrants). Seoul: Kyemyŏng University Press, 1989.

Kim Sŏkjun. "Tongyangch'ŏksik hoesa saŏp chŏn'gae kwajŏng" (The Development Process of the Oriental Development Company). In *Han'guk kŭndae nongch'on sahoewa ilbon chegukchuŭi* (The Modern Agricultural Society and Japanese Imperialism), ed. Han'guk sahoesa yŏn'guhoe. Seoul: Munhakkwa chisŏng, 1986.

Kim Sŏngho. *1930 nyŏndae Yŏnbyŏn Minsaengdan sagŏn yŏn'gu* (The Minsaengdan Incident in Yanbian in the 1930s). Seoul: Paeksan Charyowŏn, 1999.

Kim Taeguk. "Chaechungguk Hanin ch'ŏngnyun tongmaeng" (The Federation of Korean Youth Organizations). In *Chungguk Chosŏn minjok palchach'wi ch'ongsŏ* (History of the Korean Chinese in China). Vol. 2, *Pulssi*. (Kindling). Beijing: Minzu chubanshe, 1995.

———. "Wigie jingmyŏnhan Chosŏn kongsandang Manju ch'onggukkwa che 2 ch'a Kando kongsandang sagŏn." In *Chungguk Chosŏn minjok palchach'wi ch'ongsŏ* (History of the Korean Chinese in China). Vol. 2, *Pulssi* (Kindling). Beijing: Minzu chubanshe, 1995.

Kim Yongmu. "Sangjihyŏn Ojihyang esoŭi iminsari" (Life as Immigrants in Ojihyang Sangji County). In *Chungguk Chosŏn minjok palchach'wi ch'ongsŏ* (History of the Chinese Koreans in China). Vol. 4, *Kyŏlchŏn* (Final War). Beijing: Minzu chubanshe, 1991.

Ko Chunsŏk. *Chosŏn kongsandanggwa Comintern* (The Korean Communist Party and the Comintern). Trans. Kim Yŏngchŏl. Seoul: Kongdongch'e, 1989.

Kobayashi Hideo. "Manshū Nōgyō Imin no Einō Jittai" (The Management of the Peasant Emigration to Manchuria). In *Nihon Teikokushugika no Manshū Imin* (Emigration to Manchuria during Japanese Imperialism), ed. Manshū Iminshi Kenkyūkai. Tokyo: Ryūkei Shosha, 1976.

Kunan douzheng shisinian (Struggles and Hardship for Fourteen Years). Vols. 1–3. Beijing: Zhongguo dabeike quanji chubanshe, 1995.

Kwan, Hyang Suk. "Chūgoku niokeru 'Chōsentoku' no kenkyu josetsu" (An Introduction to the Study of the Korean-Chinese Community: Methodological Consideration) *Azizya Kenkyu* 47:3 (2001): 47–105.

Laclau, Ernesto. *Politics and Ideology in Marxist Theory*. London: Verso, 1977.

Laclau, Ernesto, and Chantal Mouffe. "Post-Marxism without Apologies." In Ernest Laclau, *New Reflections of the Revolution of Our Time*. London: Verso, 1990.

Lary, Diana. "Warlord Studies." *Modern China* 6:4 (1980): 439–70.

Lattimore, Owen. *Manchuria: Cradle of Conflict*. New York: Macmillan, 1935.

Lee Chaehwa. *Han'guk kŭnhyŏndae minjok haebang undongsa*. Seoul: Paeksansŏdang, 1988.

Lee, Chong Sik. *Revolutionary Struggle in Manchuria*. Berkeley: University of California Press, 1983.

Lee Chongsŏk. "Pukhan chido chiptankwa hangil mujang t'ujaeng" (The North Korean Leadership and the Anti-Japanese Armed Struggle). In *Haebang chŏnhusaŭi insik* 5 (A Study of History before and after the Liberation 5). Seoul: Han'gilsa 1989.

Lee Chŏngsu. "Ryangjach'on nongmindŭrŭi kangbak iju" (The Forced Migration of Peasants in Ryangja Village). In *Chungguk Chosŏn minjok palchach'wi ch'ongsŏ* (History of the Korean Chinese in China). Vol. 4, *Kyŏlchŏn* (Final War). Beijing: Minzu chubanshe, 1991.

Lee Hongsŏk. "Kando hyobyage taehan yuhyorongwa muhyoron" (The Validity and Annulment of the Kando Treaty). In *Chungguk Chosŏn minjok palchach'wi ch'ongsŏ* (History of the Korean Chinese in China). Vol. 1, *Kaech'ŏk* (Reclamation), ed. Pak Ch'angwuk. Beijing: Minzu chubanshe, 1999.

Lee Hun'gu. *Manjuwa Chosŏnin* (Manchuria and Koreans). Kyongsŏng: Hansŏngdosŏ chusikhoesa, 1932.

Lee, Hyongch'an. "1920–1930 nyŏndae Han'guginŭi manju imin yŏn'gu" (A Study of the Korean Emigration to Manchuria in the 1920s–1930s). In *Ilcheha Han'gukŭi sahoe kyegŭp kwa sahoe pyŏndong* (Social Classes and Social Change in the Colonial Korea), ed. Han'guk sahoesa yŏn'guhoe. Seoul: Munhak kwa chisŏng, 1988.

Lee Kanghun. "Kongsandange amsaltanghan Kim Chwa-jin changgunŭi ch'oehu" (The Last of General Kim Chwajin, Assassinated by Communists). *Pukhan* (North Korea) (August 1984): 198–207.

Lee, Kyŏnghun. "Harbinŭi p'urŭn hanŭl: 'Pyŏkkongmuhan' kwa taedonga kongyŏng" (Blue Sky in Harbin: "Pyŏkkongmuhan" and the East-Asia Co-Prosperity Sphere). In *Munhak sogŭi Fascism* (Fascism in Korean Literature), ed. Kim Cheol and Sin Hyŏnggi. Seoul: Samin, 2001.

Lee Kyŏngran. *Ilcheha kŭmyung chohap yŏn'gu* (A Study of the Financial Cooperatives). Seoul: Hean, 2002.

Lefebvre, Henri. *The Production of Space*. Oxford: Blackwell, 1991.

Li, Hongwen, Chang Cheng, and Zhu Jianhua. *Xiandai Dongbeishi* (The Modern History of Northeast China). Harbin: Heilongjiang jiaoyu chubanshe, 1986.

Liaoningsheng danganguan. *Wanbaoshan shijian* (The Wanbaoshan Incident). Jilin: Jilin renmin chubanshe, 1990.

Liaoningsheng danganguan bian (Archives of Liaoning Province). *Zhonghua minguo shizi liaoconggao diangao fenzi junfa mi dian* (Collections of Historical Documents of the Chinese People's Republic, Feudal Warlord Secret Telegrams). Vol. 1, 1919. Shenyang: Zhonghwa shuju, 1987.

Lim Ch'unch'u. *Hangil mujang t'ujaeng sigirŭl hoesang hamyŏ* (Remembering the Anti-Japanese Armed Struggle). P'yŏngyang: Chosŏn nodongdang, 1960.

Lim Hŭijun. "Hyŏksinŭihoewa chaeman ch'aekjinhoe" (The Revolutionary Assembly and Ch'aekjinhoe in Manchuria). In *Chungguk Chosŏn minjok palchach'wi ch'ongsŏ* (History of the Korean Chinese in China). Vol. 2, *Pulssi*. (Kindling). Beijing: Minzu chubanshe, 1995.

Lim Yŏngsŏ. "1910–20 nyŏndae Kando Hanine taehan Chunggugŭi chŏngch'aekkwa minhoe" (Chinese Policies on Koreans of Kan-do and Min-hwe from 1910 to 1920). M.A. thesis, Seoul National University, 1933.

"Liudaoju shangbujuzhang xianghoubao bunei ruji hanmin renshu ji xingming kaixue qing jianyou" (Report by the Head of the Department of Commerce on the Number and Names of Koreans Who Became Naturalized in Liudaoju and His Request for a Review). Jilin Yanjidao daoyin gongshu minguo sinian 114 hao anjuan, 1915 (The Head of Yanji District in Jilin Province, Number 114, 1915). Yanji: Institute of Ethnology, Yanbian University.

Luxemberg, Rosa. *The Russian Revolution and Leninism or Marxism?* Ann Arbor: University of Michigan Press, 1970.

———. *The Accumulation of Capital*. New York: Monthly Review Press, 1973.

Lytton Report. Reprint. Seoul: Tamgudang, 1986.

Manju tongp'o munje hŏbŭihoe (Committee on the Problem of Korean Compatriots in Manchuria). *Manchu tongp'o sanghwang chosa pogo* (Investigation Report on the Situation of Korean Patriots in Manchuria). Kyŏngsŏng: Misongsa, 1931.

Manzhuguoshi Vol. 1, 2 (The History of the Manchukuo) (translation of Manshūkokushi Hensan kankōkai, *Manshūkokusi*, published by Daiichihōki Shuppansha, 1971). Changchun: Dongbei shifan daxuexiao yinshuachang, 1990.

Marx, Karl. *Critique of Hegel's "Philosophy of Right."* London: Cambridge University Press, 1970.

———. *Grundrisse*. New York: Vintage, 1973.

———. *Capital*. Vol. 1. New York: Vintage, 1981.

———. *Capital*. Vol. 3. New York: Vintage, 1981.

Matsusaka, Yoshihisa Tak. *The Making of Japanese Manchuria, 1904–1932*. Cambridge: Harvard University Asia Center, 2001.

McAleary, Henry. "China under the War-Lords, Part I." *China Today* 12:4 (1962): 227–33.

———. "China under the War-Lords, Part II." *China Today* 12:5 (1962): 303–11.

McCormack, Gavan. *Chang Tso-lin in Northeast China, 1911–1928*. Stanford: Stanford University Press, 1977.

Mitter, Rana. *The Manchurian Myth: Nationalism, Resistance, and Collaboration in Modern China*. Berkeley: University of California Press, 2000.

Miyoshi, Fukushima. "Manshūkoku Tochi Seido no Genjō to Tochi Seisaku" (Conditions of the Land System and Land Policy in the Manchukuo State). Kokumuin Chiseki Seirikyoku (The Department of the Reorganization of Landownership in the Ministry of State Affairs of Manchukuo), 1937, no. 45.

Myers, Ramon. "Socioeconomic Changes in Villages of Manchuria during the Ch'ing and Republican Period: Some Preliminary Findings." *Modern Asian Studies* 19:4 (1976): 591–620.

————. *The Japanese Economic Development of Manchuria, 1932 to 1945.* New York: Garland, 1982.

————. "Japanese Imperialism in Manchuria: The South Manchurian Railway Company, 1906–1933." In *The Japanese Informal Empire in China, 1895–1937*, ed. Peter Duus, Ramon Myers, and Mark Peattie. Princeton: Princeton University Press, 1989.

Nakamura, Takafusa. *Economic Growth in Prewar Japan* (Senzenki Nihon keizai seicho no bunseki). Translated by Robert Feldman. New Haven: Yale University Press, 1983.

————. *A History of Showa Japan* (Showa shi). Translated by Edwin Whenmouth. Tokyo: University of Tokyo Press, 1998.

Nagahara, Yutaka. *Tennōsei Kokka to Nōmin: Gōi Keisei no Soshikiron* (The Emperor State and the Peasants: On Consent-Based Organization). Tokyo: Nishon Keizai Hyōronsha, 1989.

Nukaga, Makoto. "The Koreans in Manchuria." M.A. thesis, University of California, Berkeley, 1931.

Oh Sech'ang. "Chaeman Chosŏnin Minhoe yŏn'gu" (A Study of the Korean Association in Manchuria). *Paeksanhakpo* 25 (1979): 117–54.

Oh Yangho. *Han'guk munhakkwa Kando* (Korean Literature and Kando). Seoul: Munye ch'ulp'ansa, 1988.

Onda Sakubē. "Tōman Chihō ni Okeru Nōson no Genjō: Shūdan Buraku Kensetsu no Jūyōsei (Chū no Ni) and (Ni Zoku)" (Rural Conditions in Northeast China: The Importance of Constructing Collective Villages). *Manshū Hyōron* 9:8 (1935): 23–30.

————. "Tōman Chihō ni Okeru Nōson no Genjō: Shūdan Buraku Kensetsu no Jūyōsei (Chū no Yon), San (Zoku)." *Manshū Hyōron* 9:10 (1935): 24–28.

————. "Tōman Chihō ni Okeru Nōson no Genjō: Shūdan Buraku Kensetsu no Jūyōsei (Ge), San (Zoku)." *Manshū Hyōron* 9:11 (1935): 22–26.

————. "Tōman Chihō ni Okeru Nōson no Genjō: Shūdan Buraku Kensetsu no Jūyōsei (Kan), San (Zoku)." *Manshū Hyōron* 9:12 (1935): 23–27.

Ong, Aihwa. *Flexible Citizenship: The Cultural Logics of Transnationality.* Durham: Duke University Press, 1999.

Pak, Ch'angwuk [Piao Changyu]. "Chimnyage riyongharyŏnŭn ilcheui Chosŏnin imin chŏngch'aek" (The Japanese Immigration Policy Used in the Invasion). In *Chungguk Chosŏn minjok palchach'wi ch'ongsŏ* (History of the Korean Chinese in China). Vol. 2, *Pulssi* (Kindling). Beijing: Minzu chubanshe, 1995.

————. "Simyang, Musun chigueso" (In the Shenyang and Musun Regions). In *Chungguk Chosŏn minjok palchach'wi ch'ongsŏ* (History of the Korean Chinese in China). Vol. 2, *Pulssi* (Kindling). Beijing: Minzu chubanshe, 1995.

Pak Hyŏnch'ae. *Minjok kyŏngjeron: Pak Hyŏnch'ae p'yongronsŏn* (On the National Economy: Selected Works of Pak Hyonch'ae). Seoul: Han'gilsa, 1978.

Pak Ilcho. "Yonbyŏnesŏ songhaengden 'Chŏnminjedo'" (A Popular Practice, Chŏnminje, in Kando). In *Chungguk Chosŏn minjok palchach'wi ch'ongsŏ* (History of the Korean Chinese in China). Vol. 2, *Pulssi* (Kindling). Beijing: Minzu chubanshe, 1995.

Pak Kŭmhae. "Chaeman chosŏnjoge taehan min'gukchŏngbuŭi kipbon chŏngch'aek"

(The Republican Government's Basic Policy Toward Koreans). In *Chungguk Chosŏn minjok palchach'wi ch'ongsŏ* (History of the Korean Chinese in China). Vol. 1, *Kaech'ŏk*. Beijing: Minzu Chubanshe, 1999.

Pak Sunyoung. "The Relationship between the Chinese Communist Party and the Comintern with Regard to the Manchuria Provincial Committee (1930s)." Manuscript.

Pak Yŏngsŏk. *Manbosan sagŏn yŏn'gu* (A Study of the Manbosan Incident). Seoul: Asea munhwasa, 1978.

Peattie, Mark. "The Japanese Colonial Empire, 1895–1945." In *The Cambridge History of Japan*. Vol. 6. ed. Peter Duus. Cambridge: Cambridge University Press, 1988.

Perelman, Michael. *The Invention of Capitalism*. Durham: Duke University Press, 2000.

Piao Changyu [Pak Ch'angwuk]. "Riben diguo zhuyi zaidongbei zhimin tongzhi shiqi chaoxianzu nongmin suo xingde 'zigengnong chuangding' shilun" (A Study of the Program to Create Independent Farmers among the Koreans in Northeast China during Colonial Rule). In *Zhongguo chaoxianzu lishi yanju* (A Study of the History of the Korean Chinese in China). Yanbian: Yanbian University Press, 1995.

Pongch'ŏn Hunga hyŏphoe. *Chaeman Chonsŏnin t'ongsin* (Korean Communication in Manchuria). Vol. 72 (November 1939). Fiengtian.

Poulantzas, Nicos. *Classes in Contemporary Capitalism*. London: Verso, 1975.

———. *State, Power, and Socialism*. London: Verso, 1980.

Read, Jason. "Primitive Accumulation: The Aleatory Foundation of Capitalism." *Rethinking Marxism* 14 (2002): 24–40.

Ryu Pyongho. "Samsim nyŏndae Chosŏnjok imin" (Korean Immigrants in the 1930s). In *Chungguk Chosŏn minjok palchach'wi chongsŏ* (History of the Korean Chinese in China). Vol. 3, *Ponghwa* (Beacon). Beijing: Minzu chubanshe, 1989.

———. "Ch'amŭibuŭi panil kŭn'gŏji" (The Anti-Japanese Base of the Ch'amŭibu). In *Chungguk Chosŏn minjok palchach'wi ch'ongsŏ* (History of the Korean Chinese in China). Vol. 2, *Pulssi* (Kindling). Beijing: Minzu chubanshe, 1995.

———. "Chongŭibuŭi panil kŭn'gŏji" (The Anti-Japanese Base of the Chŏngŭibu). In *Chungguk Chosŏn minjok palchach'wi ch'ongsŏ* (History of the Korean Chinese in China). Vol. 2, *Pulssi* (Kindling). Beijing: Minzu chubanshe, 1995.

———. "Namman chigu panil t'ongil tanch'e: Kungminbuŭi ch'angnip" (The Anti-Japanese Organization in South Manchuria: The Establishment of Kungminbu). In *Chungguk Chosŏn minjok palchach'wi ch'ongsŏ* (History of the Korean Chinese in China). Vol. 2, *Pulssi* (Kindling). Beijing: Minzu chubanshe, 1995.

Ryu Eun Kyu. *Ich'ojin hŭnjŏk: Sajinŭiro ponŭn Chosŏnjok 100 nyŏnsa* (Forgotten Traces: The Hundred Year History of the Korean Chinese in Photographs). Seoul: Art public com Korea, 2000.

Sahoe kwahak ch'ulp'ansa. *Hangil mujang t'ujaengsa* (The History of the Anti-Japanese Armed Struggle). P'yŏngyang: Sahoe Kwahak Ch'ulp'ansa, 1980.

Sahoe Kwahagwŏn yŏksa yŏn'guso. *1926–1945 nyŏn Chosŏn munhaksa* (The History of Korean Literature, 1926–1945). Reprint; Seoul: Yŏlsaram Press, 1981.

———. *Chosŏn kŭndae hyŏngmyŏng undongsa* (The History of the Modern Revolutionary Movement). Reprint; Seoul: Hanmadang, 1988.

Scalapino, Robert, and Lee Chong Sik. *Communism in Korea, Part I.* Berkeley: University of California Press, 1972.

Schmid, Andre. "Colonialism and the 'Korea Problem.'" *Journal of Asian Studies* 59 (2000): 951–76.

Seki-Otu, Ato. *Fanon's Dialectic of Experience.* Cambridge: Harvard University Press, 1996.

Selden, Mark. *China in Revolution.* New York: M. E. Sharpe, 1995.

Senman Takushoku Kabushiki Gaisha Mansen Takushoku Kabushiki Gaisha Gonenshi (The Five-Year History of the Korea-Manchuria Company and the Manchuria-Korea Company). Changchun: Senman Takushoku Kabushiki Gaisha Mansen Takushoku Kabushiki Gaisha, 1941.

Shao, Dan. "From Homeland to Borderland: Manchus and Manchuria in the Early Twentieth Century." Unpublished manuscript.

"Shengzhang miling hanmin guihua anchaosong rishi zhaohui ji neiwubu zifu weijiaobu wengao qingchao zhaoyou" (The Objection of Japanese Consuls to the Naturalization of Koreans and the Order to Follow the Policy of the Chinese Ministry of Foreign Affairs). Jilinsheng gongshu mixunling di 67 hao, ling Jilin Yanji daoyin, minguo wu nian, 9.19 (The Decree of Jilin Province, Number 67, the Order to the Head of Yanji District in 1916, September 19). Yanji: Institute of Ethnology, Yanbian University.

Shin Chubaek. *Manju chiyŏk haninŭi minjok undongsa, 1920–45* (The Korean National Movement in Manchuria, 1920–45). Seoul: Aseamunhwasa, 1999.

———, ed. *1930 nyŏndae minjok haebang undongron yŏn'gu II* (Study of the National Liberation Movement in the 1930s). Seoul: Saekil, 1990.

Shin, Gi-Wook. "Agrarianism: A Critique of Colonial Modernity in Korea." *Comparative Studies in Society and History* 41:4 (1999): 784–804.

Shim, Yŏch'u. *Yŏnbyŏn chosa sillok.* (A History of Yanbian). Yanbian, 1930. Reprint; Yanbian: Yanbian University Press, 1987.

Smart, Barry. *Foucault, Marxism and Critique.* London: Routledge, 1983.

Smith, Anna Marie. *Laclau and Mouffe: The Radical Democratic Imaginary.* New York: Routledge, 1998.

Smith, Neil, and Cindi Katz, "Grounding Metaphor: Towards a Spatialized Politics." In *Place and the Politics of Identity*, ed. Michael Keith and Steve Pile. New York: Routledge. 1993.

So Chaeyŏng, ed. *Kando Yurang 40 nyŏn* (Forty Years of Journeying in Kando). Seoul: Chosŏnilbosa, 1989.

Sohn-Rethel, Alfred. *Intellectual and Manual Labour: A Critique of Epistemology.* Translated by Martin Sohn-Rethel. London: Macmillan, 1978.

Sŏk Chŏngsong. "Ilbonimindanŭi t'oji yakt'al" (The Plundering of Land by the Japanese). In *Chungguk Chosŏn minjok palchach'wi ch'ongsŏ* (History of the Korean Chinese in China). Vol. 4, *Kyŏlchŏn* (Final War). Beijing: Minzu chubanshe, 1991.

Son, Ch'unil. *Manjugugŭi chaeman hanine taehan t'oji chŏngch'aek yŏn'gu* (A Study of the Manchukuo Policy on the Land Rights of the Koreans in Manchuria). Seoul: Paesan Charyowŏn, 1999.

———. *Haebangjŏn tongbuk Chosŏnjok t'oji kwan'gaesa yŏn'gu.* Vol. 1 (A Study of the Land Relations of Koreans in Northeast China before Liberation). Jilin: Jilin Inmin ch'ulp'ansa, 2001.

Suh, Dae-sook. *The Korean Communist Movement, 1918–1948.* Princeton: Princeton University Press, 1967.

———. *Kim Il Sung: The North Korean Leader.* New York: Columbia University Press, 1988.

Suleski, Ronald. *Civil Government in Warlord China: Tradition, Modernization and Manchuria.* New York: Peter Lang, 2002.

———. "The Rise and Fall of the Fengtien Dollar, 1917–1928: Currency Reform in Warlord China." *Modern Asian Studies* 13:4 (1979): 643–60.

Tamanoi, Mariko. "A Road to 'A Redeemed Mankind': The Politics of Memory among the Former Japanese Peasant Settlers in Manchuria." In *Harbin and Manchuria: Place, Space, and Identity,* ed. Thomas Lahusen. *South Atlantic Quarterly* 99:1 (winter 2000): 163–92.

The Tanaka Memorial. San Francisco, n.p., n.d.

Tanaka, Stefan. *Japan's Orient: Rendering Pasts into History.* Berkeley: University of California Press, 1993.

Tian Zhihe and Pan Jinglong, *Jilin jianzhimogegaishe* (An Outline of the Establishment of Jilin Province). Changchun: Jilin renmin chubanshe, 1990.

Tōa Kangyō Kabushiki Gaisha Jūnenshi (The Ten-Year History of the Asian Agricultural Company). Tokyo: Tōa Kangyō Kabushiki Gaisha, 1933.

Tōhoku Kankensho Hatsu Hainichi Hōrei Shū (Collection of the Chinese Laws against Japan in Northeast China). Minami Manshū Tetsudō Kabushiki Gaisha, 1931.

"Toudaoju shangbujuzhang xiangcha ming ruji Hanmin xingming houbao qingjian you" (The Report by the Head of the Department of Commerce on the Number and Names of Koreans Who Became Naturalized in Toudaoju). Jilin Yanjidao daoyin gongshu minguo sinian 114 ao anjuan, 1915 (The Head of Yanji District in Jilin Province, Number 114, 1915). Yanji: Institute of Ethnology, Yanbian University.

Tōyō Takushoku Kabushiki Gaisha Sanjūnenshi (The Thirty-Year History of the Oriental Development Company). Tokyo: Tōyō Takushoku Kabushiki Gaisha, 1939.

Trautmann, Thomas. *Aryans and British India.* Berkeley: University of California Press, 1997.

Tribe, Keith. *Genealogies of Capitalism.* London: Macmillan, 1981.

"Tuan Manzhoushengwei gongzuo dagang (1931, 1. 16)" (The Major Tasks of the Manchuria Committee of the CCP, 1931, 1. 16), in *Dongbei diqu geming lishi wenjian huiji,* Jia 7, ed. Zhongyang danganguan et al. Jilin: Jilinsheng gongshanglian yinshuachang, 1988.

"Tuan Manzhoushengwei xiaohe xunshi nanman gongzuo baogao—guanyu nanman zhengzhi jingji zhuangkuang, geming xingshi ji jinhou de yijian, banfadeng (1931,

11. 17)" (Report on Southern Manchuria—The Political and Economic Conditions in Manchuria and Assessments of Revolutionary Conditions, 1931, 11. 17), in *Dongbei diqu geming lishi wenjian huiji*, Jia 9, ed. Zhongyang danganguan et al. Jilin: Jilinsheng gongshanglian yinshuachang, 1988.

"Tuanshengwei tepaiyuan Zhong guanyu dongman fanri douzheng qingkuang de baogao (1934, 12. 4)" (Report Concerning the Anti-Japanese Struggle in East Manchuria, 1934, 12. 4), in *Dongbei diqu geming lishi wenjian huiji*, Jia 20, eds. Zhongyang danganguan et al. Harbin: Harbin hulan yinshuachang, 1990.

Vlastos, Stephen. "Agrarianism without Tradition." In *Mirror of Modernity: Invented Traditions of Modern Japan*, ed. Stephen Vlastos. Berkeley: University of California Press, 1998.

Wada Haruki. *Kim Il Sung kwa Manju Hangil chŏnjaeng* (Kim Il Sung and the Anti-Japanese War in Manchuria). Seoul: Changjakkwa Pip'yŏng, 1992.

Wales, Nym, and Kim San. *Song of Ariran: A Korean Communist in the Chinese Revolution*. San Francisco: Ramparts, 1941.

Wangqing xian zhengzhi baoguoshu (Wangqing County Political Reports). Vols. 1–2. Yanji: Institute of Ethnology, Yanbian University.

"Wangqing zhishi xiangbao hanqiao guihua shishi jianming biaoyou" (The Magistrate's Report on the Naturalization of Koreans in Wangqing County). Jilin Yanjidao daoyin gongshu minguo wunian 60 hao anjuan, 1916 (The Head of Yanji District in Jilin Province, Number 60, 1916). Yanji: Institute of Ethnology, Yanbian University.

"Wang Runcheng gei zhongyang daibiaotuan de baogao—guanyu 1935 nian—1936 nian dongman dongbu gongzuo qingkuang (1937, 1. 17)" (Report from Wang Runcheng Submitted to the Central Representative Committee, 1937, 1. 17), in *Dongbei diqu geming lishi wenjian huiji*, Jia 28, ed. Zhongyang danganguan et al. Jilin: Jilinsheng gongshanglian yinshuachang, 1989.

"Wei ruji hanmin bujia kenmin mingchen" (An Order Not to Call Naturalized Koreans Kanmin). Archives of the Yanbian Autonomous Prefecture, 36 hao quanzong 2 hao anjuan 661, 1919.

"Xiangwei rijing zaimaoshanqian chuanxun kenmin Zhang Guowu sanming qingchahe" (The Investigation on the Matter in which Japanese Policemen Arrested and Interrogated Three Koreans, Including Zhang Guowu at the Mao Mountain). Yanbianzhou danganguan (Archives of the Yanbian Autonomous Prefecture), 21–6–29, 1915.

"Xunanshi chizhi Hanmin qingqiu ruji yifaban lizhuan xing daozhao you" (On the Implementation of the Law on the Koreans' Application for Naturalization). Jilin xunanshi gongshuchi di 48 hao minguo sinian (Jilin xunanshi, order number 48, 1915). Yanji: Institute of Ethnology, Yanbian University.

"Xunanshi chizhi teding qiaomin shishi jianming chazhao you" (Instructions for the Investigation of the Naturalization of Special Koreans). Jilin xunanshi gongshu michi di 142 hao minguo sinian (The Secret Order of Jilin Xuanshi, number 142, 1915). Yanji: Institute of Ethnology, Yanbian University.

Yamabe, Kentaro. *Ilche kanjŏmhaŭi han'guk kŭndaesa*. (The Modern History of Korea under Japanese Occupation). Translated by Lee Hyŏnhee. Seoul: Samkwang, 1988.

Yang Zhaoquan and Li Tiehuan, eds. *Dongbei diqu manxianren geming douzheng ziliao xuanji* (The Archives of the Revolutionary Struggle of Koreans in Northeast China). Liaoning: Liaoning minzu chubanshe. 1992.

Yim Sung-Mo. "Manjuguk Hyŏphwahoeŭi ch'ongnyŏkchŏn ch'eje kusang yŏn'gu: 'Kungminundong' nosŏnŭi mosaekkwa kŭ sŏnggyŏk" (The Planning of the Total War System in Manchukuo: Search for the 'National Movement without Nation' of the MCA). PhD diss., Department of History, Yonsei University, 1997.

Yoda Yoshiie. "Manshū ni Okeru Chōsenjin Imin" (Korean Emigration to Manchuria). In *Nihon Teikokushugika no Manshū Imin* (Emigration to Manchuria under Japanese Imperialism), ed. Manshū Iminshi Kenkyūkai. Ryūkei Shosha, 1976.

Yŏmaeng p'yŏnjip wiwŏnhoe (Publications Committee of the Women's Federation). *Suryŏngkke ch'ungjikhan yugyok kŭn'gŏji yŏsŏngdŭl* (Women in Guerrilla Bases Who Were Loyal to the Great Leader). Vols. 1–4. P'yŏngyang: Women's Federation, 1969.

Yŏnbyŏn Chosŏnjok yaksa p'yŏnch'anjo. *Chosŏnjok Yaksa*, (A Short History of the Koreans). Yanbian: Yonbyon Inmin ch'ul'ansa. Reprint; Seoul: Nonjang Press, 1989.

Yoon, Hwitak. *Ilcheha Manjuguk Yŏn'gu* (A Study of the Manchukuo State under Japanese Rule). Seoul: Ilchogak, 1996.

Young, Louise. *Japan's Total Empire*. Berkeley: University of California Press, 1998.

Zaiman Chōsenjin Gaikyō (The General Condition of Koreans in Manchuria). Zaiman Nihon Teikoku Taishikan Hensan, 1934.

Zaiman Senjin Appaku Jijō (The State of Korean Oppression in Manchuria). Minami Manshū Tetsudō Kabushiki Gaisha, 1928.

Zenman Chōsen Jinminkai Rengōkai Kaihō (The Official Magazine of the Federation of the Korean Association in Manchuria), 1933–1937.

Zhang Deliang and Zhou Yi. *Dongbei junshi* (The Military History of Northeast China). Shenyang: Liaoning daxue chubanshe, 1987.

Zhengxie Zhenyangshi weiyuanhui wenshi ziliao yanjiu weiyuanhui bian (Department of Archival Studies of the Committee of Politics and Negotiations, Shenyang), *Shenyangwenshi Ziliao* (Shenyang Archives), vol. 11, *Zhang Xueliang jiangjun shiliao xuanji* (Collected Histories of General Zhang Xueliang). Shenyang: Zhengxie Zhenyangshi weiyuanhui wenshi ziliao yanjiu weiyuanhui bangongshi chuban, 1986.

Zhengxie Zhenyangshi weiyuanhui wenshi ziliao yanjiu weiyuanhui bian (Department of Archival Studies of the Committee of Politics and Negotiations, Shenyang), *Shenyangwenshi Ziliao* (Shenyang Archives), vol. 12, *Zhang Zuolin shiliao xuanji* (Collected Histories of Zhang Zuolin). Shenyang: Zhengxie Zhenyangshi weiyuanhui wenshi ziliao yanjiu weiyuanhui bangongshi chuban, 1986.

"Zhonggong dongman dangtuan tewei gongzuo baogao—muqian yiban zhuang-kuang, jieshou zhongyang luxian yianhou de qingxing (1933, 10. 25)" (Report of the Eastern Manchuria Special Committee on the General Conditions and the Situations before and after the Receipt of the CCP Policy, 1933, 10. 25), in *Dongbei diqu geming lishi wenjian huiji, Jia 30*, ed. Zhongyang danganguan et al. Jilin: Jilinsheng gongshanglian yinshuachang, 1989.

"Zhonggong jichang quwei shiyi yuefen gongzuo baogao (1927, 12. 1)" (Report of the Jichang Committee of the CCP on November Tasks, 1927, 12. 1), in *Dongbei diqu geming lishi wenjian huiji, Jia 1*, ed. Zhongyang danganguan et al. Liaoning: Liaoning meishu yinshuachang fenchang, 1988.

"Zhonggong Manzhousheng linwei guanyu muqian gongzuo jihua jueyian (1927, 12. 24)" (Resolution on the Immediate Tasks of the Manchuria Committee of the CCP, 1927, 12. 24), in *Dongbei diqu geming lishi wenjian huiji, Jia 1*, ed. Zhongyang dangan-guan et al. Liaoning: Liaoning meishu yinshuachang fenchang, 1988.

"Zhonggong Manzhousheng linwei zhengzhi dangwu baogao—Manzhou de zhengzhi jingji xingshi ji dang de gongzuo qingkuang (1928, 2. 12)" (Report of the Man-churian Provincial Committee–Political Economic Conditions and the Situations of the Tasks of the Party, 1928, 2. 12), in *Dongbei diqu geming lishi wenjian huiji, Jia 1*, ed. Zhongyang danganguan et al. Liaoning: Liaoning meishu yinshuachang fen-chang, 1988.

"Zhonggong Manzhoushengwei gei zhonggong de baogao—guanyu Manzhou zheng-zhi jingji zhuangkuang ji jixiang juti kongzuo wenti (1931, 4. 24)" (Report of the Manchurian Provincial Committee Submitted to the CCP: The Political Economic Conditions of Manchuria and the Concerned Specific Tasks of the Party, 1931, 4. 24), in *Dongbei diqu geming lishi wenjian huiji, Jia 8*, ed. Zhongyang danganguan et al. Jilin: Jilinsheng gongshanglian yinshuachang, 1988.

"Zhonggong Manzhoushengwei guanyu chunhuang douzheng de jueyi (1933, 2. 28)" (The Manchurian Provincial Committee of the CCP on the Strategy on the Spring Struggle, 1933, 2. 28), in *Dongbei diqu geming lishi wenjian huiji, Jia 12*, ed. Zhongyang danganguan et al. Harbin: Harbin hulan yinshuachang, 1988.

"Zhonggong Manzhoushengwei guanyu Manzhou Hanguo minzu wenti jueyian (1931. 5. 26)" (The Manchurian Provincial Committee's Resolution on Koreans in Man-churia, 1931, 5. 26), in *Dongbei diqu geming lishi wenjian huiji, Jia 8*, ed. Zhongyang danganguan et al. Jilin: Jilinsheng gongshanglian yinshuachang, 1988.

"Zhonggong Manzhoushengwei jidong xunshiyuan (wu) zhi dongman tewei de xin—guanyu dongman fanri youji yundong, tongyi zhanxian, fan Minshengtuan dou-zheng decelue ji danghevqunzhong kongzuo deng wenti (1935, 2. 10)" (Report on the Eastern Manchurian Special Committee from Wu, an Agent of the Manchu-rian Provincial Committee—Problems of the Anti-Japanese Movement, the United Front, the Anti-Minsaengdan Struggle, and the Mass Mobilization, 1935, 2. 10), in *Dongbei diqu geming lishi wenjian huiji, Jia 21*, ed. Zhongyang danganguan et al. Jilin: Jilinsheng gongshanglian yinshuachang, 1988.

"Zhonggong Manzhoushengwei tepaiyuan Ji Zi baogao di yi hao—guanyu Jilin, Chang-chun de zhengzhi jingji xingshi, dangqun gongzuo ji jin hou de gongzuo buzhi (1931, 10. 2)" (First Report from Ji Zi, an Agent Sent from the Manchurian Spe-cial Committee of the CCP, Concerning the Political and Economic Conditions in Jilin and Changchun, 1931, 10. 2), in *Dongbei diqu geming lishi wenjian huiji, Jia 9*, ed. Zhongyang danganguan et al. Jilin: Jilinsheng gongshanglian yinshuachang, 1988.

"Zhonggong Manzhousheng weiyuanhui huiyijilu—guanyu zhongdonglu douzheng, fandi yundong, dang de zu zhi deng wenti (1930, 4. 2)" (Meeting Report of the Manchurian Provincial Committee of the CCP—on the Struggle in Zhongdonglu, the Anti-Imperialist Movement, and the Party's Concerns, 1930, 4. 2), in *Dongbei diqu geming lishi wenjian huiji, Jia 4*, ed. Zhongyang danganguan et al. Liaoning: Liao-ning meishu yinshuachang fenchang, 1989.

Žižek, Slavoj. "Class Struggle or Postmodernism? Yes, Please!" In Judith Butler, Ernesto Laclau, and Slavoj Žižek, *Contingency, Hegemony, Universality: Contemporary Dialogues on the Left*. London: Verso, 2000.

INDEX

Hyun Ok Park is an assistant professor in the
Departments of East Asian Studies and Sociology
at New York University.

✿

Library of Congress Cataloging-in-Publication Data
Park, Hyun Ok.
Two dreams in one bed : empire, social life, and the
origins of the North Korean revolution in Manchuria /
Hyun Ok Park.
p. cm. — (Asia–Pacific : culture, politics, and society)
Includes bibliographical references.
ISBN 0-8223-3625-1 (cloth : alk. paper)
ISBN 0-8223-3614-6 (pbk. : alk. paper)
1. Capitalism — Social aspects — China — Manchuria —
History — 20th century.   2. Koreans — China —
Manchuria — History — 20th century.   3. Manchuria
(China) — Ethnic relations — History — 20th century.
I. Title: Empire, social life, and the origins of the
North Korean revolution in Manchuria.   II. Title.
III. Asia–Pacific. HB501.P295 2005
951.'8042 — dc22
2005010058